Places of Encounter

Encounter

VOLUME I

Places of Encounter in Global Perspective

St. Petersburg

Istanbul/
Constantinople

Gallipoli

Athens

Samarkand

Babylon

Xian

Nagasaki

Shanghai

Varanasi

Dubai

Calcutta/
Kolkata

Mecca/
Makkah

Hadar

Malacca

Kilwa

Makapansgat

Cape Town

Places of **Encounter**

Time, Place, and Connectivity in World History

VOLUME I

ARAN MACKINNON

ELAINE MACKINNON

EDITORS

Routledge
Taylor & Francis Group
New York London

First published 2012 by Westview Press

Published 2018 by Routledge
711 Third Avenue, New York, NY 10017, USA
2 Park Square, Milton Park, Abingdon, Oxon OX14 4RN

Routledge is an imprint of the Taylor & Francis Group, an informa business

Every effort has been made to secure required permissions for all text, images, maps, and other art reprinted in this volume.

Editorial production by Lori Hobkirk at the Book Factory.
Typeset in 9.5 Plantin by Cynthia Young at Sagecraft.

Library of Congress Cataloging-in-Publication Data

Places of encounter : time, place and connectivity in world history / Aran MacKinnon, Elaine MacKinnon, editors.
       v. cm.
   Includes bibliographical references and index.
      ISBN 978-0-8133-4737-0 (v. 1)—ISBN 978-0-8133-4738-7 (v. 1 : ebook)—
      ISBN 978-0-8133-4739-4 (v. 2)—ISBN 978-0-8133-4740-0 (v. 2 : ebook)
      1. World history.   2. World history—Sources.   3. Cities and towns—History.   4. Cities and towns—History—Sources.   5. Social change—History.   6. Social change—History—Sources.   7. Cultural relations—History.   8. Cultural relations—History—Sources.
   I. MacKinnon, Aran S.   II. McClarnand MacKinnon, Elaine.
   D21.3.P56 2012
   909—dc23

                                                                                   2012000612

ISBN 13: 978-0-8133-4737-0 (pbk)

All maps have been created by International Mapping.

Aran MacKinnon dedicates Places of Encounter
to his co-editor/author and wife, Elaine,
whose shared love for South Africa inspired this project,
and to their fellow traveler, Kieran.

Contents

VOLUME I

6. CARTHAGE: *Gateway to the World Beyond the Mediterranean (800 BCE–700 CE)* 91

7. CONSTANTINOPLE/ISTANBUL: *A Vortex of Peoples and Cultures (324 CE–1500)* 111

8. MECCA: *Pilgrimage and the Making of the Islamic World (400–1500)* 127

List of Features

Maps

Primary Documents' Credits

Chapter 1

Lucy's Legacy: The Quest for Human Origins, by Donald Johanson and Katy Wong, copyright © 2009, 2010 by Donald C. Johanson and Kate Wong. Used by permission of Harmony Books, a division of Random House, Inc.

Chapter 3

Excerpts from *Gilgamesh* reprinted with the permission of Free Press, a Division of Simon & Schuster, Inc., from GILGAMESH: A New English Translation by Stephen Mitchell. Copyright © 2004 by Stephen Mitchell. All rights reserved.

Chapter 4

Lysias, "On the Killing of Eratosthenes," in *Trials from Classical Athens*, edited by Christopher Carey (London: Routledge, 1997), 34.

Thucydides, "The Funeral Oration of Pericles," from *The Peloponnesian War: Thucydides, The Crawley Translation*, translated by T. E. Wick and Richard Crawley (New York: McGraw Hill, 1982), 108–110.

J. M. Moore, "The Constitution of the Athenians," *Aristotle and Xenophon on Democracy and Oligarchy*, copyright © 1975 by J. M. Moore, published by the University of California Press; From *Aristotle and Xenophon on Democracy and Oligarchy*, by J. M. Moore, published by Chatto and Windus. Reprinted by permission of The Random House Group Ltd.

Chapter 5

Tong, Xiao, "Two Capitals Rhapsody," *Wen Xuan or Selections of Refined Literature, Vol. 1*, copyright © 1982 by Princeton University Press. Reprinted by permission of Princeton University Press.

"Miss Ren," from *Chinese Literature 3: Tales of the Supernatural*, by H. C. Chang. Copyright © February 28, 2011, Columbia University Press. Reprinted with permission of the publisher.

Chapter 6

"Politica" translated by Jowett from Politics & Economics from The Oxford Translation of Aristotle edited by W. D. Ross (Volume X, 1921) 782w. By permission of Oxford University Press.

Chapter 7

Letter on Constantinople, by Benjamin of Tudela, from Sandra Benjamin, ed., *The World of Benjamin of Tudela* (Madison, NJ: Farleigh Dickinson University Press, 1995), 129–132. Reprinted with permission of Associated University Presses.

Cyril Mango, ed., *The Art of the Byzantine Empire, 312–1453* (Englewood Cliffs, NJ: Medieval Academy of America, 1986), 83, 85, 91; "The clear sky . . . the living God," English translation by Paul Magdalino. Reprinted with permission of the Medieval Academy of America.

Chapter 8

The Travels of Ibn Battuta, excerpt from *One Thousand Roads to Mecca,* copyright © 1997 by Michael Wolfe. Used by permission of Grove/Atlantic, Inc.

Chapter 10

Poems of Kabir and Tulsi, from Paras Nath Tivari, *Kabir Granthavali,* and Ramcandra Sukla et al., eds., Tulsi-*Granthavali,* both quoted *in Songs of the Saints of India,* edited by John Stratton Hawley and Mark Juergensmeyer (New Delhi, India: Oxford University Press, 1988), 52, 53, 163.

Reading 2: Songs of the Saints of India by John Stratton Hawley (1989); from Kabir Granthavali, verse 178, 24 lines, 151 words. By permission of Oxford University Press, Inc.

Reading 3: Songs of the Saints of India by John Stratton Hawley (1989); from Kabir Granthavali, verse 46, 13 lines, 101 words. By permission of Oxford University Press, Inc.

Reading 4: Songs of the Saints of India by John Stratton Hawley (1989); from Tulsi Das' Kavitavali, verse 7.73, 16 lines, 96 words. By permission of Oxford University Press, Inc.

Where possible, in any electronic edition, a link is set up to our own website (URL www.oup.com)

Chapter 13

José de Acosta, *Natural and Moral History of the Indies,* edited by Jane E. Mangan, introduction by Walter D. Mignolo, translated by Frances M. López Morillas (Durham, NC: Duke University Press, 2002), 172–173. Copyright © 2002 Duke University Press. Reprinted with permission.

Chapter 14

J. V. G. Mills, trans. and ed., Ma Huan *Ying-yai Sheng-lan: The Overall Survey of the Ocean's Shores [1433]* (Cambridge: Cambridge University Press for the Hakluyt Society, 1970), adapted from 109–114. Copyright © 1970 Cambridge University Press. Reprinted with the permission of Cambridge University Press.

About the Contributors

Barbara Watson Andaya

Barbara Watson Andaya is a professor of Asian studies at the University of Hawai'i, where she teaches courses on gender, religion, and the evolution of Southeast Asian studies. She is currently involved in research on the localization of Christianity in pre-twentieth-century Southeast Asia. The author of several books and articles on the history of the Malacca Straits region, including a co-authored *A History of Malaysia* (University of Hawaii Press), she lived in Malaysia in the early 1970s, and still returns regularly to visit.

Leonard Y. Andaya

Leonard Y. Andaya is a professor of history at the University of Hawai'i, where he teaches courses on Southeast Asian history and a senior tutorial on Asia and the Pacific. He has written extensively on the precolonial period of Malaysian history and has coauthored *A History of Malaysia* (University of Hawaii Press) with Barbara Watson Andaya. He returns regularly to Malaysia as visiting professor to different Malaysian universities. He is currently writing a history of eastern Indonesia in the early-modern period using a sea perspective.

Melanie Sue Byrd

Dr. Byrd is a professor of history at Valdosta State University, where she teaches various courses on eighteenth- and nineteenth-century Europe, ancient history, and cultural history. Her dissertation research focused on the history of archaeology and the interest in ancient Egypt that arose from the French Occupation of Egypt under Napoleon Bonaparte, 1798–1801.

Julia Clancy-Smith

Julia Clancy-Smith is a professor of history at the University of Arizona, where she teaches courses on North Africa, the Middle East, and Islam as well as women's and world history. She has just published a monograph, *Mediterraneans: North Africa and Europe in an Age of Migration, c. 1800–1900* (University of California Press). Clancy-Smith is currently finishing a book on the history of French colonial education. Her first encounters with North Africa were in 1971 as a student and then in 1973 and 1974 as a Peace Corps volunteer. She has been returning to the region regularly for research ever since.

Nina Ergin

Nina Ergin is an assistant professor of art history at Koç University in Turkey, where she teaches courses on Ottoman architecture and the history of Istanbul, among other topics. Since 2005 she has been a permanent resident of the city, after already having spent several years working there and researching the history of Turkish bathhouses for her PhD.

Erik Gilbert

Erik Gilbert is a professor of history at Arkansas State University, where he teaches world history, African history, and heritage studies. He is currently working on a history of the Indian Ocean and the history of rice in East Africa. He grew up in West Africa but spent several years of his adult life in coastal East Africa, including a year as a Fulbright Scholar in Zanzibar, where he did research on the dhow trade.

Reuel R. Hanks

Reuel Hanks is a professor of geography at Oklahoma State University and serves as the editor of the *Journal of Central Asian Studies*. Dr. Hanks was a Fulbright Scholar in Tashkent, Uzbekistan in 1995 and has published more than a dozen articles and book chapters on Central Asia and Islam, nationalism and identity, foreign policy, and political geography.

Andy I. R. Herries

Andy Herries is part of the archeology program at the School of Historical and European Studies and a member of the faculty of humanities and social sciences department at La Trobe University in Melbourne, Victoria, Australia.

Christopher Howell

Christopher Howell is a professor of history and anthropology at Red Rocks College, where he teaches courses in archaeology and ancient history and is currently involved in research on the role of seafaring in shaping Africa past and present. He has visited Africa numerous times over the past decade, including the Hadar region in Ethiopia, carrying out field research on a variety of historical and anthropological topics.

Keith N. Knapp

Keith Knapp is a professor and the head of the history department at the Citadel, where he teaches courses on East Asian history and researches the history and culture of early medieval China (100–700 CE). He has spent three and a half years living in China and Taiwan; besides visiting Xian numerous times, he has also participated in an archaeological excavation there.

Nita Kumar

Nita Kumar is a professor of history at Claremont McKenna College, where she teaches courses in modernity, everyday life, history, and culture and is currently involved in research on education, children, and families. She has spent thirty years visiting and working on Banaras/Varanasi, studying it from various angles: urbanism, artisans, women and gender, and, now, education. She is also the honorary director of NIRMAN, a nonprofit based in Banaras/Varanasi that works for children, youth, and the arts.

Maritere López

Maritere López is an associate professor of history at California State University, Fresno, where she teaches courses in early-modern European history, including the Renaissance, Reformation, and Enlightenment periods. She is currently involved in research on gender and education during the Italian Enlightenment. She has traveled multiple times to Italy, conducting research and learning the ways of the Italians.

Michael Christopher Low

Michael Christopher Low is a PhD candidate in international and global history at Columbia University. He is the author of the article, "Empire and the Hajj: Pilgrims, Plagues, and Pan-Islam under British Surveillance, 1865–1908" from the *International Journal of Middle East Studies* (2008), which he is currently expanding into a dissertation. His research and teaching interests include the Ottoman Empire, the Arabian Peninsula, and the Indian Ocean. Although his travels throughout the Islamic world have taken him across much of North and West Africa, the Middle East, and India, his longest sojourns and favorite destinations for research and language training in Arabic and Turkish have been Sana'a', Yemen, and Istanbul, Turkey.

Aran S. MacKinnon

Dr. Aran S. MacKinnon is a professor of history and director of the Center for Interdisciplinary Studies at the University of West Georgia. He is the author of *The Making of South Africa* (Prentice Hall) and coauthor of an *Introduction to Global Studies* (Wiley-Blackwell) as well as numerous scholarly articles on South African history. He earned his PhD from the University of London and his MA in history from the University of KwaZulu-Natal in South Africa, where he lived and taught for over four years. He currently teaches courses on South African, African, and world history as well as global studies.

Elaine McClarnand MacKinnon

Elaine MacKinnon is a professor of Russian and Soviet history at the University of West Georgia. She is the translator and editor of *Mass Uprisings in the USSR* (M. E. Sharpe), and has written an array of journal articles, book chapters, and review essays on Russian and Soviet history. She earned her MA and PhD in modern European history at Emory University, and she currently teaches courses on world history, Russian and Soviet history, and the Cold War.

Jane E. Mangan

Jane Mangan is an associate professor of history at Davidson College, specializing in colonial history of Latin America. She lived in Potosí while researching her first book, *Trading Roles: Gender, Ethnicity, and the Urban Economy in Colonial Potosí* (Duke University Press, 2005), and followed a trail of silver inheritance from Potosí to Spain as the inspiration for her second book project on transatlantic families in the sixteenth century.

Nadejda Popov

Nadejda Popov is an assistant professor of history at the University of West Georgia, where she teaches courses in Greek and Roman history as well as the first half of the world history survey. Her research focus is Greek and Roman warfare. She grew up in Israel and has traveled extensively throughout the Mediterranean, especially Greece.

Preface

Note to the Student

Welcome to *Places of Encounter.* This text offers a new approach to learning about world history by taking you to the places where major developments in our past have occurred. Each chapter is designed to send you on a journey to a specific location associated with momentous historical events and epochs. Both volumes of this text are inspired by our desire to share with you the passion we have for the places we study and conduct our research as historians. We want to convey the excitement we feel in the places where major changes in human history occurred. Like you, we started learning the stories of our past as readers. We too discovered that we are connected to many places in the world through our common human ancestry and through the interactions of people and societies over time and across the globe. We wondered what it would be like to travel back in time to the places we read about but could only imagine. We realized that being in a historical place unlocks a portal to the past and allows us to see the intersections of land, environments, and human structures that lie at the heart of historical processes.

Themes

Places is organized around three main principles: change over time, connectivity, and the recurrence of certain themes throughout human history.

- To show change over time, the text offers a basic chronological sequence of history that begins in Volume I with the emergence of hominids (early humans) in Ethiopia and ends in Volume II with the emergence of the global, postindustrial city of Dubai in the United Arab Emirates. The volumes cover important turning points in human history, from the formation of the earliest human communities and towns through the foundation of cities, states, and empires and the development of industrialization, to the emergence of postindustrial globalization.

- To demonstrate the second principle, connectivity, both volumes present individual locations as part of a global nexus of historical and geographic connections. Each chapter identifies key regional and global connections among societies, places, peoples, and eras, demonstrating that world history is very much about connections and interactions across time and space. Each place in these volumes developed through linkages to previous historical eras and in turn shaped future historical actors and movements. Geography and environment also shaped the links people forged. In some cases, these links were regional—connecting people along a coastline with others in the interior, as in Cape Town, South Africa, or within areas of oceanic trade in the Atlantic or Indian oceans. In other cases global connections spanned outward from major urban centers such as Carthage or London in search of resources, territory, and labor, building land- and sea-based empires in the process. Similarly, technologies in the form of ships, airplanes, and even rocket-propelled weapons provided for global strands of connectivity.

- Third, the text emphasizes significant thematic elements that recur in human history. History is so vast that, in order to find some meaning in it, historians study it through different lenses or viewpoints that reflect what we deem important in our own lives. In *Places* we have emphasized themes that include migration (where and why people moved around the continent or globe); class, race, ethnicity, and gender (how humans form social and economic identities); urbanization and colonialism (how they organized themselves spatially and politically); and technology, trade, and commerce (what they built and the values they placed on those things). In the thematic table of contents you'll see all these major themes and which chapters emphasize which themes.

Overall, as you will see, the picture of our past that emerges from these volumes is like a satellite map of the world at night: as a particular place becomes important, it glows and then fades as another location takes preeminence. Like a mosaic with endless links connecting the different locations, *Places* spotlights individual pieces, inextricably linked to the others, together making up the picture of each epoch. *Places* will show you a picture of history not as a simple sequential process but rather a dynamic, multitextured combination of overlapping eras—like overlapping notes in a musical chord. We hope you will appreciate the chapters both individually and collectively, as they provide a broader landscape of the ways people and places interacted to shape our past.

Reading and Using Places of Encounter

Places is intended to allow you to engage with history in various locations around the world, even if you cannot actually be there. When you've studied history before, it was probably narrated like a story, with one event following another in a linear way. Instead of telling a linear story, this book uses place-based history to illustrate the past. If you have ever visited a historical site like an old house or a historic location like a battlefield, you're familiar with place-based history. The chapters are organized similarly:

- **A Personal Prologue** outlines the author's personal engagement with the place—how he or she came to be interested in that particular place and why. Consider how and why the authors found their passion in a particular place and time. Do you have a similar interest in a historical place or have you been inspired by a visit or tour to a historical monument marking an important political, religious, or cultural event that happened there? Perhaps you've visited a location where your ancestors lived or emigrated?

- **The main narrative of the chapter** introduces the place in a particular time. Understanding the historical context—including geographic and environmental features; available technologies and skills; and ethnicity, language, gender, nationalism, and religious beliefs—is essential to understanding the history of the place you are reading about. Imagine, for example, what your life would be like without cars or computers (technology), or how your life would be different if you lived in a society where some people were enslaved due to their race, gender, or ethnic background.

- **The Global Connections** section of the chapter shows the linkages of this place and time with other parts of the region or the world as well as how this chapter relates to the chapters that come before and after. Because human encounters are often the precursors to historic developments as a result of the exchange of ideas and goods or the clash of cultural and religious beliefs, these connections tell the story of this place's role in world history.

- **The Encounters as Told: Primary Sources** section gives you a chance to read firsthand accounts about those human encounters in the sources they left behind. These sources range from travelogues and diaries to government documents and treatises related to historical developments. Questions and notes at the beginning of each document will help you explore the relationship between the documents and the chapter narrative. You will also need to consider the context of the documents by asking questions such as: Who wrote the document and who was the intended audience? What was the writer's intent—to write a newspaper article, a government document, a propaganda piece, or something else? What sorts of things are left out or hidden in the document? Are women or indigenous people mentioned, and in what context? How do the writer's gender and socioeconomic class compare to those of the people mentioned in the document? What sorts of biases can you see in the source? How does the document help you better understand the chapter you just read? Does it refer to the physical place or perhaps to different people in the location? Does it depict people or place positively or not?

- **Maps** will show you the relationship of the place to the rest of the world and the region with which it is associated as well as the important spatial features that are referred to in the body of the chapter.

- Finally, each chapter provides a list of **additional resources** divided into two main categories. The first is further reading resources authors have recommended. Although these are not an exhaustive list of what other historians have written on the topic, they will enable you to get a deeper, more detailed understanding of some of the key developments that occurred in each location and to consider why these places are so important to world history. The second is a list of Internet URLs or web page references. These websites provide important visual materials and discussion of related ideas and analyses, and they are well worth exploring. Although you may not be able to travel to every place in the text, the chapters and secondary readings and recommended secondary readings may be the next best thing, providing you with significant insight into these places and the important roles they played. We hope that *Places of Encounter* will inspire you to ask questions of the past and the places in which it took shape as well as to undertake your own journeys of discovery to visit some of these locations—and others—that are part of the living history of our world.

Read on, and may you find the world to be as exciting a place as we and our fellow authors do!

Aran and *Elaine MacKinnon*, editors

Note to the Instructor

Welcome to *Places of Encounter.* This text provides a unique approach to world history. It is designed to allow students to experience the places where major developments took shape and to feel the excitement that comes from imagining historical events as and where they happened. It is inspired by the connections the authors have to the locations they have studied and visited as well as their belief that students share their excitement about world history as they are introduced to these places. It builds on well-established approaches to writing history by situating stories in a specific place to show how the local experience can be relevant to broader global experiences. It also goes beyond these studies by taking advantage of new approaches in environmental and place-based history. These approaches emphasize the importance of the historical and imagined relations between people and the land, and they show how these can be understood by considering the connections people make between place and the past. Additionally, *Places of Encounter* takes these place-based relationships and connects them to the wider currents of global history. Each chapter shows the reader how and where its place is connected temporally and spatially to other historically significant regions and developments. In these ways it seeks to provide students and instructors with both new perspectives and new tools for looking at major developments in world history.

The text is divided into two volumes, one for each of the major chronological blocks of time that are most often taught in two-term courses at college and universities. (For courses with different chronological breaks, each chapter is also available in digital form so that the book can be easily customized to fit every course.)

Places of Encounter can be assigned in at least two ways. First, by supplementing the content with lecture material, instructors can assign *Places* as a main text, guiding students along the overall arc of chronological history through the chapter progression. Volume I begins this progression with the emergence of modern humans in Hadar, Ethiopia, and South Africa, and then it takes the students through the development of early settled human communities and urban complexes in Mesopotamia, China, and the Mediterranean. It shows how and where trade-based societies and their cultures emerged and made connections in the Middle East, Africa, and Europe, and how these then connected to the emergence of imperial ventures and global commercial connections from Europe to the Americas and elsewhere on the globe.

The arc continues in Volume II and guides students through the early-modern period of burgeoning empires and the expansion of merchant-capitalism in the Atlantic world and Asia to the emergence of major industrial metropoles in Europe and East Asia. It then turns to the era of competition and conflict through the World Wars and into the global Cold War, ending with the era of intensified decolonization, globalization, and urbanization.

Alternatively, the volumes can be used to supplement a traditional survey text. The place-based approach allows for more detailed studies of the major developments and themes addressed in a survey textbook, providing a foundation for discussion and analysis of multiple topics and themes for each location. The primary source documents, called "Encounters as Told," can be the foundation for primary source analyses in class.

Chapters have a consistent structure, including the following components (described in the Note to the Student, above):

- **Personal Prologue** discusses the author's personal connection to the place, often including the author's own physical and cultural encounters with the locality and its people.

- **The Chapter Narrative** explains how and why particular places became important. Additionally, they provide a compelling and focused case study of how the local environment intersects with major historical developments.

- **Global Connections** in each chapter show how broader regional and global developments are tied to various places that were central to specific historical eras and movement.

- **Maps** show the relationship of the place to the rest of the world and the region with which it is associated as well as the important spatial features that are referred to in the body of the chapter.

- **Encounters as Told: Primary Sources** provide opportunities for students to consider voice, biases, and agency in history.

- **Further Reading and Web Resources** provide more detail on select topics as well as ways to further explore the location in the context of the latest historiographical approaches to the field.

Places is organized to be flexible and can be used in a number of ways:

1. Most obviously, successive chapters can be assigned in the rough chronological order the book reflects. Each chapter then shows how broader regional and global connections and developments are tied to various nodes, places that were central to specific historical developments. Thus, the chapters help explain how and why particular places became important. Additionally, they provide a compelling and focused case study of how the local environment intersects with major historical movements.

2. Because the chapters are based around a series of major themes, an instructor might choose to cut across chronology and follow these categories of analysis across time and space. The thematic table of contents shows the thematic connections among chapters. Instructors can select one or more themes to revisit as they move through the world history sequence to see how these themes differed from place to place and over time. For example, students can compare and contrast how people interacted with their environments as early hominids in Ethiopia and as globalized investors developing real estate in Dubai. Alternatively, chapters can be selected to supplement the instructor's own lectures or a traditional text.

3. The regional table of contents shows which chapters touch on which global regions. A list of regional connections provides the possibility of showing students how various locations intersect and influence each other. As with many approaches to world history, we believe the links and contingencies among societies and regions are fundamental to understanding world history. Each chapter, therefore, makes explicit links to other chapters, regions, and time periods as well as to broader developments that relate to a given region.

4. *Places of Encounters* takes advantage of exciting new Internet-based technologies to enhance the ways students can see and engage with the chapter locations. Each chapter concludes with suggested websites. Using Google Earth, readers can see the geographical location in a global context and may use Google Earth tours to see more details about particular places.

We would like to thank the many reviewers whose careful reading of the chapters provided helpful insights to make this book a better fit for their classrooms:

Brett Berliner, Morgan State University

Gayle K. Brunelle, California State University, Fullerton

Samuel Brunk, University of Texas at El Paso

Alister Chapman, Westmont College

Arthur T. Coumbe, Troy State University

Eugene Cruz-Uribe, California State University, Monterey Bay

Edward Davies, University of Utah

Margaret Handke, Minnesota State University, Mankato

Paul Hatley, Rogers State University

Andrew J. Kirkendall, Texas A & M University

Ari Daniel Levine, University of Georgia

Senya Lubisich, Citrus College

Harold Marcuse, University of California, Santa Barbara

David Meier, Dickinson State University

Chad Ross, East Carolina University

Quinn Slobodian, Wellesley College

Evan R. Ward, Brigham Young University

Jeffrey Wilson, California State University, Sacramento

Special thanks to the students in Eugene Cruz-Uribe's world history class at Cal State Monterey Bay, who read and evaluated chapters from the book.

Read and enjoy, and hopefully together we can inspire students to follow in our footsteps!

Aran and *Elaine MacKinnon*, editors

Volume I.
Thematic Table of Contents

	Class and social stratification	Cultural exchange: synthesis & syncretism	Environment	European colonialism	Labor	Migration	Race and ethnicity	Religion	Technology	Trade and commerce	Urban environment and urbanization	War and conflict	Women and gender
HADAR			X			X	X						X
MAKAPANSGAT			X			X	X	X	X				
BABYLON		X						X		X	X	X	
ATHENS	X	X				X		X		X	X	X	X
XIAN		X						X		X		X	
CARTHAGE		X	X			X				X	X	X	
CONSTANTINOPLE /ISTANBUL		X				X		X		X	X	X	X
MECCA		X		X		X		X		X			X
KILWA	X	X	X			X		X		X			
VARANASI	X	X	X	X			X	X					X
SAMARKAND		X	X		X		X			X	X		
VENICE	X		X			X		X		X	X		
POTOSÍ	X	X		X	X	X	X	X					X
MALACCA	X	X		X						X	X		

Volume I.
Regional Table of Contents

	Africa	Atlantic Ocean World	Europe	Indian Ocean World	Latin America	Mediterranean	Middle East	Southeast Asia	Pacific Ocean World
HADAR	X								
MAKAPANSGAT	X								
BABYLON						X	X		
ATHENS			X			X			
XIAN								X	X
CARTHAGE	X		X			X			
CONSTANTINOPLE /ISTANBUL			X			X	X		
MECCA							X		
KILWA	X					X			
VARANASI				X				X	
SAMARKAND							X		
VENICE			X			X			
POTOSÍ		X			X				X
MALACCA				X				X	

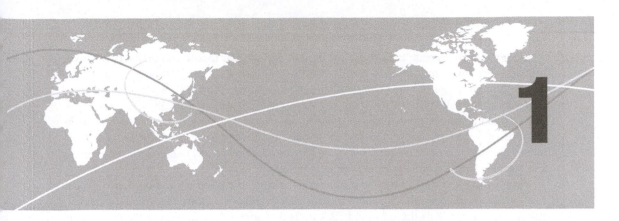

Hadar

The Legacy of Human Ancestors

(4,000,000–100,000 BCE)

CHRISTOPHER HOWELL

THE AREA OF HADAR FIRST MADE HEADLINES IN THE 1970S WITH THE DISCOVERY of the most famous of the *Australopithecine* fossil remains, nicknamed "Lucy" by the paleoanthropologist who discovered her, Dr. Donald Johanson. Lucy was one of the most complete fossil skeleton hominids ever recovered. She was a rarity in a world where modern fossil hunters or paleontologists celebrated even an occasional tooth find. Her incredible state of completeness and preservation hinted at just how special Hadar would become as a source for hominid prehistory and history. Lucy continues to be the unofficial "spokesperson" for Hadar and its unparalleled ability to help us address what it means to be human.

To visit Lucy's homeland, one needs to return to her African roots, specifically the region of Hadar in Ethiopia, where the world's richest fossil database on human ancestors continues to yield fascinating new windows into the ancient world of hominids. I first visited the region a decade ago while working on an archaeology expedition seeking clues of ancient seafaring along the African coast. Political instability and red tape led to a number of unexpected free days, and some of us decided to head inland to visit the land of our ancestors in Ethiopia. Dr. Johanson's finds had made Hadar and the Afar Triangle famous. Perhaps we would find a "Lucy" or other significant fossil, we thought. Well, we had no such luck, but during our journey we learned why the Rift Valley and Hadar were yielding so much information on hominids.

Hadar is a proverbial "gold mine" of human and animal fossils and artifacts from six million years ago to modern times. This is the very time postulated in evolutionary theory for the emergence of humans from earlier primate animal forms. The action of plate tectonics produced the Great Rift Valley, the Afar Triangle, and, specifically, the Hadar depression. Thus, the earth is literally splitting apart and exposing ancient deposits from millions of years ago. These deposits of soil and rock are what have fossilized and protected the remains of our ancestors. If we listen and observe at Hadar, we learn that we are not so different from these early bipedal species.

Even in modern times Hadar promotes adaptation to changing environments. To get to the Hadar area, we hired a car and driver to help us negotiate the volatile political, tribal climate as well as the sand and rock trails that sometimes substitute for roads. Our driver was well versed in local road and political conditions, and he handled the necessary small gift exchanges (bribes) that allowed us to pass various checkpoints—some official and some not so much. After a grueling twelve-hour car trip we reached Elowha village in the heart of the Afar triangle. My colleagues were road weary, so they decided to visit a local market known for indigenous goods, find something to eat, and then do an exploration on their own; they were sick of the car. I was too, but I asked the driver to take me to a local bar so I could refresh myself. The driver and I ended up at a local "bar"—really just a watering hole, locally known as Lussy's and named for the famous find of Lucy. I learned that we were only thirty miles (fifty kilometers) from Afar Locality 288, where thirty-one-year-old Dr. Donald Johanson and Tom Gray first found Lucy in 1974. Refreshed, I began to get the "fever" that every person who shares a fascination with finding remains of the past gets. In less than thirty minutes by Land Rover, I found myself amidst the sandy slopes that held Lucy's secrets for over three million years. I took a walk around the sandy slopes in the blazing sun. Maybe it was the sun or the weary trip, but I felt like I was walking in the steps of Lucy across the same landscape our ancestors did millions of years ago and just as the Johanson expedition did over three decades ago.

Fossils of animals and human ancestors are quite prevalent in the area. As this chapter will show, over four million years ago in East Africa human ancestors began to walk upright (bipedalism) as an adaptation to a mixed landscape of riparian forests and savannah grasslands. Known as "hominids" in modern scientific terms, their ability to walk upright resulted in physical and behavior adaptations such as tool making and use, nutrient-rich diets, and, eventually, larger brain size. These adaptations allowed for migrations out of Africa and the spread of modern humans across the globe, thus leading to the modern world we know today.

Yet it was not at all clear that early hominids would survive and thrive in East Africa just because they could walk upright and use simple stone tools to adapt to a changing environment. The fascinating story of how our hominid ancestors survived and thrived is best "read" through fossils and artifacts recovered at East African sites along the Rift Valley, where bipedalism and tool use first occurred in hominid populations between six million years ago and the emergence of modern humans starting around two hundred thousand years ago.

HADAR AND THE WORLD: The Center of Humanity

The site of Hadar in the Afar Triangle at the north end of the Rift Valley in Ethiopia is considered the most important site and area for telling the story of the emergence of humanity. (See Map 1.1.) Hadar is a depression landform located in the Afar triangle about 1,640 feet (500 meters) above sea level. The Afar Triangle is geologically famous as the

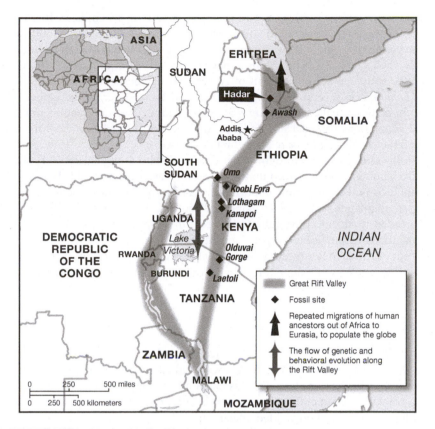

Map 1.1. Migration Out of East Africa and the Great Rift Valley

The Great Rift Valley of East Africa is produced by plate tectonic activity in the earth's subsurface layers. In northern Ethiopia, three plates collide in the Afar Triangle, with Hadar at the heart of the collision zone, providing a unique geographic setting that has been the backdrop environment for the earliest human evolution. The Rift Valley has proven to be an evolutionary "highway" with early human ancestors moving north out of Africa and departing Hadar for the rest of Eurasia and the world ever since human ancestors began to walk upright.

meeting place of three tectonic plates—Nubia, Somalia, and Arabia—that form the African Rift valley system, home of some of the most important early human ancestral fossils in the world. Like much of Africa, Hadar is a hard place to get to because of geography, weather, and political climate. The hot summer days and cool winter nights remind us of just how contrasting and extreme human ancestral adaptation has been for the past few million years. Africa's topography is not so different today from what it was like six million years ago. Wind and water have heavily eroded Hadar's 262 feet (80 meters) of sandy deposits, revealing fossilized bones from the origins of human time. This landscape holds the key to understanding how humanity emerged from our complex relationship with and adaptation to the environment.

From sites like Hadar, researchers known as paleoanthropologists are reconstructing this story in fascinating detail. Due to their efforts, we know that numerous species associated with two genera in particular, *Australopithecus* and *Homo*, were and are key to understanding the physical and cultural evolution adaptations that led to us and our modern human civilization.

Recent finds at Hadar and in the Rift Valley of East Africa also indicate that Lucy's relatives did not just walk upright but also utilized early tools—simple stone tools for cutting and concussing. It is thus with Lucy that the first signs of being human emerge. She recently finished a tour of US museums in her first journey "out of Africa." Her genus, the *Australopithecines*, never made it out of Africa, but her descendants did. This was the genus *Homo* that in several waves spread out of Africa and across the globe. Today we modern humans are called *Homo sapiens sapiens*, and we owe our success to these early physical adaptations (bipedalism) and cultural-behavior adaptations (tool making) that Lucy and her *Australopithecine* relatives first developed.

Thus, the ability to walk upright—specifically, "habitual bipedalism"—is what led to the modern human world. It freed up the hands, increased vision, and led to complex diet and brain growth. But of utmost importance, walking upright gave rise to the most critical human adaptation of all: tool making and tool use. With tools, bipedal hominids no longer needed to change physically for successful adaptation to an environment; they could manufacture and use tools that changed the environment for them. Lucy finally did make it out of Africa in her recent tour, ironically on complex tools like jets and ships that were made possible by her adaptations, which she helped "test out" almost four million years ago!

Lucy: The Find That Made Hadar

For fossil finders around the globe, nothing comes close to the excitement Donald Johanson and colleagues felt the day they discovered Lucy, one of the most complete sets of *Australopithecine* remains found to this day. The team arose at sunrise, and after a cup of thick, black Ethiopian coffee (Ethiopia is the original birthplace of coffee beans), they headed for an area that had yielded ancient animal remains a short drive away. Animal fossils had been found in the area suggestive of a riparian or stream environment, though from a different time and sedimentary layer from those that usually yielded fossilized hominid remains. Nonetheless, Johanson and graduate student Tom Gray wanted to explore the area further anyway. They dropped off geologists and then combed the area for several hours before Johanson spotted a hominid elbow. This was followed by what eventually became the fossilized remains of a 65 percent complete hominid. Johanson and Gray were beside themselves! They could not wait to get back to camp and share their find.

Lab analysis revealed the remains to be those of an adult female *Australopithecus afarensis*. Johanson had made the find of finds: a relatively complete fossilized skeleton of an upright hominid from over three million years ago that helped fill in the so-called "missing link" of human evolution. This was the supposed gap that many critics of evolution suggested existed between ancient, primate-like fossils that did not walk upright and more recent, human-like fossils that clearly did walk upright. Lucy resembled an upright chimpanzee in some ways but had other features suggestive of later hominids.

But the find needed a name. Over the next few days several were proposed, including *Dinkinesh*, meaning "you are marvelous" in local Amharic vocabulary. However, Johanson's girlfriend, Pamela Alderman, proposed the name we know as the group celebrated over a campfire dinner of roasted goat, fried potatoes, and Bati beer. The tape player wafted the lyrics from "Lucy in the Sky with Diamonds" across the cooling desert night. The song was from the Beatles' album *Sgt. Pepper's Lonely Hearts Club Band*, and the name stuck. Today Lucy and the Hadar region continue to inspire a new generation of fossil hunters seeking to answer pressing questions of evolution and hoping to make a field-changing discovery just as Johanson did over three decades ago—a find made by walking the landscape just as our ancestors did for millions of years at Hadar.

Hadar as the Center of Humanity

Beginning in the late 1970s and continuing today, thousands of fossilized bones and tools have been discovered at Hadar. The area's geomorphology (short-term land-form processes), geology (long-term land-form processes) along with limited modern-population impacts are partly responsible for the unique preservation and exposure of fossils at Hadar. Its ancient climate and biome must also have been a great draw for hominids. The animal fossils, pollens, and erosion evidence indicate that Hadar was a much wetter region during early fossil hominid times. Its environment oscillated several times between forested streams and receding forests. As the forests and water supply receded, grassland savannas took over. Together these factors resulted in the attraction, protection, fossilization, and then, finally, exposure of the greatest number of ancient potential human ancestors ever found. The database that continues to emerge at Hadar may turn out to be greater than the entire global database for all non-Hadar (Afar Triangle) databases combined! As of 2010 both the quantity and quality of these fossils is unparalleled when compared with any other paleontology site in the world.

Today we classify this general group of bipedal, upright species and possible relations and ancestors as *Hominoidae*. Dr. Johanson prefers the term "hominid" for bipedal issues, but modern researchers also use the term "hominin." We will utilize hominid in honor of Lucy (*Dinkinesh*) as the first major discovery at Hadar and the one that placed Hadar on the map. Today Hadar is the preeminent place to search for answers to the question, "What does it mean to be human?" It is a question at the very heart of our existence.

Lucy and the First Family

Lucy was not alone at Hadar. Counting Lucy, the fossil specimens of *Australopithecus aferensis* found at Hadar to date number over 360 individuals—far more individual specimens than are known from any other paleontology site in the world. It is not clear, however, if this means that the ancient Hadar region between three to four million years ago held a greater population density due to better environmental resources or if that this is simply due to the unique preservation traits and modern geologic exposure traits underway at Hadar.

This collection of 360 individual fossilized remains, discovered over the past three decades, is collectively and affectionately known as the "First Family" of humanity. It is by far the largest concentration of an ancient species of hominids ever found. Only at Hadar can paleoanthropologists who study fossil remains of past human ancestors hope to find detailed answers to their questions about hominids. These include biological and social questions concerning adaptation, origins, and quality of life as well as questions about social groups, diet, and lifespan. Today we know that Lucy and her species were only one of several *Australopithecine* species in the African savannahs and forest lands between four and one million years ago. Her species was particularly gracile, or slightly built, but with variable heights from 3 to 5.5 feet tall, weighing around a hundred pounds, and having brain casings around 400 to 500 cubic centimeters. Lucy and her kind walked upright regularly and had larger brains than modern primates such as chimpanzees. They ate mostly a fruit, plant, and insect diet that would be unfamiliar to us today, whether vegetarian, omnivorous, or carnivorous. Lucy and her companions lived only to thirty years or so if they made it to adult status. Modern humans average twice the lifespan and have a brain three times the size of Lucy's. Hence, Lucy was closer in build and lifespan to early *Homo* genus species like *Homo habilis* from around 2 million years ago than she was to modern humans. The *Homo* genus first emerged alongside or perhaps from the *Australopithecines* around 2.6 million years ago in East Africa, including at Hadar. *Homo* migrated out of Africa as efficient bipedal species that made and used stone tools. Several species of the genus migrated across the globe in waves that eventually led to modern humans, or *Homo sapiens sapiens*.

Although there is debate over whether the *Australopithecines* genus developed tools even earlier than *Homo*, researchers have found at Hadar the earliest stone tools definitely associated with the *Homo* genus, dating from 2.6 million years. These are called Olduwan-style stone tools, and they are common across Hadar. Olduwan stone tools were the first stone-tool industry in the world, and they show up first in the Rift Valley between 2.6 and 1.7 million years ago. Olduwan tools are characterized by simple choppers made from breaking river cobble in half to obtain a sharp cutting and concussing edge but with a smooth, round hand-hold on the opposite side. Additionally, simple uniface and biface scrapers as well as cutting tools characterize the Olduwan tool industry. Unifaces and bifaces are stones that hominids worked purposefully on one or both sides to obtain a sharp edge for cutting but not usually for concussing.

The *Australopithecines* (4 million to 1 million years ago) and the *Homo* genus lines (2.6 million years ago to present) overlap each other in time and space at Hadar and in Africa in general, making interpretations of culture difficult. The concentration of Lucy-like individuals at Hadar and the presence of various stone-tool assemblages all suggest basic social organization for the purposes of adaptation to a mixed forest and savannah-like environment several million years ago. At Hadar, hominid groups needed to access stone tool–making material, water, and food in territorial units that matched their social unit size. Researchers believe such basic social units as a family or band would be necessary, as infants could not care for themselves for at least the first few years of life.

Unfortunately, the inability of relative and absolute dating systems to narrow the times for hominid fossil and tool discoveries to more than a few thousand years currently makes it impossible to explore the exact nature of the relationships between *Australopithecines* and the *Homo* genus lines or even to distinguish culture traits at sites with mixed associations. So currently researchers cannot address whether these two genera were in contact with each other between the span of 2.6 million years ago, when *Homo* first appears, and 1 million years ago, when *Australopithecines* die out at Hadar and East Africa in general.

What researchers can be certain of is the early hominid relationship with the environment at Hadar. The small size of hominids, whether late *Austrolopithecines* or early *Homo*, indicates a limited range in terms of how far individuals and groups could cover in a day or a season. Animal fossils and sediment layers indicate that Hadar's location on an ever-expanding Rift Valley system in East Africa may have been key. This was a land of climate and biome change, albeit over thousands of years. Thus, many species of plants and animals called it home over the course of hominid times. Hominid species could take advantage of the concentration of resources along the north-south-running Rift Valley in East Africa by walking to the resources and utilizing basic tools to adapt to those resources. Perhaps the emerging and changing Rift Valley system promoted migration up and down its length. Perhaps certain hominid groups simply moved within a local landscape to seasonal resources or to resources that varied by elevation and landscape. We can never know for sure because the environments changed across six million years of hominid occupation at

Hadar. Although early hominids were not nearly as efficient at habitual bipedalism as modern humans are, the basic gait of *Australopithecines* such as Lucy was good enough to get individuals and small groups from one resource base to the next.

This increasing complexity in terms of physical adaptation and cultural-behavior adaption are evident in the fossils and stone tools at Hadar from between six million and three hundred thousand years ago. The varying environmental conditions across this span of time in this region apparently helped select or promote certain successful adaptations to the environment. In the fossil remains of hominids at Hadar several adaptations are clearly evident, including body- and brain-size increases, evolution of more efficient parts in the skeleton for walking, and increased dexterity in the hands. In turn these adaptations were tied to behavioral adaptations, such as construction and use of stone tools, migration or patterned movements to key resources like water and food, and increasing complexity in the diets as more and more animal products supplemented a plant-based diet.

First Human and First Culture

In 1994 Hadar again made headlines. Already famous for Lucy and the First Family, researchers made a second astounding discovery: 2.3- to 2.6-million-year-old fossils of a partial *Homo* genus jawbone along with many teeth. These became the oldest known direct human ancestor fossils by several hundred thousand years. But that was not the end of the story. Subsequent excavations yielded over a dozen stone tools consisting of sharp-edged flakes knocked off several stone cores. Some of the flakes fit back onto the cores from which they were formed. This meant that Hadar not only yielded the oldest known remains of the human genus *Homo* but also the oldest human-associated tools. We might consider this a type of "First Human" and "First Culture." In other words, if we think of culture as behavioral adaptation to the environment, then the stone tools at Hadar are the oldest known examples of human culture in the world. So hundreds of thousands of years after Lucy and First Family populations were walking across the Hadar landscape, another species associated with bipedal locomotion was also exploring and adapting to the savannah highlands and river forest lowlands at ancient Hadar. We cannot determine the exact species, but we are certain, based on the teeth and jawbone, that it is a human ancestor—a human ancestor that may have sat down among the remains of *Australopithecines* to craft some of the earliest tools in human history.

Stone-tool (lithic) production is usually associated with the need for a sharp cutting edge (flakes) and a heavy concussing tool (hammerstones) to not only help process food supply such as plant and animal material but also dig, defend, and attend to other purposes. We call this behavioral adaptation phase the Paleolithic Period, or "old stone age" in human history, and it is a clear sign of behavioral rather than just physical adaptation to an environment. No longer did hominids need to develop biologically sharper claws or teeth for cutting or stronger bones and muscles for concussing. Stone and other materials could be modified and utilized as tools between hominids and the environment. Behavioral adaptation had moved into the realm of tool making.

Biological adaptation now had a new and powerful partner: behavioral adaptation in both social groups and physical modification of the environment. This changed everything. The species we know as humans today is a direct result of these developments, for better or for worse. The basic stone-tool kit would be with hominids and, especially, the *Homo* genus for the next two million years. The combination of bipedalism, social groupings, and tools gave the *Homo* genus increased access and processing capabilities to varied environments and food supply. For instance, hammerstones could be used to break up carrion animal long-bones, and sharp stone knives could be used to remove soft tissue such as marrow. Indeed, East African hominid sites are full of just such evidence. Yet we know from fossilized teeth and analysis on stone tools that the human ancestral diets were omnivorous. Based on analysis of residues on the stone tools as well as C3 and C4 (carbon ratios) from human bones, this omnivorous diet consisted of an increased nutrient base that included wider varieties of flora and fauna as the transition from *Australopithecines* to the *Homo* genus line took place at Hadar and across East Africa. Hadar is well known for its fossil remains of animals such as antelope and savannah game; tools allowed for easier processing of both plants and animals and are clearly evident at later *Homo* genus sites.

This increased interaction with the environment in turn led to further changes toward an increasingly modern human anatomy. Brain sizes grew toward one thousand cubic centimeters, and this was only possible with a more complex, nutrient-rich diet. The *Homo* genus also increased their environmental ranges, albeit in haphazard growth and shrinkage patterns, across Africa and then across the globe, giving access to increased nutrient bases for brain-growth need. Modern human civilization today can be tied back to Hadar some 2.3 to 2.6 million years ago with First Human and First Culture.

Ardi

In 2009 results of finds made in the 1990s would yet again place Hadar at the center of the debate of what it is to be human. Perhaps the most important biological individual set of remains discovered at Hadar were found only forty-six miles (seventy-five kilometers) from the Lucy location. These were identified as belonging to *Ardipithecus ramidus*, one of the earliest known hominid species. Nicknamed "Ardi" after the genus, this individual set of female remains, though nearly as complete as Lucy, required years of preservation work before they could be studied fully in 2009. Ardi proved to be even older than Lucy and far more difficult to categorize. Ardi and her kind dated to 4.5 million years ago and earlier. She had skeletal traits associated with tree-dwelling primates as well as bipedal capabilities. The implications were astounding for paleoanthropology and human evolution: Ardi appeared to be a link between early tree-dwelling (arboreal) primates of great antiquity and the more recent habitually bipedal hominids such as Lucy and modern humans that had adapted to mixed environments of forests, waterways, and grasslands.

Various theories are posited to explain Ardi's unique characteristics. At the heart of the issue is the cause or need for bipedalism. No doubt bipedalism frees up the hands, elevates the vision center, realigns the spinal nerve center, and, of course, allows for long-distance migrations. Increased linkages between hands, eyes, and brains also result along with increased access to a variety of nutrients and environments. But Ardi challenges the idea that bipedalism was a direct adaptation to grasslands as forests shrank due to climate changes. On one side researchers, such as Tim White, who helped discover and preserve Ardi, believe we have to rethink the so-called "savannah theory," consisting of bipedalism emerging in adaptation to loss of forest habitat and increase of grassland habitat. White believes that ancestors of *Ardipithecus* are not much like chimps and monkeys of today, even though humans share 98 percent of their genetic material with chimpanzees.

An alternate theory based on Ardi's physiology is the "food-for-sex theory." *Ardipithecus ramidus* needed both arboreal and bipedal adaptations because males who accessed a broader food base from forests and grasslands successfully won out in reproduction access to females. The finding of thirty-five additional *Ardipithecus ramidus* remains at

Hadar that are associated with the female Ardi bolster this theory. These show little sexual dimorphism (differences between males and females), as they have similar-sized, small canine teeth and similar body sizes. Such characteristics are associated with mating displays among modern primates. This could result from dual-locomotion capabilities for forests and savannahs, but it could also result from behavioral practices of social-group adaptations or perhaps a combination of the two. However, if White is correct, then Ardi and her kind have little in common with Lucy and her kind other than bipedalism. *Ardipithecus* has no known stone tools, lived in forested environments, and may even have had different reproduction and food gathering practices when compared to *Australopithecines* at Hadar, who may have had stone tools and adapted to a more mixed environment.

As with other finds at Hadar, Ardi's kind were associated with detailed evidence of the environment in which they existed. During the time of *Ardipithecus ramidus* at Hadar the environment was a forested woodland rather than the dry, eroded landscape it is today. Over six thousand animal fossils were recovered from Ardi's time. Antelope, monkey, arboreal birds, and seeds of fig and palm trees hint at the landscape that Ardi thrived in and adapted to. Wear patterns and isotope samples from *Ardipithecus ramidus* teeth indicate a diet of fruits, nuts, and forest foods. No stone tools were recovered in association with Ardi, and this may be key. As soon as stone tools show up in the record after Ardi's time and toward the end of Lucy's time, a wider diet was accessed. Fauna shows up on the menu with the arrival of tool making and usage with the later *Australopithecine* and *Homo* genus lines. Stone tools become common by the time of *Homo habilis* and especially *Homo erectus* from 1.6 million years ago. They are so plentiful that the term "Olduwan" is used to describe early humans' use of the stone-tool set across Africa.

Such statements are only possible because of the incredible record of prehistory available at Hadar. The richness of evidence and its exposure at Hadar in particular and the Afar Triangle in general is in contrast to other hominid sites, even those in fossil East Africa and its Rift Valley, of which Hadar and Afar are a part. We currently have more *Australopithecine* and *Ardipithecus* specimens from Hadar and Afar than we do from the rest of the world combined.

First Child and Australopithecine Tools

Just recently in the new millennium yet more findings at Hadar turned the paleoanthropologist world upside down again. The discovery in 2000 by Zeresenay Alemseged of yet another *Australopithecus aferensis* known as the "Dikika child" sparked this upheaval. Dikika is just across the shallow riverbed from Hadar. Even for the Hadar region, this specimen was amazingly complete, with preserved skull, baby teeth, fingers, torso, a foot, and a tiny kneecap. Dated to over 3.3 million years ago, the Dikika child is fairly near the 3.18-million-year date postulated for Lucy. Some even called her Lucy's child, though that would be a stretch. At only three years of age, the Dikika child, or "First Child" as she is now known, allows for amazing insights into the early development of infants for *Australopithecines*. Comparing infant growth and development among humans, chimpanzees, and ancient hominids now became possible. First Child was similar in bone growth and development to early human infants but not as similar to modern chimpanzees or, probably, prehominid fossils such as Ardi, who used both arboreal and terrestrial locomotion. Thus, early researchers may have been justified in placing Lucy, First Child, and First Family closer to other hominids than to early ancestors such as Ardi.

Another discovery associated with First Child, however, has made the bond between full hominids such as *Australopithecines* and the *Homo* genera even stronger. Researchers have long struggled with the issue of the break in the hominid line associated with diet and stone tools. *Australopithecines* were smaller, had no definite tools associated with them, and appeared to have eaten fewer if any large animals compared to the generally later, larger, and more omnivorous *Homo* genus line. Stone tools, however, were common at *Homo* sites and were often associated with processing food, based on common finds of animal remains with processing marks from stone tools. In 2011 near Hadar the results of analysis of two animal bones from Dikika challenged those interpretations of Homo as the only tool-making and -using genus. The bones date to a layer of deposits known to be 3.4 million years old. This was a time when only *Australopithecus afarensis* individuals and groups like Lucy, First Family, and First Child occupied the region. Analysis results indicate that the animal bones have cut marks from stone tools. The evidence is very similar to evidence seen for later stone-tool processing of animal bones at *Homo* sites. So it is possible that *Australopithecines* and the *Homo* genera were both processing animal remains for food supply. Still, the findings are preliminary, and other researchers have noted that no actual stone tools have been found and that the animal bones are several hundred feet from the nearest *Australopithecine* remains.

For hominid descent lines the implications would be enormous if the find stands up to scrutiny. Researchers like Donald Johanson have long suspected and speculated that *Australopithecine* sites likely have stone tools associated with them, but the mixed deposits and presence of later stratigraphic layers associated with the genus *Homo* make this difficult to prove. If *Australopithecus afarensis* was processing and eating large animals, this would be perhaps the final bond between *Australopithecines* and the overlapping but generally later-arriving *Homo* genus. Thus, in locomotion, diet, culture, tool use, and tool making, the two genera are much more similar than previously thought and more likely to share descent associations. This would provide an enormous step back in the human descent line and complete a major relationship in the hominid family.

Hadar and the Future

One thing is certain: Hadar will likely keep its place as the center of the debate on human origins and identity. More fossils and related environmental data are found with each expedition. Hadar is the largest outdoor classroom in existence concerning human ancestry, and its "field lab" will only get bigger. The level of preservation of individual specimens, the enormous sample size of group populations, and the equally significant environmental database make Hadar the ultimate source on all things hominid.

Even now, however, Hadar can answer certain questions. The simplistic ideas that humans and our ancestors have never physically changed or, at the opposite end of the spectrum, have changed beyond all recognition from our ancestors must be discarded. The Hadar database indicates bipedalism has been around since the time of Ardi and became more efficient through the time of Lucy into our own human genus today. Brain size increased with time, as did territorial expansion through migration. Body size, however, has oscillated, as Ardi was only 4 feet tall and Lucy 3.5 feet tall, but some of Lucy's relatives were 5.5 feet tall. Similar variations are seen in the later *Homo* line. Tool making and usage indicates some of the first development of what modern humans call "culture" or behavioral adaptation. It too provides a mixed message at Hadar. We cannot be sure, but we suspect that Lucy's genus may have been involved with stone tools based on the Dikika finds, but that Ardi and the *Ardipithecine* genus was not. Our human genus Homo was certainly involved, but maybe with more refined versions of stone tools than those dating from the time of Lucy.

Environment, breeding practices, behavior adaptations such as tool making, and more all combined at Hadar to leave us a complex message about the past. In addition to simplistic ideas being debunked, Hadar has done the same with idealistically driven theories about ancient life. Claims that human ancestors were somehow unique and this is what differentiated us from other living organisms do not hold up in the face of overwhelming evidence at Hadar, be they artifacts, genetic data, or skeletal remains. The record also does not substantiate theories that human ancestors were only vegetarian, strictly hunters of live game, the only tool makers and users, or the only bipedal genus. Instead, Hadar suggests a much more broad-based approach to surviving and thriving, with lots of overlap, success, and failure.

Human ancestors did not rule out anything when it came to survival and have much more in common with us today than we might at first think. Like us, they walked upright, used complex tools, sought out complex foods, and adapted to a great variety of environments. Perhaps most importantly, they survived and thrived for millions of years in East Africa and then spread across the globe as the *Homo* genus. Modern humans differ mainly in our attempts to settle down permanently in the last few thousand years, a process called "sedentism," in direct contrast to the long successful "nomadic" lifestyle hominids practiced at Hadar for millions of years. It remains to be seen if we as modern humans will succeed in going against the legacy of Hadar or if we can equal the incredible Hadar hominid track record extending across seven million years of successful adaptation!

Many adaptations, many successes, and many failures are all parts of the complex story. The differences between us and our ancestors appear to be mainly in scale. Later developments, such as cooking foods to acquire higher nutrient return, help explain such differences in degree. Today modern humans with complex social networks and even more complex tool kits occupy every part of the globe. We even use complex tools to aid us in adapting to extreme environments in space and in the oceans.

Today there are over six billion humans spread across the globe, each with an average brain size of fourteen hundred cubic centimeters and an amazingly complex set of social, food, and tool-kit networks at the heart of that expansion. This expansion is one whose roots can be traced back to places like Hadar some millions of years ago. Hadar may also hold the key as to where we are headed in the future. The Hadar database is unparalleled in framing what questions we can ask—such as: What is it to be human? What was life like for our human ancestors?—and what answers we can develop concerning our past. Ardi, Lucy, First Child, First Family, and First Human have the answers, and they can be found only at Hadar, the current center of human origins and human identity, whatever that may ultimately be.

GLOBAL ENCOUNTERS AND CONNECTIONS:
Adaption, Evolution, and Migration

The world of paleoanthropologists is not a world of certainty. Most of the database concerning the human past has disappeared with the ravages of time. What is left can be interpreted in a variety of ways. Yet Hadar has forever changed the direction of those interpretations concerning early hominids. The database is too large to ignore or explain away. The time depth with associated vegetation and climate changes is too long and the fossil evidence too great not to ask questions about adaptation and evolution. We are compelled to investigate the linkages of Lucy and all hominids at Hadar.

Yet there are some questions that Hadar cannot address, at least not currently. One of those is the emergence of modern humans across the globe. For those answers, researchers are looking to southern Africa to address how and when modern humans emerged and possibly spread out of Africa. (See Chapter 2 on Makapansgat.) Sites such as those in the Makapansgat Valley in northern South Africa and Blombos Cave on the South African coast may hold the key. Just as Hadar contains an unparalleled record on early hominids, the Makapansgat Valley and its associated caves have yielded similar evidence for later hominids from the time of *Australopithecines* 3.5 million years ago. At Makapansgat a large database on the emergence of modern humans from a few hundred thousand years ago to the present exists. These two sites, when paired with Hadar, provide a near-continuous record of hominid evolution from 6 million years ago to modern day.

Almost a century ago early hominid researchers such as Raymond Dart began sifting through the caves and the limeworks factory at Makapansgat, as factory workers were reporting large numbers of fossils. Makapansgat possesses an excellent database on hominids and the *Homo* genus in Africa, and this is useful for cross-checking interpretations at Hadar. For instance, the body and brain-casing sizes of *Australopithecus aferensis* can be compared between Hadar and Makapansgat, as can dates of existence for genus and species up and down East Africa and the Rift Valley.

Additionally, South Africa has another site that can help fill in the gaps at Hadar concerning the emergence of anatomically modern humans a few hundred thousand years ago. This is Blombos Cave on the coast of South Africa, where evidence indicates fully modern anatomical humans were utilizing red ochre, making shell beads, and harvesting a rich variety of both marine and land animals for food supply somewhere around or just after one hundred thousand years ago. Like Hadar, the evidence from Blombos continues to grow, allowing researchers to address key questions in evolution.

For example, one of the most compelling current debates in paleoanthropology centers on whether or not early *Homo* genus species like *Homo erectus* migrated out of Africa across Eurasia between two million and one million years ago to form "pockets" of local populations that eventually evolved into modern humans. Based on the large number of *Homo erectus* sites around Eurasia that emerge after the development of the species in East Africa, researchers generally agree that the migrations took place. This migration or set of migrations would have been associated with sites like Hadar and Makapansgat. This is known as the original "Out of Africa" theory. A second version of the theory holds that such an early migration did occur but that a later wave of migrations of fully modern anatomical humans from around two hundred to one hundred thousand years ago replaced these early *Homo* populations across Eurasia. Additionally, genetic evidence suggests that modern humans emerged in East Africa between two hundred and one hundred thousand years ago. This is supported by sites in East Africa like Hadar, Makapansgat, and Blombos Cave, which all contain evidence of the emergence of modern humans in East Africa during that time span.

However, the traditional debate on the "Out of Africa" theory has recently seen another variable added. Migrations may have taken place not only by land but also by sea, as suggested by a recent discovery on Crete Island in the Mediterranean just north of Africa. Researchers have uncovered 130,000-year-old stone tools on Crete, thus indicating that modern humans had seafaring capabilities at that time. Because Blombos Cave was occupied slightly later than Crete, at around 85,000 years ago, and contains evidence of modern humans harvesting sea resources, its occupants may have also had coastal seafaring capabilities.

Adding in seafaring as an additional means of migration out of and even into Africa certainly complicates the traditional "Out of Africa" debate. It also forces researchers to rethink the roles of Hadar and Makapansgat in this debate in particular and in evolution in general. Obviously, hominids who can travel by sea might adapt differently in behavior or even in physical structure from hominids migrating by land. Or maybe not. Whatever the final conclusions from databases in East Africa and around the world, Hadar will continue to be the most important early hominid site in world history because of the quantity, quality, and continued discovery of ancient hominid fossils.

ENCOUNTERS AS TOLD: PRIMARY SOURCES

For many who enter the world of paleoanthropology and commit themselves to a life of fossil hunting as well as endless "translation" and interpretation of the past record, there comes a moment when the academic work and the fieldwork of exploration come together. For the most famous paleoanthropologist of our time, Donald Johanson, that moment came when he discovered "Lucy" in 1974. These fossilized skeletal remains were 65 percent complete, by far the most complete ever recovered for early hominids. The find captured the public's attention, generating publicity for and interest in humans' early ancestors.

Lucy's Legacy, by Donald Johanson and Katy Wong

Not only did the recovery of Lucy challenge and help rewrite our interpretations of human evolution, but the fossil also indicated just how unusual and rich the fossil beds of Hadar were. The very time of hominid evolution was exposed in the sedimentary layers eroding onto the surface at Hadar between six million and three hundred years ago. The level of preservation and the quality and quantity of fossil remains both animal and hominid would prove to be unmatched anywhere else in the world. In the following primary source, Dr. Johanson vividly discusses the excitement and fortunate circumstances associated with the discovery of Lucy. As you read through the source, ponder the following questions:

- How fortunate was Donald Johanson to have found the fossils of Lucy on November 24, 1974?

- What role does "field work" play in how paleontologists interpret the past?

- Why does Lucy continue to have such an impact on how we view Africa and our concept of humanity?

Never in my wildest fantasies did I imagine that I would discover a fossil as earthshaking as Lucy. When I was a teenager, I dreamed of traveling to Africa and finding a "missing link." Lucy is that and more: a 3.2-million-year-old skeleton who has become the spokeswoman for human evolution. She is perhaps the best known and most studied fossil hominid of the twentieth century, the benchmark by which other discoveries of human ancestors are judged.

Whenever I tell the story, I am instantly transported back to the thrilling moment when I first saw her thirty-four years ago on the sandy slopes of Hadar in Ethiopia's Afar region. I can feel the searing, noonday sun beating down on my shoulders, the beads of sweat on my forehead, the dryness of my mouth—and then the shock of seeing a small fragment of bone lying inconspicuously on the ground. Most dedicated fossil hunters spend the majority of their lives in the field without finding anything remarkable, and there I was, a thirty-one-year-old newly minted Ph.D., staring at my childhood dream at my feet.

Sunday, November 24, 1974, began, as it usually does for me in the field, at dawn. I had slept well in my tent, with the glittering stars visible through the small screen that kept out the mosquitoes, and as sunrise announced a brilliant new day, I got up and went to the dining tent for a cup of thick, black Ethiopian coffee. Listening to the morning sounds of camp life, I planned with some disinclination the day's activities: catching up on correspondence, fossil cataloging, and a million other tasks that had been set aside to accommodate a visit from anthropologists Richard and Mary Leakey. I looked up as Tom Gray, my grad student, appeared.

"I'm plotting the fossil localities on the Hadar map," he said. "Can you show me Afar Locality 162, where the pig skull was found last year?"

"I have a ton of paperwork and am not sure I want to leave camp today."

"Can you do the paperwork later?"

"Even if I start it now I'll be doing it later," I grumbled. But something inside—a gut sense that I had learned to heed—said I should put the paperwork aside and head to the outcrops with Tom.

A couple of geologists joined us in one of our old, dilapidated Land Rovers, and in a cloud of dust we headed out to the field. I sat in the passenger seat enjoying the passing landscape peppered with animal fossils. Flocks of quacking guinea fowl ran for cover, and a giant warthog, annoyed by our intrusion, hurried off, its tail straight up in the air. Unlike many mammals that had been hunted to extinction in the area, the Hadar warthogs were left alone by the Afar locals, whose Islamic faith forbade eating pork. Tom put the Land Rover through its paces, and as we picked up speed in the sandy washes, my mind switched gears into fossil-finding mode. After we dropped off the geologists, who needed to inspect an important geological fault that had disturbed the sedimentary layers near Locality 162, Tom and I threaded our way along smaller and smaller gullies.

"Somewhere around here," I said. "Pull over." Then I laughed as it occurred to me that in the remote desert you don't have to pull over, you just stop driving. We got out and spent a few minutes locating the cairn that had been left to mark the pig skull's locality, a little plateau of clay and silt sediments bordered by harder layers of sandstone. A year earlier, a geologist had been out on a mapping mission and the plateau was obvious on the aerial photographs we had toted along; otherwise we might have overlooked it. After carefully piercing a pinhole into the aerial photo to mark the spot and labeling it "162" on the reverse side, we lingered. I was reluctant to return to camp and my paperwork. Even though the area was known to be fossil poor, we decided to look around while we were there. But after two hours of hunting all we had to show were some unremarkable fossil antelope and horse teeth, a bit of a pig skull, and a fragment of monkey jaw.

"I've had it. When do we head back?" Tom said.

"Right now." With my gaze still glued to the ground, I cut across the mid-portion of the plateau toward the Land Rover. Then a glint caught my eye, and when I turned my head I saw a two-inch-long, light brownish gray fossil fragment shaped like a wrench, which my knowledge of osteology told me instantly was part of an elbow. I knelt and picked it up for closer inspection. As I examined it, an image clicked into my brain and a subconscious template announced hominid. (The term hominid is used throughout this book to refer to the group of creatures in the human lineage since it diverged from that of chimpanzees. Some other scholars employ the word hominin in its place.) The only other thing it could have been was monkey, but it lacked the telltale flare on the back that characterizes monkey elbows. Without a doubt, this was the elbow end of a hominid ulna, the larger of the two bones in the forearm. Raising my eyes, I scanned the immediate surroundings and spotted other bone fragments of similar color—a piece of thighbone, rib fragments, segments of the backbone, and, most important, a shard of skull vault.

"Tom, look!" I showed him the ulna, then pointed at the fragments. Like me, he dropped to a crouch. With his jaw hanging open, he picked up a chunk of mandible that he wordlessly held out for me to see. "Hominid!" I gushed. "All hominid!" Our excitement mounted as we examined every splinter of bone. "I don't believe this! Do you believe this?" we shouted over and over. Drenched in sweat, we hugged each other and whooped like madmen.

"I'm going to bring the ulna to camp," I said. "We'll come back for the others." I wanted to mark the exact location of each bone fragment scattered on the landscape, but there were too many pieces and time was short.

"Good idea. Don't lose it," Tom joked, as I carefully wrapped the ulna in my bandanna. I decided to take a fragment of lower jaw, too, for good measure. I marked the exact spots where the bones had lain, scribbled a few words in my field notebook, and then got back into the Land Rover. . . .

[Back at the camp] I jumped out of the Land Rover and everyone followed me to the work area, where a large tent fly protected our plywood worktables. Still in a state of semidisbelief, I sat and unpacked the precious remains. Reassured that they were in fact real, I sighed with relief. Everyone leaned over to see the tiny fragments of arm and jaw. The questions came fast and furious. Is there more? Where'd you find it? How did you find it? And then there was a stunned silence as the import of what we'd found sunk in. It hit me that if I had walked just a few more paces and looked to my left rather than my right, the bones would still be there on the slope. And in the ever-changing landscape of the Afar, a single desert thunderstorm could have washed them off the plateau, over a cliff and into oblivion, forever. . . .

We celebrated the discovery with a delicious dinner of roasted goat and panfried potatoes washed down with a case of Bati beer my students had somehow managed to smuggle into camp. Conversation became less animated and more technical, focusing on morphology and size. I felt from the beginning that the fossils belonged to a single individual because there was no duplication of parts in the remains we collected; the pieces all had the same proportions and exhibited the same fossilization color. I further argued that the skeleton was a female specimen of *Australopithecus*—a primitive human forebear—because of the small size of the bones relative to those of other *australopithecines*. All *australopithecines* were sexually dimorphic, which is to say males and females exhibited physical differences beyond those pertaining to the sex organs. So if the lightly built ulna we discovered were from a male, then a female would have to be unbelievably tiny.

While we were all talking, Sgt. Pepper's Lonely Hearts Club Band was playing on a small Sony tape deck. When "Lucy in the Sky with Diamonds" came on, my girlfriend Pamela Alderman, who had come to spend some time in the field with me, said, "Why don't you call her Lucy?" I smiled politely at the suggestion, but I didn't like it because I thought it was frivolous to refer to such an important find simply as Lucy. Nicknaming hominid fossils was not unheard of, however. Mary and Louis Leakey, giants in the field of paleoanthropology, dubbed a flattened hominid skull found in Tanzania's Olduvai Gorge "Twiggy," and a specimen their son Jonathan found received the moniker "Jonny's Child." But most of the scientists I knew wouldn't give their fossils a cute name based on a song by the Beatles. The next morning, however, everyone wanted to know if we were going to the Lucy site. Someone asked how tall Lucy was. Another inquired how old I thought Lucy was when she died. As I sat there eating my breakfast of peanut butter and jelly on toast, I conceded that the name Lucy had a better ring to it than A.L. 288, the locality number that had been assigned to the site.

At my request, the government representative from the Antiquities Administration who had escorted our expedition sent word to the director general of the Ministry of Culture, Bekele Negussie. He arrived a few days later with some of his colleagues. While I answered their questions, I resisted referring to our australopithecine as Lucy because I was uncomfortable about an Ethiopian fossil bearing an English name. When the team returned that afternoon from the site bursting with news of more Lucy fragments, additional information about Lucy, endless speculations about Lucy, my discomfort grew. After dinner Bekele and I sat outside the dining tent looking up at a brilliant starlit sky. I talked about the implications of the discovery, how it might impact prevailing theories about hominid evolution. And we discussed arrangements for a press announcement in Addis Ababa in December.

He listened in silence, then regarded me very seriously and said, "You know, she is an Ethiopian. She needs an Ethiopian name."

"Yes!" I agreed, relieved. "What do you suggest?"

"Dinkinesh is the perfect name for her."

I mentally inventoried my Amharic vocabulary, which was just enough to shop for basics, greet people, ask directions, and, most important, order a cup of the best coffee in the world. The word Dinkinesh wasn't there. "What does it mean?"

With a broad smile, as if he were naming his own child, he answered, "Dinkinesh means 'you are marvelous.'"

He was right, it was the perfect name. Of course, today most of the world, including nearly every Ethiopian I have spoken to, calls her Lucy. And Lucy is the name that has appeared in crossword puzzles, on *Jeopardy!*, in cartoons, and on African Red Bush Tazo tea bags. In Ethiopia she has lent her name to numerous coffee shops, a rock band, a typing school, a fruit juice bar, and a political magazine. There is even an annual Lucy Cup soccer competition in Addis Ababa. Once, while driving through the town of Kombolcha on the way back to Addis after a field season, years after the discovery, I spotted a small sign that said LUSSY BAR. I brought the car to a screeching halt and my colleagues and I went in to have a beer. When we asked the proprietress how the place got its name, she explained in a solemn voice that many years ago a young American found a skeleton named Lucy in the Afar region, and that she took great pride in naming her bar after the fossil that proved Ethiopia's status as the original homeland to all people. With a grin, I told her I was the American who had found Lucy. She shrieked in delight and insisted that we have our picture taken together to mount on the wall. I sent the photo to her, and for all I know, it hangs there still. But sometimes I still think of Lucy as Dinkinesh, because she truly is marvelous.

Source: Donald Johanson and Katy Wong, *Lucy's Legacy* (New York: Crown-Random House, 2009), 10–11.

Further Reading

Johanson, Donald C., and Kate Wong. *Lucy's Legacy.* New York: Crown-Random House Press, 2009.

Radosevich, Stefan, Gregory Retallack, and Maurice Taieb. "Reassessment of the Paleoenvironment and Preservation of the Hominid Fossils from Hadar, Ethiopia." *American Journal of Physical Anthropology* 87 (1992):15–27.

Shreeve, Jamie. "Oldest Skeleton of Human Ancestor Found." *National Geographic.* October 1, 2009. http://news.nationalgeographic.com/news/2009/10/091001-oldest-human-skeleton-ardi-missing-link-chimps-ardipithecus-ramidus.html.

Taieb, Maurice, and Donald Johanson. "Plio-Pleistocene Discoveries in Hadar, Ethiopia." *Nature* 260 (1976): 293–297.

Web Resources

Arizona State University public workshop on Hadar/Afar Triangle paleontology sites: www.public.asu.edu/~edimaggi/Pictures/GK-12_STEM-dimaggio_compress.pdf; and Becoming Human, Institute of Human Origins, www.becominghuman.org/.

ICOMOS World Heritage Hominid Sites, www.international.icomos.org/centre_documentation/bib/worldheritage-hominidsites.pdf.

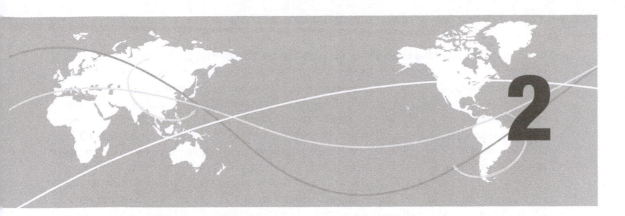

Makapansgat and Pinnacle Point

Three Million Years of Human Evolution in South Africa*

(3,000,000–2,000 BCE)

ANDY I. R. HERRIES

I N 1997 I WAS FINISHING MY UNDERGRADUATE DEGREE IN ARCHAEOLOGICAL SCIENCE and was invited to work on the early hominin-bearing sites (hominin refers to fossils on the human evolutionary line) of South Africa for the first time. Drawn by the desire to answer the question, "where do we come from?," I was eager to explore the series of extremely ancient caves found at Makapansgat. These caves in the interior of

---

*This work is the result of research with numerous colleagues in Africa over the past
fifteen years. In particular, Kaye Reed, Kevin Kuykendall, Charlie Lockwood, John McNabb,
Anthony Sinclair, and Alf Latham at Makapansgat; Phil Hopley and Brian Kuhn at Taung;
Colin Menter at Drimolen; Darryl De Ruiter, Robyn Pickering, Paul Dirks, and Lee Berger

southern Africa chart the evolution of the early human lineage and contain hints of the lives of species important for our understanding of the transition from more apelike hominins (*Australopithecus*) to members of our own genus, *Homo* (our species being *Homo sapiens*).

We drove up to Makapansgat from Johannesburg in the dark, a journey of around 300 kilometers (186 miles). We were staying at the small hut the early researchers built, and the entire place seemed steeped in history, with the various shelves and cupboards full of an assortment of items collected from around the valley over the last fifty years. When the sun rose and drove us out of our tents around the little research house, the full spectacle of the Makapansgat Valley lay before us. At the valley's head rose hundreds of meters of imposing red quartzite cliffs being circled by black eagles. The Red Cliffs mark the point where the ancient Makapansgat cave system would have begun its life over 4 million years ago. High up above us on the western side of the valley, railway tracks swung in the cool breeze as they dangled out into midair, remnants of the mining and subsequent excavations that had taken place at the Cave of Hearths. The site contains Paleolithic stone tools covering parts of the Early (less than 2.6 million years), Middle (less than 500,000 to 300,000 years) and Later (less than 50,000–30,000 years) Stone Age (ESA-MSA-LSA) as well as later Iron Age occupation (last two thousand years). However, its oldest Early Stone Age deposits contain Acheulian stone tools and hominin remains dated to sometime between 780,000 and 400,000 years ago. These are just a couple of the many fossil and archaeological bearing caves that occur at Makapansgat, which also includes Buffalo Cave, a rare 1-million-year-old hyena den. Being an avid cave explorer with the University of Liverpool Potholing Club for a few years, I was not sure if I was more excited about exploring the caves or, as was the wish of most of us, finding our first African hand-axe, the classic tool type of the Acheulian Industry, which began about 1.8 million years ago, and an iconic image of African archaeology.

During our first visit to the Makapansgat Limeworks cave, the location of the various *Australopithecus africanus* fossil finds, immediately I was struck by its size. It was more of an open cast mine in many places than a cave, and light reached almost every corner of the series of massive mined tunnels and chambers. I felt at home immediately, which was a good thing, as unknown to me at the time I would spend the next six years exploring every corner, trying to unlock its mysteries. As it turns out, for me this was the beginning of fifteen years of working on a variety of archaeological and fossil-bearing sites, covering the last three million years and almost every corner of South Africa.

Whereas my early work looked to identify the beginnings of the Genus *Homo* and how more apelike hominin species (australopithecines) evolved into more humanlike hominin species, my later work concentrated on finding the beginnings of our own species, *Homo sapiens* (modern humans). This quest took me to the Pinnacle Point Caves, which I first visited three days after submitting my PhD in 2003. The caves are located just outside of Mossel Bay on the southern Cape coast of South Africa, about 250 miles (400 kilome-

at Malapa; Tim Partridge and Darren Curnoe at Sterkfontein; Justin Adams and Jason Hemingway at Gondolin, Hoogland, and Haasgat; James Brink and John Gowlett at Cornelia, Kilombe, and Chesowanja; David Braun, Naomi Levin, and Laura Bishop at Elandsfontein and Koobi Fora; Lyn Wadley at Sibudu and Rose Cottage Cave; and Curtis Marean and Kyle Brown at Pinnacle Point. This work was supported by ARC Discovery Grants DP0877603. Thanks also to the many students of the Makapansgat Field Schools between 1997 and 2002 and the Pinnacle Point Excavations between 2003 and 2010. A final thanks to Matt Caruana for many talks and laughs regarding the ODK.

ters) east of Cape Town. (See Map 2.1.) Pinnacle Point is one of a series of cave localities along the coast that contains stone tools characteristic of the Middle Stone Age (MSA) and charts the behavioral origins of early modern humans.

My first interest in human evolution and the Paleolithic time period came when listening to lectures at a university about half man–half ape creatures from Africa that lived millions of years ago and, according to Australian anatomist Raymond Dart (1957) at least, lived by "greedily devouring livid writhing flesh." Naturally, this grabbed my attention immediately. The story of our human origins was something that I had very little knowledge about, and it seemed to be something that science still did not understand very well. My discipline continues to amaze me to this day; almost every year in the last fifteen there seems to have been a discovery that has changed or sometimes overturned our view of early human history. During this time genetics has revolutionized our understanding of modern human origins and shown that we all originate from Africa. Amazingly, it appears that all humans alive today may have originated from an effective breeding population of just six hundred individuals in one area of Africa, and modern humans have come close to extinction on more than one occasion in our two hundred thousand–year history.

Although I have worked on most of the South African hominin-bearing sites throughout my career, it is Makapansgat and Pinnacle Point that hold special places in my heart. Makapansgat was the first African site that I worked on and is the largest and the most impressive visually of all the South African sites. Makapansgat's distance from Johannesburg, compared to the Cradle of Humankind, is one of its charms. Researchers do not pop out to the site and back in a day. When I worked there, we would camp from four to eight weeks in the mountains surrounding the sites, cooking mostly on an open fire with a *braai* (barbeque) or a *Potjkie* (South African version of a dutch oven). In contrast, Pinnacle Point is fully part of the modern bustling world, located on a cliff face below a golf course just outside Mossel Bay. Yet the golf course is only a recent occurrence, and once you leave the cliff-top realms of the rich and descend the ten-year-old rickety wooden staircase to the rock shoreline and caves below, you step back in time 164,000 years. This is where early modern humans battled out an existence in a period of intense aridity and cold, where they first learned to harness the riches of the sea and think symbolically about things other than what was for dinner. Here is perhaps where we began, out of a small group of humans on the tip of Africa, close to extinction, but at the beginning of a long journey eventually to reach all corners of the globe. The site amazes as much visually as it does for the sweeping expanse of its history. Giant waves rip against the shore while dolphins, seals, and whales play within the waters offshore. It is little surprise that this is where man first learned to harness the riches of the sea over 160,000 years ago. Regardless of where my base of operations has been, from the United Kingdom to Bulgaria and then to Australia, the lure of these places has remained constant.

At 3 to 2.6 million years old, Makapansgat is the oldest human fossil site in South Africa. (See Map 2.2.) I worked there between 1997 and 2002, during a period of intense social change when the "new" South Africa was still finding its feet after the abolition of apartheid, the system of racial segregation and discrimination that the country's white minority leadership enforced. With apartheid over, free elections and a Truth and Reconciliation Commission were just some of the many changes overtaking the country. What did not change, however, was the wealth of knowledge to be found about the early human lineage in the area's ancient caves.

The majority of evidence for the beginning of the human lineage (7–4 million years), the origins of the genus *Homo* (2.5–1.9 million years), and the anatomical and behavioral beginnings of our own species, *Homo sapiens* (200,000–50,000 years), has come from East and South Africa. This chapter outlines South Africa's contribution to these issues and will progress from the first evidence for hominins in South Africa around 3 million years to the first evidence for early modern humans around 200,000–150,000 years. The question of a recent (in the last 50,000 years) or early (200,000–70,000 years) origin for modern human cognition will also be briefly discussed.

MAKAPANSGAT AND THE WORLD:
Hominin Origins and the Evolution of the Human Lineage

Four of the best-known early hominin fossil–bearing localities in South Africa are Makapansgat, Taung, Sterkfontein, and, more recently, Malapa. Sterkfontein and Malapa are located approximately 31 miles (50 kilometers) northwest of Johannesburg. Taung is located approximately 186 miles (300 kilometers) west, and Makapansgat 186 miles north in the Strydpoort Mountain range. (See Map 2.1.) The area containing these cave sites was designated as a World Heritage site in 1999, called the Cradle of Humankind (see Map 2.1) and has a series of fossil-bearing deposits ranging in age from perhaps four million years at the dawn of humanity to the early twentieth century.

From Makapansgat and other African sites, it now seems clear that there were a number of fundamental leaps during the course of human evolution. The most numerous human fossils that have been recovered from the Cradle of Humankind are of the genus *Australopithecus*. Though a human ancestor, *Australopithecus* was still quite apelike, with a small brain and large teeth, but was capable of bipedal locomotion (upright walking). Bipedalism appears to be the first fundamental character that distinguishes hominins from other apes. The first evidence for bipedalism is equivocal, and a range of fossils attributed to different species between 7 and 4 million years have been argued to be the first bipedal ape and, thus, hominins. *Australopithecine* remains the oldest definitive hominin genus, with concrete evidence in the form of an extensive fossil record and fossil footprints preserved in ash at Laetoli in Tanzania 3.6 million years ago. The partial skeletons of the early human species *Australopithecus afarensis*, known as Lucy (approximately 3.2 million years), and other skeletons from 3.9 to 2.0 million years from East and South Africa provide further evidence for this. Although the question of why hominins became bipedal is a matter of intense debate, it has often been linked to increasing aridity and an opening up of the environment and the spread of Savanna grassland due to climate change in Africa, resulting in a move to a more ground-based existence and foraging strategy that perhaps occurred over a larger area. This may have necessitated movement between more isolated areas of wooded habitat separated by bush or grassland.

Evolution is often viewed as a linear process, with one species evolving into the other and with the earlier species disappearing. In reality evolution is like a tree with numerous branches. Random mutations constantly occur in the genomes of organisms, creating genetic variation in a species that may in turn diverge to create different species. If these mutations give a particular population a selective advantage over another population, the population with the mutation will survive to reproduce, and that mutation will eventually become the norm within the population, thereby creating a new species. If in direct competition, then the original species may perish. In this model both the new species and the old species will be contemporaneous for at least a short period of time. The period between roughly 2.5 and 1.5 million years ago is just such a time period, when several different human species coexisted on the African landscape and during

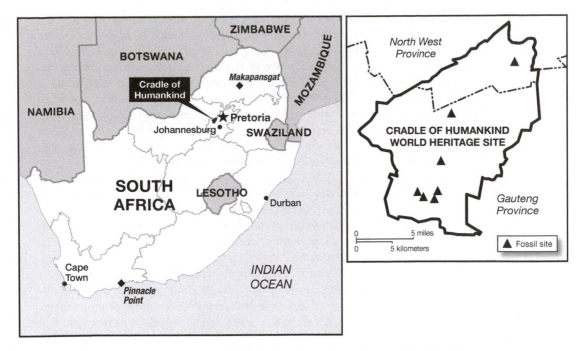

Map 2.1. Early Hominin-Bearing Sites in the Cradle of Humankind World Heritage Area

Although early hominin-bearing sites have been identified in southern Africa, the majority are clustered in a small region of dolomite-containing caves just to the northwest of Johannesburg in a World Heritage area called the Cradle of Humankind. The australopithecine-bearing sites of Makapansgat and Taung are located in other small outcrops of this dolomite, some three hundred kilometers to the north and west of Johannesburg, respectively. In contrast, the greatest collection of modern human and Middle Stone Age–bearing sites are a series of quartzite sea caves stretching along the southern Cape coast of South Africa, including the new sites at Pinnacle Point near Mossel Bay.

which time the transition occurred from the more apelike *Australopithecus* to the more humanlike first member of our own genus, *Homo*. However, there are a number of contenders for this title. In East Africa a recent find identified as *Australopithecus garhi* has been dated to about 2.5 million years ago and marks the end of *Australopithecus* in East Africa. Until recently it was impossible to date many of the South African species, and it was assumed that *Australopithecus* occurred in East and South Africa at the same time, even though they were classified as a different and perhaps more humanlike species, *Australopithecus africanus*.

Recently, all of the South African *Australopithecus africanus*–bearing deposits have been dated to between 3 and 2 million years ago, which is much younger than previously thought. Moreover, originally it was thought only one species of *Australopithecus* occurred in South Africa, but recent finds at Malapa and Sterkfontein show that two other species potentially occurred, the approximately 2 million-year-old *Australopithecus sediba* and a third as yet unclassified species represented by the 2.3- to 2.2 million-year-old littlefoot skeleton from Sterkfontein.

Although *Australopithecus africanus* appeared more humanlike in many ways, these new dates seemed to suggest that this species was perhaps less likely to be ancestral to

Homo, as a series of fragmentary fossils from East Africa dated to between 2.4 and 1.8 million years ago have already been defined as the first evidence of *Homo*. These are sometimes referred to as *Homo habilis, Homo rudolfensis,* or, more often, just early *Homo*. However, it is still possible that these specimens of *Homo* evolved from earlier representatives of *Australopithecus africanus.* Moreover, some researchers believe that many of these potential early specimens of *Homo* should in fact still be classified as *Australopithecus* (e.g., *Au habilis*) and that *Homo* should really start with *Homo ergaster,* which has a more modern body stature, larger brain, and first occurs in East Africa sometime around 1.8 to 1.8- to 1.7 million years ago. *Homo ergaster* is also the first species to leave Africa, with similar 1.8- to 1.7 million-year-old fossils discovered at Dmanisi, Georgia.

Recent studies suggest that the oldest fossils of *Homo ergaster* may actually come from the South African site of Swartkrans sometime between 2.3 and 1.8 million years ago. Moreover, the new 1.98-million-year-old species *Australopithecus sediba* has recently been suggested to have traits of both the earlier species *Australopithecus africanus* and the later species *Homo ergaster* and, as such, represents a transitional species between the two. The completeness of the *Australopithecus sediba* remains in the form of two partial skeletons, and its mosaic nature also suggest that more fragmentary fossils during this time period could be classified as different species even if they actually came from the same individual. This leads to the question as to whether we can accurately assign more fragmentary specimens to a particular Genus, let alone species. It is also in part an argument over what actually represents the Genus *Homo*. If it were confirmed that Australopithecus in South Africa gave rise to *Homo ergaster* directly, this would be a major change in the traditional view that *Homo* arose in East Africa. The problem is that the earliest fossils of *Homo ergaster* and *Au. sediba* are very close in age, and so it seems difficult for one to have given rise to the other unless older specimens of *Au. sediba* are found.

Thus the advantage of the South African sites is that they can provide partial skeletons that enable us to see what the entire hominin looked like and more accurately assess its taxonomic status. The majority of fossils discovered are often very fragmentary, which can make it extremely difficult to reconstruct exactly what the individual looked like, how fossils relate to each other (i.e., what evolved to what), and how body size and shape may have varied between males and females (sexual dimorphism) as well as juveniles and adults (developmental history). If the entire or partial skeleton is preserved, then an understanding of these features and processes is a lot easier, especially if both male and female or both adult and juvenile skeletons are present. Evidence that these early hominins may have moved around in family groups comes from some 3.6-million-year-old fossil footprints from Laetoli in Tanzania. Set inside the larger adult tracks are a set of smaller juvenile tracks, suggesting that the younger *Australopithecus afarensis* individual was following in the footsteps of the older parent, just as a modern child might do so on the beach today. Equally, at Malapa, a series of adult and juvenile fossils are found together and were buried rapidly, suggesting they may have fallen into the cave together.

The Hunter or the Hunted? Makapansgat and Australopithecine Lifeways

The first stone tools occur at Gona in Ethiopia around 2.6 to 2.5 million years and occur around the same time as the earliest potential evidence for *Homo* in East Africa. The earliest tools are classified as the Oldowan Industry, after the famous site of Olduvai Gorge in Tanzania where they were first found. Determining which species made these tools or if more than one did is difficult because there are very few associations of stone tools with hominin remains. It was often assumed that *Homo habilis* was the first stone tool user,

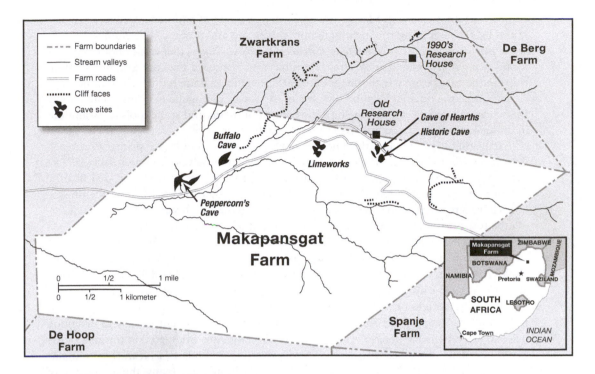

Map 2.2. Makapansgat Farm

The Makapansgat Farm is located near the town of Mokopane in Limpopo Province, South Africa. A number of fossil-and archaeological-bearing cave sites occur in the valley. The Makapansgat Limeworks is the oldest at 3.0 to 2.6 million years ago, yielding Australopithecus africanus remains. Buffalo Cave has revealed vertebrate fossils dating to between 1.1 and 0.8 million years ago, whereas the Cave of Hearths has yielded the remains of archaic Homo sapiens (aka Homo rhodesiensis) dating to younger than 780,000 years ago. Historic Cave and Peppercorn's Cave contain Iron Age occupations.

rather than the more apelike *Australopithecus;* however as *Homo habilis*'s place in the evolutionary tree or even within *Homo* has been debated, its "handy man" status as a tool user has been questioned. The 2.5 millioni-year-old *Australopithecus garhi*, which is associated with cut-marked bone, but not stone tools, is another potential tool user. After 2 million years, with the evolution of the larger-brained and -bodied *Homo ergaster*, a broader hominin diet is seen in the archaeological record, the first hominins leave Africa, and, by 1.8 to 1.5 million years, a more complex stone-tool technology, the Acheulian, is developed. Rather than the simple technology of the Oldowan, where flakes of stone were removed from cobbles, the Acheulian is characterized by a number of specific end-products, hand axes, and cleavers. Hand axes have often been described as the penknife of the Stone Age, having probably been used for a variety of tasks, from butchering animals to processing plant remains.

At between 3 and 2.6 million years old, the Makapansgat Limeworks is the oldest of the South African hominin-bearing sites. The Limeworks is an ancient cave system that was systematically mined for speleothem (secondary mineral deposits such as stalagmites and stalactites) after roughly 1918. The speleothems were burned in kilns to make lime, used both in construction and a cyanidation process for extracting gold. The invention of this technique in 1890 created a boom for the lime-mining industry in the

early twentieth century and led to the discovery of many of southern Africa's early hominin localities, making the technique both a blessing and a curse. The mining has enabled the recovery of fossils, such as *Australopithecus africanus*, that would not have been
found using conventional excavation. Yet it has also obscured the stratigraphic relationships in the caves from which the fossils were recovered, making it difficult or impossible
to determine the original location of some of the fossils or engage in appropriate dating.
In archeology and paleoanthropology, the context of fossils and stone tools is paramount
in understanding their age and association to each other.

Excavating fossils to elicit this knowledge is extremely difficult (see primary sources).
The caves from which the fossils are recovered have themselves become fossilized. The
caves have become completely in-filled with sediments and then partly eroded like the
dolomite rocks around them. Many of the fossils that would originally have been in the
caves have already been lost due to erosion. As such, at many sites excavating and collecting the fossils is crucial, lest they are eroded away and lost forever.

The first fossil of *Australopithecus africanus* was discovered at the Buxton-Norlim
Limeworks near the South African town of Taung in 1924 and nicknamed the Taung
Child. Australian anatomist Raymond Dart's description of the fossil as an early human
ancestor in 1925 caused huge controversy (see primary sources), and most researchers of
the time believed it to be nothing more than a monkey. Until this time most early human
fossil finds had come from Europe, and because of this, a Eurocentric view of evolution
existed, whereby many people believed that modern humans originated in the area of the
world populated by civilized societies. The discovery of a number of Neandertal remains
in Europe between 1829 and 1856 reinforced this view, and, for many, the excavation of
the Piltdown Man fossil in England in 1912 confirmed it. Although the Piltdown fossil
was a fake reconstruction of a modern human cranium and an orangutan jaw with filed-
down teeth, despite many scientists' reservations as early as 1913, not until 1953 was the
fossil finally confirmed as a fraud with the advent of more scientific techniques. Other researchers noted that the living great apes, to which man was more closely related, lived in
Asia and Africa. However, Dart's discovery of *Australopithecus africanus* at Taung in 1925
and finally at Makapansgat in 1947 eventually established Africa as the cradle of humankind and South Africa as an important region in the story of human origins.

Wilfred Eitzman, a local schoolteacher, discovered the first fossils at the Makapansgat
Limeworks in 1922 after learning about them from a local lime miner (see primary
sources). The finds were sent to Raymond Dart, who recognized them as the remains of
extinct primates similar to those associated with the Taung Child. Due to the interruption
caused by World War II, however, researchers did not visit the site until 1940, by which
time much of the material had been mined away, leaving the stratigraphy in disarray, with
most of the cave deposits and fossils emptied onto the hillside above. Not until 1945 did
the University of the Witwatersrand, led by Philip Tobias, conduct the first "official" expeditions. These expeditions recovered the first primate fossil from the site, eventually
leading to the recovery of over seven thousand more fossils.

Many of the bones from Makapansgat were black, and Dart took this to represent evidence of early fire use and human occupation despite no evidence of human fossils or
stone tools. Dart believed that this suggested that from man's earliest origins he possessed
a number of behavioral traits that separated him from other animals on the landscape. We
now know that many of the developments that separate man from other animals came
much later, with altered stone–tool use from 2.6 million years ago, fire from perhaps
800,000 years ago, and evidence of more symbolic thought first occurring at sites such as

Pinnacle Point soon after 200,000 years ago. The earliest australopithecines in effect were perhaps little more than bipedal apes, living out an existence not too dissimilar from many of the other great apes.

Inspired by the evidence of fire, however, Dart named the fire makers a new species of hominin, *Australopithecus prometheus*, after the Titan Prometheus, who stole fire from Zeus. (Today, the fossils are normally all classified as *Australopithecus africanus*) However, some researchers suggest that more than one species of *Australopithecus* occurs at both Makapansgat and Sterkfontein, and as such, the term *Australopithecus prometheus* may one day be resurrected as the name of this second species if the type specimen from Makapansgat is included. Dart also concluded that many of the bones from the Makapansgat Limeworks represented the pre-stone tools of the fire maker *Australopithecus prometheus*. This was in stark contrast to his earlier views after the discovery of the Taung Child, when he, perhaps more rightly, theorized that *Australopithecus africanus* was a scavenger barely eking out an existence in the African savannah. Dart referred to this industry as the Osteodontokeratic Culture (ODK), meaning bone-tooth-horn culture, and helped perpetuate the idea of the "Killer Ape Theory" and set the foundation for the view of "Man the Hunter," with humans hunting animals from their earliest ancestry. Throughout the 1950s, 1960s, and 1970s Dart and anthropologist Robert Ardrey published an amazing series of papers and books describing, with some poetic license, the use of these tools in graphic detail: "man's predecessors . . . seized living quarries by violence, battered them to death, tore apart their broken bodies, dismembered them limb from limb, slaking their ravenous thirst with the hot blood of victims and greedily devouring livid writhing flesh" (see Dart in Further Reading). These ideas became so entrenched in society that a number of films and books have encompassed the ideas Dart suggested from the Makapansgat evidence, the most notable of which is the opening sequence of *2001: A Space Odyssey* as well as themes in *Planet of the Apes*. However, detailed studies of the bones from the Makapansgat Limeworks have shown that this was not the case; instead, hyenas, not australopithecines, accumulated them. Early man was the hunted, not the hunter.

In Dart's vision hunting behavior was not limited to other animals but also included cannibalism of australopithecine individuals. Cannibalism is a reoccurring theme in the study of early humans and was still practiced among tribes in Papua New Guinea until the 1970s, although there are still some reports of it happening today. Obtaining a reliable account of cannibalism is difficult, as it is often used to describe rival or unknown groups in a negative way. However, a number of human fossil remains demonstrate purported evidence of cannibalism. The oldest is a 1.8 million–year-old hominin fossil (StW53) from Sterkfontein in South Africa that has evidence of stone-tool cut marks, suggesting disarticulation of the jaw from the skull. No stone tools are found in association with this speciman or indeed the bulk of hominin remains prior to 2 million years, although some do occur with stone-tool cut-marked bone. It has generally been assumed that specimens attributed to early *Homo* were responsible for the first stone-tool use, and one of the earliest potential *Homo* candidates from Ethiopia at 2.3 million years is one of the few associated with stone tools. However, with the view that *Homo ergaster* represents the first species of *Homo*, stone tool use becomes an australopithecine trait. Moreover, several researchers argue that the first stone tools at 2.6 million years already show a complexity that some tool use must have come before, even if it was the use of archaeologically invisible, unmodified stone or wood. After all, our closest cousin the chimpanzee uses such tools today.

Many scholars have also debated whether the cut-marked Sterkfontein fossil (StW53) is actually *Australopithecus*, akin to *Homo habilis* or a new species of *Homo* altogether. This fossil is certainly younger than 1.8 million years, and by that time, *Homo ergaster* already occurred at the site of Swartkrans across the river. As such, the cut marks on StW53 may represent early contact between the smaller-brained and more apelike *Australopithecus* and the larger-brained and more humanlike *Homo ergaster*. It is likely that *Homo ergaster* would have just seen *Australopithecus* as another animal and food source on the landscape in the way chimpanzees hunt monkeys today.

Studies of the bones themselves can also be used to understand how the bones got into the caves where they were found, an area of study known as taphonomy. Traditionally scholars believed that these early humans lived in the caves, much like later human species, such as *Homo neanderthalensis* (Neandertals), or the earliest of our own species, and that they were responsible for the bone accumulations. Tooth marks on the bones of many of the fossils, however, again suggest that *Australopithecus* and *Paranthropus* (a specialized hominin genus universally seen as a side branch in human evolution) were the hunted, not the hunter, being simply part of the assemblage of bones accumulated by hyenas and leopards or, in the case of the Taung Child *Australopithecus africanus* fossil, an eagle.

Diversified Food Sources Mark the Transition from Scavenger to Hunter

The development of more scientific techniques in archaeology from the 1960s onward led eventually to the formal dismissal of the claims for fire, the ODK, and the theory of *Australopithecus africanus* as a hunter. The blackening of the bones Dart received from Makapansgat was shown to be simple mineral staining due to precipitation of manganese dioxide from the dolomite walls of the cave. In addition, *Australopithecus africanus* was shown to be the hunted when the bone accumulations were attributed to hyenas and leopards. Our evidence for whether *australopithecines* were still scavengers and ate meat is limited. No stone tools have been found in direct association with any species of *Australopithecus* in South Africa, and these have often been associated with the beginnings of meat eating. However, isotopic analysis of *australopithecine* teeth suggests that *Australopithecus africanus* and *Australopithecus afarensis* from between four and two million years ago may have eaten some form of meat, but how much of the diet this composed is hard to determine, and much of it may be from eating things such as termites.

If any of these earlier hominins did eat meat, they were certainly scavengers. Whether hominins or carnivores were accessing the meat first can be evaluated by looking at the relationship of tooth marks and cut marks on the bones. If cut marks can be seen to cover carnivore tooth marks, then the hominins were certainly scavenging. However, if the stone-tool cut marks come first, then the hominins may have had more direct access to the carcasses. Unfortunately such evidence is rare and one of the only direct lines of evidence of what these early hominins were doing. In some rare cases residues are still preserved on the stone tools, suggesting that the hominins were using them to process a range of material, including meat, wood, and plants.

After two million years ago and certainly with the development of a more complex stone-tool technology (the Acheulian) associated with *Homo ergaster* and later species, greater evidence for meat eating is seen in the archaeological record. Soon after two million years hominins at Koobi Fora in Kenya have been documented to eat a range of food, including crocodile, fish, turtle, and a variety of antelopes. Such diversification of food sources, especially those high in protein, may have lifted constraints on brain size and led to the evolution of larger brains in later species of *Homo*. Processing meat with stone tools probably also led to other anatomical traits in *Homo*, such as changes in tooth morphology, a character of *Homo*.

Modern theories do not see early humans as hunters until after about five hundred thousand years ago. Some of the earliest evidence for hunting comes in the form of wooden spears from Schöningen in Germany around four hundred thousand years ago. It is possible that hominins were using such wooden tools much earlier than this, but because wood rarely preserves, they are simply not preserved in the archaeological record. This makes identifying the transition from scavenging to hunting extremely difficult.

Adaptations through the Use of Tools

The first stone tools found in South Africa, dated to sometime between 2.0 and 1.8 million years ago, come from Wonderwerk Cave and Swartkrans Cave and are designated as part of the Oldowan industry. The more complex stone-tool technology, known as the Acheulian, developed soon after 1.8 million years ago in East Africa and may have also occurred from a similar early time in South Africa. Unfortunately, the dating of the South African sites is currently not good enough to assess this with certainty, and many early Acheulian sites, such as the Vaal River sites and Sterkfontein, may be younger than 1.5 to 1.4 million years old. The Oldowan and Acheulian are defined together as the Early Stone Age. The Acheulian industry is the longest-lived stone tool tradition made by multiple species of hominin, and it is replaced by the Middle Stone Age in Africa sometime between 550,000 and 280,000 years ago.

The first stone-tool types that are characteristic of the Middle Stone Age began to occur between 550,000 and 280,000 years ago in both East and South Africa. Of these, blades occurred first, followed by projectile points and a technique of making stone tools called the Levallois technique. This technique is known as a "prepared core technology," meaning preparations are made in advance so as to standardize the end product. Forms of prepared core technology first occur in the Early Stone Age for making large flakes that were in turn used to make hand axes.

Due to a dearth of fossils or the difficulty of dating known fossils, little is known about the hominins that existed in the period less than 1.4 million years ago in Africa. In some cases this lack of fossils may reflect their preservation due to geological factors, but it may also relate to the greater ability of these middle Pleistocene hominins to defend themselves through the use of tools. In many cases all that is left are the cultural remains of the species that once inhabited the region. Millions of hand axes, a characteristic stone tool of the Acheulian industry, scatter the landscape of Africa from end to end, suggesting a period of relative stasis in the human lineage. However, based on the stone tools they left behind, there is increasing evidence for increased complexity in what these hominins were doing starting about a million years ago and certainly from 500,000 years onward. The hand axe persists until perhaps 280,000 years ago and, in some cases, as early as 125,000 years ago, but a trend toward smaller, more complex, flake-based technology such as points and blades, characteristic of the Middle Stone Age, begins from about 500,000 years ago in Africa. Reconstructing what these hominins were like and how they lived is, therefore, extremely difficult from this time period in Africa, and the various human fossils are attributed to an array of species names, including *Homo erectus, Homo heidelbergensis, Homo rhodesiensis, Homo helmei,* or just archaic *Homo sapiens.* Far more is known outside of Africa in places such as Europe, where a vast array of limestone caves preserve the evolution of the Neandertal lineage over the last 500,000 years or more.

GLOBAL ENCOUNTERS AND CONNECTIONS:
The Spread of Humans Out of Africa

The various trends in human evolution did not necessarily take place at the same time in different parts of Africa, let alone the world. *Homo ergaster* was the first hominin to leave Africa shortly after 2 million years ago, as shown by the fossils from Dmanisi, Georgia. Hominins identified as *Homo erectus* had reached Asia by perhaps 7 to 1.5 million years, and they managed to cross open ocean to the island of Flores in Indonesia by 1 million years ago. Here they appear to have evolved in isolation to become *Homo floresiensis*, also known as the Hobbit, and survived here until eighteen to twelve thousand years ago. Parts of the world that required a bigger sea crossing, such as the Americas and Australia, however, were not occupied until after twenty thousand and seventy thousand years ago, respectively, and then exclusively by modern humans. Hominins entered Europe later, about 1.2 million years ago, where they are often termed *Homo antessesor*. In Europe *Homo antessesor* may have evolved into *Homo heidelbergensis* or Europe may have been occupied a number of times by different species, again originating in Africa. However, it seems certain that *Homo heidelbergensis* evolved to *Homo neandetalensis* in Europe, forming a distinct lineage.

The Spread of Early Technology

Like their contemporary African counterparts, the Dmanisi *Homo ergaster* fossils are associated with the earlier simplistic Oldowan technology. In fact, even the earliest hominins to enter Europe at 1.2 million years ago, *Homo antecessor*, were also still using Oldowan-style technology, despite the Acheulian being widespread by this time in Africa. This may suggest an Asian origin for these first Europeans perhaps descended from the earliest *Homo ergaster* to inhabit the region. In eastern Asia, where the earliest *Homo ergaster* evolved to *Homo erectus* and the Acheulian is completely absent, although an Acheulian-like industry does occur in China at Bose by 800,000 years ago. Many researchers see this as an independent development of hand-axe-like tools, and as such the Acheulian appears to have never reached East Asia. This also suggests that, unlike what was previously thought, the first hominins to leave Africa and even to enter the much colder climate of Europe did so with a technology not much more complex than the first stone tools from 2.6 million years ago. Moreover, they may also have achieved this without fire, another technology that scholars originally saw as a prerequisite for movement out of Africa and into harsher, colder climates. This may explain why the early archaeological record of Europe is poor, with hominins unable to gain a permanent foothold in the cold climate of that region until much later and with the development of more complex Acheulian technology and perhaps fire use after 900,000 years ago.

Fire is important for a number of reasons. First, it provides warmth and protection from predators. Second, it breaks down toxins in certain foods and renders meat more digestible, helping hominins to diversify to new food sources more easily when moving into different regions of the world. The earliest suggested evidence for fire comes from a series of sites, such as Chesowanja in East Africa around 1.5 million years ago. However, distinguishing this early purported hominin fire use from natural bushfires is extremely difficult, so most scientists remain skeptical. The oldest accepted evidence for fire is from the Acheulian site of Gesher Benot Ya'aqov in present-day Israel soon after 780,000 years ago and perhaps also at the site of Swartkrans in South Africa at around the same time. However, extensive use of fire is not found until after 500,000 years ago at later Acheulian sites, such as Beeches Pit in the United Kingdom.

When compared to East Africa, in South Africa the Acheulian technology appears to have first occurred slightly later, at sometime between 1.6 and 1.4 million years ago at sites on the Vaal River and at Wonderwerk and Sterkfontein Caves. Again, the associated hominin is usually defined as *Homo ergaster* or *Homo erectus*. By the time *Homo rhodesiensis* (also often designated as *Homo heidelbergensis* like the European species) is seen in South Africa, as at the Cave of Hearths at Makapansgat and other sites slightly younger than 1 million years ago, the Acheulian is still being used, but new technologies such as the Victoria West Core are then being introduced. Victoria West technology is a type of "prepared core technology" that creates standardized blanks for making hand axes. This technology suggests an increased cognitive capacity in this post-1-million-year-old hominin species. This is a process that flourishes fully with prepared core technology in the Middle Stone Age. As such, despite the fact that different hominin species used this changing technology, over time there is a trend in technology in Africa that suggests against the early idea of stasis within the Acheulian. As such, the technologies appear to transcend the pigeonholing of biological species and perhaps continued links between the various groups of hominins living there. Outside Africa and the Near East the older Oldowan technology still persisted until perhaps 800,000 years ago, suggesting that links among the various groups did not occur.

Species Migration and Exchange

There is often very little account taken of whether species that left Africa and evolved in Asia or Europe may have re-entered Africa again at a later stage. It often seems to be assumed there was only one-way traffic "Out of Africa." It is possible that *Homo erectus*, which could be considered to have exclusively evolved in Asia, may have later migrated back into Africa, where fossils similar to those in Asia are found dating to around 1 million to 800,000 years ago. Some researchers use the occurrence of *Homo erectus* in Africa at ~1 million years to suggest that *Homo ergaster* and *Homo erectus* are not distinct species. Soon after this period Acheulian technology is more widely seen in other areas of the world, such as India and Europe, perhaps suggesting further migrations of hominins out of Africa or an increased connection with hominins in other regions. Reconstructing the biogeography of these early hominins can be done only on the basis of finding new fossils and dating the deposits in which they occur. Complications related to taphonomy and whether the specific geology even allows the preservation of fossils makes this difficult. Scholars originally believed, based on the numerous finds in Europe and at Kebara Cave in Israel, that Neandertals lived only in Europe, with perhaps some occasional migrations into the Near East during extreme cold phases. More recent finds in Okladnikov Cave in southern Russia and reevaluation of remains from Teshik-Tash in Uzbezikstan, however, now suggest that these hominins ranged over a much greater area, including northern Asia.

In many cases the occurrence or absence of Neandertals has been defined by the occurrence of the Mousterian stone-tool technology, a scraper-rich industry exclusively attributed to Neandertals in Europe. Recently there have been a number of discoveries of young fossils with more archaic features, suggesting that these species survived in tandem with younger species, including *Homo sapiens,* and there are suggestions that other species also used Mousterian stone-tool technology. This makes identifying particular species in a region based on stone tools alone difficult. Additionally, recent DNA work on fossils that are older than 50,000 years from Denisova Cave in southern Siberia suggest hominins there split from the lineage that eventually evolved to modern humans around the same time as the Neandertals, around three hundred thousand years ago, and soon after diverged again from the Neandertal line. The only modern humans that share traits with the Denisovans come from Papua New Guinea, suggesting that the Denisovans interbred with these modern humans' ancestors or, perhaps, even once resided in Southeast Asia. This is particularly interesting given the occurrence of a number of scraper-rich, Mousterian-like industries in southern China at this period.

In a similar way all non-African modern humans are more closely related to Neandertals than African modern humans. This again suggests that at some point early modern humans leaving Africa interbred with Neandertals, most likely in the Near East. Tantalizing evidence for this comes in the form of early modern humans also using Mousterian stone-tool technology in Israel around 100,000 years ago rather than a Middle Stone Age technology, as occurred in Africa. This all suggests that links did occur between the various hominin populations in different areas of the world, but that it was generally sporadic. Such links also question whether Neandertals should be considered a completely separate species or, as some researchers suggest, merely a subspecies, *Homo sapiens neandertalensis,* thus making us *Homo sapiens sapiens.*

"We Are All Africans": The Origin of Modern Humans

Despite this complexity DNA evidence clearly indicates that all modern humans alive today came from a small population in Africa that likely arose around 177,000 years ago. The fossil evidence supports this age with fossils classified as the earliest anatomically modern humans from Herto and Omo in Ethiopia, dated to sometime between 200,000 to 150,000 years ago. The rich fossil-bearing sites in and around Makapansgat also contribute to this evidence with many Middle Stone Age deposits at the Cave of Hearths. However, whether these early modern humans would have been behaviorally modern is still a matter of debate. Some researchers believe that abstract thought and modern human cognitive ability arose rapidly around 40,000 years ago in Europe, as shown by the wide variety of cave art, engravings, and burials that occurred in the Upper Paleolithic of Europe. The wealth of symbolic and artistic material found in Europe suggests to some that an "Upper Paleolithic Revolution" took place at this time.

Others believe that the evolution to behavioral modernity was a gradual process, with clear early examples of more modern behaviors seen in the Middle Stone Age. South African examples include the utilization of engraved ochre (iron oxide nodules) at Blombos Cave and Pinnacle Point between 164,000 to 70,000 years ago as well as the heat treatment of stone tools and exploitation of shellfish at Pinnacle Point 164,000 years ago. This exploitation of shellfish is the last major change in the human diet until the invention of agriculture starting perhaps 12,000 years ago in the Middle East. Some researchers argue that the reliance on shellfish as a major part of the hominin diet signals complex thought, as that would be necessary so as to understand tides and lunar cycles rather than only sun cycles. The introduction of shellfish into the human diet may also have changed gender roles in society, as shellfish collecting was traditionally a gathering rather than a hunting behavior, and gathering was traditionally a woman's activity. Unlike before, women would, therefore, be responsible for collecting the bulk of the protein in the group's diet.

Not everyone agrees, and some researchers suggest that not only did modern humans undertake such practices but also that Neandertals and perhaps other species such as *Homo erectus* also exploited the sea. However, other researchers point out that occasionally collecting shellfish from the sea is very different from a true coastal adaptation as seen in early modern humans. A move to exploiting seafood would also have been vital to colonizing the final areas of the world, such as Australia and the Americas, and would have fueled rapid migration along the world's coastlines. This would have allowed humans to spread rapidly out of Africa and inhabit the entire globe. Seafood essentially gave early humans a stable and constant food source that helped them survive extremely harsh conditions. Originally scholars suggested that the Americas would have been colonized by crossing the Bering Straits between Russia and Alaska when it was frozen solid and a land bridge existed; however, recent finds off the Californian coast may suggest that the earliest colonizers were in fact seafaring people, and this in part explains the apparent rapid colonization of both North and South America after twenty thousand years ago.

Furthermore, early evidence for the heat treatment of stone tools indicates that early modern humans knew that they could alter the properties of stone by using heat, and to do so, they would have had to have achieved a good control over the temperature within the fire (between 300 and 400°C). It is likely the temperature to which the rocks were heated was controlled by burying them in sand beneath the fire. Until recently this was a technique that scholars thought did not occur until the last thirty thousand years because it is a front-loaded technology in which a great deal of preparation goes into the object before it is used. As such, it must have had a special purpose or must have had a major selective advantage for a particular activity. In other words, modern humans, unlike previous species, were no longer creating stone tools for the moment they were currently living in; they were looking to the future and anticipating what they might need, suggesting a modern view of time.

From as early as 164,000 years ago at Pinnacle Point hominins also appear to have collected shells for their beauty rather than simply for food, indicating interests and thoughts beyond the day-to-day activities of getting food and perhaps even ideas of trade and exchange of goods. A microscopic study of the shells shows abrasion from being washed in the surf and on the beach. This practice at Pinnacle Point may have been the forerunner of shell beads found at other sites from about 82,000 years ago.

Also at Pinnacle Point, one of the caves (13B) has revealed evidence for ochre use as far back as 164,000 years ago. Although the oldest ochre is not engraved like the material from Blombos, it was ground to a powder and was likely used as a body paint, perhaps as part of group identification or some other ritual. Inferences for this come from the study of modern hunter-gatherers, in which ochre is almost always associated with ritual practices. In particular, ochre is often linked to coming-of-age rituals and, in particular, menstruation. At Pinnacle Point, however, the use of ochre is simply part of a package of innovations that suggest that the people living there were thinking more and more as way we do today. Further evidence against the Upper Paleolithic Revolution of Europe comes from the other side of the world in Australia. At Lake Mungo, 42,000 years ago modern humans were already covering their dead with ochre and perhaps also cremating them, suggesting again a rich symbolic lifeway existed far away from Europe at this time. Instead the current evidence suggests continuity and gradually increasing complexity from the Middle Stone Age through to the Upper Paleolithic.

The Later Record of South Africa in Contrast to the Rest of the World

The later archaeological record of southern Africa is very different from other parts of the world. In the Middle East the first move toward a more settled way of life began around 23,000 years ago at the beginning of the Epi-Paleolithic and this was followed by early agriculture starting around 12,000 years ago. Southern Africa differs in that hunter-gatherers still occupied the Cape region until the first European explorer, Portuguese Bartolomeu Dias, arrived in 1487. These populations still subsisted by a purely hunting and gathering lifestyle, just as their ancestors had for the previous 200,000 years. The Bantu-speaking Iron Age pastoralists and farmers made it into South Africa only about 2,000 years ago, first settling in northern South Africa and then slowly spreading into the southeast. However, identifying the spread of Bantu populations into South Africa is in itself a challenge because many seem to have reverted back to a more hunter-gatherer way of life but, now, with the addition of domestic animals. Moreover, some hunter-gatherer populations likely took up the new ways of life and technology of these Bantu immigrants—not as agriculturalists but instead as herders as well as traders, using pottery as a means of commerce. Today South Africa is a complex melting pot of cultures, with white English- and Afrikaans-speaking South Africans along with different Bantu origin groups as well as the Khoesan. The Khoesan, however, were almost entirely wiped out in South Africa, and many of the groups that reside there today are immigrants themselves, refugees of the extended 1966–1989 South African war in South-West Africa (now Namibia and southern Angola). But because many remember only the legacy of apartheid and the persecution of the dominant 2,000-year-old immigrant Bantu population of South Africa, the Khoesan remain the forgotten true indigenous population of southern Africa, having a direct ancestry there at least 164,000—if not millions—of years ago.

ENCOUNTERS AS TOLD: PRIMARY SOURCES

This section contains excerpts from three primary documents that reflect debates on and approaches to recording early hominin finds in southern Africa. An exchange between Raymond Dart and Sir Arthur Keith illustrates the debate over early human ancestors, whereas two documents on excavations—one from the site of the Taung Child and the other from the Makapansgat Limeworks—serve as a contrast between an in-the-moment recording of an excavation and decades' old recollections. As techniques have changed, the modern archaeologist's task is in part as much about reconstructing the actions of early researchers and excavators as it is about excavating new sites.

Letter to the Editor, by Raymond A. Dart and Sir Arthur Keith

This first primary document is Raymond Dart's response to comments made by Sir Arthur Keith regarding Dart's discovery and description of the Taung Child *Australopithecus africanus* fossil as an early human ancestor. This was the first potentially early human ancestor discovered in Africa after the more humanlike Kabwe skull was found in Zambia in 1921, and few scientists initially believed the discovery. This is followed by comments from Arthur Keith, who did not believe Dart's claims. This type of exchange is common in science but often treads a fine line between helping to prove claims made by one researcher and becoming a personal battle.

- What is the first defining characteristic that separates a hominin from an ape?

- Is the idea of a "missing link" valid given what we now know of the hominin record and the nature of evolution? Should *Australopithecus sediba* be considered a missing link?

- Which is the first species that all researchers agree is part of the genus *Homo*?

In *Nature* . . . Sir Arthur Keith has attempted to show first that I called the Taungs skull a "missing link," and secondly, that it is not a "missing link."

As a matter of fact, although I undoubtedly regard the description as an adequate one, I have not used the term "missing link." On the other hand, Sir Arthur Keith in an article entitled "The New Missing Link" in the *British Medical Journal* pointed out that "it is not only a missing link but a very complete and important one." After stating his views so definitely in February, it seems strange that, in July, he should state that "this claim is preposterous." . . .

In view of these facts, there is little justification for the attempted witticism that in making the "African ancestors typified by the Taungs infant" the "foundation stone of the human family tree"—whatever that may be—I am making "a mistake identical with that of claiming a Sussex peasant as ancestor of William the Conqueror." . . .

Sir Arthur need have no qualms lest his remarks detract from the importance of the Taungs discovery—criticism generally enhances rather than detracts. Three decades ago Huxley refused to accept *Pithecanthropus* [now called *Homo erectus*] as a link. Today Sir Arthur Keith regards *Pithecanthropus* as the only known link.

Raymond A. Dart

. . .

Prof. Dart is under misapprehension in supposing that I have in any way or at any time altered my opinion regarding the fossil . . . discovered at Taungs. From the description and illustrations given by him the conclusion was forced on me that *Australopithecus* was a member of "the same group or sub-family as the chimpanzee and gorilla." In the same issue of *Nature* Prof. G. Elliot Smith expressed a similar opinion, describing *Australopithecus* as "an unmistakable anthropoid ape that seems to be much on the same grade of development as the gorilla and chimpanzee without being identical with either." . . .

The position which Prof. Dart assigns to the Taungs ape in the genealogical tree of man and apes has no foundation in fact.

Sir Arthur Keith

Source: Raymond A. Dart and Sir Arthur Keith, "Letter to the Editor," *Nature* 2917 (1925): 462–463.

"The Taungs Ape," by Aleš Hrdlička

The second primary source outlines Italian paleoanthropologist Aleš Hrdlička's 1925 excavation of the discovery site of the Taung Child fossil soon after its discovery in 1925. Today scholars generally believe that Hrdlička excavated a second, younger deposit compared to that containing the Taung Child *Australopithecus africanus* fossil. The Pinnacle of rock where he excavated it still bears his name and is only about twenty meters from the Dart Pinnacle, where the skull was likely found. Unlike Dart, who merely studied fossils from the site, Hrdlička actually visited the site, and most of what we know about the location of the fossil and its potential context comes from his early photographs. Hrdlička wrote this document soon after the discovery of the fossil and he excavated the site.

- What are some of the primary problems in reconstructing the context and, therefore, the evolutionary relationships of the various South African early hominin fossils?

- Name the genus and species of the fossils from Malapa. What are the problems with classifying the fragmentary hominin fossils into species compared to more complete skeletons?

- How did Raymond Dart's view of the lifestyle of *Australopithecus* change between finding the Taungs Child and the Makapansgat *australopithecine* fossils?

The quarrying for the limestone was begun in the face of the cliffs and the same method is followed today. A very large amount of material has already been removed producing a large, roughly semilunar space, along most parts of which intensive blasting goes on. The depth of the quarry from the original rock face to the farthest part of the walls as they now stand, is about 300 feet, and for a considerable portion of this distance the workingmen have noted the large cave-crevice and also several tunnels filled in with the pinkish, less valuable rock. In the rock of these old holes and according to report also in the large crevicecave, petrified remains of animals have been found on repeated occasions. . . .

Another such cave-tunnel existed in the back or western wall of the quarry not far from the stalactite cave; and in this solidly filled hole, following a blast one day in the latter part of 1924, Mr. G. L. de Bruyn, one of the mine overseers, discovered in the broken rock something that looked like a larger petrified skull. From what he could see he thought it was possibly

the skull of a young Bushman. Mr. de Bruyn saved the specimen and delivered it to Mr. Spiers in whose office it lay for some weeks. It so happened that just about this time the fossil discoveries of the Buxton quarry were brought to the attention of Professor Dart by Miss Josephine Salmons, Student Demonstrator of Anatomy, and shortly afterwards Professor R. B. Young, who was informed of these finds by Dart, having an occasion to visit the location, brought the fossil in question together with some additional pieces to the Johannesburg University.

In manipulating the pieces of rock brought back by Professor Young, Dr. Dart found that "the larger natural endocranial cast articulated exactly by its fractured frontal extremity with another piece of rock, in which the broken lower and posterior margin of the left side of a mandible was visible." After cleaning the rock mass, the outline of the hinder and lower part of the facial skeleton came into view; and a careful development of the solid limestone in which it was embedded finally revealed the almost entire face of a very interesting new form of anthropoid ape. . . .

After examining what remains of the tunnel that gave the anthropoid skull and of the remnants of the large cave a short distance to the right of this, the writer was led to the northern wall of the quarry, where a part of the original limestone elevation abutting on the dry ravine to the north of it has been left standing. In this wall, a little over 30 feet from its base and about the same distance from the top, there could be seen the pinkish fillings of another tunnel, somewhat less than 3 feet in diameter. Upon fastening a rope above and climbing up with its help, it was possible to reach the now solidly filled cavity. Fragmented bones in the rock filling the cavity were found after a very little search, but with the uncomfortable position and great hardness of the rock it was impossible to remove anything except in small pieces. An effort was made then to drill a small hole just below the filling, in order to blast out a small portion; but the tools of the native who climbed up for the purpose and tied himself at the hole with a rope were so ineffective that the attempt was abandoned. Mr. Rielly then arranged for three successive small blasts about the filling, laying half a stick of explosive in a depression of the rock and covering it with mud. These explosions made much noise, but removed only small portions of the rock. However, enough was uncovered of the filling to see additional bones including half of a monkey (probably baboon) skull. The next day the writer worked on the exposure for several hours. He tried a cold chisel, but the rock proving too hard, a heavy hammer was hoisted up and piece after piece of the rock was broken off with the hammer. This work, necessitating a suspension against the middle of a vertical wall with only here and there a little edge or nook for the feet, was not easy, nor was it enjoyed for it was felt to be a sort of vandalism, it being impossible to obtain a single specimen unbroken.

Source: Aleš Hrdlička, "The Taungs Ape," *American Journal of Physical Anthropology* 8 (1925): 379–392.

"Reminiscences of Makapansgat Limeworks and Its Bone-Breccial Layers," by Wilfred I. Eitzman

Author Wilfred Eitzman visited the Makapansgat Limeworks in the 1920s. Around thirty years later, in 1958, he described his visits to the site, when it was still being mined, from which *Australopithecus africanus* was later recovered.

- Compare the preceding primary source with the one that follows. Are there any reasons that one source might be more reliable than the other?

- How old are the first stone tools, and which species likely made them? Was *Australopithecus africanus* a hunter?

Not until the middle of May could I return to the limeworks. Then I entered the tunnel made into what obviously had previously been a cavern and was amazed at what I saw! The reports received from schoolboys and from natives were not exaggerated. The interior was a charnel house! There were thick seams of bone on both sides of the tunnel; bones were mixed with rubble and blocks, dislodged the day before by dynamiting. A thick high heap of bone was exposed about 40–50 feet from the entrance.

The tunnel was now 35 feet across, 20 feet high and had been excavated to a depth of nearly 70 feet from the entrance. I should have been there every day to watch the situation so as to recover any promising material but my work as a science and mathematics teacher had to be attended. To my mind the best material was lost in those few weeks in May 1925 when the most important parts of the bone bearing breccias were being dynamited and destroyed.

On that occasion I took the photograph that appeared in the star of August 10th. . . . It has also faded but it is the only photographic evidence available today of what the Makapansgat cavern looked like before the lime and bone-breccia had been almost completely removed from them. . . . In 1929 I conducted Professor Cipriani and his colleagues through the Makapansgat workings. There was still much of the bone deposits to be seen in those days. . . . I saw the layers and seams of Makapansgat limeworks so often that their arrangement is indelibly imprinted in my mind.

At least 60,000 tonnes of lime had been removed from the cavern made at the Limeworks during the fifteen years from 1922 to 1937 when I last saw it. . . . In 1925 a complete fossil man was found just near the end of the great first tunnel in a crevice above the grey breccia . . . on the east side. The fossil was destroyed and cast into the lime kilns. A certain person employed by the Northern Limes was responsi-

ble. The truth of this was beyond doubt; schoolboys heard about it independently. I questioned many natives who worked at the quarry and they confirmed it. The same person boasted about it as late as 1929 in the presence of Professors de Sitter, Gates and others.

His successors left were more co-operative but so much had already been destroyed that it was almost impossible to reconstruct the extent of the once intact breccia. . . . Finally when the lime company stopped working the final damage was done by another company, not deliberately, by removing from the dumps even the lowest grade of limestone to put into kilns in Potgietersrust. One or two of the dumps were sifted and the walls inside the old workings were scraped for several years until the tunnels began to collapse and became unsafe for mining.

The voracious demand for lime and the resorting of the dumps, along with the antipathy of hostile miners, explain why only a fraction of the original bone-breccia has been recovered despite the systematic sorting of the dump areas. . . . It also explains why so few *australopithecine* remains have been found at Makapansgat.

Source: Wilfred I. Eitzman, "Reminiscences of Makapansgat Limeworks and Its Bone-Breccial Layers," *South African Journal of Science* 54 (1958): 177–182.

Further Reading

Barham, L., and P. Mitchell. *The First Africans: African Archaeology from the Earliest Toolmakers to Most Recent Foragers.* Cambridge: Cambridge World Archaeology, 2008.

Brain, Charles Kimberlin. *The Hunters or the Hunted? An Introduction to African Cave Taphonomy.* Chicago: University of Chicago Press, 1981.

Dart, Raymond A. "*Australopithecus africanus*: The Man-Ape of South Africa," *Nature* 115 (1925): 195–199.

Deacon, H. J., and J. Deacon. *Human Beginnings in South Africa: Uncovering the Secrets of the Stone Age.* Walnut Creek, CA: Altamira Press, 1999.

Derricourt, R. "The Enigma of Raymond Dart," *International Journal of African Historical Studies* 42 (2009): 257–282.

Green, Richard E., Johannes Krause, Adrian W. Briggs, et al. "A Draft Sequence of the Neandertal Genome," *Science* 328 (2010): 710–722, www.sciencemag.org/content/328/5979/710.full.

Grine, Frederick E., John G. Feagle, and Richard E. Leakey, eds. *The First Humans: Origin and Early Evolution of the Genus Homo.* New York: Springer, 2009.

Marean, C. W. "When the Sea Saved Humanity." *Scientific American* 303 (2010): 54–61. doi:10.1038/scientificamerican0810-54.

Web Resources

Archaeomagnetism, Caves & Human Origins, www.archaeomagnetism.com.
Becoming Human, www.becominghuman.org/.
Hominid Species, TalkOrigins.org, www.talkorigins.org/faqs/homs/species.html.
Human Evolution, Australian Museum, http://australianmuseum.net.au/Human-Evolution.
Institute of Human Origins, http://iho.asu.edu/home.
Science & Nature: Prehistoric Life, BBC, www.bbc.co.uk/sn/prehistoric_life/human/species/.
3D Collection, Smithsonian National Museum of Natural History,
     http://humanorigins.si.edu/evidence/3d-collection.

Biographical Note

In addition to the works included in Further Reading, the following sources provide
information and analysis of particular relevance to the topics discussed in the chapter.
L. R. Berger, D. J. De Ruiter, S. E. Churchill, P. Schmid, K. J. Carlson, P. H. G. M. Dirks, and
J. M. Kibii, "*Australopithecus sediba*: A New Species of *Homo*-Like Australopith from South
Africa," *Science* 328 (2010): 195–204; Charles Kimberlin Brain, *The Hunters or the Hunted?
An Introduction to African Cave Taphonomy* (Chicago: University of Chicago Press, 1981);
K. S. Brown, C. W. Marean, A. I. R. Herries, Z. Jacobs, C. Tribolo, D. Braun, D. L. Roberts,
M. C. Meyer, and J. Bernatchez, "Fire as an Engineering Tool of Early Modern Humans,"
Science 325 (2009): 859–862; D. R. Braun, J. W. K. Harris, N. E. Levin, J. T. McCoy,
A. I. R. Herries, M. K. Bamford, L. C. Bishop, and M. Kibunjia, "Early Hominin Diet
Included Diverse Terrestrial and Aquatic Animals 1.95 Ma in East Turkana, Kenya,"
Proceedings of the National Academy of Sciences of the United States of America,
107 (2010), 10002–10007; Raymond A. Dart, "*Australopithecus africanus*: The Man-Ape of
South Africa," *Nature* 115 (1925): 195–199; Raymond A. Dart, "The Osteodontokeratic
Culture of *Australopithecus promethius*," Transvaal Museum Memoir, Transvaal Museum,
Pretoria, no. 10 (1957): 105; H. J. Deacon, and J. Deacon, *Human Beginnings in South Africa:
Uncovering the Secrets of the Stone Age* (Walnut Creek, CA: Altamira Press, 1999);
R. Derricourt, "The Enigma of Raymond Dart," *International Journal of African Historical
Studies* 42 (2009): 257–282; N. Goren-Inbar, N. Alperson, M. E. Kislev, O. Simchoni,
Y. Melamed, A. Ben-Nun, and E. Werker, "Evidence of Hominin Control of Fire at Gesher
Benot Ya'aqov, Israel," *Science* 304 (2004): 725–727; R. E. Green, J. Krause, A. W. Briggs,
T. Maricic, U. Stenzel, M. Kircher, N. Patterson, and S. Pääbo, "A Draft Sequence of the
Neandertal Genome," *Science* 328 (2010): 710–722; A. I. R. Herries, P. Hopley, J. Adams,
D. Curnoe, and M. Maslin, "Geochronology and Palaeoenvironments of the South African
Early Hominin Bearing Sites: A Reply to 'Wrangham et al., 2009: Shallow-Water Habitats
as Sources of Fallback Foods for Hominins,'" *American Journal of Physical Anthropology*
143 (2010): 640–646; C. W. Marean, "Pinnacle Point Cave 13B (Western Cape Province,
South Africa) in Context: The Cape Floral Kingdom, Shellfish, and Modern Human
Origins," *Journal of Human Evolution* 59 (2010): 425–443; C. W. Marean, M. Bar-Matthews,
J. Bernatchez, E. Fisher, P. Goldberg, A. I. R. Herries, Z. Jacobs, A. Jerardino, P. Karkanas,
T. Minichillo, P. J. Nilssen, E. Thompson, I. Watts, and H. W. Williams, "Early Human Use of
Marine Resources and Pigment in South Africa during the Middle Pleistocene," *Nature* 449
(2007): 905–908; S. P. McPherron, Z. Alemseged, C. W. Marean, J. G. Wynn, D. Reed,
D. Geraads, R. Bobe, and H. A. Béarat, "Evidence for Stone-Tool-Assisted Consumption
of Animal Tissues before 3.39 Million Years Ago at Dikika, Ethiopia," *Nature* 466 (2010):
857–860.

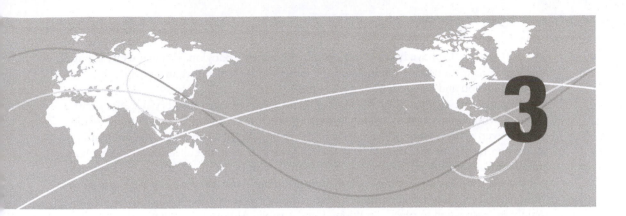

Babylon

Rise of a Complex Urban Civilization

(ca. 3700–539 BCE)

MELANIE SUE BYRD

T HE NAME BABYLON EVOKES A SENSE OF MYSTERY AND REMOTENESS. EVEN THE name is poetic: it means "gateway of the gods." Today little remains of the city except some brownish, crumbling ruins and partial reconstruction dating from the era of Saddam Hussein. To the Greeks, however, Babylon was a place of astonishing, legendary wonders, such as the hanging gardens, which they described in travel guides. Herodotus, the famous Greek historian who lived in the 400s BCE, found Babylon impressive, but his colorful account had many exaggerations and inaccuracies. For instance, he erroneously stated that women were required to prostitute themselves at temples to strangers, which added to the image of Babylon as a place of sexual license. Then to the Jews, Babylon was a place of alienation and oppression, to which they had been deported forcibly, and they feared assimilation into a foreign culture with a polytheistic religion. Our vision of Babylon remains that of an infamous city, doomed for its extravagance and excess. Many people today associate Babylon with biblical stories like the destruction of the Tower of Babel or the account of Belshazzar's feast, when divine handwriting appeared on the wall of the palace, foretelling the collapse of the Babylonian monarchy. Over time, these episodes were imaginatively represented in the visual arts, opera, and film, thereby the way we perceive ancient Babylon. Even the television science fiction series *Babylon 5* used the themes of religion, dreams, prophecies, power, conflict, and destruction that have become associated with ancient Babylon. Today the city's name still stands as a cautionary reminder of the dangers inherent in urban society driven toward expansion and consumption of resources.

I first became captivated by Mesopotamia through works of mystery novelist Agatha Christie, who was married to an archaeologist and wrote vividly of her adventures on digs in Iraq, even setting some of her novels in the region. What really made the ancient culture come to life for me, though, was the discovery of a small collection of Babylonian cuneiform tablets hidden away in our university archives. In the 1920s, a president had purchased them as a teaching tool so that students from rural south Georgia could "touch the Holy Land"; like others of his era, our president thought of Mesopotamia mainly in connection to places mentioned in the Bible. Although Babylonia did have biblical connections, these tablets tell a different kind of story. They are transactions of average people doing ordinary, everyday business and record keeping. The new archivist at our university wanted to use the tablet collection for teaching once again. My students always enjoy seeing the oldest texts in our library, and one young man even exclaimed, "Wow! They look just like Post-it Notes!" In fact, the tablets are like Post-it Notes in the sense that they are memoranda from a long gone civilization. Through them we encounter the day-to-day transactions that underpinned a civilization that has been shrouded in legend.

Any bureaucrat who has ever traveled on an expense account can perhaps identify with an ancient courier who was paid in rations. The tablets opened up an entire world. Mesopotamia became fascinating to me precisely because it was so remote, and elusive. Despite being written, first-hand sources, ancient tablets are sometimes vague. Surviving accounts do not cover all aspects of every period in Mesopotamian history. Because of this, scholars disagree and contradict one another on many aspects of Mesopotamian history. There are discrepancies in dating systems and chronologies. What's more, because scholars of Mesopotamia are such highly trained specialists, much of what they write is incomprehensible to non-specialists. I wanted to discover the accessible, human side to Mesopotamia.

I found it in the celebrated *Epic of Gilgamesh*. The friendship between Gilgamesh and Enkidu, as well as Gilgamesh's grief over his friend's painful death, is moving. Furthermore, it is not only the first "buddy story" in which two men brawl with each other and end up friends but also the first instance of the "best friend dying" motif so beloved of Hollywood. Perhaps my favorite episode in the story is when Gilgamesh, in his quest to understand life and death, encountered the ale brewer Siduri. She told him how to find the man who held the key to immortality but also reminded the distraught hero that death is part of the human condition. Maybe this is the first example of somebody like a bartender dispensing solace and advice! I was even more intrigued to discover that before the era of Hammurabi, women did, in fact, participate in ale and beer manufacture, and were protected by special patron goddesses, like Ninkasi. In short, the study of Mesopotamia is fascinating because it keeps raising interesting questions, and like Gilgamesh, the student of Babylon keeps on searching for answers.

To gain some perspective on Mesopotamia, we must look at it in relation to other civilizations of the Bronze Age. Like Mesopotamia, Egypt and India developed sophisticated civilizations in fertile river valleys. Along the Nile, Egypt prospered as a civilization of small villages, united under a monarchy. In the region that today is Pakistan and northern India, Harappan or Indus Valley civilization flourished. Cities like Mohenjo-Daro and Harappa (ca. 2600–1700 BCE) offered impressive urban planning and elaborate water storage facilities. Unfortunately, the language of the Indus Valley civilization remains un-deciphered, so the details of city life and social organization are not accessible to us. Babylon was a unique city of its era, so it is no wonder that it acquired an enduring legendary mystique. From roughly 3700 to 539 BCE, Mesopotamia saw the rise of a complex urban civilization and the development of territorial kingdoms and empires.

BABYLON AND THE WORLD: A City of Many Historical Firsts

To us in the twenty-first century, the names and places of ancient Mesopotamia only exist in connection to contemporary wars. Yet Babylonia offers some of the oldest written records in the world. The beginning of written communication distinguishes history from prehistory, so Babylonia is a place where we encounter many historical "firsts." We can see some of the earliest attempts of people to meet the challenges of living in large cities and dealing with complex social, professional, economic, and political systems. Babylonians voiced some of the first lamentations over the destructiveness of war, made some of the first observations of stars and planets, and wrestled with concepts of what justice meant, both in the cosmic and social sense. They created the sweeping epic as a form of storytelling that is still the basis of our adventure, fantasy, and science fiction stories today.

For a long time Babylon was part of a lost civilization. Much of the built environment of Mesopotamia was mud brick, so it did not survive over the centuries, and the ancient languages fell from use. Fortunately, travelers and antiquarians remained curious about places like Babylon and Nineveh, whose names endured. Most sites were simply mounds of stratified rubble called tells. Correctly identifying and mapping them was difficult. Many ancient texts survived, though, and as competitive European states expanded their commercial and imperial interests in the Middle East, Europeans began to take an active interest in the history and artifacts of Mesopotamia. By the mid-nineteenth century, scholars had deciphered enough of the ancient languages that the civilization became recognized for its impressive cultural achievement. France, England, and Germany plunged into archaeological rivalry to excavate the famous sites. Owning pieces of the first cities and empires gave a cachet of power and cultural prestige to the industrial nations, who perhaps saw Mesopotamia as the ancestor of their own cities and empires.

The best way to understand the world of ancient Babylon is to look at its geographic setting within the larger region of the ancient Near East. The city was located in southern Mesopotamia, a Greek term that means "Land between the rivers." (See Map 3.1.) The two rivers that defined Mesopotamia are the Tigris and the Euphrates, and southern Mesopotamia is known as Babylonia. Its environment is characterized by hot, parched plains, and, near the coast of the Persian Gulf, marshes. Here, the volatility of the rivers, especially the Tigris, made irrigation a necessity for agriculture and urban life. Northern Mesopotamia is called Assyria, and its landscape features hills and fertile plains watered by rainfall. Generally speaking, ancient Mesopotamia encompassed most of modern-day Iraq, plus parts of Iran, Turkey, and Syria. Because of its location between the Mediterranean area and Central Asia, Mesopotamia has always been at the intersection of many civilizations.

Mesopotamian people interacted with those of the Levant (the east coast of the Mediterranean) to the west, Anatolia to the north, the Iranian Plateau to the east, and the Persian Gulf to the south. Much of the contact came through commerce. Trade was vital, because Babylonia lacked many resources. It sought tin from Asia Minor and lumber from Lebanon and Syria. Late in the third millennium BCE Mesopotamia traded

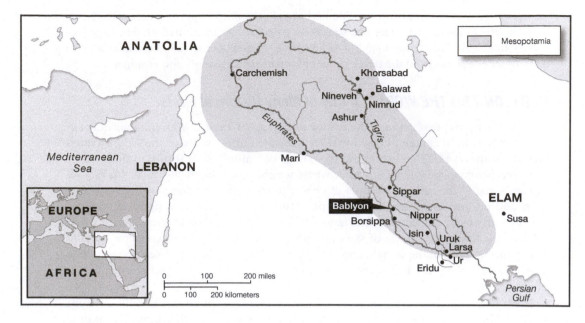

Map 3.1. Mesopotamia

Proximity to the Tigris and Euphrates rivers as well as the Persian Gulf had an important impact on the development of Mesopotamian civilization. Some scholars speculate that the shoreline of the Persian Gulf was closer to the southern cities before the climate started to become drier around 3700 BCE.

with Dilmun, probably the modern island of Bahrain, Magan or Makan, (a source of copper), what is northern Oman today, and Meluhha, identified as the sophisticated Indus Valley, or Harappan, civilization. Moreover, because much of Mesopotamia consisted of plains with few natural barriers, various groups, especially nomads from surrounding regions, were attracted to the area. Though Mesopotamian sources often depict the arrival of nomads as invasions that caused instability and the collapse of empires, these arrivals added to the dynamism of the region and became part of the fabric of the civilization. Amorites, for instance, established dynastic, monarchical rule that first made Babylon a powerful city and empire. Kassite rulers became the first people in Mesopotamia to breed horses specifically for chariot warfare. Thus terms like Mesopotamia and Babylonia do not refer to a single ethnicity or kingdom, but instead added to a dynamic culture in which people shared traditions, religious beliefs, and social organization. Mesopotamia saw political unity only when ambitious rulers arose and built empires.

Mesopotamia is part of the broad region sometimes dubbed the "Fertile Crescent" that curved in an arc north from the Persian Gulf down to the coast of the East Mediterranean. In this area the domestication of foodstuffs like wheat, barley, lentils, rye, sheep, pigs, and cattle began around 9000 BCE. As a result, small agricultural communities appeared in northern Mesopotamia by 6000 BCE. Between 6000 and 4000 BCE, Mesopotamians began to make pottery and use mud brick as a construction material. By the fourth millennium BCE, they were using the potter's wheel. The first metal that humans worked was copper. Around 3000 BCE, Middle Eastern metallurgists learned how to combine tin and copper to form bronze, which was stronger than copper alone. The resulting proliferation of bronze tools and weapons marked the beginning of the Bronze Age in the Middle East. During the Bronze Age was when Babylonian civilization began to flourish.

City, Kingdom, and Empire

The most intriguing aspect of Babylonia is that it offers us a glimpse of the first urban culture. The city was at its heart. The urban revolution—when towns grew into cities—began in the southern plains of Babylonia near the Persian Gulf around 3700 BCE. We refer to this region as Sumer and the civilization as Sumerian, even though there was no ethnically distinct group of people identifiable as Sumerian. Scholars debate the details of who the peoples of Sumer were, how their language evolved, where they came from, and when they arrived in the south, but they agree that Sumerian civilization laid the foundation for subsequent Mesopotamian cultural traditions.

The inhospitable environment of Babylonia required significant human alteration to make it suitable for living. Experts used to believe that mastering irrigation projects like draining marshes and digging canals contributed to the rise of cities, but more recent archaeology indicates that urbanization preceded such large-scale projects. Land reclamation enabled agricultural surpluses, which in turn contributed to population growth. Scholars debate the exact reasons why urban expansion occurred in southern Mesopotamia. The arrival of outsiders, perhaps because of climate change, also might have contributed to this demographic growth. Regardless, urban centers flourished and grew into independent, complex city-states, with the early cities having populations of perhaps 10,000 to 50,000. Each city-state had a dynastic leader called an *ensi* (governor) or *lugal* (usually translated as king) who oversaw centralized institutions that organized society and the economy. Uruk, called Warka today, has often been called the first true city. Scholars debate whether it is literally the oldest urban center, but nonetheless, it was an impressive site. Its walls stretched for six miles and were protected by hundreds of towers. Uruk had a variety of private houses whose construction and embellishment reflected differences in wealth. It was an economic center and also boasted monumental temples. The city of Eridu was also extremely ancient and emerged as a principal religious center, with a shrine that dates back to around 5000 BCE. Another important early city was Ur, which was once a coastal city, in a prime location for trade with Arabia. In the 1920s, the noted archaeologist Leonard Woolley discovered a cemetery filled with spectacular treasures at Ur, reflecting the wealth enjoyed by the elite. Famously, according to tradition, Ur was the original home of the biblical figure Abraham, who is recognized by Jews, Christians, and Muslims as a founding patriarch.

Because each city-state was autonomous, they were often rivals who fought one another over water and agricultural land. Shifting power was a characteristic of these early cities. For instance, Nippur came to replace Eridu as a holy city. Some scholars believe that in the 2000s BCE cities formed a league or confederation, perhaps to confront threats from external enemies. Around 2340 BCE, a ruler known as Sargon from the area of Akkad, which was just to the north of Sumer, built an empire that lasted roughly two hundred years and forced a degree of unity on the Sumerian city-states. The Akkadian empire was the first regional state in Mesopotamia. It expanded to encompass the Persian Gulf area, part of Asia Minor, and part of the Levant. It was the first multiethnic, polyglot (multilingual) empire in recorded history. Akkadians spoke a language from the Semitic language family (the same family as Hebrew and Arabic), which was quite different from the somewhat mysterious Sumerian language. The empire made Akkadian the official language of governing and business in Mesopotamia.

Sargon forged his empire by military conquest and governed by placing Akkadian governors in charge of Sumerian city-states. He built infrastructure to facilitate trade, but ultimately held his conquests together by force. The concept of unified empire was new to Mesopotamia, and the city-states of Sumer clung to their local identities. The moment imperial power weakened, Sumerian city-states asserted autonomy. After the demise of Sargon's empire, the Sumerian city of Ur enjoyed supremacy in the south around 2100 BCE. Rulers of this Third Dynasty of Ur (ca. 2112–2004 BCE), like Ur-Nammu and his son Shulgi, built the first multilevel ziggurats, like the one dedicated to the moon god Nanna at Ur. Religious architecture reflects how central religion was to Mesopotamian life. A ruler's power to govern was believed to come directly from the gods, and Mesopotamian art often shows rulers interacting with gods. For instance, the top portion of the Hammurabi Code visually illustrates Hammurabi receiving power from Shamash, the sun god. The whole institution of monarchy was believed to have been divinely created.

To show their power and piety, rulers built, expanded, or maintained temples. Mesopotamians conceived of gods as anthropomorphic (looking like humans) and immortal. Gods controlled all aspects of nature, like weather and fertility, which were of great importance to an agricultural society. Further, gods were unpredictable and required reverence from their human servants. During religious celebrations, deities manifested themselves in their temples to accept offerings. Each deity resided in the temple of his or her particular city and also could be represented by statues in temples in other cities. The temple was the center of the divine presence that protected and maintained the life, prosperity, and security of each city-state. After a century, however, famine, ecological problems, and invasions ended Ur's power. A famous piece of poetry, the "Lamentation over the Destruction of Ur," depicts the goddess of Ur, Ningal, beseeching the leading gods of the pantheon, to no avail, to spare her city from invasion.

Meanwhile, a new group of semi-nomadic, Semitic-speaking people called Amorites, moved into Mesopotamia from the north and west. Amorites adopted Mesopotamian culture, and some established themselves as rulers of city-states. Under an Amorite dynasty, Babylon first achieved prominence. Though the town already existed, during the era of the famous Amorite King Hammurabi and his dynasty (ca.1800–1600 BCE) it grew into an important city and the center of a thriving empire. Hammurabi was a conqueror who brought southern Mesopotamia under his control. Today, scholars use the term Babylonia to designate the southern portion of Mesopotamia. With Babylonian expansion, the city's deity, Marduk, gained prominence in the Mesopotamian pantheon and came to be seen as the king of the gods who had vanquished the primeval forces of chaos during the creation of the cosmos. Marduk possessed great wisdom and magical powers that could be used against evil forces in the cosmos. Most importantly, Marduk was believed to have built Babylon as an earthly abode for the gods. Babylon became the religious heart of Mesopotamia and the locus of the cultural traditions that had developed from the time of the Sumerians. Babylonian scribes compiled important literary works, like the famous *Epic of Gilgamesh*.

In addition to literature, Hammurabi's reign is very well documented with records of trade and diplomacy. The most famous written source from Babylonia that gives us insight into the structure of that society is the Hammurabi Code. Though it is not the earliest Babylonian law code, it is the most complete. Scholars disagree about the Code's function in the everyday practice of law, but agree that it reflects a society in which the king stood between the gods who empowered him and the people he ruled. The law code shows Hammurabi receiving power from Shamash, the god of justice, and the prologue depicts the king as powerful, pious, and a protector of the oppressed. However, the code was not a law code in the modern sense; it offered no general or universal principles. Instead, it is a compilation of specific rulings. Some scholars have interpreted it as a political testament, a summary of Hammurabi's reign or a literary model to train scribes. It was remarkably comprehensive, covering criminal law and civil matters such as business, property, slavery, inheritances, marriage, and family relations. By modern standards, these laws were harsh; for instance, breaking into a house was punishable by death. To Babylonians, justice meant retribution, or what is called Talon Law. The most famous example of Talon Law from the Hammurabi Code is the concept of "an eye for an eye, a tooth for a tooth." Hammurabi's laws were not like modern statutes, and existing records of legal cases do not refer to his code specifically. Scholars continue to debate how the famous code was used in the society. It is also important to remember, that what constituted an appropriate retaliation depended entirely on a person's social status. If a person of a higher rank did bodily harm to one of lower rank, the guilty party merely paid a fine. The legal status of Babylonians depended on social rank (royal, landowner, or commoner), gender, and whether they were free or slaves. Babylonian society was stratified, with social mobility an option only for those near the top. There was no sense that people had rights. They received protection from the king, who presented himself as a father figure and shepherd of his flock.

The social structure of Babylon was complex, and the details of social hierarchies and social interactions are not explained in documents. Terminology for social groups that appears in records depends on specific context or relationship between the persons described. For instance, a highly ranked, elite palace official could still be referred to as the "slave" of the king. The term "house," which appears in Babylonian records as a description of social relationship, had a variety of meanings. It could refer to a single nuclear family household, a manufacturing establishment, an institution such as a temple estate, the household of the king, or to a clan or tribe. The Hammurabi Code mentions three specific social categories: free man (*awilum*); dependent (*mushkenum*), and slave (*wardum*); scholars do not know the precise nuances of these terms and what they meant to people of Hammurabi's time. One aspect of Babylonian society is quite clear, though: it was patriarchal. Women were under the control of their fathers until they married, at which time they came under the control of their husbands. Children belonged to their father's family. A man had complete control over his wife and children. Though marriage was usually monogamous, a childless woman was required to allow her husband to take a second wife in order to produce heirs. However, women could apparently retain some control over their dowries after marriage and also could accumulate property of their own through investments. A woman whose husband abandoned her could remarry after five years.

Babylon Reaches Its Height

Hammurabi's empire did not survive long after his death around 1750 BCE. Despite upheaval, invasion, and a sack of the city by Hittites from Anatolia (ca. 1595), Babylon endured. Kassites, originally from the Zagros Mountains, had moved into Mesopotamia in the 1700s BCE. By approximately 1475, they controlled Babylonia and ruled for nearly four hundred years of relative stability. They embraced the culture of Babylonia, and continued many of the achievements of Hammurabi's era, such as the development of a unified, regional monarchy as opposed to independent city-states. They participated in trade networks, providing items like horses and chariots in exchange for gold and timber. Late in the Kassite Era, civilizations of the east Mediterranean region experienced a variety of crises. During the Bronze Age, expansive trade networks emerged for the exchange of tin and copper needed to make bronze, as well as a variety of other goods connected the East Mediterranean, Aegean, Egypt, and western Asia. Goods traded included gold, timber, minerals, precious stones, and shells. Various trade routes that extended from the Indus Valley through the Iranian Plateau to Anatolia, Cyprus, Crete, and southern Greece passed through Mesopotamia. (See Map 3.2.) Between roughly 1200 and 1100 BCE, however, the trade networks that had characterized the Bronze Age disintegrated, and many regions in the Middle East faced severe pressures. Scholars vigorously argue over what caused the end of the Bronze Age, but they agree that it involved conflict, disruption of trade, and population migrations. The Hittite Empire collapsed, and Egypt faced invasion. Elamites, who lived to the east of Babylonia, sacked the city and carried the famous law code of Hammurabi back to their capital, Susa. Then, after 1100 BCE, Arameans, semi-nomadic pastoralists of unclear origin, raided Mesopotamia. Food shortages and inflation added to the general chaos.

By the 800s BCE, the center of power in Mesopotamia moved northward. Ashur or Assur, to the north of Babylon, had emerged around 1809 BCE as an independent kingdom with a king. Its process of expansion to become the Assyrian Empire was slow and characterized by setbacks. Assyria survived the collapse of the Bronze Age relatively intact, and gradually built a powerful army that used new iron technology along with bronze for weapons. Further, an important innovation was incorporation of cavalry into the army. Horses allowed mounted warriors to maneuver rapidly on rough terrain. The Assyrian Empire employed the first large-scale army, which included military engineers skilled in siege craft. Assyria is chiefly remembered for its military might and forceful treatment of subject peoples. Defeated populations were often deported so as to break up regional ties. Assyrian art and propaganda tended to emphasize military conquest and brutal punishment of enemies.

When Assyria launched its formidable imperial venture in the 700s BCE, Babylonia fell to its might. Assyrian cities like Assur and Nineveh became the new sites of political power. At its height the Assyrian Empire stretched from Sumer, north into Syria, down the coast of the Mediterranean, and into Egypt. Babylonia, however, retained its religious and cultural prestige.

Then, with the collapse of the Assyrian Empire in 605 BCE, power shifted back to Babylonia. The city of Babylon reached its apogee as the center of a splendid civilization and the cultural and religious center of the Near East (ca. 604–560 BCE). It was the center of the last great empire originating in Mesopotamia. Today, we call this period and empire Chaldean, after a people who first appeared in historical records in the 800s BCE and quickly became important in Babylonia. The city was very wealthy and cosmopolitan, with residents from the Levant, Persia, and Egypt engaging in trade. Many successful family businesses flourished. A few large-scale family enterprises even dealt in slave trading, real estate, and major commercial transactions throughout Babylonia and into West Iran.

Babylon also became a center of scholarship, especially in mathematics and astronomy. Sumerians had developed a mathematical system based on sixty (sexagesimal system). They developed the concept of a 360-degree circle and 60-minute hour, which we still use today. They used cuneiform symbols for numbers, and, over time, Babylonians worked out practical problems relevant to commerce and engineering. Mathematical tables allowed them to work out square roots, cube roots, and exponential functions.

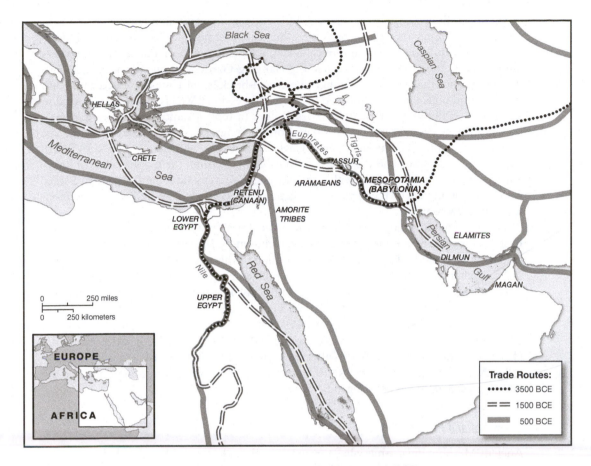

Map 3.2. Trade Networks Through Mesopotamia, 3500–500 BCE

Mesopotamia's location made it an important link in key trade networks that flourished between Central Asia and the Mediterranean. Open frontiers allowed migrants, such as Arameans, to enter the region easily, and Mesopotamian city-states and kingdoms engaged in a variety of relations with neighboring civilizations.

Though they never developed underlying theories to explain mathematics, they laid the foundation for the later Greek and Muslim achievements in that field. The belief that heavenly bodies were deities and that celestial phenomena influenced human activities encouraged Babylonians to observe the skies. Though motivated by belief in the super-natural, the observations that Babylonian astronomers made enabled them to calculate movements of the sun, moon, and planets, even predicting lunar and solar eclipses. They also developed a lunar calendar composed of twelve months of thirty days. Egyptians, too, used sophisticated astronomy to develop both a 360- and a 365-day calendar to align the pyramids and determine the annual flooding of the Nile. During the Hellenistic Era (ca. 323-30 BCE) Egyptian and Babylonian astronomy converged in the famous Egyptian city of Alexandria, laying the foundation for much Western understanding about the heavens up until the time of Copernicus and Galileo. Babylonians can be credited with developing mathematical astronomy, and were so well known for this skill in this field that later Greeks and Romans used the term "Chaldean" as a synonym for astronomer.

Chaldean Babylon is best remembered for its monumental building. The great ziggurat (elaborate temple tower, perhaps three hundred feet high) called Etemenanki, dedicated to Marduk, inspired the biblical account of the Tower of Babel. Greek writers immortalized and perhaps exaggerated the Hanging Gardens as one of the Seven Wonders of the ancient world. The shining, blue glazed-brick Ishtar Gate decorated with lions, dragons, and bulls that once adorned the city's Processional Way is now reconstructed in a museum in Berlin, where it still dazzles visitors (a replica stands on the original site). Some of the city's great monuments date from the reign of Nebuchadnezzar II, the last great Babylonian king. The last ruler of Chaldean Babylon, Nabonidus (556–539 BCE), offended high officials and the priests of Marduk by favoring the moon god over Babylon's traditional deity. Factions within the city began secretly favoring Cyrus II of Persia, who was building his own empire. Cyrus captured Babylon in 539 BCE with little resistance and few reprisals.

Because the city enjoyed such prestige as a cultural and religious center in the Near East, Cyrus presented himself as having been chosen by Marduk to restore Babylon's religious heritage, and this use of divine justification for his conquest fit within the tradition of Mesopotamian kingship. The first empire builder, Sargon, explained his rise to power in religious terms by stating that he received the favor of the goddess Ishtar. Cyrus then made his son, Cambyses, king of Babylon. The city continued to flourish, prosper, and serve as a center of scholarship and religion under the Persian Achaemenid Dynasty (ca. 620–330 BCE), despite some economic strain and occasional revolts. It was not until the Hellenistic Era (ca. 323–30 BCE), after the death of Alexander of Macedon, (popularly called Alexander the Great), in 323 BCE, that Babylonia stagnated economically and the fabled city began to pass into legend.

Literature and Religion

Ancient Mesopotamia comes alive through its written legacy. Although scholars still debate the origins of writings, in Babylonia, writing emerged near the end of the fourth millennium BCE, and the full details of the process are unknown. As the first city-states grew in size and complexity, writing became a practical necessity for keeping records. From simple pictographs Sumerians developed complex signs in a script that modern scholars call cuneiform, meaning "wedge shaped." Clay was abundant along the river banks, so it became the principal writing material. Scribes used a reed stylus to press wedge-shaped symbols into damp clay tablets. The tablets were then sun dried or oven baked, which made them more durable. Cuneiform script was also used for inscriptions on monuments.

Though ruling elites kept extensive records, the majority of the population was illiterate. Only scribes from wealthy families who received rigorous training at a "tablet house" learned to read and write the hundreds of signs that evolved over time. Akkadians then adapted cuneiform to their language. Akkadian cuneiform became the common medium for diplomatic correspondence in the Middle East, and surviving examples, like the famous Amarna Letters, offer insight into the way ancient states interacted with one another. For instance, some of the correspondence includes requests from Kassite kings to Pharaoh Amenhotep IV of Egypt for things like a marriage alliance or better treatment of Babylonian merchants in Egypt. Rulers kept well-organized, extensive libraries and archives of information they considered important, including literature, dictionaries, and information about religious rituals. Temples and businesses also kept accounts of their activities. Although much writing was for administrative or sacred purposes, Babylonians were creative and devised clever satires about the socially pretentious, offered maxims of advice, and formulated love charms to assure sexual and romantic success.

Of all the written works that comes from Babylonia, the *Epic of Gilgamesh* is the most enduring, with its themes still central to culture today. Gilgamesh is the oldest recorded story about a hero who searched for the meaning of human existence, encountered death, and withstood many trials in the course of his quest. Gilgamesh was the semilegendary king of Uruk, believed to have been two-thirds divine. The earliest parts of the story date back to Sumer, but in Hammurabi's Babylon was where a writer compiled the ancient tales into a single, unified epic. Later a Kassite poet, Sin-lequ-unninni, prepared the standard version we know today, with its emphasis on friendship, grief, fear of death, and learning life's lessons through hardship.

Gilgamesh was an abusive king, so the gods sent Enkidu, a "wild man" from the steppes beyond the city, to challenge him. Scholars frequently interpret Enkidu as representing nomads. His process of civilization through seduction by the beautiful temple priestess Shamhat is perhaps an early form of the "beauty and the beast" myth. The two men fought in a contest of masculine strength, but then became best friends. Later, in the course of the adventures they shared, they offended the powerful goddess Ishtar, so Enkidu sickened and died as punishment. Following the death of his friend, the grief-stricken Gilgamesh began to seek the reason for human mortality. In one of the most famous episodes of the tale, Gilgamesh sought wisdom from Utnapishtim, the only man to have survived the great flood that had destroyed the world. He revealed to Gilgamesh the secret of a plant that would confer immortality. Gilgamesh found the plant, but a snake seized and ate it while he was bathing. Thus, in the end, the hero discovered that immortality was reserved exclusively for the gods. Gilgamesh did not despair completely, though. He had gained much wisdom about the human condition through his mythic journeys and returned to Uruk a better king who was glad to see his splendid city once again.

Gilgamesh experienced his adventures in a world of volatile gods who often seemed vengeful or inscrutable. As the hero learned, humans were made of clay to serve the gods. Divine rewards and punishments for human conduct occurred in this life. Thus in one form or another, religious beliefs permeated Babylonian society. Rudimentary temples were central to the earliest Sumerian cities, and they became increasingly elaborate. At first, temples were simply raised above ground on a platform. Eventually, however, the multilevel, stepped ziggurat that reached the heavens came to characterize urban religious complexes. Ziggurats were artificial mountains that that allowed priests to climb nearer to the realm of the gods. The temple was literally the household of the patron deity and housed a cult statue. Temple communities were part of the social and governing elite, owned land, conducted business, and participated in the economic life of cities. A large temple like the Esagila, the temple of Marduk at Babylon, had thousands of staff workers and owned hundreds of acres of agricultural land. As such, Babylonian society is often described as theocratic because religious and civil institutions were interconnected. Children of royal or wealthy families became priests and priestesses, like Enheduanna, daughter of Sargon, who was appointed priestess of the moon god Nanna at Ur. Sometimes entire families worked at temple communities.

Each city had a local patron deity. An, the sky god, was the patron of Uruk. Ur was the home of Nanna, the moon god, whereas Nippur, which became an important religious center, was sacred to Enlil, the god of air and storms. Enlil was the king of the gods and the agent who bestowed authority to govern on mortal rulers. When Babylon rose to preeminence, the Babylonian creation epic, the "Enuma Elish," explained how Babylon's god, Marduk, replaced Enlil as the head of the pantheon. Leaders of cities and rulers of empires had to oversee religious rituals to assure prosperity and divine protection. There were numerous, cyclical public observances on the Babylonian calendar. The New Year's festival, which came to be celebrated at the spring equinox during the Chaldean era, was an especially important civic function. Although many of its elaborate ceremonies involved the ruler and priests exclusively, ordinary people encountered the divine presence by joining together to watch public processions in which a statue of the god was carried along a parade route. However, scholars do not know exactly what role ordinary people played in these celebrations or how they perceived them because records about religion come from the literate, priestly elite.

Aside from official functions, Mesopotamians saw omens and supernatural forces at work in their daily lives. Perhaps because they lived in a harsh physical environment and faced periods of upheaval, people understandably viewed their world as terrifying. They believed that personal suffering and sickness were punishment for sin. They also believed in a variety of demons, ghosts, and monsters that interacted with humans. Numerous charms, spells, prayers, and incantations protected individuals against the omnipresent fear of evil and helplessness.

While Babylonians experienced the supernatural on a daily basis, a group of people with a different set of religious beliefs encountered important religious transformations in Babylon. Ethical monotheism had begun to evolve with early Hebrew and Israelite beliefs and practices, influenced by contact with Canaanite and Mesopotamian civilizations. For instance, the concept of a flood that destroyed creation was Mesopotamian in origin. The term Eden, as in the Garden of Eden, derives from the Sumerian word *edin*, for wild steppe land beyond the urban built environment. The earliest account of a divinely ordained flood that destroyed creation is Sumerian. Over time religious practices of Hebrews and Israelites took on distinctive features and became increasingly monotheistic. Hebrew religious reformers emphasized the belief that their deity, Yahweh, required sincere ethical conduct rather than priestly rituals from followers. Though wrathful, Yahweh was not capricious and could be swayed by moral, devout behavior.

When Nebuchadnezzar defeated the small Kingdom of Judah (in modern-day Israel) in 586 BCE, he maintained the Assyrian policy of deporting conquered peoples. As many deportees from Jerusalem to Babylon felt alienated in the foreign environment, they confronted these new challenges and subsequently adapted religious practices that built the foundation of Judaism. Prophets began to stress the idea that upheaval and military defeat were divine punishment. Though belief in divine retribution was common in Mesopotamian culture, Jews expressed it in the context of monotheism: Yahweh deliberately used Babylonian conquest to punish followers for lack of devotion. Thus, explicitly, there was only one, universal deity, Yahweh, in control of the actions of all peoples. More importantly, Yahweh came to be understood as an abstract deity who lived in the heavens and was not exclusively tied to the Temple in Jerusalem. Many modern religious scholars also suggest that while in Babylonia, Jews began to assemble previously written traditions into the Torah, the foundation of their sacred scriptures. The fundamental aspects of monotheism and the characteristics attributed to Yahweh in Jewish scripture became part of Christian and Muslim beliefs, so Babylon was a place of profound and enduring religious encounters.

GLOBAL ENCOUNTERS AND CONNECTIONS:
Babylonia as a Nexus Point for Civilization and Empire

Ironically, one of the most legendary encounters in the history of Babylon occurred well after the heyday of Mesopotamian-centered empires. The glamour, wealth and splendor of Babylon impressed the Greeks and in 331 BCE, Alexander of Macedon, whose life and career became the stuff of myth, entered the city during his rapid, dramatic conquest of the Persian Empire. As he took control of the Empire, Alexander increasingly acted like a Persian ruler and assumed the aura of divinely sanctioned power that had long been part of the Mesopotamian tradition. His sudden death from unknown causes, perhaps an acute disease, in Babylon in 323 BCE, while planning further conquests, added to the mystique of both Alexander and Babylon. Paradoxically, Greeks had gone to war against Persia because they viewed it as the ultimate "other," the exact opposite of their own cultural values and traditions. In fact, the varied cultural traditions of Greece had connections to the diverse civilizations of the Near East; most famously, the Babylonian contribution to Greek math and astronomy has long been recognized. Though Babylonians did not devise abstract theories, they worked out calculations that Pythagoras and Euclid would later explain.

In the twentieth century scholars started to examine parallels between the adventures of Gilgamesh and tales of Greek heroes like Hercules, as well as the Homeric epics. Mesopotamian accounts of the origin of the gods, likely transmitted via the Hittites of Anatolia (Hittite New Kingdom ca. 1412–1200 BCE), perhaps influenced Greek views on the formation of their pantheon. After all, neither Greek civilization nor Mesopotamian civilization existed in a vacuum. Trade took people and ideas from both cultures into a wider world. The expansion of the Assyrian Empire into the Levant brought a major Mesopotamian empire to the coast of the Mediterranean, where Phoenician (Canaanite) cities played a role in wide-reaching trade networks that involved the Greeks. In the 1980s, scholars coined the term "orientalizing revolution" to describe the early interactions among Greeks and cultures of the Levant, Egypt, and Mesopotamia in the 800s and 700s BCE.

Of course the most extensive, well-documented encounters between Greeks and Babylonians occurred in the wake of Alexander's Empire, during the Hellenistic Era, when Greek settlers and merchants came to the kingdoms of Alexander's successors. In cities at least, a certain amount of syncretism, cultural mixing and borrowing, took place. Hellenistic Greek scholars encountered the Persian Mazdian priests, who passed on their knowledge of Babylonian astronomy and astrology. The Greeks also borrowed the term *magi* for these learned men, and it is the basis of our word *magic*. It is somehow appropriate that a word that conveys mystical power should have origins in remote encounters that take us back to the ancient ancestor of our own civilization.

With its open frontiers and geographic location close to the Levant, Egypt, the Iranian Plateau, and Anatolia, Mesopotamia was well situated to become a crossroads for wide-ranging trade networks. Trade for resources that were scarce, like metals, stone, and timber, brought Mesopotamians into contact with other peoples. In fact, control of trade routes may have been a factor that prompted Sargon to forge the first empire. As city-states vied with one another for supremacy and empires rose and fell, economic prosperity remained a constant, important factor in Mesopotamian life. Pastoral migrants were attracted to cities and absorbed Mesopotamian traditions. The wealth of cities allowed for the construction of monumental architecture, like temples. Urban elites created a literary tradition that preserved the memory of Mesopotamian culture.

Babylon stands out as the most memorable Mesopotamian city because of its powerful rulers, like Hammurabi and Nebuchadnezzar, under whom the riches and prestige of the city increased. Although the Jews who had been forcibly deported to Babylon may have disliked the foreign culture, they were part of the process of cultural encounters, and some remained in Babylon after the Persian conquest. Whereas people remember the negative image of Babylon from the Bible, the Babylonian Talmud, an important piece of Jewish religious writing compiled in Babylon from the third to fifth centuries CE, is a reminder of the diverse interactions that speak to Babylon's enduring mystique.

ENCOUNTERS AS TOLD: PRIMARY SOURCES

Although many written sources certainly exist for Babylonia, some are in poor condition or are incomplete. In addition, the language and writing style are very different from easy-to-read, flowing narratives. Scholars who read Sumerian and Akkadian are highly trained specialists and often have to guess what passages mean and then support their assertions with comparisons to similar ancient texts and references to interpretations of other modern scholars. Often, a significant amount of research is needed simply to translate a single sentence. Thus, translated works from Mesopotamia often seem stilted or fragmented to modern readers. So reading Babylonian texts requires imagination. The following selections illustrate aspects of life in Babylonia.

The Valdosta Tablet

Commerce was central to the cities of Babylonia. Scholars use the term "redistributive economy" to describe systems in central institutions that gathered and stored circulated goods. Thousands of surviving tablets related to business and economic matters have been discovered around the remains of Ur, Nippur, and other sites in Babylonia. These tablets reveal information about transactions and exchanges in an era before coinage. Taxes and tribute, in the form of goods such as livestock, were sent to regional centers, for counting and redistribution. Some of the taxes, along with offerings, went to maintain temples and pay temple personnel. Other income was for workers, such as messengers, who were part of the bureaucratic hierarchy. Manufacturing establishments, such as textile workshops, also kept track of their payments to workers.

- What details about life and work in Babylonia can you glean from the following extracts from economic tablets?

- How did workers get paid?

- How did Babylonians date records?

- Can you think of any modern professional situations that compare to the differing payments and grades of status accorded to workers in the tablets?

- What does the excerpt illustrate about the hierarchical nature of the society?

VALDOSTA TABLET NO. 5

One pot [ca. 20 liters] of dida beer, five sila [ca. 5 liters] of high quality beer, one ban [ca. 10 liters] of bread and two shekels [ca. 30cc] of oil and two shekels of alkali, three fish and three bunches of onions, Agu'a, the messenger sent to Persia. One pot of dida beer, six shekels of oil, one ban of bread, two shekels of oil, two shekels of alkali, three fish and three bunches of onions, Ilka the messenger. . . . Three sila of beer, two sila of bread, two shekels of oil, two shekels of alkalai, one fish, one bunch of onions, Dugamu the . . . Total: two pots of average quality dida beer [made with] one ban [of barley]; total: five liters of high quality beer; total: 6 shekels of oil; total 2 ban 2 sila of bread; total: six shekels of oil; total: six shekels of alkali; total: seven fish; total: seven bunches of onions. On the 7th day, month: "Bricks are placed in the moulds" [Month 2] The year after: "The boat of Enki was caulked."

VALDOSTA TABLET NO. 7

. . . cows and five, . . . 28 sheep and 3 goats, . . . have been slaughtered for the kitchen, for the soldiers, on the second day; booked out of [account of] Duga, by means of Nur-Adad, the scribe. . . . Year: the boat [named] "'the ibex of the Abzu'" was caulked."

VALDOSTA TABLET NO. 8

Six old small "weaver" garments, two old . . . garments . . . (for) the weavers. Two small "weaver" garments, one moth-eaten "weaver" garment.

Source: Valdosta State University Archives. The translations and notes in parentheses were done by cuneiform expert Dr. Cale Johnson for the Cuneiform Digital Library Initiative. This project puts translations of tablets from around the world on the Worldwide Web so that all scholars have access to them: www.valdosta.edu/library/find/arch/online_exhibits/babylonian/Cuneiform%20Digital%20Library%20Journal.htm. Dr. Johnson's translation appears in the Cuneiform Digital Library Journal (2006), 2.

Code of Hammurabi

The Hammurabi code exists on a black stone stele (marker) that is on display in the Louvre Museum in Paris today. Translators are not certain about all of the nuances of the terms used as designations of social rank, but they agree that the Code is a valuable source on the social hierarchy of Babylon. The provisions in the Code take the form of a simple declaration stating an action and the consequence. There is little evidence to suggest if or how the Code reflected actual legal practice. The term "man" in this context probably means free man of at least moderate prosperity and possibly a landowner.

- Which excerpts show a concern for equality and justice and indicate that the king cared for the welfare of his people?

- Based on the following excerpts, how do you think women were regarded in Babylonian society?

- What excerpts best exemplify the concept of Talon Law?

- Why do you think laws were so harsh?

- How is the king presented?

- What kind of social structure do these laws reflect?

#14: If a man has stolen a man's son under age, he shall be slain.

#16: If a man has harboured in his house a fugitive male or female slave of the palace, or of a plebeian; and has not brought them to the order of the commandant, that householder will be slain.

#21: If a man has broken into a house, before the breach shall he be slain, and there buried.

#26: If a captain or a soldier has been ordered upon "the way of the king," and has not gone, but has hired a substitute, that captain or soldier shall be slain. The substitute shall take his house.

#27: If a captain or a soldier has been taken in a "misfortune of the king," and his field and garden given to another to administer; when he returns and regains his city, he shall receive back his field and garden and shall administer them.

#48: If a man is liable for interest, and the god Adad has flooded his field, or the harvest has been destroyed, or the corn has not grown through lack of water; then in that year he shall not pay corn to his creditor. He shall dip his tablet in water, and the interest of that year he shall not pay.

#129: If the wife of a man is found lying with another male, they shall be bound and thrown into the water; unless the husband lets his wife live, and the king lets his servant live.

#131: If a man's wife is accused by her husband, but has not been found lying with another male, she shall swear by the name of God and return into her house.

#134: If a man has been taken prisoner, and there is food in his house, and his wife forsakes his house, and enters the house of another; then because that woman has not preserved her body, but has entered another house, then that woman shall be prosecuted, and shall be thrown into the water.

#142: If a woman hates her husband, and say "Thou shalt not possess me," the reason for her dislike shall be inquired into. If she is careful, and has no fault, but her husband takes himself away and neglects her; then that woman is not to blame. She shall take her dowry and go back to her father's house.

#150: If a man has given to his wife a field, garden, house, or goods, and has given her a sealed tablet; then after her husband [has gone to his fate] her children have no claim. The mother can give what she leaves behind to the children she prefers. To brothers she shall not give.

#154: If a man has known his daughter, that man shall be banished from his city.

#157: If a man after his father has lain in the breasts of his mother, both of them shall be burned.

#195: If a son has struck his father, his hands shall be cut off.

#196: If a man has destroyed the eye of a free man, his own eye shall be destroyed.

#198: If he has destroyed the eye of a plebeian, or broken the bone of a plebeian, he shall pay one mina of silver.

#199: If he has destroyed the eye of a man's slave, or broken the bone of a man's slave, he shall pay half his value.

#200: If a man has knocked out the teeth of a man of the same rank, his own teeth shall be knocked out.

#201: If he has knocked out the teeth of a plebeian, he shall pay one-third of a mina of silver.

202: If a man strike the body of a man who is above him, he shall receive sixty lashes with a cowhide whip in the assembly.

#209: If a man strike the daughter of a free man, and cause her foetus to fall, he shall pay ten shekels of silver for her foetus.

#210: If that woman die, his daughter shall be slain.

#213: If he has struck the slave of a man, and made her foetus fall; he shall pay two shekels of silver.

#229: If a builder has built a house for a man, and his work is not strong, and if the house he has built falls in and kills the householder, that builder shall be slain.

Source: Chilperic Edwards, *The Oldest Laws in the World: Hammurabi* (London: Watts & Co., 1906), http://books.google.com/books?id=4gI3AAAAIAAJ&printsec=frontcover#v=onepage&q&f=false.

The Epic of Gilgamesh

The *Epic of Gilgamesh* was originally written as a poem to be recited or perhaps sung at feasts, and would have had repeated certain passages extensively. In the first part of this excerpt, Enkidu has a dream in which he foresees himself in the land of the dead. In the second half, Gilgamesh has roamed the earth after the death of his friend, seeking the means to attain immortality. He encountered a woman tavern keeper at the edge of an ocean and she admonished him.

- Based on these excerpts, how did Mesopotamians understand life and death?

- How did they understand the place of humans in the cosmos?

- What factors might explain those views?

- Do you think that Mesopotamians can be characterized as completely pessimistic in their outlook? Why or why not?

- What does this passage indicate about the relationship between gods and humans?

- Compare and contrast these passages from *Gilgamesh* to other epic stories that you are familiar with from other eras or modern culture.

> . . . Those who dwell there squat in the darkness,
> dirt is their food, their drink is clay,
> they are dressed in feathered garments like birds,
> they never see light, and on the door and bolt
> the dust lies thick. When I entered the house,
> I looked, and around me were piles of crowns,
> I saw proud kings who had ruled the land,
> who had set out roast meat before the gods
> and offered cool water and cakes for the dead.
> I saw high priests and acolytes squatting,
> exorcists and prophets, the ecstatic and the dull. . . .

> . . . When the gods created mankind,
> they also created death, and they held back
> eternal life for themselves alone.
> Humans are born, they live, then they die,
> this is the order that the gods have decreed.
> But until the end comes, enjoy your life,
> spend it in happiness, not despair.
> Savor your food, make each of your days
> a delight, bathe and anoint yourself,
> wear bright clothes that are sparkling clean,
> let music and dancing fill your house,
> love the child who holds you by the hand,
> and give your wife pleasure in your embrace.
> That is the best way for a man to live.

Source: Stephen Mitchell, *Gilgamesh: A New English Version* (New York: Free Press, 2006).

Further Reading

Bottero, Jean. *Everyday Life in Ancient Mesopotamia.* Translated by Antonia Nevill. Baltimore: Johns Hopkins University Press, 2001.

Foster, Benjamin, ed. *From Distant Days: Myths, Tales, and Poetry of Ancient Mesopotamia.* Bethesda, MD: CDL Press, 1995.

Kramer, Samuel Noah. *History Begins at Sumer: Thirty Nine Firsts in Recorded History.* Philadelphia: University of Pennsylvania Press, 1981.

Leick, Gwendolyn. *The Babylonians: An Introduction.* New York: Routledge, 2003.

Nemet-Nejat, Karen Reha. *Daily Life in Ancient Mesopotamia.* Peabody, MA: Hendrickson, 2002.

Roaf, Michael. *Cultural Atlas of Mesopotamia and the Ancient Near East.* New York: Facts on File, 2000.

Stiebing, William H. *Ancient Near Eastern History and Culture*, 2nd ed. New York: Pearson Longman, 2009.

Trustees of the British Museum. *Babylon: Myth and Reality.* London: The British Museum, 2009.

Web Resources

ABZU Bibliography, Electronic Tools and Ancient Near East Archives, www.etana.org.abzu/.

Babylonian Clay Tablets at South Georgia State Normal College (Valdosta State University), www.valdosta.edu/library/find/arch/online_exhibits/babylonian/babylonian.htm.

Iraq's Ancient Past, University of Pennsylvania Museum of Archaeology and Anthropology, www.penn.museum/sites/Iraq/?p=958.

Royal Graves of Ur, The British Museum, www.britishmuseum.org/explore/highlights/article_index/r/the_royal_graves_of_ur.aspx.

Athens

The Cradle of Western Civilization

(900 BCE–324 CE)

NADEJDA POPOV

M Y INTEREST IN ALL THINGS ANCIENT CAN BE TRACED BACK TO WHEN I WAS in elementary school and came across a thick volume of Greek and Roman myths. The stories were fascinating, although a little strange, and—in retrospect—not age-appropriate reading. Determined to learn more about the ancient world, however, I began studying Latin in high school, and the summer before college I began studying Ancient Greek as well. I spent my college career blissfully ignoring anything more recent than the Middle Ages while becoming very well acquainted with the languages, literature, history, art, and civilization of Ancient Greece and Rome. Thus, by the time I first visited Athens as a graduate student in a summer session at the American School at Athens, I had already been studying all things related to Greek civilization for six years. As a result, I brought more questions and assumptions with me than the typical visitor and was especially eager to see how the modern city related to the remains of the Athens with which I was more familiar from my studies—the self-sufficient city-state of the fifth and fourth centuries BCE.

The American School, where I was staying during my first visit, was founded in 1881 and since then has served as the home away from home for generations of students of antiquity from American universities. The school's location by the Lykavittos (meaning "Hill of the Wolves") was originally on the outskirts of the city. Today, however, the wolves have been replaced with expensive boutiques, and the area is part of the upscale neighborhood of Kolonaki, home to Athens' modern aristocracy.

On my first afternoon in Athens, along with the rest of my fellow-students and our professor, I hiked up the Lykavittos. From the top of the hill, where a nineteenth-century chapel of St. George shares quarters with a restaurant and a theater, we were able to see all of Athens and the environs, including the Acropolis and, at a distance, the Piraeus, the harbor town of ancient Athens and now a city in its own right. What struck me even more than the breathtaking view, however, was the professor's remark that on a clear day one could see the Peloponnese from the Lykavittos. This was a powerful reminder of the proximity of Athens to its neighbors. The location of Athens made constant interaction—whether peaceful or otherwise—with the surrounding city-states unavoidable from its earliest days to the present day, when the city remains a popular tourist destination.

Athens today is the capital of Greece and, thus, has a political significance that is entirely modern. Yet the motives that draw tourists to Athens are mainly the same as mine: to see the remnants of the ancient city. Athenians themselves, therefore, are forced to live in the past as much as in the present because much of their income depends on it. As a result, the city today is a perfect blend of old and new, with reminders of the Classical city integrated into some of its most modern upgrades. Nowhere is this exemplified as clearly as in the new subway stations, where ancient artifacts found underground when the particular station was built are on display.

Although for some Athenians today this encroachment of the ancient city into their daily lives is a disruption—indeed, media debates flare up every time construction in the city is delayed because, inevitably, ancient artifacts have been found at a site—this bizarre mixture of old and new is precisely what makes Athens so exciting for me. Notably, educational tourism is not just a modern phenomenon in Athens; prominent at first mainly as a commercial and naval power, Athens at its height proudly dubbed itself the "School of Hellas," an intellectual capital of the Greek world, with "Hellas" being the ancient Greek term for the Greek world as a whole. The story of Athens is, therefore, a story of its evolution from a trading capital and a naval empire into a center of philosophy and knowledge in the Ancient Mediterranean and, ultimately, the cradle of Western civilization.

ATHENS AND THE WORLD: A Model of Culture and Politics

From the eighth century BCE to the Macedonian conquest of Greece in the mid-fourth century BCE, the definitive model of settlement in the Greek world was the city-state (*polis*, singular; *poleis*, plural). Each city-state was fully independent and self-sufficient, with its own system of government, law, economy, civic life, and the military. But from a grand total of over fifteen hundred known city-states, the vast majority of surviving archaeological, literary, and historical evidence derives from one—Athens. Through the evidence a story emerges of a small polis that grew into a large commercial and naval empire as well as a cultural center whose intellectual influence over the Mediterranean and the Near East survived the Roman conquest of Greece and continues today.

The name Athens forever connects the city with its patron divinity, Athena, goddess of wisdom, crafts, and war. The origins of this connection were significant to the Athenians, as evidenced by the existence of two different myths explaining how the city had acquired Athena's protection and name. In the more famous of these myths, Athena and Poseidon, god of the sea, held a contest, judged by the other gods, for the right to name the city. Each gave the city a gift: Poseidon, a salt spring; Athena, an olive tree. Because the gods deemed Athena's gift to be more valuable, she won. This myth became part of the landscape of the historical city, as the location of both gifts on the Acropolis (the citadel) was common knowledge in the Classical period (490–323 BCE). Moreover, the myth made its way into Athenian law: to cut down an olive tree was a crime. Offenders were tried in the Areopagus Court, the same court that tried the most severe murder cases. The significance that this myth grants to the olive tree is a powerful reminder of the importance of olive products in Athens and the rest of the Greek world. Olive oil, more than just a food and cleaning agent, was liquid currency.

The second myth presents an intriguing alternate version of the event. In it the people of the region, rather than the gods, held a vote to determine whether Athena or Poseidon should become the patron deity of their city. All men voted for Poseidon, a male god. All women voted for the goddess Athena. Because women outnumbered men by one at this vote, they carried the day. To appease the upset Poseidon, however, this vote was to be the women's last. This myth provides an explanation for the status quo in the historical period: women were not full citizens and were not allowed to participate in the democratic process of the Classical city. In fact, the idea of women participating in government seemed so ludicrous to the Athenians that around 390 BCE the comic playwright Aristophanes wrote a comedy, *The Assemblywomen,* in which the women of Athens take over the government of the city by a trick, effectively disfranchising the men. Hilarity and chaos ensue.

Taken together, the two myths about the origins of the city's name encapsulate Athenian pride in the connection of its citizens to Athena as well as a veritable obsession with matters of law and citizenship—two concepts that in the Athenian mind were inextricably connected to the stability and success of its democratic government during the Classical period, when Athens was at its height both culturally and politically.

Geography, Settlement, and Expansion: From the Bronze Age to the Classical Period

Thucydides, Athenian general and historian of the last third of the fifth century BCE, appears to have foreseen the Athenian domination over the historical record of the Greek city-states. Early in his *History of the Peloponnesian War,* Thucydides remarks on the visible and invisible greatness of Athens and Sparta, the two most powerful Greek poleis of his day. Although both are undeniably great, argues Thucydides, if they were suddenly to become desolate and subject to judgment by posterity solely based on their archaeological record, no one would ever believe that Sparta was a great city-state. The power of Athens, however, would be judged to be twice as significant as it actually was. Thucydides refers, by this remark, to the Athenian emphasis on monumental building and beautifying the city. This monumental architecture was, in reality, a symptom of the lofty pride and imperialistic ambitions of fifth-century Athens. Its most proud achievement was the Parthenon, the temple of Athena Parthenos (the Maiden) on the Acropolis. (See Map 4.1.)

The Athenian statesman Pericles began constructing the temple in 447 BCE and scandalously used funds from the treasury of the Delian League, a league of allied poleis led by Athens. Athenian use of the funds to build a magnificent temple in the heart of Athens was an arrogant gesture of imperialism, and Athens' allies certainly interpreted it as such, although they were not powerful enough to prevent it. The completed temple became a symbol of the power and greatness of Athens and still stands proudly today. Indeed, the Parthenon is known around the world today as a symbol of Athens and Greece in general, an example of the persistence of the cultural heritage of Classical Athens. It is a testament to the incredible skill of its architects that the temple had even survived an explosion in

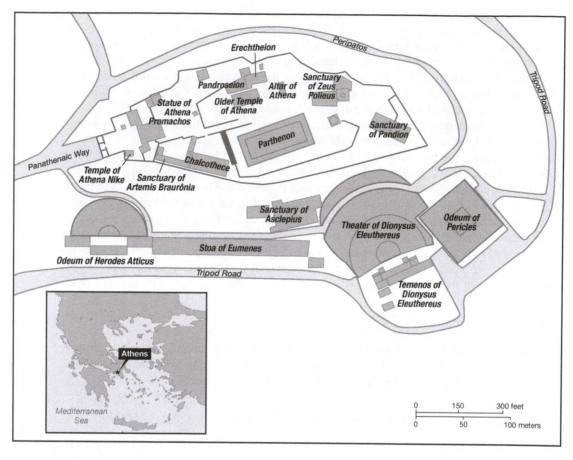

Map 4.1. Acropolis of Athens

Continually occupied since the Neolithic period, the Acropolis was the earliest inhabited point of the city. From the Archaic period (800–480 BCE), it was the religious and symbolic center of the city as well as a place of entertainment. Tragedies and comedies were performed at the Theater of Dionysus. An additional performance venue was constructed in 161 CE by Herodes Atticus, a Greek philosopher and prominent Roman politician. The Odeum of Herodes Atticus is still used today for outdoor concerts and recitals.

1687 CE, when a Venetian attack ignited the ammunition stores the Ottoman Turks kept inside, as they were in possession of Athens at the time.

Athens of Thucydides's day was the largest *polis* in the Greek world, with a total population of around two hundred thousand in 431 BCE. Indeed, few other cities in the Mediterranean were larger. At its height Carthage had a population of five hundred thousand, whereas Rome alone reached the one million mark. Archaeological evidence reveals, however, that although Athens was culturally and politically at its height in the second half of the fifth century BCE, the easily defensible nature of the Acropolis made it an attractive location for settlement from the earliest periods of human history. A hill sharply rising from the plain, with a flat area on top and steep cliffs all around, the Acropolis was the first settled point of the eventual city. However, the location did not offer many resources other than defensibility. The poor quality of the agricultural land was a running joke in Classical Athenian literature, as only olive trees grew easily in the region. Wheat and barley—the main grain crops grown in Attica—required considerable effort. Furthermore, the only precious metal in the region was silver in the mines of Laurion, located thirty-seven miles from the city, in the southeastern corner of Attica. However, Athenians eventually found commercial uses for such agriculturally worthless resources as their exceptionally iron-rich clay, which was perfect for pottery making. Similarly, the local marble turned out to be ideal for public building. Finally, the location of the Acropolis, slightly inland but only six miles from a harbor, made the settlement easy to defend against attacks from the sea while still allowing easy access to naval trade routes through which Athenian-made pottery and artwork were able to be shipped out.

Already occupied in the Neolithic period, the site became a significant settlement in the Mycenaean era (the final part of the Bronze Age in Greece, ca. 1600–1100 BCE). Among the findings from the Mycenaean era are wealthy tombs from the fourteenth century BCE, containing luxury imports from Crete, the Near East, and possibly Egypt. Examples include numerous ivory pins and barrettes most likely from the Near East, gold jewelry, and a Cretan relief stone vase with a carving of a youth vaulting over a bull, a typical motif in Minoan Crete. These findings suggest that the inhabitants of the area in the late Bronze Age already had trade connections, whether direct or indirect, to the eastern Mediterranean. Because the only items that have been found from the period are luxury goods, however, it appears that this early trade was limited to items of use for the aristocracy alone. Notably, the borrowing of the Greek alphabet from the Phoenician script sometime before 800 BCE is another tantalizing reminder of the interaction of Athens and the Greek world with the Near East and Phoenicia, the trade capital of the Bronze Age Mediterranean.

Additionally, fortification walls and a water-supply system from the late thirteenth century have been discovered. Their presence shows that the inhabitants of the area were ready for the eventuality of an attack and, particularly, a siege. It appears, however, that early Athens focused more on trade than war and was already experimenting with pottery production. Samples have been found of locally made pottery with marine decorations, such as octopodes. Whether Athens had already begun exporting its pottery this early on is unknown, however. Athens does not play a significant role in the account of the mythical Trojan War in Homer's *Iliad*, which suggests that Athens was not a major military power at the time the epic was created. The *Iliad*, an orally composed epic poem, had reached its final form in the eighth century BCE, and its description of major heroes and armies involved in the Trojan War is likely representative of the greatest cities of the Late Bronze Age and the Early Archaic period (ca. 800 BCE).

Archaeological evidence indicates that Athens remained stable during the Dark Ages (ca. 1,000–800 BCE), a period of relative poverty and cultural decline throughout the Greek world following the mysterious collapse of the Mycenaean palace civilization around 1100 BCE. Although this period is also known as the Iron Age for the discovery of iron throughout Greece and the Near East, in Athens iron appears to have taken the backseat to a more financially advantageous discovery. During this period Athens vied with Corinth, its close neighbor to the south, for the title of the pottery capital of the Mediterranean world. Made in different sizes and shapes for specific purposes, pottery was widely used in everyday life for storage (for grain, olive oil, wine, perfume), household tasks such as fetching water, and as tableware, including mixing bowls and drinking cups. Although plain styles were certainly available, decorated vases were affordable and in demand. It is in Athens that the new Geometric style of pottery decorating was developed by 900 BCE. With its use of geometric shapes and stylized human and animal figures in decoration, Athenian Geometric pottery was a widely traded commodity throughout the entire Mediterranean.

One measure of its success is that other producers at the time borrowed this style of decorating. Over the next three centuries Athenian vase painters adapted to the ever-changing demands of their various markets. By 600 BCE Attic vase painters had learned from the Corinthians the black-figure method of decoration, a technique of painting and incising silhouette-like figures in black onto the red clay surface of the vase. Finally, around 525 BCE Athenian vase painters invented the red-figure style, in which red figures were used to decorate the background of the vase, which was painted black. This red-figure style is still the most easily identifiable as Athenian today, and modern audiences find it the easiest to appreciate because it portrays human figures and their coloring is the most realistic. Notably, Athenian vase painters of both the black- and red-figure styles clearly considered themselves true artists and took special pride in their work; quite a few vases bear the signature of the artist or the workshop where they were decorated. One example of an especially well-documented artist is the so-called Amasis Painter, a black-figure painter active in the second half of the sixth century BCE; over ninety of his works are known today because of the signature on each vase: "Amasis made me." Notably, his name is Egyptian, which suggests the intriguing possibility, unattested in the written sources, that Egyptian craftsmen were able to settle and flourish in late-Archaic Athens.

Although Corinth attempted to compete with Athens, it proved unable to match the quantity and quality of the Athenian wares. By the middle of the sixth century BCE Corinth stopped producing vases for export, and Athens became the undisputed capital of pottery exports in the Mediterranean, with an especially strong market in Etruria (northern Italy) as well as the Greek settlements in southern Italy and Sicily. Given Corinth's location immediately to the south of Athens, it is difficult not to wonder how this economic rivalry affected the relationship between the two city-states over the following century. Indeed, the bitterness of Corinth over Athenian imperialistic tendencies in the fifth century could have its roots in this earlier competition for the control of the Mediterranean pottery markets.

As the Athenian exporting trade blossomed over the course of the Dark Ages and the early Archaic period (800–490 BCE), the city itself grew in circles, expanding outward from the Acropolis. Early in the Dark Ages the area northwest of the Acropolis developed into a potters' neighborhood, the Kerameikos, with an adjacent cemetery by the same name. Archaeological excavations of the area revealed potters' workshops and debris from pottery making. Given the prominence of the pottery trade in Athens, it is not surprising that by the early fifth century BCE this area became the Athenian Agora, the civic and commercial center of the Classical city. The earliest known meaning of the term *agora* is "general assembly"; Homeric epics regularly use the term to refer to army assemblies. The use of the Agora in Athens as well as in other Greek city-states as not only a place of unofficial assembly and discussion for citizens and visitors but also as the location of some of the law courts and the main place of trade shows how closely intertwined the commercial and the civic spheres were in the Greek polis.

By the seventh century BCE Athens eventually incorporated all of Attica (the surrounding region of about 965 square miles) into the city-state. (See Map 4.2.) This newly added area, mostly consisting of small farms, was organized into 139 *demes* (villages). Walls surrounded the city of Athens proper, and all residents of Attica could go inside the city walls for safety during time of war. This happened, for instance, in the beginning of the Peloponnesian War (431–404 BCE). Then, in the mid-fifth century BCE, the Long Walls were built, connecting Athens to its harbor town, Piraeus. Finally, by the fourth

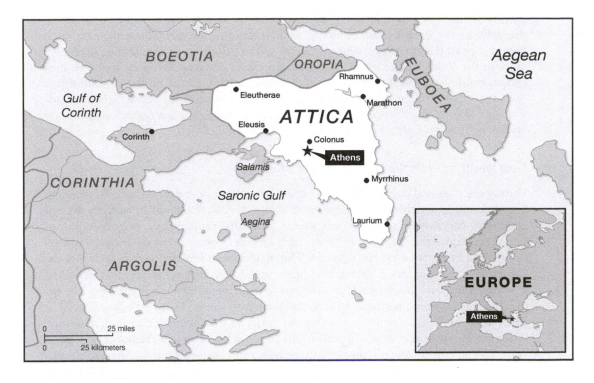

Map 4.2. Athens and Attica

While Athens in the Classical Period (480–323 BCE) dominated the sea, controlling most of the Greek islands, Attica was surrounded by cities and regions hostile to her—Boeotia and Corinth as well as Aegina, a rival naval empire. This proximity to perennial enemies led to the rise of border forts in towns such as Rhamnus and Eleutherae in the fourth century BCE, in order to protect the borders from invasion.

century BCE most of the demes on the borders of Attica were equipped with watchtowers and were responsible for alerting the city in case of an imminent invasion, a system dubbed by one modern scholar as "Fortress Attica."

The Athenians' continuing obsession with defensive-wall building in all periods of their history was certainly justified. Every Greek city-state was proud of its freedom and independence, and each viewed the possibility of submitting to anyone else's rule as slavery. In addition, all Greek city-states were fiercely competitive, for both ideological reasons and the desire to acquire additional resources. Most Greek city-states were within mere hours' march from a number of other poleis, and Athens was no exception to that rule. Attica stretched to the Aegean on the east, and its closest neighbor from that direction was the island of Euboea, fifty miles away. There were, however, powerful neighbors close by on the other three sides. The most powerful of these neighbors was Thebes, located thirty-three miles to the north of Athens proper but significantly closer to the border with Attica. Thebes was an archenemy of Athens for the entirety of the Classical period, a sentiment reflected in the Athenian tragedians' obsession with portraying Thebes and the Thebans negatively in their plays. To the west was Megara, whose relations with Athens were often uneasy as well, culminating with the Megarian Decree, passed in the winter of 433/432 BCE. The decree was a trade embargo that barred

Megarian merchants from all ports of Athens and her allies in the Delian League, effectively destroying the Megarian economy. To the southwest was Corinth on the isthmus, a tiny strip of land connecting mainland Greece to the Peloponnese. Finally, just seventeen miles to the south lay the island of Aegina. An island sea power, Aegina was a rival of Athens, vying for control over other islands in the Aegean. Living under constant threat from these powerful neighbors on three sides, Athens nonetheless had a significant advantage over the other Greek poleis: a much larger territory and, as a result, a significantly greater population from which to recruit an army in time of war.

From the Athenian Empire to the "School of Hellas"

During the Classical period Athenians believed that they were autochthonous, meaning that their ancestors, the earliest inhabitants of the area, were literally born from the soil of Athens. Archaeological evidence indeed indicates the same people, presumably, continually occupied the site, as there are no signs of violent conquest or destruction and reoccupation of the area by other groups. The myth of autochthony ideologically set the Athenians apart from the inhabitants of other city-states, such as the Spartans, who had to conquer the land that they settled, and gave the Athenians a feeling of an especially intimate connection to their land. In addition, during this period the myth contributed to the Athenian obsession with maintaining the purity of the Athenian race and, therefore, strictly regulating access to citizenship. In fact, the statesman Pericles in 451 BCE passed a Citizenship Decree, also known as the Law of Autochthony, restricting citizenship to only those individuals who had two Athenian parents and two sets of Athenian grandparents.

Athenians viewed the world, therefore, in two simple categories: Athenians and others. The Athenian determination to keep these two categories separate in order to protect their interests intensified during the main wars that Athens underwent in the fifth century BCE: the two Persian Wars of 492–490 and 480–479 BCE as well as the Peloponnesian War of 431–404 BCE. These wars, for whose outbreak the aggressors (Persia and Sparta respectively) blamed Athens, proved to be formative conflicts in the history of the Greek world in general and for Athenian history in particular, as they forced Athens, originally loyal to the isolationist ideal of all Greek city-states, to interact more extensively than ever before with other cultures both within and outside Greece. Furthermore, each of these wars indirectly resulted in Athens transforming into a very different polis than it was before. Athens' performance in the Persian Wars, which contributed to a victory of the united army of the Greek city-states in both Persian invasions of Greece, led others to recognize Athens as a naval superpower. As a result, the city transformed from being chiefly an economic empire into a military one. After the war Athens gradually expanded its sphere of influence over the vast majority of the islands both in the Aegean and along the coast of Ionia, becoming a full-fledged empire by 454 BCE.

The Athenian Empire was not typical, however. Whereas the Persian Empire, for instance, expanded through conquest, Athenian influence on her allies was cultural and constitutional. Most notably, Athens urged members of her empire to adopt a democratic form of government. Still, others saw Athenian influence over the islands in the same light as the Persian threats to Greek freedom earlier on. The fear of Athens' continuing growth was, according to Thucydides, the real reason for Sparta's decision to enter the Peloponnesian War, a twenty-seven-year-long conflict that involved the entire Greek-speaking world and was the greatest war ever known to man so far—if we trust Thucydides. Although Athens lost the war to Sparta, the aftermath, ironically, was that both the loser and the winner became weaker. The diminished military strength of the two strongest states in Greece then left a power vacuum, which contributed to the rise of new military states over the course of the fourth century BCE, first Thebes and later Macedon.

The Peloponnesian War was a brutal conflict during which the previously observed unofficial rules of war throughout Greece disappeared and were replaced by a "total war" mentality, which became prevalent in Greek warfare afterward, thus showing the danger of precedent. And yet it was during the Peloponnesian War that Athens rose to its cultural height. This was the period of the great tragedians Sophocles and Euripides, the comic playwright Aristophanes, the historian Thucydides, and the philosopher Socrates, mainly known from the writings of his student Plato. Predictably, the inspiration for many of the literary works of the period was the war itself. In these writings antiwar sentiment predominates. The comedies of Aristophanes resort repeatedly to the plot motif of clever antiwar heroes who save the day and end the Peloponnesian War on the stage. In *The Acharnians*, produced in 425 BCE, the protagonist is an Athenian farmer who is so frustrated by the war and the war-hawking ways of contemporary Athenian politicians that he brokers his own individual peace with Sparta. In *Peace* (421 BCE) another Athenian farmer tries a more creative approach to ending the war: he fattens up a dung beetle in order to fly to the sky for a conference with Zeus, king of the gods. Finally, the protagonist of Aristophanes's *Lysistrata* (411 BCE) is an Athenian wife, Lysistrata, who is unhappy over her husband's frequent absence from home because of campaigning. She gathers wives from city-states throughout Greece, including Sparta, and convinces them to go on a sex strike to force their husbands to end the war.

The protagonists in all three plays succeed in their aim. These plays, which put Athenian civilians on the stage, represent the popular view of the war. They highlight both individual Athenians' frustration with the long duration of the war and civilians' ability to end the war more effectively than the politicians and the armies could—a sentiment with which the Athenian audience certainly identified.

In spite of the frustration with the war's long duration, its role as an intellectual breeding ground was not lost on its contemporaries. In the winter of 431–430 BCE the Athenian statesman Pericles delivered the Funeral Oration, quoted by Thucydides, publicly eulogizing those Athenians who had fallen in the first year of the war. In his oration he described Athens as "the School of Hellas," meaning the model polis, whose government, legal system, intellectual milieu, and bravery had a profound influence on any states that came into contact with it. Although Pericles's description of Athens as a model for Hellas—the Greek world—may have sounded grandiose to his contemporaries, the art, literature, culture, philosophy, and political thought from late fifth-century Athens were more influential on Western civilization than the contributions from any other period or location in the Greek world. It is during this time that the Hippocratic physicians wrote the first Greek medical treatises, Athenian drama was at its height with the works of Sophocles and Euripides, Thucydides's history presented a model for historical writing for subsequent historians, and Socrates developed his method of debating philosophical questions with the public.

Democracy and Law in Classical Athens

Pericles's pride in the Athenian democracy was certainly not without reason. The best documented example in history of a direct democracy, its stability was remarkable. The democracy lasted with virtually no changes from 508 to 322 BCE, with the exception of two brief oligarchic coups toward the end of the fifth century BCE. On both occasions, however, the majority of the citizens successfully banded to restore the democracy just months later. The stability of the Athenian democracy was, according to Athenians, due to the ideal of *isonomia* (equality of political rights and laws for all citizens) that ruled in Athens in conjunction with *eleutheria* (political and personal freedom) and *parrhesia* (freedom of speech). The grouping of these ideals was unique to Athens in the Greek world, a striking contrast to the world today, where they are an integral part of many countries' constitutions. By contrast, the ideal of *eunomia*, which ruled in Sparta, Athens' main rival in the Classical period, literally meant good order, without implying a sense of fairness or equality for all citizens.

In typical Athenian fashion the origins of both the Athenian democracy and the Athenian legal system are buried in myth. The founder of the Athenian democracy was, according to myth, King Theseus, who in his youth traveled to Crete and killed the monstrous Minotaur. Deciding that kingship was not the best form of government, Theseus then turned his power over to the people.

Also according to myth, the founder of the first-ever trial court in Athens was none other than Athena herself. That first court, the Areopagus, was a murder court, and the myth of its creation is narrated in the third and final tragedy of Aeschylus's trilogy *Oresteia*. Orestes, an Argive prince, is being hunted by the Furies, who are angry that he had killed his mother. Orestes's murder of his mother, however, was divinely ordained, as she had killed his father and the death of one's father must be avenged. Polluted by this shedding of kin blood, Orestes is an exile until Athena orders him to go to Athens, where she would provide a fair trial for him. For this trial Athena herself selects the best of her citizens to act simultaneously as both judges and jury, a practice that continues in historical Athenian courtrooms. When the jury's votes are tied at the trial, Athena breaks the tie in Orestes's favor.

This myth of the origins of the Athenian courtroom trial system shows Athena's intervention into the process at every step: the establishment of the court in Athens, specifically, is her idea; she is the one who selects the best of her citizens for the jury; and finally, she acts as a jury member herself. The message of the myth is unmistakable: the goddess herself ordained courtroom justice in Athens, and she wants it to flourish. Attribution of divine origins and patronage to law is common. For instance, the Babylonian law code of Hammurabi was supposed to have been granted to King Hammurabi by the sun god Shamash. The law code of Hammurabi, however, did not provide any extraordinary powers to the people other than the knowledge of the laws. The Athenian creation of a "jury of one's peers," by contrast, stems from a specifically Athenian democratic ideology that all Athenian citizens can be trusted with the administration of their city.

In the historical source the law giver Solon, credited with the creation of much of Athenian law, is also considered one of the fathers of democracy. Appointed by the people of Athens as sole *archon* (chief magistrate) for the purpose of revising the Athenian constitution in 594–593 BCE, Solon was faced with a problem of debt slavery and property inequality, which had caused civic strife in the city. Following the *seisachtheia*, a one-time cancellation of all debts, Solon divided the citizens into four new property-based classes, which persisted through the Classical period. Specifically, the classes were based on the number of bushels of wheat each citizen's land produced per year. The top class, in fact, was named the *Pentakosiomedimnoi* (the five hundred bushelmen). Of these, the top three classes were land owners whereas the bottom class, the *thetes*, was composed of the poorest land owners and those citizens who did not own any land. The distinction was significant, as land owning was a prerequisite both for serving in the Athenian infantry (the hoplite phalanx) and, not coincidentally, for being eligible to hold the highest office in the democracy, the archonship. Nine archons were appointed by lot each year out of all the eligible citizens over the age of thirty. Over the course of the fifth-century BCE, as Athens began incorporating the *thetes* into the army as rowers in the navy, their political influence correspondingly rose as well.

In addition to these four classes of citizens, there were several classes of noncitizens who did not have a role in the democracy: women, slaves, and foreigners. Athenian women, just as women in the rest of the Greek world, were always under the rule of a male relative. Athenian reliance on slavery was also typical for the Greek world; every Athenian farmer, unless extremely poor, likely owned at least one slave. Notably, Greeks considered it disgraceful to enslave fellow Greeks. Athenian slaves came from such regions as Thrace, Egypt, and the Levant and were used for agricultural tasks as well as in craftsmen's shops and the silver mines. In addition to slaves, however, there were free resident-aliens in Athens, especially among the classes of craftsmen and tradesmen. Although allowed to live and work in Athens, these resident-aliens were barred from such benefits of the Athenian citizenship as voting and access to the law courts.

The Athenian practice of appointing citizens to major political office by lot rather than elections reflects the extraordinary level of trust that the polis placed in all of its citizens. Out of a grand total of twelve hundred annually appointed magistrates, including the archons, only one hundred were elected in the *ekklesia* (assembly of all citizens over the age of twenty). The rest were appointed by lot. This level of trust toward all citizens was reflected in the composition of the juries in the Athenian law courts. Jurors as well were appointed by lot from all citizens, including *thetes*, over the age of thirty. Serving as both judges and jury, the several hundred jurors—as many as five hundred in some cases—appointed for a typical Athenian trial determined by voting the guilt or innocence of the defendant, with a tie counting in favor of the defendant, which was established in the mythical murder trial of Orestes, as it is understood that Athena would be on the side of anyone for whose trial the human jurors' votes are tied. Next, the defendant and the accuser proposed penalties for the crime, and the jury selected one of these by voting. This unusual system of determining the punishment is likely a remnant from the days before the formal existence of law courts when justice was administered through arbitration and deliberation of the two sides directly.

Although most known cases concern private individuals of no political significance, the connection between the democracy and the enforcement of law in the courts is commonly highlighted in the surviving courtroom speeches. When asking to convict an attacker who had beaten him, one Athenian contrasts his attacker's poor service to the democracy with his own distinguished military career and begs the jury not to allow such a man to continue insulting citizens unpunished.

And yet although the system of trial by large citizen juries was usually a reliable method of guaranteeing a fair trial, it was not foolproof. Notably, scholars have highlighted the failure of the legal system on these occasions as a flaw in the Athenian democracy in general. Perhaps the most prominent example of such a case is the controversial trial and conviction of the philosopher Socrates in 399 BCE. Socrates was charged with corrupting the youth with such teachings as his controversial claim that the gods' approval or disapproval does not make an action right or wrong as well as urging his students to question everything around them, including the workings of the democracy. While the prosecution asked death as his penalty, Socrates asked for free meals for himself at public expense as the punishment because, as he argued, his only fault was educating the citizens, a fault that deserves a reward rather than a punishment. Faced with the selection between these two penalties, the jury sent Socrates to his death.

GLOBAL ENCOUNTERS AND CONNECTIONS:
The Ancient Roots of Modern Foundations

Modern scholars often provide a common image of ancient Mediterranean societies: frogs around the pond. The Mediterranean, named the "Corrupting Sea" in an influential book by the same title, promoted extreme connectivity and interaction among all those dwelling on its shores. Among the most obvious examples of this connectivity in action is the Greek alphabet, which the Greek world adapted from the Phoenicians sometime in the eighth century BCE. Another example is the prevalence of Athenian vases in archaeological sites all over the Mediterranean and as far away as the Black Sea littoral, indicating the Athenian control of trading networks. Clearly, the Athenians had been some of the most active and farthest-reaching frogs in the pond. The city of Athens itself, moreover, was a locus of encounters with others, whether for the purposes of war and invasion or the traffic of goods, knowledge, and philosophy.

The eventual loss in the Peloponnesian War weakened Athens militarily, but the function of the city as the "School of Hellas" only intensified over the course of the fourth century BCE and beyond, spreading its intellectual influence far beyond the Greek world. Following the Macedonian conquest of Greece in 338 BCE, Athens was respected as an educational center. Especially renowned was the Academy, the philosophical school of Plato and his student Aristotle, who had served as a private teacher to Alexander the Great. Moreover, the reputation of the Academy was so long-lasting that Raphael's painting of the Academy in 1509–1510 CE became one of the most recognizable symbols of the European Renaissance. Long before Raphael, however, Alexander's former general Ptolemy famously used Athens as his model, in his attempt to transform Alexandria, the city Alexander founded in Egypt, into the new cultural capital of the Mediterranean. Attempting to replicate the Academy on an even more lavish scale, Ptolemy built the Museum and the Great Library at Alexandria, intending them to function as a scholarly institution where the greatest minds of the world could live and study at the state's expense. One of the first scholars affiliated with the Library was the mathematician Euclid, whom Raphael included in his painting of the Athenian Academy, thus conflating the two great institutions.

The Roman conquest of the Greek World, finalized in 146 BCE, merely added a new audience eager to immerse itself in Greek—and, especially, Athenian—culture and education. Many sons of Roman aristocrats spent several years in their youth studying oratory and philosophy in Athens. The Roman poet Horace, who had studied in Athens himself, accurately summarized the Roman inferiority complex vis-à-vis Greek culture as he summed up the Roman conquest of Greece: "captive Greece took captive her rude conqueror." The Emperor Constantine's establishment of Constantinople in 324 CE finally ended Athens' role as a cultural center that was only second, perhaps, to Alexandria and Rome itself. As a new Greek-speaking capital of the Eastern Roman Empire, Constantinople fully superseded Athens as a center of Greek oratory and culture. Athens had thus gone full circle from obscurity to fame and back to obscurity.

Connections, however, reach across not only geographical space but also time. In studying the connections of Athens with other world civilizations in history, the most significant feature that has repeatedly come under scrutiny is the Athenian democracy. Studies of the references to the Athenian democracy in writings and rhetoric of the Italian Renaissance, during the French Revolution, and the American Revolution show the legacy of the Athenian democracy as a controversial ideal to be considered but, more often than not, rejected. Italian Renaissance thinkers Donato Giannotti and Niccolò

Machiavelli, for instance, saw Venice and Sparta as the ideal states, with stable mixed governments, and they condemned the Athenian ideal of freedom as excessive license for the disordered multitudes, whose participation in the government caused the city's downfall.

British thinker Thomas Hobbes, who translated Thucydides into English in the 1620s, complained that studying the Athenian democracy was dangerous because it could turn one against monarchy, a danger to which Hobbes himself was immune, perhaps because of his special appreciation of Thucydides, an avowed oligarch. For the American Founding Fathers the Athenian democracy, which allowed all adult male citizens to participate in government fully, was too democratic. For twentieth-first-century audiences, however, the nature of the Athenian democracy, a slave-owning community that excluded women and foreigners from citizenship, is not democratic enough.

ENCOUNTERS AS TOLD: PRIMARY SOURCES

Athenians in the Classical period recognized the uniqueness of the Athenian experiment with democracy and considered it to be the key for the city's economic, military, and intellectual success. The following documents showcase the Athenian pride in the city and its institutions as they also point out the citizens' responsibilities for maintaining the city's greatness.

"On the Killing of Eratosthenes," by Lysias

Sometime in the late fifth or early fourth century BCE a private Athenian citizen, Euphiletos, caught another man, Eratosthenes, in bed with his wife in his own house. According to Athenian law, a citizen who catches an adulterer in the act with his wife may kill the man on the spot, and that is indeed what Euphiletos did. The burden of proof, however, was then on Euphiletos to show the jury at his trial that the killing was justified—that Eratosthenes was indeed an adulterer and that Euphiletos had no other grudge against him. A professional speech writer, Lysias, wrote the defense speech that Euphiletos spoke at his trial. The following excerpt is from the conclusion of this speech.

- How does Euphiletos justify his actions to the jury?

- What is the significance of his claim that the punishment he meted out to Eratosthenes was not just a private one but rather one for the whole city?

- Finally, why do you think the adultery law in Athens was so severe?

In my opinion, gentlemen, this was not a private punishment for my own sake but for the whole city. For men who act in this way, once they see the prizes set up for such offences, will be less likely to commit them against others, if they see that you are of the same mind. Otherwise, it is far better to expunge the established laws and make others which will impose the punishments on men who protect their own wives and grant full immunity to men who wish to offend against them.

Source: Lysias, "On the Killing of Eratosthenes," in *Trials from Classical Athens*, edited by Christopher Carey (London: Routledge, 1997).

The Funeral Oration of Pericles

In the winter of 431–430 BCE Pericles delivered a public eulogy over the Athenian war-dead from the first year of the Peloponnesian War. The Athenian historian Thucydides was likely present at the occasion, and he included Pericles's speech in his *History*.

- According to Pericles, how does Athens differ from the rest of the Greek city-states?

- According to Pericles, what are the duties of Athenian citizens?

Our city does not copy the laws of neighboring states; we are rather a pattern to others than imitators ourselves. Its administration favors the many instead of the few; this is why it is called a democracy. If we look to the laws, they afford equal justice to all in their private differences; if to social standing, advancement in public life falls to reputation for capacity, class considerations not being allowed to interfere with merit; nor again does poverty bar the way, if a man is able to serve the state; he is not hindered by the obscurity of his condition.

The freedom which we enjoy in our government extends also to our ordinary life. There, far from exercising a jealous surveillance over each other, we do not feel called upon to be angry with our neighbor for doing what he likes, or even to indulge in those injurious looks which cannot fail to be offensive, although they inflict no real harm.

But all this ease in our private relations does not make us lawless as citizens. Against this fear is our chief safeguard, teaching us to obey the magistrates and the laws, particularly such as regard the protection of the injured, whether they are actually on the statute book, or belong to that code which, although unwritten, yet cannot be broken without acknowledged disgrace.

Further, we provide plenty of means for the mind to refresh itself from business. We celebrate games and sacrifices all the year round, and the elegance of our private establishments forms a daily source of pleasure and helps to distract us from what causes us distress; while the magnitude of our city draws the produce of the world into our harbor, so that to the Athenian the fruits of other countries are as familiar a luxury as those of his own.

If we turn to our military policy, there also we differ from our antagonists. We throw open our city to the world, and never by alien acts exclude foreigners from any opportunity of learning or observing, although the eyes of an enemy may occasionally profit by our liberality; trusting less in system and policy than to the native spirit of our citizens; while in education, where our rivals from their very cradles by a painful discipline seek manliness, at Athens we live exactly as we please, and yet are just as ready to encounter every legitimate danger. . . .

In short, I say that as a city we are the school of Hellas; while I doubt if the world can produce a man, who where he has only himself to depend upon, is equal to so many emergencies, and graced by so happy a versatility as the Athenian.

Source: Thucydides, *The Peloponnesian War: Thucydides, The Crawley Translation*, translated by T. E. Wick and Richard Crawley (New York: McGraw Hill, 1982).

The Constitution of the Athenians, by the Old Oligarch

In Athenian literature even the enemies of Athens, such as the Persians, are convinced of the superiority of the Athenian democracy, with its emphasis on the freedoms of individual citizens over all other constitutions. Not all extant sources, however, express a wholehearted approval of the democratic system. Democracy was far from universally popular in Athens, and intellectual critics with oligarchic tendencies abounded. For example, the historian Thucydides was no fan of the democratic government, although his descriptions of the democratic statesman Pericles leave no doubt as to his approval of this particular democratic leader. Outsiders could be even more critical of the Athenian democracy. Sometime between 415 and 412 BCE one such critic composed *The Constitution of the Athenians,* a description of the Athenian democracy with a running commentary regarding its strengths and weaknesses. The author's name is unknown, but scholars have fondly dubbed him the "Old Oligarch" because of the cantankerous tone and content of his work.

- According to the Old Oligarch, what are the problems with the democratic system of government in Athens? Do you agree with his assessments? Why or why not?

- What other criticisms of the democracy do you think Athenians and outsiders could present?

- How do you think Thucydides would respond to the Old Oligarch?

Now, in discussing the Athenian constitution, I cannot commend their present method of running the state, because in choosing it they preferred that the masses should do better than the respectable citizens; this, then, is my reason for not commending it. . . .

Slaves and metics [i.e., resident aliens] at Athens lead a singularly undisciplined life; one may not strike them there, nor will a slave step aside for you. Let me explain the reason for this situation: if it were legal for a free man to strike a slave, a metic or a freedman, an Athenian would often have been struck under the mistaken impression that he was a slave, for the clothing of the common people there is in no way superior to that of the slaves and metics, nor is their appearance. . . .

There is one weakness in the Athenian position: as rulers of the sea, if they lived on an island, it would be open to them to harm their enemies if they wished while remaining themselves immune from devastation of their land or invasion as long as they controlled the sea. . . .

It is my view that the common people at Athens know which citizens are respectable and which are wicked; realizing that the latter are useful to them and help them, they like them despite their wickedness, but they tend to hate the respectable citizens. They do not think that their virtue exists for the common people's advantage but the opposite. On the other hand, there are some who are truly of the common people, but are not by nature on the side of the common people. I do not blame the common people for their democracy, for anyone is to be pardoned for looking after his own interests; but a man who is not of the common people and chooses to live in a city that is ruled by a democracy rather than one with an oligarchy is preparing to do wrong, and realizes that it is easier to get away with being wicked under a democracy than under an oligarchy.

Source: Old Oligarch, *The Constitution of the Athenians,* in *Aristotle and Xenophon on Democracy and Oligarchy,* edited by J. M. Moore (Berkeley, University of California Press, 1975).

Further Reading

Christ, Matthew. *The Bad Citizen in Classical Athens*. New York: Cambridge University Press, 2006.

Horden, Peregrine, and Nicholas Purcell. *The Corrupting Sea: A Study of Mediterranean History*. Oxford: Wiley-Blackwell, 2000.

Hurwit, Jeffrey. *The Athenian Acropolis: History, Mythology, and Archaeology from the Neolithic Era to the Present*. Cambridge: Cambridge University Press, 2000.

Lanni, Adriaan. *Law and Justice in the Courts of Athens*. New York: Cambridge University Press, 2006.

Lape, Susan. *Race and Citizen Identity in the Classical Athenian Democracy*. New York: Cambridge University Press, 2010.

Loraux, Nicole. *The Children of Athena: Athenian Ideas about Citizenship and the Division between the Sexes*. Princeton, NJ: Princeton University Press, 1994.

Ober, Josiah. *Fortress Attica: Defense of the Athenian Land Frontier 404–322 B.C.* Leiden, The Netherlands: Brill, 1985.

———. *Political Dissent in Democratic Athens: Intellectual Critics of Popular Rule*. Princeton, NJ: Princeton University Press, 2001.

Oliver, Graham. *War, Food, and Politics in Early Hellenistic Athens*. New York: Oxford University Press, 2007.

Roberts, Jennifer. *Athens on Trial: The Anti-Democratic Tradition in Western Thought*. Princeton, NJ: Princeton University Press, 1997.

Web Resources

The Athenian Agora Excavations: www.agathe.gr/.

Interactive Maps of the Ancient Greek World and Athens, www.plato-dialogues.org/tools/mapindex.htm.

Internet Ancient History Sourcebook: Greece, www.fordham.edu/halsall/ancient/asbook07.html.

National Archaeological Museum of Athens, www.namuseum.gr/wellcome-en.html.

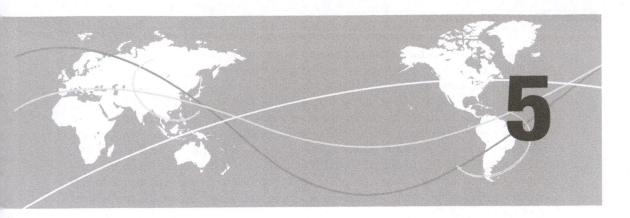

Xian

Eastern Gateway and Strategic Citadel

(1049 BCE–907 CE)

KEITH N. KNAPP

U PON MY FIRST ARRIVAL IN XIAN IN THE SPRING OF 1983, BESIDES THE remnants of its Ming Dynasty (1368–1643) wall, the place looked no different from any other Chinese city. It had endless rows of low-rise apartment buildings interrupted only by large and already decaying Soviet-style buildings. However, upon making my way to the area north of the city's Drum Tower, which is a warren of narrow streets and alleys filled with small shops, I discovered a magnificent looking structure created exquisitely in traditional Chinese style; it was the city's grand mosque, originally built in 742 CE. Unlike other monasteries and temples that the government had reconstructed in the 1980s to earn tourist dollars and demonstrate Communist religious tolerance, the mosque was a functioning place of worship that devout Chinese Muslims zealously guarded and maintained. This building, with its venerable age and once-foreign religion, brought home that Xian had been the storied Silk Road's eastern terminus. The Silk Road was a series of caravan routes that traversed the steppes and deserts of Eurasia and linked together East Asia, South Asia, and West Asia. Its eastern terminus attracted foreigners from across Eurasia who brought not only their splendid goods but also exotic religions.

Although Xian was the capital of China's earliest and most powerful imperial dynasties, visible traces of these regimes are few because Chinese built their palaces and temples with wood rather than stone. In 1992 I set out to find some of their traces by visiting the ruins of Weiyang Palace, which was the Western Han Dynasty's (221 BCE–8 CE) governmental nerve center. At the stop for a bus that would take me there, I asked a waiting farmer how far the ruins were from our location. He told me that they were very far; moreover, they were not worth visiting anyway: "It is just a big pile of dirt," he said. Undeterred, I piled into an extremely crowded bus. We went only one stop when the same farmer yelled to me that I should get off. Upon exiting the bus, I realized that the farmer had been speaking the truth: before me was a huge pile of dirt. But what a magnificent pile it was!

All that remains of the palace is its anterior hall's foundation. Emerging three or four meters from the ground, it is quite large and leaves one with the impression that Weiyang Palace was a magnificent wooden building that soared loftily above all others. From the topmost building the view of the city must have been stunning indeed. Ordinary people looking at the elevated palace from afar must have believed that they were staring at a heavenly abode. Except for a couple necking in the back of a black "Red Flag" sedan that was parked on the anterior hall's lower foundation, all of this was easy to imagine because the place was entirely deserted. The ruins showed me that, with only a little bit of imagination, envisioning the grandeur of China's imperial governments was easy.

Much as in the past, Xian continues to serve as a crossroad that draws people from all over, whether they be Uighur peddlers from Xinjiang, Chinese software entrepreneurs from the coastal provinces, or tourists from Europe, Japan, and North America. Consequently, as in the past, it functions as China's most cosmopolitan interior city. Of course, what brings people now are not exotic goods coming from faraway lands but rather archaeological treasures from the city's storied past. It is this combination of ancient splendors and the modern assimilation of diverse influences that keeps me returning to this ever-changing city.

This chapter will discuss the place of Xian in China's early history. For the first two thousand years of China's history, from the beginning of the Western Zhou Dynasty in 1049 BCE until the end of the glorious Tang Dynasty in 907 CE, no city in China was more important. We will first explore the geographical reasons for the strategic importance of the Xian area. Then we will survey its history as the seat of China's early imperial dynasties: the Western Zhou (1049–771 BCE), the Qin (221–207 BCE), the Western Han (206 BCE–8 CE), the Sui (581–617 CE), and the Tang (618–907). In our discussion of these dynasties I will underscore how interactions with foreigners constantly shaped early Chinese polities and how the Silk Road made an indelible impression on the material culture, vernacular customs, and spiritual values of the Chinese living in medieval Xian.

XIAN AND THE WORLD:
A Strategic Location for Commerce and Empire

Xian's importance in history has everything to do with its geographical location. Mountain ranges enclose all sides of the lower Wei River basin in which Xian is located. The tallest of these mountains are in the Qinling Range to the city's south; its highest peak soars to 12,389 feet. The range's height is so forbidding that it prevents humid air from the south from entering northern China, thus separating the moist south from the dry north. East of Xian lies the Xiao Range, which affords access to Xian only via the easily defended Hangu Pass, sitting at the confluence of the Wei and Yellow Rivers. Due to its mountain barriers, Xian is easy to defend, and the area was traditionally called Guanzhong "[The Land] Within the Passes" or Guannei "[The Land] Inside the Gates."

Guanzhong's soil is very fertile, but northern China's sparse rainfall does not guarantee dependable agriculture. The lower Wei River Valley, however, is blessed with eight rivers that farmers rely on to grow their harvests. Thus, due to its protective mountains, abundant water, and rich soil, the Wei River Valley was an ideal place in which to live, which is why people flocked to this area and it became one of China's oldest urban settlements. In fact, its semi-arid climate, lack of forest cover, and numerous waterways made it comparable to other early centers of civilization, such as Babylon in Mesopotamia and Harappa in the Indus River Valley.

Xian in the Western Zhou (1049–771 BCE)

Xian first became the site of a capital during the second, historically verified dynasty, the Western Zhou (1049–771 BCE). In the twelfth century BCE the Zhou people resided in what is today western Shaanxi province. From both the historical and archaeological record we know much about the Western Zhou, which controlled both the Yellow and Huai River Valleys. It shared many characteristics with the people of the first historical dynasty, the Shang. Like the Shang, noble Zhou families believed that their strength came from their powerful ancestors. They envisioned these ancestors as spirits who were interested in their descendants' success and had needs of their own. No activity, then, was more important than offering them sacrifices in either gratitude or supplication. These sacrifices occurred at the ancestral temple and were offered in the most precious wares the Zhou people owned: bronze ritual vessels. To ascertain the ancestors' wishes, nobles of both the Shang and Western Zhou made use of scapulimancy (i.e., they applied fire to the cracks of tortoise plastrons, the abdominal surface of the shell) and cow scapula to communicate with the spirit world. In some cases Shang and Western Zhou scribes wrote on the bone the questions that were put to the ancestors and the ancestors' answers. In Western literature these divination records are known as "Oracle Bones": they furnish the first evidence of writing in China.

Like the Shang, Western Zhou warriors held two-horse chariots in high esteem. These vehicles came to China from contact with central Eurasian pastoralists, who were the first to harness the horse for both transportation and war. From atop the mobile platform of the chariot, an archer could easily shoot his enemies while a second warrior with his halberd stabbed or hacked approaching foes. These military vehicles were so effective that in ancient China a state's strength was commonly measured in the number of chariots it could muster. They were expensive to build and maintain, and the warriors in the chariots were nobles who engaged in much training to master deftly using a weapon while riding the chariot. These vehicles' overriding importance is evident in many Western Zhou nobles' tombs, which bore a separate chariot pit. Within the pit is an actual chariot along with its two horses and the unlucky driver. The Western Zhou noble spent so much time in his chariot that he needed it even in death.

Although we do not know to what extent the Western Zhou engaged in commerce with their neighbors, it is clear that the Zhou had extensive dealings with northerners, who they called the Rong and Di peoples. These were bronze-making cultures that lived in permanent settlements and depended on both agriculture and stock breeding. They resided in the modern-day provinces of Xinjiang, Gansu, Ningxia, Inner Mongolia, Heilongjiang, Liaoning, and Jilin. Western Zhou grave goods reveal heavy Rong and Di influences: bronzes inspired by movable goods used by pastoralists, body ornaments with

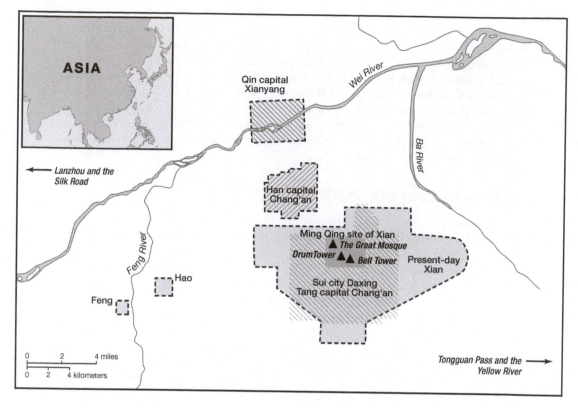

Map 5.1. Historical Xian

Xian in the Wei River valley was the capital for many of China's earliest and most powerful dynasties. This map shows the sites of the Western Zhou capitals of Feng and Hao, the Qin capital of Xianyang, Han dynasty Chang'an, and the Sui capital of Daxing, which the succeeding Tang dynasty renamed as Chang'an. By Ming and Qing times (1368–1911), the city was only a provincial capital and a mere shadow of its former self. Take note of its small size compared to the Sui/Tang city.

animal motifs, and a marked increase in horse and chariot paraphernalia. Steppe goods and art no doubt entered Western Zhou material culture sometimes through trade, sometimes through war.

By the early eighth century the Western Zhou was teetering. Non-Chinese people who were probably being pushed out of the steppe by more aggressive groups menaced the Wei River Valley. Finally, in 771, the Rong successfully invaded the capital and killed the last Western Zhou ruler, King Yu. The Zhou nobles fled eastward to Luoyang in modern-day Henan Province and established the Eastern Zhou (770–256 BCE). This forced move highlighted the Zhou government's weakness, and as a result, local lords felt emboldened to run their fiefs as autonomous states. Although the Zhou continued to exist nominally, it controlled only the capital area; the rest of Eastern Zhou China consisted of over a hundred autonomous but unstable states. Internally, threats came from hereditary nobles who had their own land and troops and frequently overthrew their rulers; externally, other Chinese states often endeavored to conquer their weaker neighbors. To protect themselves rulers distanced themselves from the old warrior nobility. They turned to infantry armies composed of commoners to fight their wars and bureaucrats to centralize their governments. The men they recruited as officials were not the powerful warrior aristocrats but rather lesser nobles known as *shi*, "knights or lower officers," and commoners who had neither independent status nor power. Due to this process, by the end of the Eastern Zhou the shi emerge as the ruling class made up of scholars and officials.

One of these shi was Confucius (551–479 BCE), who despised his era's chaos. Confucius wanted to return China to the idyllic conditions that supposedly prevailed under the first Zhou rulers who took self-perfection and the people's welfare to be of paramount importance. Self-cultivation was central to his message: a good man is one who is always striving to improve himself morally. Confucius believed that one did so by guiding his conduct through following the *Li*, the Zhou kings' rules of conduct and rituals. If a ruler could act like these ideal, ancient kings, then people from other states would flock to him. Although his disciples were prized for their extensive knowledge of court ritual, Eastern Zhou rulers declined to employ Confucius's philosophy in governance.

In the era known as the Warring States (481–226 BCE), when only seven of the largest states had managed to survive, Confucianism was only one of many philosophies vying for patronage. The northwestern state of Qin was predisposed toward a different philosophy of government, which we call Legalism. What mattered to Legalists was tweaking administrative policies and practices so that they would serve to benefit the ruler. One of the best means of doing so was by establishing a well-publicized law code that would apply to everyone equally, regardless of social class or position. The law would reward men who undertook thankless or dangerous tasks that enriched the state, such as being a farmer or soldier, and punish those who engaged in frivolous activities that weakened the state, such as merchants, who were regarded as parasites because they produced nothing. Upon becoming Qin's prime minister, the Legalist theorist Shang Yang (ca. 390–338 BCE) 1) created a nobility entirely based on meritorious service in warfare; 2) reorganized the Qin state into forty-one administrative districts—nobles no longer had independent fiefs; 3) organized the people into groups of five families that were collectively responsible for each family's crimes; and 4) turned people he considered idlers into either peasants or slaves. At first many people within Qin objected to these changes, but when they saw that the laws were applied equally, even to members of the royal family, the new rules gained popular support. These reforms attracted talented administrators and soldiers from across China and made the Qin army into the most powerful military force in East Asia.

Xian as Capital of China during the Qin (350–207 BCE)

In the seventh century BCE the Qin government moved its capital from eastern Gansu Province to the western part of Shaanxi Province. Around 350 BCE, due to its impregnable defensive position, its significance as a crossroads, and its easy access to the North China Plain, Shang Yang moved the capital to the Xian area. He established the capital just north of the Wei River and called it Xianyang. Significantly, the first word of this name means "to complete" or "to unify," whereas the second word "yang" denotes the city's geographical position south of a mountain and north of a river.

Although Shang Yang laid the foundation for Qin to become the most powerful state in China, it was Ying Zheng (259–210 BCE), the renowned First Emperor of the Qin, who conquered the remaining six states and established China's first imperial empire. He did so in less than ten years, from 230 to 221. To stress his singular accomplishment, he gave himself a new title, *huangdi*, "The August Deity or Emperor." To run the country from the capital and rule as an autocrat, Ying Zheng abolished all independent fiefdoms and organized the whole country into thirty-six administrative districts. To oversee the empire, he created a centralized bureaucracy that had 24,000 officials and was divided into nine bureaus. In order to be able to dispatch his army promptly to any place within his territory, he made well-built roads that connected the capital to all of the frontiers. Soon his empire stretched from northern Vietnam in the southwest to western Manchuria in the northeast. To prevent rebellions, he forcibly moved 120,000 of the most influential families from the provinces to the capital region. To eliminate regional differences, he unified weights, measures, axle lengths, coinage, and Chinese written characters. True to the Legalist teachings, the First Emperor also set forth a comprehensive law that governed many aspects of life. In short, he created a centralized state based on an egalitarian law code and politically, economically, and culturally unified an area as large as the Roman Empire. Moreover, although ruling families would change, the basic governmental framework that the First Emperor forged would last until 1911. Therefore, it is no wonder that our word China is probably derived from the word "Qin."

On its northern frontier the Qin faced people who were engaged in a relatively new form of livelihood. Between the sixth and fourth centuries BCE several groups along the northern frontier took up pastoral nomadism; that is, they became herders who each year moved with their flocks of livestock to predetermined pasturages. They lived in yurts (round tents covered with layers of felt) and ate dairy products such as milk, yogurt, and cheese. They needed to exchange their surplus animals and animal byproducts for goods and foods they could not produce themselves, such as iron, salt, and grain. If their agrarian neighbors refused to trade with them, they took what they wanted through raiding; they excelled in warfare as mounted archers. In the third century BCE, in the Ordos Region, inside of the bend of the Yellow River, there emerged a pastoral nomadic group known as the Xiongnü.

A legacy of the interaction between the pastoral nomads and Warring States Chinese was the adoption of cavalry. Our first indication of when this happened is a record of a court debate in 309 BCE, in which the king of Zhao argues that part of his army should be made up of cavalry and that the cavalrymen should be dressed in barbarian clothes— that is, a tight-fitting tunic, trousers, and boots. Interestingly, he sees this not only as a method to keep the pastoral nomads at bay but also as a way to attack other Chinese states. From this point on, all Chinese armies incorporated cavalry into their forces. In fact, the famous Qin Terracotta warriors of Xian are organized into three units: an infantry unit, a command unit in which the leaders ride in chariots, and a cavalry unit.

The Qin state had extensive contact with the pastoral nomads, but their relationship became contentious once the Qin unified China. There were so many similarities between the Qin and pastoral nomads that other Chinese states viewed the Qin as semi-barbarian. Both the Qin state and its private merchants frequently engaged in trade with the northerners. They would provide gold and silk in exchange for horses and furs. This relationship began to falter, though, during the First Emperor's reign. To solidify his northern borders, the First Emperor's armies drove the Xiongnü north of the Yellow River. Then, to prevent raiding, the First Emperor's generals built a defensive wall. They did this in part by reusing the defensive walls of the old six states and in part by constructing new walls to connect the old ones. These walls went all the way from modern-day Gansu province in the far west to the Bohai Sea in the east. Today we refer to this structure as the Great Wall and think of it as continuous. However, Qin and Han people called this barrier "long walls," made not of stone but of layer upon layer of tamped yellow earth. Elsewhere, forbidding mountains or other geographical features kept invaders out.

Of course no discussion of Qin grandeur would be complete without mention of his underground city: his mausoleum, which is located about thirty miles east of Xianyang in the town of Lintong. Qin laborers constructed a massive tumulus, or pile of earth, above his tomb known as Mt. Li. From written accounts we know that within the First Emperor's tombs there was a miniature world with models of palaces, towers, people, and even rivers flowing with mercury. Although his mausoleum has not yet been excavated, three side pits have revealed a marvelous life-like and life-sized army of six thousand terracotta soldiers. When interred, the clay warriors were painted in multiple colors and armed with bronze weapons. Recent excavations have disclosed that there were also figurines of entertainers, civil officials, and birds, so it could well be that the tomb was a reconstruction of the world. The 1974 discovery of the Terracotta Warriors, as they are popularly known, quickly gained international attention and continues to draw travelers to Xian today.

Xian as the Forever Peaceful City in the Han (206 BCE–8 CE)

Although the governing institutions the First Emperor established would last until 1911 CE, his regime did not survive his son's reign. In 209 BCE a number of revolts broke out across China. One rebel commander put Xianyang to the torch; there were so many palaces that they burned for three months. In 202 BCE the Western Han dynasty was founded, with its capital established south of the Wei River, a few miles northwest of Xian's present location. This city was named Chang'an ("Forever Peaceful" or "Long-lasting Tranquility"). As the Western Han expanded into present-day North Korea and Xinjiang (also known as Chinese Turkestan) and penetrated deeper into Vietnam, this empire was even larger and more extensive than the Qin.

Each block in the city was surrounded by a tamped earth wall, each side of which had a gate. The gates were secured at nightfall so no one could go either in or out. Of course, during the day people were free to move about and meet with whomever they wished. Chang'an had 160 of these wards. Each ward had a supervisor who was in charge of the gates and twenty *bao* (groups of families) who were collectively responsible for each other's behavior. The purpose of the wards was both to protect the inhabitants during times of war and to keep them under strict control during times of peace. All other Han cities were also divided into wards for the same purposes.

During the Western Han's first half, Chang'an was a huge city that probably had 250,000 residents, but its palaces did not overwhelm the rest of the city in size or grandeur. This probably reflects the early Han rulers' advocacy of the Warring States philosophy of Daoism. Proponents of this school believed that there was an order inherent in nature called the *Dao* ("The Way" or "The Path"). This order was most apparent in the unfolding of the seasons and the alternation between day and night. Those whose lives accorded with the rhythms of the Dao would prosper and live long; those whose actions contravened the Dao would fail in their enterprises and die early. As a result, people should live naturally and simply; they should lessen their desires and avoid extravagance. Daoist rulers set an example for their people through their own frugality; thus, their harems were modest, building projects few, public expenditures low, and their burials simple. In many ways Daoism was strikingly different from Confucianism: it deemphasized the importance of public service and the performance of lavish rituals and instead emphasized the importance of reclusion and simple living. Nevertheless, the two philosophies shared many concerns: both esteemed self-cultivation and leading by example, and both abhorred war. Given this overlap, the Chinese found practicing both Confucianism and Daoism easy. It is often said that a literatus was a Confucian while in office and a Daoist at home. The Western Han government's embrace of the laissez-faire practices of Daoism generated a long period of peace and prosperity.

Shortly before the year 200 BCE, in response to being driven from their homeland, a charismatic leader named Modun unified the Xiongnü and formed them into a state headed by a hereditary leader, the *Shanyu*. In 198 his forces defeated a Han army. The Xiongnü state demanded gifts and trade, and the Han government signed a number of peace treaties that manifested the "Harmony through kinship" policy. In exchange for the Xiongnü not raiding, the Han government recognized the Xiongnü state as a diplomatic equal; married a Chinese princess to the Shanyu; furnished annual payments in silk, wine, and grain; and opened border markets. Although this policy secured peace for a while, the Xiongnü would often demand more. The Xiongnü state also dominated the agriculturally and commercially rich oasis cities of the Tarim Basin, which is in present-day Xinjiang Province and was an important segment of the Silk Road.

This uneasy peace lasted until the reign of the long-lived Han Emperor Wu (r. 141–87), the Martial Emperor. Desperate to find another means of dealing with the Xiongnü, in 139 BCE, he sent an envoy named Zhang Qian to the far northwest to find allies. Although unsuccessful in doing so, Zhang may have traveled as far as Iraq; he returned with an extensive knowledge of Eurasia's peoples. Emperor Wu then decided to send large cavalry armies to attack the Xiongnü, forcing them to move north of the Gobi Desert. At the same time, to prevent them from obtaining the oasis cities' resources, Han armies invaded the Tarim Basin; by 101 BCE Han armies conquered Ferghana (in present-day Kyrgyzstan), thereby bringing the area completely under Chinese subjugation.

By controlling the Tarim Basin, the Han now for the first time had access to the Silk Roads. The western terminuses of the silk roads were Antioch, Constantinople, and Damascus; Chang'an now became the eastern terminus. (See Map 5.2.) Given that any goods transported along the silk routes had to be carried by camel, only luxury items traveled far. Ordinary commodities were also transported but only for short distances. The most prestigious Chinese export item was silk; the Greeks in fact called China *Seres*, or the "land of silk." Yet many other Chinese goods were in demand, such as lacquerware, steel products, gold and silver utensils, goods made from bamboo, peaches, pears, and oranges. At the same time, Chinese were eager to receive foreign goods, such as horses from Central Asia, sandalwood and incense from India and Southeast Asia, coral from Persia and Sri Lanka, and glass from Persia and Central Asia. Although we often think of the Silk Road connecting China with Rome, there was little if any direct contact between the two. Chinese silk commanded a high price in Rome, but it usually was shipped from the Kushan Empire, which controlled Central Asia and Northwestern India.

From the subjugation of the Tarim Basin in 101 BCE until the collapse of the Silk Road around 1750 CE, Xian was the gateway into China and the Silk Road's eastern terminus. By means of the Silk Road China established diplomatic relations with a number of countries. The most frequent visitors were envoys from the Tarim Basin's oasis cities. These visitors acknowledged Han's China superiority by paying China tribute in exchange for protection and trading privileges. Other countries sent envoys, including several Indian kingdoms and the Parthian Empire in Persia. Many countries viewed sending envoys to China as a trading opportunity: the Chinese would reward the envoys with rich presents and would look the other way when they did business on the side; in fact, oftentimes foreign envoys were merchants. The Silk Road trade immensely enriched the

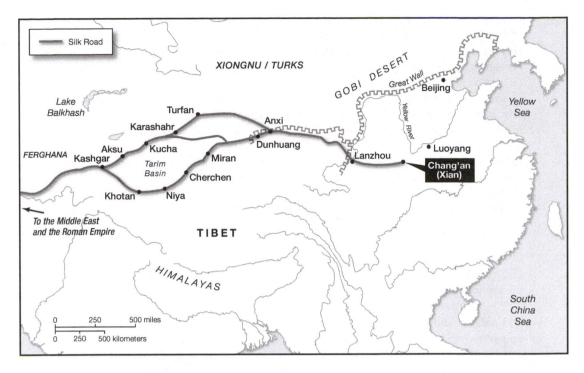

Map 5.2. Xian and the Silk Road

Xian was the eastern terminus of the Silk Road, which connected East Asia with Europe, the Middle East, and South Asia. To ensure the security of this trade route, early Chinese governments frequently controlled the Tarim Basin. Early Chinese governments constantly came into contact with pastoral nomadic groups to the north, such as the Xiongnu during the Qin and Han dynasties and the Turks during the Sui and Tang.

inhabitants of Xian. Chinese merchants could buy exotic goods in Chang'an and then sell them in other parts of country at a substantial markup. Because foreigners craved Chinese-manufactured goods, such as lacquerware, the capital was also filled with workshops producing export goods. Other residents could always find gainful employment in industries that catered to foreign envoys and Chinese and foreign merchants. The state also reaped tremendous benefits from the Silk Road. Attracting foreign envoys from afar generated much prestige for the regime, especially because it reaffirmed the notion that China was the "central kingdom"—that is, the center of the world. Foreign trade also brought not only much revenue in the way of tariffs but also the luxury goods that the upper class used to distinguish itself from the rest of society.

Cosmopolitan Sui-Tang Chang'an (581–907)

In 316 CE, after a Xiongnü chieftain named Liu Yao seized Chang'an, it no longer served as a capital city. For the next one hundred years different steppe groups, such as the Xiongnü, the Xianbei, and the Di, established short-lived regimes that ruled over parts of northern China. By 440 a tribe from the steppes united northern China and established the Northern Wei Dynasty (386–535). Four other dynasties subsequently rose and fell between 535 and 580. In 581 Yang Jian, a successful general whose family had intermarried with elite steppe families for generations, established the Sui Dynasty (581–617). He became known as Emperor Wen (r. 581–605). In 589 he conquered the last southern dynasty, thereby uniting China once again. Although the dynasty would last only until 617, Emperor Wen established the foundation on which the glorious Tang (618–907) would be built.

Emperor Wen built a new capital city, Daxingcheng, southeast of the old Han dynasty city. In 618, when the Li family overthrew the Sui and established the Tang dynasty, Daxingcheng was renamed Chang'an and continued to serve as the capital. Both the Sui and Tang Dynasties' founders undoubtedly chose the Xian area as their capital because of its ideal geographical location: it was in a strategically important area that was also economically vibrant; moreover, one could not only dominate the Yellow River Valley from this vantage point but also control the Silk Road and its lucrative trade.

The city was so big that some precincts had more farms than people. Like its Western Han predecessor, there were three gates in each wall, and the palace city's wall towered over them. Each of Chang'an's main gates was in line with one of the four cardinal directions. The main avenue split the city into eastern and western sides and was an enormous 155 meters wide. Chang'an under the Tang was home to probably close to one million inhabitants.

The city's two halves were quite distinct. The eastern half was more sedate because it had palaces and the residences of nobles. The western half was much more boisterous and active; many commoners and foreigners lived there. Each side of the city had its own official market, which was enclosed by a rammed earth wall. The Eastern Market mostly sold domestic goods, whereas the western market, which was much more active, sold foreign goods that came by means of the Silk Road. Merchants from across the empire and well-heeled citizens of Chang'an came to this market to buy precious goods such as amber, gems, glass and crystal vessels, horses, cattle, and gold and silver coins from Persia and Byzantium, which were used as jewelry. Foreign traders flocked to Chang'an to buy Chinese goods that were in high demand in West Asia. These goods included tea, porcelain, silk, paper, tapestries, embroideries, damasks, pearls, and Chinese medicines. Japanese and Korean envoys and merchants bought books in Chang'an's used-book market. These merchants were of many different origins: Arab, Persian, Indian, Uighur Turk, and Sogdian. The marketplace was filled with "Persian shops" and "Persian workshops." The poet Li Shangyin (813–858) maintained that the expression "poor Persian" was a contradiction in terms. Uighurs were oftentimes horse merchants or usurers. Some foreign merchants needed translators to transact business. Probably the most numerous foreign traders were Sogdians from Samarkand in Central Asia. Sogdians excelled in trading and usually could speak four or five different languages; in fact, they were so ubiquitous along the Silk Road that Sogdian became the trade route's lingua franca. The markets were also places of entertainment, where one could take in the acts of street performers and acrobats or visit wine shops and brothels. Executions were also performed there.

Like the founder of the Sui dynasty, the founders of the Tang, Li Yuan (Emperor Gaozu, r. 618–626) and his talented son Li Shimin (Tang Taizong, r. 627–649) were generals from the northwest whose family had for generations intermarried with Steppe aristocrats. They were equally comfortable with Chinese and Turkish customs (at this time, the Turks were in Mongolia, which was their homeland). In fact, Li Shimin's heir preferred Turkish music and dress, lived in a yurt, and surrounded himself with Turkish retainers. Unlike traditional Chinese rulers who distanced themselves from warfare and patiently waited to succeed or schemed to assume the throne, Li Shimin followed steppe customs by personally engaging in combat, ambushing two of his elder brothers, and forcing his father to retire to gain the throne. In 618 Li Shimin captured Chang'an with the aid of the Eastern Turks; he gained their help by promising to reestablish the lucrative tributary system and giving them all of the loot netted in the campaign. However, the same Turks soon became the main threat to the northern Chinese frontier. In 626 the Eastern Turks launched a raid that nearly reached Chang'an, but in 629 Li Shimin took advantage of a civil war among the Eastern Turks, launching an expedition that successfully ended their empire. In the aftermath Eastern Turkish commoners were allowed to settle in northern China while their leaders became the vanguard of Li Shimin's army. In 640, in the Tarim Basin, they led Tang armies to victory over the Western Turks, allowing China to once again control the eastern leg of the Silk Roads. The Sino-steppe origins of the Yang and Li families allowed them to create empires that could effectively deal with northern threats. Because they had a much greater understanding of steppe culture, Sui and Tang rulers were much better at playing steppe rulers against each other and fracturing brittle tribal confederations. Consequently, Li Shimin was recognized not only as the Chinese Son of Heaven; he was also the Khan of the Turks. Given their bicultural upbringing, Sui and Tang rulers could envision a society in which Chinese and foreigners could peacefully live side by side. It was this combination of steppe martial strength and Chinese economic and organizational resources that made the Tang the greatest power and civilization in East Asia.

GLOBAL ENCOUNTERS AND CONNECTIONS:
Cultural Convergence Creates an Ancient Melting Pot

During the Sui-Tang period China was more open than ever before to things from afar, whether it was foreign dress, music, dance, or religion. In this era an unprecedented number of foreigners lived in Chang'an. After the Eastern Turks surrendered, there were at least fifty thousand of them living in the capital. There were so many Sogdians that the government established an office of the Sogdian "caravan leader," who enforced laws and settled disputes within his community. Foreigners were indeed everywhere in Chang'an. They owned many inns, wine shops, food shops, and bakeries. Chinese particularly liked to visit foreign-owned wine shops, where they could sip grape wine and be served by comely foreign women with green eyes. Both musicians and entertainers were frequently Central Asian or Persian. Foreigners also set up their own religious establishments: the city was home to Islamic mosques, Nestorian Christian churches, Jewish synagogues, and Buddhist monasteries as well as Manichean and Zoroastrian temples.

The Cosmopolitan Tang: Political, Social, and Religious Melding

To some extent foreigners also wove themselves into the fabric of Chinese society. Foreign merchants often wore Chinese clothes and married Chinese wives or took on Chinese concubines. No doubt present-day China's Chinese Muslim minority, known as the Hui, had their origins in Arab and Persian merchants who married Chinese women beginning during the Tang. Foreigners also led Tang armies. In 751, deep in Central Asia at the Battle of Talas, an Arab army defeated a Chinese one commanded by a Korean general. The Tang general An Lushan, who had a Turkish mother and a Sogdian father, was an imperial favorite—that was, until he nearly ended the dynasty in a bloody revolt known as the An Lushan Rebellion (756–763); ironically, the rebellion was put down only after a Uighur Turk cavalry came to the aid of the Tang forces. Further, foreigners served in the Tang government as well as the military. In the mid-ninth century the son of an Arab merchant passed the highest test in the civil service examinations and obtained high office.

Interactions with foreigners had a profound effect on many different aspects of Sui-Tang daily life. Reflecting steppe tastes, northern Chinese favored yogurt over tea and lamb over fish. The people of Chang'an particularly loved West Asian pastries, such as pancakes, crepes, and sesame seed buns. In terms of dress, by the early Tang Dynasty nearly all men in China, regardless of ethnicity, wore the West Asian style of clothing: tightly sleeved and belted tunics, trousers, and boots. An area where foreign influence on behavior was particularly evident was in the activities of women. According to Confucian precepts, women were supposed to stay at home, keep apart from non-kin males, and, if her husband dies, never remarry. In contrast, steppe women had much freedom and played an essential public role in the life of their tribes. Sui-Tang–period women were likewise free to engage in activities outside the household; they even rode horses and learned archery. Violating Confucian mores, they sometimes had premarital sex, chose their spouse, divorced, and remarried. The Tang even had China's only female emperor, Wu Zetian (r. 685–705), who had a male harem; by all accounts she was a very effective ruler.

Without a doubt the greatest impact that the Silk Road had on China was the introduction of the Indian religion of Buddhism. This religion affected nearly every aspect of medieval China. The grandiose Chinese literary tradition was now rivaled by its Indian counterpart. Educated Chinese had to learn a whole new literary corpus. To do so, a few learned a foreign, written language, Sanskrit, while many others struggled to master difficult concepts and words in newly translated and numerous Buddhist texts. Life-loving and worldly Chinese now also had to accept a worldview that underscored life's effervescence and the sensory world's unreality. Buddhism created new social groups—monks and nuns—that were outside normal society and opted out of China's all-important family system. Monasteries too were a new social institution that soon became a significant economic player, owning a great deal of land and commanding enormous resources. Buddhism, in fact, nearly became Sui-Tang China's national religion and caused medieval Chinese to reassess who they were and what they believed.

In conclusion, Xian has played an incredibly significant role in China's early history. Due to mountain defenses, fertile soil, and easy access to river highways, it was simple to defend and use as a base to attack the Yellow River plain. Its easy access to the caravan routes that led west to the rich oasis cities of the Tarim Basin and beyond made it a lynchpin to east-west communications. Owing to these favorable circumstances, Xian served as the capital to five of China's strongest and most important polities: the Western Zhou that established control over all of northern China; the Qin that unified all of what we now consider China proper; the Han that not only consolidated the Qin's achievement but also connected China with the Silk Road; the Sui, which reestablished Chinese control over China proper; and the Tang, without a doubt one of East Asia's greatest dynasties. Nevertheless, Xian owed much of its wealth and grandeur to the commerce that came to the city in its role as the eastern terminus of the Silk Road. Being the gateway to China brought foreign merchants to Xian, who enriched both the government through paying tariffs and bribes and the economy by bringing an insatiable appetite for Chinese goods. At the same time, the Silk Road enriched Chinese culture by stimulating hunger for new items and ideas; most importantly, it caused Chinese to wonder whether they truly were the center of the world.

ENCOUNTERS AS TOLD: PRIMARY SOURCES

The following three selections present different perspectives on life in Xian and under the Han and Tang dynasties. The first, a literary piece combining prose and poetry, reflects on the merits of Chang'an. The second relays the impressions of Chang'an by two ninth-century Arab travelers. The final document presents a fictional story from eighth-century Chinese literature that reveals patterns of daily life from that time. Each highlights the vibrant, flourishing city that was Xian during the Han and Tang dynasties.

"Two Capitals Rhapsody," by Ban Gu

Historian Ban Gu (32–92 CE) describes Western Han Chang'an in a *fu* (rhapsody). Rhapsodies were literary pieces that combined both prose and poetry to describe places and objects with a tremendously varied and rich vocabulary and were often employed to praise a city. The excerpt here is a section of a larger rhapsody called the "Two Capitals Rhapsody," in which Ban Gu describes the glorious merits of both Chang'an, the Western Han capital, and Luoyang, the Eastern Han (25–220 CE) capital. Note that he calls much attention to the geographical strengths of the area. Although obviously exaggerated, his description of Chang'an's markets gives us a vivid sense of how popular they were. The excerpt ends by talking about the powerful local families whom the Western Han government had forcibly moved to the mausoleum towns north of the city so that the regime could keep an eye on them—they ended up producing many of the Western Han's most important officials.

- What geographical features made Xian an ideal place for the capital?

- What was the design of the capital?

- What was life like within the city?

- Who lived in the suburbs?

There was a Western Capital guest questioning an Eastern Capital [Luoyang] host, "I have heard that when the Great Han first made their plans and surveys, they had the intention of making the He-Luo [Luoyang] area the capital. But they halted only briefly and did not settle there. Thus, they moved westward and founded our Supreme Capital. Have you heard of the reasons for this, and have you seen its manner of construction? The host said, "I have not. I wish you would

I

Unfold your collected thoughts of past
    recollections,
Disclose you hidden feelings of old
    remembrances;
Broaden my understanding of the imperial way,
Expand my knowledge of the Han metropolis.

The guest said, "Very well." The Capital of the
    Western Han
Is located in [the ancient province of] Yongzhou;
It is called Chang'an.
To the east it relies on the barriers of Han
    Valley and the Two Yao,

With the peaks Taihua and Zhongnan as its
　　landmarks.
To the west it is bordered by the defiles of
　　Baoye and Longshou,
And is girdled by the rivers He, Jing, and Wei.
With its pubescent growth of flowers and fruit,
It has the highest fertility of the Nine Provinces.
With its barriers of defense and resistance,
It is the safest refuge of the empire.
Therefore, its bounty filled the six directions,
And thrice it became the Imperial Domain.
From here the Zhou rose like a dragon,
And Qin leered like a tiger.
When it came time for the great Han to receive
　　the mandate and establish their capital:
Above, they perceived the Eastern Well's
　　spiritual essence;
Below, they found the site in harmony with the
　　River Diagram's numinous signs.
Lord Fengchun established the plan;
The Marquis of Liu [Liu Bang or Han Gaozu
　　(r. 206–195 BCE), the founder of the
　　Western Han] carried it to completion.

Heaven and Man acted in concordant
　　resonance,
Thereby sharpening imperial discernment.
Then, looking around, our founder gazed
　　westward,
And this, verily, he made the capital!
In this place
One could look out on Qin Mound,
Catch a glimpse of the Feng and Ba [Rivers],
And recline on the Longshou Hills.
They planned a foundation for one million
　　years;
Ah! An immense scale and a grand
　　construction!
Beginning with Emperor Gao [Liu Bang] and
　　ending with Ping
Each generation added ornament, exalted
　　beauty,
Through a long succession of twelve reigns.
Thus, did they carry extravagance to its limit,
　　lavishness to its extreme.

II

They erected a metal fortress a myriad
　　spans long,
Dredged the surrounding moat to form a
　　gaping chasm,
Cleared broad avenues, three lanes
　　wide,
Placed twelve gates for passage in and out.
Within, the city was pierced by roads and
　　streets,
With ward gates and portals nearly a
　　thousand.
In the nine markets they set up bazaars,
Their wares separated by type, their shop rows
　　distinctly divided.
There was no room for people to turn their
　　heads,
Or for chariots to wheel about.
People crammed into the city, spilled into the
　　suburbs,
Everywhere streaming into the hundreds of
　　shops.
Red dust gathered in all directions;
Smoke blended with the clouds.
Thus, the people being numerous and rich,

There was gaiety and pleasure without end.
The men and women of the capital
Were the most distinctive of the five regions.
Men of pleasure compared with dukes and
　　marquises;
Shopgirls were dressed more lavishly than
　　ladies Ji or Jiang.
The stalwarts from the villages,
The leaders of the knights-errant,
Whose sense of honor emulated Lord
　　Pingyuan and Mengchang,
Whose fame equaled that of Lord Chunshen
　　and Xinling,
Joined in bands, gathered in groups,
Raced and galloped within their midst.
One gazes upon the surrounding suburbs,
Travels to the nearby prefectures,
Then to the south he may gaze on Du
　　[Emperor Xuan's mausoleum] and Ba
　　[Emperor Wen's mausoleum]
To the north he may espy the Five
　　Mausoleums,
Where famous cities [the mausoleum towns]
　　face Chang'an's outskirts,

And village residences connect one to
another.
It is the region of the prime and superior
talents,
Where official sashes and hats flourish,
Where caps and canopies are thick as
clouds.
Seven chancellors, five ministers,
Along with the powerful clans of the provinces
and commanderies,
And the plutocrats of the Five Capitals [the
empire's five foremost cities],

Those selected from the three categories,
transferred to seven locations [The three
categories of people selected to be
transferred to the mausoleum towns were
high officials, wealthy individuals, and
powerful magnates],
Were assigned to make offerings at the
mausoleum towns,
This was to strengthen the trunk and weaken
the branches,
To exalt the Supreme Capital and show it off to
the myriad states.

Source: Ban Gu, "Two Capitals Rhapsody," in *Wen Xuan or Selections of Refined Literature*, vol. 1. edited by Xiao Tong, translated by David R. Knechtges, 99–109 (Princeton, NJ: Princeton University Press, 1982).

Nubian Geography, by Abu Zayd Hasanibn Yazid Sirafi and al-Tajir Sulayman

Seven centuries after Ban Gu's fu an Arab work known as the *Nubian Geography*, written by Abu Zayd Hasanibn Yazid Sirafi and al-Tajir Sulayman (tenth century), relayed the testimony of two Arab travelers who had visited Tang China. Each man went to China separately—one in 851 and the other in 867. This account shows the impressive layout of Tang Chang'an as well as how clearly segregated nobles were from commoners. Those who come to the Western Market are not the nobles or officials themselves but rather their servants and underlings.

This text was translated into French by Eusebius Renaudot (1646–1720) and then translated into English in 1733. Capitalizations of the eighteenth-century translation have been retained. Eighteenth-century spellings have been modernized, replacing "f" for "s" in necessary instances.

- What was the layout of Tang Chang'an?

- How were social strata reflected in the divisions of the city?

We asked Ebn Wahab many Questions concerning the City of *Cumdan* [Chang'an], where the Emperor keeps his Court. He told us that the City was very large, and extremely populous; that it was divided into two great Parts, by a very long and very broad Street; that the Emperor, his chief Ministers, the Soldiery, the supreme Judge, the Eunuchs, and all belonging to the imperial Household, lived in that Part of the City which is on the right hand Eastwards: that the People had no manner of Communication with them; and that they were not admitted into Places watered by Canals, from different Rivers, whose Borders were planted with Trees, and adorned with magnificent Dwellings. The Part on the left hand Westward, is inhabited by the People and the Merchants, where are also great Squares, and Markets for all the Necessaries of Life. At the break of Day you see the Officers of the King's Household, with the inferior Servants, the Purveyors, and the Domestics of the Grandees of the Court, who come, some on foot others on Horseback, into that Division of the City, where are the public Markets, and Habitations of the Merchants; where they buy whatever they want, and return not again to the same Place till the next morning.

This same Traveller related that this City has a very pleasant Situation, in the midst of a most fertile Soil, watered by several Rivers. Scarce any Thing is wanted, except Palm-Trees, which grow not here.

Source: Abu Zayd HasanibnYazid Sirafi and al-Tajir Sulayman, *Nubian Geography*, in *Ancient Accounts of India and China: By Two Mohammedan Travellers Who Went to Those Parts in the 9th Century*, translated by Eusebius Renaudot, first printed in London in 1733 (New Delhi: Asian Educational Services, 1995), 58–59.

Miss Ren, by Shen Jiji

The last source, *Miss Ren*, is an excerpt from a fictional story about a virtuous fox fairy, from a genre of Chinese literature called *chuanqi* ("transmitting the unusual"), in which people in ordinary circumstances happen upon the extraordinary. The author, Shen Jiji (late eighth century), was an official in the history office of the Tang Dynasty. These stories are important to the historian because their authors strived to make the narratives' events sound as if they were plausible. They tell us not only much about medieval views of the supernatural but also the patterns of daily life. The passage below is valuable because it illustrates life in Chang'an's residential wards, the freedom of women, social class, entertainment, and the city's cosmopolitan flavor. Note that the Xin-an mentioned in the story is not Xian.

- How should Tang women behave?

- How does Miss Ren behave?

- What does this tell us about relations between men and women during the Tang?

- What is the social position of Cheng Sixth?

Miss Ren was a fox spirit. There was the Prefect Wei Yin, who was, on his mother's side, grandson of the Prince of Xin-an, ranking ninth among his cousins, and who, in his youth, was wild and fond of drinking. One of Yin's female cousins married Cheng Sixth, whose personal name I have forgotten; though accomplished in the military arts and fond of wine and women, Cheng was so poor that he had no home of his own and lived with his wife's relations. Yin and Cheng were best of friends and quite inseparable.

In the sixth month of the ninth year (750) of the Tianbao reign, Yin and Cheng were in a street in the capital of Ch'ang-an, going together to a feast in Xinchang Ward. On reaching the southern end of Xuanping Ward, Cheng excused himself, saying that he would join Yin later, and while Yin turned eastwards on his white horse, Cheng went south on his donkey, entering the north gate of Shengping Ward. Three women happened to be walking in the street, one of whom, dressed in white, was unusually beautiful, Cheng was much attracted and contrived now to precede and now to follow them, timidity only restraining him from addressing them. But the woman in white would often look at him, as if susceptible to his attentions, whereupon Cheng said in jest, "So fine a lady should not be pacing the streets of Ch'ang-an." The woman said laughing, "If some people who are mounted would not lend us their beast, what may we do?" Cheng then said, "A donkey is hardly fit to carry a lady, but have mine for the present. I shall be content to follow on foot." And Cheng and the women looked at each other and burst out laughing; her companions presently joining in the exchanges, all were soon on familiar terms. Cheng followed them eastwards to the Pleasure Gardens, by which time it was dusk, and they stopped outside a gate in a mud wall, behind which rose an imposing residence. The woman in white said to Cheng, "Pray stay a moment" and went in, and one of her companions, a servant girl left behind by the gate, asked Cheng his name and rank in the family. Cheng gave his reply and proceeded to ask about her mistress, and the girl said, "She is Miss Ren, and twentieth among her cousins." Soon afterward, Cheng was invited in. Having tied his donkey by the gate and placed his hat on the saddle, he was greeted by a woman over thirty, who turned out to be Miss Ren's sister. Candles were lit and food spread out; the wine flowing freely, they were joined by Miss Ren, who had changed her clothes, and all three passed a merry evening, drinking to their hearts' content. It being then late, Cheng retired with Miss Ren, whose peerless beauty, aided by her melodious voice, pealing laughter and graceful movements, made her seem divine, not of this world.

Before dawn, Miss Ren said to Cheng, "You must go! My brother, who is in the employ of the Bureau of Entertainment, is on duty in the Southern Hall of the Palace, and will come out at dawn. Do not tarry!" Having made her promise they would meet again, Cheng left. The gate of the Ward still being locked, a Tartar pastry-seller in his shop by the gate had just lit his lamp to start a fire in the stove, and while waiting for the drum to sound, Cheng took shelter under the pastry-seller's curtain and chatted to the man. Pointing in the direction of the place where he had spent the night, Cheng said, "If you turn east from here, you will see a gate; whose house does it open into?" The pastry-seller replied, "It is all waste land behind a wall; there is no house." Exclaiming, "But I just passed a house! Why do you say there is none?" Cheng began to argue heatedly with the man, who suddenly nodded to himself and said, "Oh, I know what it is! There is a fox here who lures men to her lair in the waste ground. I have seen it happen three times. I suppose you, too, have been enticed by her." Ashamed, Cheng denied this, and when it was broad daylight, went back to the spot and found the gate and mud wall, though which he glimpsed only a neglected market garden overgrown with weeds.

Source: H. C. Chang, *Chinese Literature 3: Tales of the Supernatural* (New York: Columbia University Press, 1984), 45–47.

Further Reading

Di Cosmo, Nicola. *Ancient China and Its Enemies: The Rise of Nomadic Power in East Asian History*. Cambridge: Cambridge University Press, 2002.

Kiang, Heng Chye. *Cities of Aristocrats and Bureaucrats: The Development of Medieval Chinese Cityscapes*. Honolulu: University of Hawai'i Press, 1999.

So, Jenny F., and Emma C. Bunker. *Traders and Raiders on China's Northern Frontier*. Seattle and London: Arthur M. Sackler Gallery & University of Washington Press, 1995.

Whitefield, Susan. *Life along the Silk Road*. Berkeley and Los Angeles: University of California Press, 1999.

Wu Hung. *Monumentality in Early Chinese Art and Architecture*. Stanford, CA: Stanford University Press, 1995.

Xiong, Victor Cunrui. *Sui-Tang Chang'an: A Study of Urban History in Medieval China*. Ann Arbor: Center for Chinese Studies, University of Michigan, 2001.

Xue Pingshuan. "The Merchants of Chang'an in the Sui and Tang Dynasties." *Frontiers of History in China* 2 (2006): 254–275.

Zou Zongxu. *The Land within the Passes: A History of Xian.* Translated by Susan Whitfield. New York: Viking Press, 1991.

Web Resources

A Digital Reconstruction of Tang Chang'an, www.sde.nus.edu.sg/changan/#.
A Visual Sourcebook of Chinese Civilization, http://depts.washington.edu/chinaciv/.

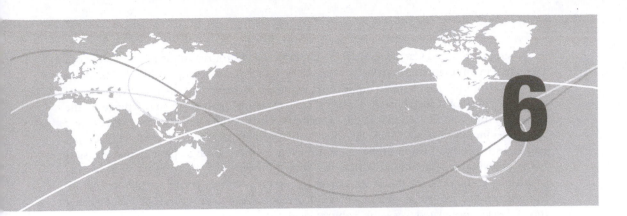

Carthage

Gateway to the World Beyond the Mediterranean

(ca. 800 BCE–700 CE)

JULIA CLANCY-SMITH

IN THE SUMMER OF 1973 A CHARTERED PLANE LANDED AT THE TUNIS-CARTHAGE airport on the last leg of its journey from the United States to North Africa. On board were scores of new Peace Corps volunteers, recent graduates from American universities intending to teach English as a foreign language. I was among the volunteers, unaware at the time that this first encounter with Tunisia would grow into a lifelong friendship. I was assigned to teach in a high school in the ancient Islamic city of al-Qayrawan (or Kairouan) in the interior, founded in 671 CE during the Arab-Berber Muslim conquests of North Africa. Nevertheless, I spent much time in Tunis, with its seductive *madina* (old city) as well as nearby coastal villages—La Marsa, Sidi Bou Said, La Goulette, and, above all, Carthage, whose hold over my imagination proved the most enduring. My undergraduate history courses probably first introduced me to Carthage, mainly as the rival to and then city vanquished by Rome. In addition, the verdant nature of this suburb, with its leafy, shaded streets; wonderful Moorish residential architecture; and numerous cafes acted as a lure. After all, my Peace Corps teaching site was in the semi-arid interior many hours away on creaking public buses; the Mediterranean splendor of Carthage drew me back whenever possible.

When I first visited Carthage in 1973, the transnational tourist industry was taking off. I watched in amusement as busloads of travelers, mainly from Europe, toured archeological sites around Byrsa Hill with guidebooks in hand. Over the years, as I returned repeatedly to Tunisia for research in the archives, I always made the trip out to Carthage on the little local train and noticed that in the twenty-first century the tourists come from all over the globe, including Japan. Their favorite destinations are the restored ports, the Roman baths, and the refurbished archeological museum where I have spent many pleasant hours enjoying the exhibitions. Although I myself am not a golf fan, many visitors now play eighteen holes at the "Golf du Carthage" and stay in swanky five-star hotels along the coast. Since my initial encounter with Carthage thirty-eight years ago it has grown into a densely populated, very chic suburb; its glorious views of the sea and its luxury villas and condos make it one of the most fashionable addresses in the capital city region. Land values are among the highest in the country. Indeed, the former French ambassador to Tunisia selected Carthage as his retirement residence. What's more, recently Carthage was declared a UNESCO world heritage protected site. But it was not always that way.

Whether arriving by ship, as I myself did several times, or putting into the Gulf of Carthage several millennia ago, travelers experience an enchanting sight in terms of sheer physical beauty. The Gulf's eastern wing is bordered by the Cap Bon Peninsula, which is pierced by jagged mountains, the Jabal Zaghawan and Bu Qarnayn, as twin islets, Zembra and Zembretta stand like sentinels, guarding the entryway to terra firma.

A number of geographical features have rendered the Carthage-Tunis region a place of dense human inhabitation and strategic importance for centuries. First, it is relatively well watered by winter storms that fill household cisterns with potable water and support complex agrarian enterprises, such as olive cultivation, fruit trees, and other rain-fed crops. And ample deposits of many-hued marble dot the area, offering building materials. Second, the region is adjacent to the lush Cap Bon jutting out into the Sea; on clear moonless nights one can dimly perceive the lights of Sicily in the distance. Only 182 miles separate this northernmost tip of Africa, the Cap Bon peninsula, from the Mediterranean's biggest island, Sicily, situated dead center in the Sea. Third, the configuration of Tunisia's continental shelf makes it one of the few places with substantial daily tides—as much as three feet. These produce unusually plentiful banks of coral, sponge, fish, and shellfish, which have attracted fishermen for millennia. Finally, unlike much of the African coast, where either forbidding deserts or towering mountains approach and often block the sea, Carthage lies on a great plain whose resources potentially provided the infrastructure essential for the existence of centralized states. In short, Carthage was superbly located for travel, commerce, agriculture, urban construction, and warfare.

This chapter interprets the history of Carthage from its earliest establishment by Queen Dido, the beautiful daughter of the king of the Phoenician city-state of Tyre, around 814 BCE, until 698 CE when it was largely abandoned. Reconstructing the history of Carthage in this period, however, poses a number of problems because of the nature of the evidence. Due to Rome's destruction of the city and its records at the end of the Third Punic War, scant primary historical sources remain. A few Punic texts were translated into Greek and Latin, but the main accounts were penned by Greek and Roman philosophers or historians, such as Herodotus, Aristotle, Polybius, Livy, and Appian. Many of these writers identified with states that competed with Carthage for trade routes as well as access to precious metals and other resources. For the most part their interpretations of Carthage tend to be harsh; the few authors who regarded the African-Mediterranean empire favorably have not survived. Nevertheless, Punic inscriptions on monuments and buildings discovered in North Africa, Sicily, Sardinia, and elsewhere in the Mediterranean where the Carthaginians built fortresses, walls, emporia, or structures represent counter-sources to hostile foreign accounts. Recent archeological excavations have revealed much new material that contradicts the conventionally negative view of Carthage and its historical legacy. (The Carthaginian language, Punic, was a dialect of Phoenician used in the Carthage region well into the Christian era, long after the language had ceased to be spoken elsewhere. The word "Punic," from the Latin *Poenicus* and later *Punicus*, refers to the civilization of Carthage but derives from the Greek *Phoinikes*, meaning "Phoenician.")

This chapter argues that Carthage not only illustrates but also connects the grand currents of ancient African, Mediterranean, Near Eastern, and European histories. At its apogee, Carthage controlled most of the coastal central and western Mediterranean—North Africa, France, and Spain—as well as critical big islands, such as Corsica, Sardinia, and western Sicily, and smaller islands like Malta, Lampedusa, and Ibiza, which were strategically important. Its emergence as a maritime imperial force to be reckoned with by the sixth century BCE was the consequence of large-scale political transformations across Afro-Eurasia—the pressures of the rising Babylonian Empire on the eastern Phoenician states, centered in Tyre (present-day Lebanon) and the movement of the Greeks into the western Mediterranean. The presence of a strong city-state and maritime empire like Carthage, together with its subordinate or allied states, cities, or ports in the central Mediterranean, impeded the extension of Greek hegemony over the entire Inner Sea. Finally, the three wars that the Carthaginian Empire fought with the ascendant Roman state between 264 and 146 BCE had world historical consequences that shaped the nature of Rome's empire in the Mediterranean and Asia Minor.

CARTHAGE AND THE WORLD:
A Nexus for Travelers, Traders, and Empires

According to the Greek philosopher Plato (426–346 BCE), the peoples inhabiting the Mediterranean Basin's rim resembled "frogs round a pond" because of the sea's geography, which nurtured—indeed encouraged—movements and displacements. As a tricontinental hub, the Mediterranean forms one of the globe's greatest water highways. However, it is not a single entity but rather a complex of seas, peninsulas, gulfs, and narrows; its multitude of islands, islets, and archipelagos means that it is both a maritime and land transport system. In ancient times, during the spring and summer sailing season, from May to September, ships dotted the Mediterranean when winds and visibility were favorable and storms posed fewer dangers. Between the winter months and the spring or March equinox, the sea lanes of the Mediterranean were most likely less crowded, as ships and crews wisely sought shelter in home ports. This is because the Atlantic influence, predominant during those months, brings northerly winds, severe storms, and unsettled conditions on water and land.

Around 500 BCE Mediterranean shipbuilders made significant changes to war vessels, increasing their speed and maneuverability by arranging files of rowers on each side of the ship from bow to stern; gradually ships were built that could accommodate at least 300 rowers plus 120 marines. Carthage was known for its shipbuilding savvy. One of the drivers for warfare was the location of scarce but critical resources: above all, metals such as tin, gold, and silver, and grains. Conflicts among Greek, Phoenician, Etruscan, and Roman states often translated into struggles to control Mediterranean regions that contained valuable ores or agricultural resources in abundance—for example, Spain's ample silver deposits and Sicily's rich grain harvests. Merchant ships and smaller sailing vessels, varying greatly in size and carrying capacity, benefitted from these maritime developments. They carried passengers, dispatches, and goods, particularly those needing rapid transport to prevent spoilage, such as wheat. Underwater archeologists have uncovered a number of galleys loaded with amphora or storage jars sunk during storms or warfare; the sea floor remains littered with thousands of jars once containing olive oil or wine. Depending on size, merchant galleys were powered either by humans laboring at the oars, supplemented by auxiliary sails, or, for larger vessels, by sails with rowers used only when entering or leaving port. By the middle of the third century super cargo ships, with capacities of as much as 1,300 tons, moved between Rome, Alexandria, and Sicily, often stopping in Carthage. The wreck of a seventh-century BCE craft revealed kitchen facilities for the crew and passengers that were far more advanced than the primitive cooking arrangements on board Columbus's ships in 1492, over seven centuries later!

Countless people earned their living as seafarers, fighters, pirates, and traders on the Mediterranean's deep blue waters. These activities nurtured land-based industries for shipbuilding and providing naval stores, thus involving hinterland agrarian communities, such as the Cap Bon. Some of the large naval fleets boasted one hundred ships, which meant that thousands of men—rowers, officers, and other personnel—had to be fed. Because vessels could carry rations for only a few days, the solution was either to bring supply ships or put ashore to obtain food supplies, which resulted in Phoenician and Greek outposts across the Mediterranean. This in turn stimulated agriculturalists to produce more to meet higher demand. Because grains were essential for daily diets, the wheat Sicily and North Africa produced explains rivalry among Greece, Carthage, and Rome for control of the central Mediterranean. Thus, the pursuit of power and prosperity on water also had an impact on social, economic, and political relationships on land and, above all, in adjacent villages, towns, and cities. Additionally, changes in land transportation between 600 and 300 BCE allowed some communities in the arid interiors of northern Africa and Asia to become more firmly integrated into sea-land circuits by employing camel or horse power to move humans and goods within reach of ports.

Eastern Phoenicians: Traders and Founders of Carthage

The first great trans-Mediterranean traders—and the founders of Carthage—were the Syrians, or eastern Phoenicians. Originally a Semitic people who pushed into the coastal Levant prior to 1500 BCE, the Phoenicians were the seagoing branch of a larger group, the Canaanites. The height of their mercantile empire, situated along the shores of present-day Lebanon, came between 1200 and 700 BCE. (See Map 6.1.) Prior to about 800 the main focus for eastern Phoenician commerce was Egypt because of its abundant supplies of grain and its role as intermediary in the Red Sea–Indian Ocean trade. From both the Nile Delta and Valley, Levantine merchants—and later Carthaginian traders—acquired grains and precious spices that they exchanged for timber or textile dyes. Gradually a Phoenician trade diaspora spread across the central and western Mediterranean as well as beyond Gibraltar and down the coast of West Africa, going as far as the present-day Spanish Sahara. The westward movement of these peoples was driven in part by rising demand in southwest Asia for silver and other metals. Because mines existed in southern Spain, particularly around the present-day city of Cadiz, the Phoenicians established emporia there. The Phoenicians did not settle Italy proper but instead created trading stations in western Sicily, Malta, and Sardinia; similar establishments, like Carthage, linked the shores of North Africa with the eastern Mediterranean. However, Carthage was more than a mere trade outpost, for it soon outstripped Tyre.

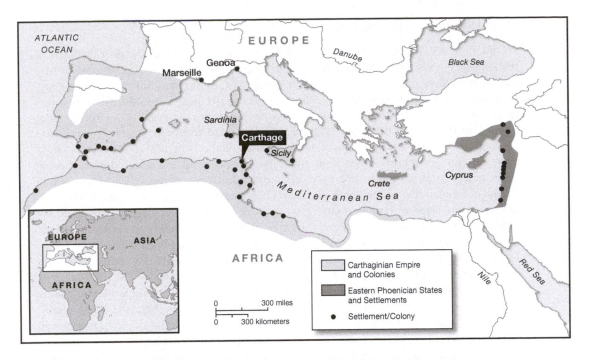

Map 6.1. Eastern Phoenician Colonies, Western Phoenician Settlements, and Carthaginian Empire, ca. 1500–264 BCE

The early eastern Phoenician maritime trading states and later Carthaginian (western Phoenician) Empire began with outposts that grew into colonies in both the eastern and western Mediterranean world. These ringed the sea to tap into sources of grains and metal ores as well as to gain access to commercial routes; the only exception was in eastern Libya where the desert approaches the Mediterranean. Together these two, overlapping the Phoenician trading and colonization systems, brought into sustained contact far-flung regions of the Inner Sea. That system and the rise of the Carthaginian Empire in the central Mediterranean triggered centuries of conflict with Greek and later Roman states and colonies for mastery of the Sea.

Phoenician merchants exchanged textiles and pottery from the Levant for silver, slaves, and wheat from Spain or northern Africa. Because maritime technology favored coastal sailing, the Phoenicians used their strings of trading posts also as restocking stations, taking on board supplies of food and water between Spain and their home base, Tyre. Phoenician seamen and their ships controlled much of the central and western Mediterranean until roughly 750 BCE.

After 700 BCE Mesopotamian conquerors, first the Babylonians and subsequently the Persians, reduced the Phoenician mother state at Tyre in size and prosperity. However, its African and Mediterranean colonial outposts persisted as commercial centers. Carthage alone, superbly located where the central Mediterranean narrows, eclipsed the eastern Phoenicians. By the early sixth century BCE the Carthaginians had assumed control over most of the Phoenician trading commonwealth and exerted an enormous impact on indigenous North Africans, the Berbers, as well as upon the peoples and cultures of adjacent Mediterranean islands. For the Greeks and later the Romans, they represented the principal contenders for mastery of the Inner Sea as well as important trading and commercial partners.

The Establishment of the "New City"

As noted, the deeply indented Gulf of Carthage offers some of the best port facilities on the African shores of the Mediterranean. Although a Phoenician trading outpost or way station may have existed before the ninth century BCE, the area did not yet boast any substantial settlement, although the Phoenician city of Utica, some twenty miles away, had been established earlier. According to mainly Latin sources, notably the Roman poet Virgil (70–19 BCE) in the *Aeneid*, Carthage was founded around 814 by a woman, Dido ("Wanderer"). Also known as Elissa or Elisha, she was the king of Tyre's firstborn. However, her younger brother, Pygmalion, murdered her husband and seized power, causing Dido and a large retinue to flee Tyre on an extended voyage, possibly to Cyprus and Malta, before landing on the Tunisian coast. There she founded a new capital for her followers: "Qart Hadasht" or "new city," from whence the name Carthage is derived. However intriguing the story, Carthage may have been created to relieve overpopulation in the mother state, Tyre, which seems to have been the case with Greek colonization in Sicily. Legend has it that Queen Dido peacefully obtained the land on which Carthage was built from a local lord through an ingenious agreement today known as the "Theorem of Dido." According to this myth, the queen from the east requested land the size of an ox hide as a temporary refuge; she then cut the hide into thin slivers that, after being placed end to end, encompassed a substantial elevated region commanding the sea, known even today as "Byrsa" ("hide" in Latin and Greek; "fortress" in Punic) Hill.

Eventually the city boasted a double harbor that was virtually impregnable from either land or sea and enjoyed access to the rich, fertile agrarian hinterland watered by the Mejerda River system. Carthage was constructed on a triangular peninsula covered with gentle hills; the nearby lake offered abundant fish and secure anchorage. There wheat and fruit grew plentifully and Berber or Libyan pastoralists raised flocks of sheep and cattle. Carthage's location allowed it to command commerce moving in both directions across the Mediterranean. And the constant influx of migrants from the Levant meant that religious ideas, laws, and customs of Southwest Asia continually melded with traditions prevalent among the original peoples of North Africa within the crucible of Carthaginian society and state.

By the sixth century BCE the former refugees and migrants from Tyre had gradually been transformed into Carthaginians. Merchants along with mercantile interests and attitudes structured the sociopolitical order as much as the ethos of warfare and the warrior. Because the inhabitants of Carthage distinguished between civil and military authorities, military leaders were generally kept out of politics, which was unique for the times. Power was shared among free citizens, aristocrats, and monarchs; although a popular assembly of citizens existed, the magistrates and smaller, aristocrat-ruled senate dominated the government. Unlike the Greek city-states, however, citizens generally did not serve in the army. Again in contrast to Greece, Carthage constituted a true empire in that it gradually incorporated diverse ethnoracial groups and communities into its institutions. Whereas Carthaginians manned the all-important naval fleet, the largely mercenary army was composed of heterogeneous peoples drawn from far-flung campaigns around the Mediterranean—from Italy, Spain, the Balearic Islands, and North Africa itself.

Among the gods and goddesses the Carthaginians worshipped was Baal Hammon, the chief deity of ancient Semitic religions, and Tanit, a female fertility goddess found in the Levant's pantheon since the Bronze Age. However, by about the fifth century BCE Tanit became the supreme goddess of Carthage. Connected with the heavens, she was principally a mother goddess and symbol of fertility. Originally only the chief god's consort, her cult eventually eclipsed that of Baal Hammon in importance. Pictorial carvings of the goddess often portray her along with dolphins or other fish because, in addition to being the protector of Carthage, she was the patroness of sailors.

Outside of North Africa the cult of Tanit gained a large following on Malta, Sardinia, and in Spain. As such, she was the equivalent of the Greek Astarte, the evening star deified and a goddess associated with fertility, sexuality, and war. Current excavations in Malta, however, reveal that worship of Tanit and Astarte comingled on the island. The remains of a many-layered temple have been uncovered that dates back to the sixth century BCE, when the Carthaginians established control of the Maltese archipelago. It seems that for three hundred years both Astarte and Tanit were venerated together (or perhaps as a single amalgamated goddess) in a sumptuous temple. In 218 BCE, during the Second Punic War (see below), Malta fell to the Romans. The conquerors built on the existing temple but incorporated the older goddess cult into veneration for the Roman Juno Caelestis, an example of cross-cultural borrowing and synthesis involving African, European, and Asian components.

Those Punic texts that have come down to us reveal the existence of a highly organized caste of ritual specialists or temple priests whose physical appearance marked them off from the rest of the population—they wore no beards. Rhythmic dancing was often employed in ceremonies. *Stelae* (decorated commemorative slabs inscribed with the names and titles of persons remembered) of limestone representing Punic religious culture and art have been uncovered in large quantities throughout North Africa as well as in western Sicily. Most stelae were erected to mark the internment of human remains in large, open-air sanctuaries.

The Berbers: Vital Pastoralists and Soldiers for Carthage

Until the arrival of Queen Dido ethnic groups named Libyans by Greek writers and Berbers by modern historians peopled the North African lands. Classified as a subset of the larger Afro-Asiatic language grouping, the Berbers spoke languages akin to ancient Egyptian, Semitic, and Chadic. Not a racial designation, the word Berber is derived from the Latin *barbari*, that is, "barbarian," those speaking neither Greek nor Latin. By the time Carthage was founded, the Berbers had fanned across northern Africa and the Sahara, developing three principal modes of life—settled agriculture, pastoralism, and transdesert trading. As the Punic cities never boasted sufficient citizens, they drew heavily on the surrounding Berber populations for military might and labor.

Carthage's expanding presence exposed interior Berber societies either directly or indirectly to a more complex, urban civilization that in turn influenced but did not necessarily entirely replace the Berbers' older way of life, language, and beliefs in the countryside. However, Carthaginian cities fused Berber and Punic cultures, so much so that Greek and Roman writers later referred to these populations as "Libyo-Phoenicians." Yet the cultural exchange was not simply one sided. Berber customs and attitudes toward the place of women, which allowed for female warriors, oracles, and military leaders, may have played a part in elevating the goddess Tanit to the equal of Baal Hammon. By the third century BCE centralized Berber kingdoms, with relatively complex forms of political organization, emerged in the territory lying between what is today eastern Morocco and western Tunisia; at times, these kingdoms also allied with Rome against Carthage. Berber states, however, tended to be ephemeral because a stable principle governing succession to power and throne did not exist, whereas a merchant-citizen oligarchy generally ruled Carthage (see Aristotle's commentary below).

Undergirding these kingdoms were evolving local economies based on settled farming, manufacturing, and trade connected to the port cities. The Berbers were also integrated more firmly into Mediterranean-wide circuits through warfare. Although Carthaginian generals were drawn mainly from notable families, the merchant class held little personal enthusiasm for warfare, and thus, Berber warriors were recruited for campaigns against Greek and Roman rivals.

During the first centuries of their existence Carthage and its dependent cities, stretching as far as Morocco, were primarily oriented to local and international Mediterranean trade and commerce. However, the rise of Rome and the series of Punic-Roman Wars starting in 264 BCE brought profound transformations.

The New City: Organization, People, and Activities

Carthage had grown into a very large, densely populated city and empire, whose navy, commerce, and way of life were the envy of competitors. Thanks to the descriptions from the Roman historian Appian of Alexandria (ca. 95–165), the ports are better known than other parts of the city. Their design made distinctions between commerce and warfare: a rectangular port was devoted to trade and a second round port for military use. Although a channel connected these two, the commercial port gave directly onto the sea; whereas the naval port surrounded an island containing a structure permitting the admiral to survey fleet movements. Over two hundred ships could be accommodated in the port, which offered quays, docks, and storage facilities. Nearby was the agora, a vast esplanade lined by sumptuous buildings, including a temple dedicated to the god Baal Hammon, the walls of which were embellished with gold. Adjacent to the agora were main streets with residences reaching as high as six stories. Though narrow, the streets were laid out in grid-like patterns.

The city seems to have expanded from south to north. The most recent archeological evidence reveals the nature of residential life in the southern part of the city. Houses from the third and second centuries BCE were divided into square or rectangular rooms that gave onto interior courtyards; floors were inlaid with mosaics in geometric patterns. Domestic buildings were equipped with devices to trap rainwater for daily use, and public foundations were maintained throughout the city. At the urban limits were found the cemeteries, which have also yielded up material objects about Punic culture and beliefs. Beyond the cemetery was a semirural zone of irrigated gardens and orchards sheltering summer villas. Perched above the city was the walled citadel on Byrsa Hill. At its pinnacle was the most splendid built structure of all—the temple to the god Eshmoun, fronted by a monumental staircase. Just prior to the third war with Rome, a twenty-two mile fortification defended the city proper, suburbs, and citadel. Included within these defense works were stables large enough for three hundred elephants and four thousand horses, storage facilities for grain and forage, and military barracks for thousands of cavalry and foot soldiers.

This infrastructure supported some three hundred thousand people at Carthage's height, making it one of the most densely populated city-states in the Mediterranean. The upper social strata were composed of the aristocrats claiming ancestry to the original settlers from Tyre. Merchants, literati, and skilled artisans formed a middling stratum, followed by mercenary soldiers, seamen, and unskilled laborers. At the bottom of the social pyramid were slaves from all over the Mediterranean world. The most feverish human activity took place at the commercial port, where ships unloaded imported metals and wood, which were scarce in the Carthage region, or exported manufactures produced by local craftsmen—textiles, finished leather, ceramics, glass, weapons, tools, and so on. Agricultural products from satellite villages, such as olive oil, grain, wine, honey, and beeswax were critical to commercial exchanges as well. In a sense, Carthage resembled seventeenth-century England or Holland in that its merchants and traders traveled far and wide—to Portugal and even down the coast of West Africa—to conduct business. Indeed, they were reputed to "know all of the languages" necessary for striking deals. Carthage even sent caravans into sub-Saharan Africa; in the latter its manufactured and agricultural goods were traded for gold, salt, timber, live animals such as apes or peacocks, and hides. From northern European regions Carthage sought amber, tin, silver, gold, and furs; spices produced in or transiting through Arabia, east Africa, and India were obtained from Egypt and then redistributed in the central and western Mediterranean. Finally, as was the practice throughout the ancient world, human beings—enslaved persons—were traded in enormous numbers. Some were seized during raids or bought in markets, but most were taken during warfare. As was true of Greece and Rome, Carthage sent enemy warriors captured during military campaigns into slavery, although it is important to note that the status of slave was not tied to any particular race or ethnicity.

Rivals and Allies: Greeks and Etruscans

In the sixth and fifth centuries BCE warfare repeatedly erupted between Greece and Carthage as Greek merchants, backed by the state, attempted to oust the Carthaginians from commercial posts in Spain and the islands. In 535 BCE Carthage's navy and army blocked further colonization by driving Greek forces out of a newly created settlement on Corsica. However, the real bone of contention was, as always, Sicily. Yet peaceful interludes brought lively commercial exchanges even between avowed enemies; Greeks of southern Italy traded with North Africa, and both Carthaginian and Greek merchant ships carried goods back and forth. Upper-class members of Carthaginian society came to appreciate Greek artisans, sometimes luring them to the imperial center through patronage or having local artists imitate Greek decorative styles for pottery.

In part, the Carthaginian victory of 535 BCE was due to its alliance with Etruscan kings. In central Italy the Etruscans, predecessors of the Romans, moved into the western Mediterranean. Between the mid-sixth and mid-fifth centuries BCE, kings ruled from the Po River in the north to the Campania in west central Italy. Indeed, the Etruscans may have introduced the notion of the city-state as a form of government to much of central Italy, borrowing it from the Greeks. The rise of Etruscan power created a three-way struggle between Greek colonies, on the one hand, and the Carthaginians and their allies, the Etruscans, on the other. This alliance prevented the Greeks from fully dominating the Mediterranean. In contrast to Carthage, the Etruscans never established a true maritime empire; rather, they maintained a loose confederation or alliance system, whose main task was to ward off the Greek menace. This became a pressing duty in their southern realms, as Greek colonists from the Aegean and Asia Minor aggressively pushed into eastern Sicily and up the boot of Italy. Disaster came in 474 BCE when a Greek navy from the powerful city-state of Syracuse in southeastern Sicily devastated the Etruscan fleet. The remainder of the century saw Etruscan maritime power cede to that of the Greeks, as political upheavals in the Italian Peninsula brought their demise. By the third century BCE, Etruscan kings and lords had been shoved off the stage of political history and had inadvertently laid the groundwork for the rise of Rome.

Between roughly 800 and 550 BCE three groups—Phoenicians, Etruscans, and Greeks—had brought most of the Mediterranean and Black Sea coasts under their commercial, cultural, and political sway. They accomplished this principally through trade, warfare, and migration or colonization. If the Etruscans fought off Greek navies, they also eagerly purchased Greek products, such as pottery, or imitated Greek artistic styles, as did the Carthaginians. Yet both the Carthaginians and Etruscans evolved their own unique styles and exported fine products to the eastern and western limits of the Mediterranean world. In the fourth century BCE female terra cotta figurines manufactured by Carthaginian artisans were exported to southern Spain, where they were used in religious ceremonies. Finally, all three drew heavily on their respective hinterlands for resources, supplies, and human labor. Indeed, these hinterlands continually moved outward in space. In this way, peoples quite distant from the sea were more closely involved in the economic and cultural rhythms of the Mediterranean.

True connectivities had been created across the Mediterranean by the time of the Punic-Roman Wars, beginning in 264 BCE. These represented genuine trans-sea connections because any trading or population node in the system could potentially be linked up with other such nodes around the Mediterranean Basin. Indeed, the regions from Gibraltar to the Indian Ocean became more firmly integrated as long-distance commercial exchanges on sea and land along with local commerce merged to provide a wide array of products to increasing numbers of people. Carthage played a considerable role in constructing those trans-sea, transcontinental connectivities and represented the most important maritime empire on the Mediterranean's southern and western flanks.

Prolonged Warfare with Rome (264–146 BCE)

Its concentration of wealth, population, and power drew Carthage into a series of deadly clashes with ascendant Rome that might be characterized as "island conflicts." The first Punic War (264–241 BCE) initially erupted over control of Sicily, but its long-term world historical consequences would prove decisive. Enduring twenty-three years, this was the longest military conflict of the period, and it drew the Roman army out of the Italian Peninsula and onto the islands as well as into North Africa for the first time. Carthage's fleet was larger and its seamen boasted superior naval knowledge, so much so that the Romans, whose fleet was negligible, built their ships using a model of a captured Punic vessel. As indicated by the ancient remains of a Punic warship with numbered timbers, suggesting mass production, Carthaginian ship builders appear to have discovered the principle of prefabrication.

Nevertheless, the Roman army enjoyed an advantage because it was largely composed of citizens and thus may have been more numerous. In contrast, Punic forces drew heavily on mercenaries (paid fighters) and subject peoples, such as the native Berbers, who were often required to pay tribute to Carthage and more likely to desert. This first war ended in Carthage's defeat in 241 BCE and the forced evacuation of Punic trading posts in Sicily. Rome acquired its first overseas territories in Sardinia and western Sicily, and as a result, its imperial vision widened across the Mediterranean into the Aegean. (See Map 6.2) Carthage reacted to this loss by focusing on Tunisia's fertile rain-fed coast, notably the Cap Bon Peninsula, whose large agrarian estates produced valuable cash crops—as they do today—such as olive oil, grains, and wine, which were traded throughout the Sea. These enterprises were so appreciated that the Romans later undertook to translate Carthaginian farming manuals into Latin so as to mine them for agricultural knowledge and techniques.

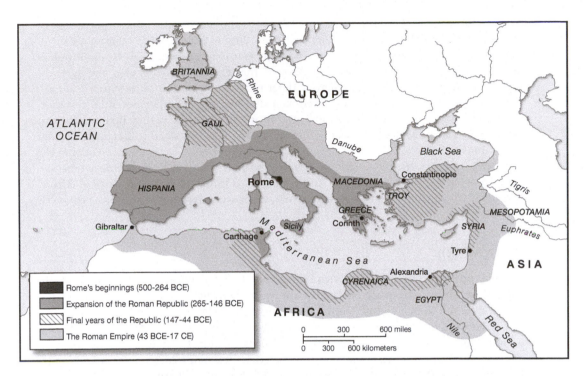

Map 6.2. Territorial Expansion of the Roman Republic and Empire, 500 BCE–117 CE

The four phases of Rome's expansion from a central Italian kingdom to a super-state by 117 CE integrated three continents within a single empire. It also brought into sustained contact the Mediterranean world, northern Africa, the near East, and Europe south and north of the Alps. Rome's vast empire, one of the largest to date, came with a price. Rivals and competitors, such as the Greeks and Carthaginians, had to be vanquished.

The next round occurred as Rome moved into Spain, which had long been a key Carthaginian commercial partner, especially for the traffic in metals. During the Second Punic War (218–201 BCE) Hannibal, a Carthaginian citizen, led an overland invasion of Italy from bases in Spain; in fact, his troops, including elephants, marched across the Alps in a stunning attack. Although the initial Carthaginian victories constituted a serious threat to the continuation of Roman rule over Italy, Hannibal's defeat at the Battle of Zama in 202 BCE resulted in surrender. Not content, the Romans concluded pacts with Berber North African chiefs, such as Masinissa, in the interior around Carthage in order to surround their enemy with allied tribes faithful to Rome. Carthage was also forced to sign a humiliating treaty and pay tribute to Rome, which it did until 151 BCE.

The Third Punic War (149–146 BCE) erupted when the leaders of the Roman Republic claimed that Carthage had violated the terms of the treaty ending the Second War. Demographic and economic forces, however, were at work. By the middle of the second century Rome's population was exploding, with as many as four hundred thousand people. Provisioning the capital city with sufficient food was a political necessity to dampen urban unrest—and Carthage boasted rich agricultural lands. In 149 BC the Republic declared war against Carthage, which sought to appease its enemy by sending hundreds of noble Carthaginian children as hostages to Rome in exchange for peace, but to no avail. After the Romans declared their intent to burn Carthage, its inhabitants prepared to withstand a siege that lasted several years. During the long, bitter siege, as weapons gave out, the women of Carthage, according to legend, used their own hair to make bowstrings for the archers and sold their jewels to buy supplies. Rome invaded and utterly destroyed the city; salt was "sown" throughout its urban area and agricultural lands to symbolize the conquerors' determination to annihilate its future productivity. Furthermore, that act also served as a dire warning to other potential rivals or rebels. The city's inhabitants were put to the sword or enslaved, or they fled into the interior regions. The adjacent Berber town and citadel of Tunis, allied to Carthage during the wars, was also leveled to the ground. Rome eventually incorporated Carthage's other dependent port cities, such as Utica, into a single polity. A Roman *praetor* (magistrate enjoying judicial functions), residing in Utica, administered the province of Africa until 27 BCE, when former Carthaginian territories were designated as a new province, *Africa Proconsularis*.

Carthage Reborn

The city proper lay largely abandoned until about 105 BCE, when military land grants to soldiers serving Rome were initiated. However, given the region's fertility, *latifundia* (large agricultural estates) had earlier been established; these were held by Roman citizens who were often absentee land holders and relied on local labor to produce mainly agricultural products. Rome reconstructed Carthage after 27 BCE, when the descendants of some of its former inhabitants repeopled it, although soldiers and poor peasants from the Italian Peninsula also arrived as colonists. Eventually, Carthage, with more than three hundred thousand people, became one of the three most important cities of the empire, principally for its cereals; two-thirds of its harvest was exported—hence its title, "Granary of Rome." Therefore one crucial transformation Roman rule introduced was that Carthage's older maritime trading and commercial identities, which had structured its social hierarchy, were subordinated to the interests of land-owning elites. At the same time, new colonies were established during the early second century CE, notably in present-day Algeria, where the cities of Timgad and Lambessa served strategic military purposes, shielding the more populous and prosperous coastal regions and cities from attacks originating in the interior from either nomadic warriors under tribal chieftains or Berber kingdoms.

Roman colonizers remained in the cities and drew sharp boundaries between land-owning aristocrats and the subdued native population laboring on the land. A three-tiered hierarchy emerged composed of citizens, Romanized Africans—often from prominent indigenous families—and unassimilated African Berbers. This socioeconomic and legal pecking order influenced language and religion. It is significant that Latin was mainly an urban tongue while Berber and Punic dialects continued to be spoken, above all in the countryside. However, Roman imperial cults exerted little impact on much older Punic and Berber beliefs, rituals, and practices.

One little-known historical fact is that Roman Africa converted to Christianity earlier than many parts of Western Europe; indeed, historians argue that conversion to Christianity constituted a form of local protest against pagan Rome's domination. The first bishopric was established in 180 CE. Augustine of Hippo (354–430 CE), or St. Augustine, a Romanized North African, was later was named Bishop of Hippo Regius (in present-day Annaba, Algeria). His father was a Roman citizen, but his mother was a Berber. A Latin-speaking philosopher and theologian who first studied rhetoric in Carthage, Augustine's writings deeply shaped the development of Western Christianity.

The Christian presence in Carthage introduced urban changes with the building of some twenty-three basilicas; numerous Church councils were also convoked in the city. By this time Carthage had been equipped with all the monumental public structures and amenities associated with classical civilization, from a stadium to theaters. The Emperor Hadrian (r. 117–138 CE) built an aqueduct (remains of which still exist today) to supply fresh water to the city. Antoninus (r. 138 to 161) continued his predecessor's grand works on the colossal baths (*thermes*), whose size made them the third largest in the empire; he also constructed a new forum on Byrsa Hill that St. Augustine evoked in his major work, *Confessions*. Significantly, that same hill served as the imperial residences for Roman, Vandal, and Byzantine rulers, as it had originally for Queen Dido and her retinue. By the fourth century the city boasted thirty-seven miles (sixty kilometers) of underground drainage and water pipes. Some of the most magnificent Roman mosaics come from Carthage and coastal Tunisia during this period, with many of them gracing luxurious villas belonging to notables who owned vast estates.

In 429 a Germanic tribe, the Vandals, crossed the Mediterranean from Spain and conquered the region around Carthage, soon using it as a base to attack Sicily and Sardinia—a long-term pattern already seen in previous centuries. After a decade the Vandals finally took Carthage in 439 but retained most existing laws, institutions, and practices. The city suffered little destruction, although the glorious baths of Antoninus were deliberately destroyed because the Vandals feared that city inhabitants would employ the extensive facilities as a fortress to resist. In 533 a mighty Byzantine fleet appeared in the Gulf of Carthage and easily bested the Vandals, who were either enslaved or fled the city.

Under Byzantine rule for more than a century, the Carthage region became even more cosmopolitan because Greek elements from Asia Minor intermingled with the older Punic, Roman, and Berber cultures and people. The city appears to have progressively lost population during the sixth century CE, however, although basilicas, cemeteries, and other structures were built. The Byzantine Empire sought to resurrect the older Roman imperium but failed because theological disputes and doctrinal differences tore asunder the population, as its local governors in Carthage lacked sufficient manpower to repel raids from Berber tribal confederacies. Eventually, Constantinople's presence was reduced to modern-day Tunisia's coastal cities and a few strategic interior strongholds. Destabilized politically, religiously, and socially by the seventh century, Byzantine Carthage was no match for a new faith and religiopolitical movement, Islam, whose warriors embarked on extensive military campaigns across Afro-Eurasia beginning around 634 CE.

In 695 Arab-Berber armies began a first assault on Carthage, having taken Byzantine-ruled Alexandria in 643. However, a large-scale revolt in the hinterland distracted the Arab leader, Hasan ibn al-Nu'man. A female Berber warrior La Kahina (meaning priestess or sorceress) from the Awras (Aures) Mountains in Algeria led forces against the Arab armies. Allegedly wielding supernatural powers—hence her name—La Kahina held the position of queen when she assumed command of indigenous resistance to the Arabs. Seen by some modern historians as the "Berber Joan of Arc," La Kahina and her followers fought pitched battles all over Tunisia before her defeat just prior to 698. The queen fought to the death and was buried near a well that bore her name. Her long streaming hair, oracles and divinations, and ecstatic inspirations have made La Kahina the subject of myth and speculation for centuries. Her revolt, however, delayed the Arab-Muslim takeover of Carthage for three years. From 695 on, its population had begun to flee by ship for Sicily and Spain. The victors enslaved those who could not escape, and some enslaved persons were sent back to the imperial center, Damascus. Although Arabic and

Byzantine sources are contradictory regarding whether the city itself was totally destroyed, archaeological evidence suggests that defensive walls and aqueducts were demolished and the port filled in because it was too close to the sea and the redoubtable Byzantine fleet.

GLOBAL ENCOUNTERS AND CONNECTIONS:
Carthage as a Convergence Point for Civilizations

Eleven centuries elapsed before Carthage's rebirth and growth into today's tony seaside suburb. In a sense the rapid growth of Tunis, only twelve miles distant, into a major Islamic center of learning, religion, culture, commerce, and manufacturing after 700 CE kept its sister city in a state of neglect. However, building materials—*spolia*—from the Carthage site were incorporated into Islamic Mediterranean architecture, so even religious buildings from the eighth century boast Roman columns. Location on the sea rendered Carthage vulnerable to maritime attacks, but the new Muslim city of Tunis was shielded from the open water by the Lake of Tunis, a fact reflected in its Arabic name, al-Mahrusa, "The well-protected."

In 1800 the land around what had once been the capital and port was still sparsely populated. However, renewed interest in the history of Carthage, notably from European imperial powers vying for control of North Africa, such as France, Italy, and Great Britain, resulted in its growing importance as a highly contested archaeological site, and this interest served diverse ideological agendas. Throughout that same century Carthage was repeopled by urban Muslim notables from Tunis and resident European diplomats and traders for whom it became a place of summer sociability and leisure. During French colonial rule over Tunisia (1881–1956) diverse Mediterranean folk of ordinary means—Sicilians, Neapolitans, Maltese, and so forth—also took up residence in Carthage, laboring in fishing, masonry, or cafe work as well as adding to the ethnic, linguistic, and religious mix.

The city's resurrection and its re-incorporation in transnational circuits and networks were the product of imperial endeavors in the Mediterranean, Asia, and Africa as well as the emergence of global, corporate tourism, with its own peculiar sorts of connectivities and challenges. The emergence of the modern tourist industry in Tunisia by the late nineteenth century and its further development with independence from France after 1956 rendered Carthage a prime attraction. In 1985 the mayor of Rome, Ugo Vetere, and Chedly Klibi, the mayor of Carthage, cosigned a symbolic peace accord that ended the conflict between their cities, which allegedly dated back than twenty-one hundred years because the third—and last—of the Roman-Punic wars had never been concluded with a formal treaty.

As colonizers and conquerors, as were their eastern Phoenician, Greek, Etruscan, and Roman predecessors and/or rivals, the Carthaginians belie the still-prevalent notion of the Mediterranean in the Classical era as essentially a Greek and Roman lake. In truth, three major empires, which were intimately related, marked the historical trajectory of the Inner Sea during the centuries under consideration. Their cultures and even the people themselves were remarkably similar despite or because of longstanding conflicts that paradoxically nurtured civilizational borrowings and emulation. Rome owed much to Hellenic culture, but the Greeks had been deeply influenced by both the Phoenicians of Tyre and of Carthage, the latter primarily via Sicily. Carthaginian cities in Sicily proved as complex and prosperous as their Greek counterparts, and only Carthage succeeded in linking western Africa, the Sahara, and North Africa with southern Europe and Southwest Asia for extended periods of time.

The slow dismemberment and then utter destruction of the Carthaginian Empire by 146 meant that the diverse yet interconnected civilizations of the ancient Mediterranean world were subsequently controlled from the Italian Peninsula. The victory over Carthage removed the only serious obstacle to Roman hegemony throughout the entire Mediterranean and into Asia Minor. Rome retained its dominance over the Inner Sea until 246 CE, when the Emperor Diocletian's reforms divided the empire into eastern and western branches. This was the Mediterranean political world system that the Arab-Muslim armies encountered when they moved out of northern Arabia and into the Fertile Crescent and northern Africa after the Prophet Muhammad's death in 632 CE.

When describing the Tunis-Carthage region in the twentieth century, the native Tunisian writer Albert Memmi stated in his 1992 book *The Pillar of Salt* that the "List of her masters, when I came to know some history, made me giddy: Phoenicians, Romans, Vandals, Byzantine Greeks, Berbers, Arabs, Spaniards, Turks, Italian, French—but I must be forgetting some and confusing others. Walk five hundred steps in my city, and you change civilizations" (96–97).

ENCOUNTERS AS TOLD: PRIMARY SOURCES

The two documents below come from "foreign" observers—not the Carthaginians themselves. The first was composed during the height of Carthaginian power before the disastrous wars with Rome; the second account, devoted to the Roman-Punic Wars, was written long after the defeat of Carthage in the period, when Rome was beginning to recolonize the city and its hinterland, destroyed in 146 BCE. Taken together, these documents invite us to consider how the authors' identities and the historical periods in which they were writing might have influenced their interpretations of the Carthaginian state and its people. In addition, both documents illustrate the ways in which Carthage had become a sprawling Mediterranean as well as land-based empire.

The Politics, by Aristotle

Aristotle of Stagira (384–322 BCE) in Macedonia was a physician, scientist, and the greatest of the Greek philosophers, having studied under Plato. Most of his writings were lost, though some lecture notes, rediscovered in the first century BCE, have survived. Aristotle's *The Politics* literally means the "things concerning the *polis*" (*polis* means city-state; see Chapter 4 on Athens). A work of political philosophy, this is a fragment of a larger treatise or series of lectures. In the selection below Aristotle discusses the nature of Carthage's constitution in order to make distinctions between different kinds of states.

Aristotle's comparative analysis of government employs four types of political organization—democracy, oligarchy, aristocracy, and monarchy—that we still use today.

- How are the Greek philosopher's use and implicit definition of those terms different from or similar to our understanding of these concepts?

- What features does Aristotle attribute to the Carthaginian constitution, and how does it contribute to state formation in his view?

- What characteristics of the Carthaginian state provided stability?

- What aspects of Carthaginian government does Aristotle find deficient?

- What evidence leads the Greek philosopher to conclude that Carthage is an aristocracy with both oligarchic and democratic tendencies, and what information from this chapter might lead you either to agree or disagree with Aristotle?

The Carthaginians are considered to have an excellent form of government, which differs from that of any other state in several respects, though it is in some very like the Spartan. Indeed, the Spartan, Cretan, and Carthaginian states closely resemble one another and are very different from any others. Many of the Carthaginian institutions are excellent. The superiority of their constitution is proved by the fact that the common people remain loyal to it. The Carthaginians have never had any rebellion worth speaking of, and have never been under the rule of a tyrant.

Among the points in which the Carthaginian constitution resembles the Spartan are the following: The common tables of the clubs answer to the Spartan *phiditia* [common meals or banquets] and their magistracy of the Hundred-Four to the Ephors; but, whereas the *Ephors* [leader of ancient Sparta who shared power with the Spartan king] are any chance persons, the magistrates of the Carthaginians are elected according to merit—this is an improvement. They have also their kings and their Gerousia, or council of elders, who correspond to the kings and elders of Sparta. Their kings, unlike the Spartan, are not always of the same family, nor that an ordinary one, but if there is some distinguished family they are selected out of it and not appointed by seniority—this is far better. Such officers have great power, and therefore, if they are persons of little worth, do a great deal of harm, and they have already done harm at Sparta.

Most of the defects or deviations from the perfect state, for which the Carthaginian constitution would be censured, apply equally to all the forms of government which we have mentioned. But of the deflections from aristocracy and constitutional government, some incline more to democracy and some to oligarchy. The kings and elders, if unanimous, may determine whether they will or will not bring a matter before the people, but when they are not unanimous, the people decide on such matters as well. And whatever the kings and elders bring before the people is not only heard but also determined by them, and any one who likes may oppose it; now this is not permitted in Sparta and Crete. That the magistrates of five who have under them many important matters should be co-opted, that they should choose the supreme council of One Hundred, and should hold office longer than other magistrates (for they are virtually rulers both before and after they hold office)—these are oligarchic features; their being without salary and not elected by lot, and any similar points, such as the practice of having all suits tried by the magistrates, and not some by one class of judges or jurors and some by another, as at Sparta, are characteristic of aristocracy.

The Carthaginian constitution deviates from aristocracy and inclines to oligarchy, chiefly on a point where popular opinion is on their side. For men in general think that magistrates should be chosen not only for their merit, but for their wealth: a man, they say, who is poor cannot rule well—he has not the leisure. If, then, election of magistrates for their wealth be characteristic of oligarchy, and election for merit of aristocracy, there will be a third form under which the constitution of Carthage is comprehended; for the Carthaginians choose their magistrates, and particularly the highest of them—their kings and generals—with an eye both to merit and to wealth.

But we must acknowledge that, in thus deviating from aristocracy, the legislator has committed an error. Nothing is more absolutely necessary than to provide that the highest class, not only when in office, but when out of office, should have leisure and not disgrace themselves in any way; and to this his attention should be first directed. Even if you must have regard to wealth, in order to secure leisure, yet it is surely a bad thing that the greatest offices, such as those of kings and generals, should be bought. The law which allows this abuse makes wealth of more account than virtue, and the whole state becomes avaricious. . . .

The government of the Carthaginians is oligarchic, but they successfully escape the evils of oligarchy by enriching one portion of the people after another by sending them to their colonies. This is their panacea and the means by which they give stability to the state. Accident favors them, but the legislator should be able to provide against revolution without trusting to accidents. As things are, if any misfortune occurred, and the bulk of the subjects revolted, there would be no way of restoring peace by legal methods.

Sources: Aristotle, *The Politics*, translated by Benjamin Jowett (New York: Modern Library, 1943), 1272b24–1273b25; LIVIUS: Articles on Ancient History, Livius.Org.

History of Rome: The Punic Wars, by Appian

Appian of Alexandria (ca. 95—165 CE) was born into a wealthy Greek family, worked as a barrister in Rome sometime after 120 CE, and became a procurator after 147. He composed numerous works, most notably a *History of Rome*, which appeared before 162, but he is most remembered for his writings on the civil wars, and these have survived in their entirety. In the text below, Appian gives an account of the three wars between Rome and Carthage. His history raises a number of questions.

- Given Appian's background, upbringing, and when he was writing, what kinds of biases would one expect from his interpretation of these wars?

- To what factors does Appian attribute the rise and power of the Carthaginians?

- Appian states that the Roman General Scipio "razed Carthage to the ground and forbade the rebuilding of it." Does Appian provide any clues in his narration of why the Romans would utterly destroy Carthage—instead of seizing it and making it their own colony?

The Phoenicians settled Carthage, in Africa, fifty years before the capture of Troy. Its founders were either Zorus and Carchedon, or, as the Romans and the Carthaginians themselves think, Dido, a Tyrian woman, whose husband had been slain clandestinely by Pygmalion, the ruler of Tyre. The murder being revealed to her in a dream, she embarked for Africa with her property and a number of men who desired to escape from the tyranny of Pygmalion, and arrived at that part of Africa where Carthage now stands.

Being repelled by the inhabitants, they asked for as much land for a dwelling place as they could encompass with an ox-hide. The Africans laughed at this frivolity of the Phoenicians and were ashamed to deny so small a request. Besides, they could not imagine how a town could be built in so narrow a space, and wishing to unravel the mystery they agreed to give it, and confirmed the promise by an oath. The Phoenicians, cutting the hide round and round in one very narrow strip, enclosed the place where the citadel of Carthage now stands, which from this affair was called Byrsa, "hide."

Proceeding from this start and getting the upper hand of their neighbors, as they were more adroit, and engaging in traffic by sea, like the Phoenicians, they built a city around Byrsa. Gradually acquiring strength, they mastered Africa and the greater part of the Mediterranean, carried war into Sicily and Sardinia and the other islands of that sea, and also into Spain. They sent out numerous colonies. They became a match for the Greeks in power, and next to the Persians in wealth. But about 700 years after the foundation of the city the Romans took Sicily and Sardinia away from them, and in a second war Spain also.

Then, assailing each the other's territory with immense armies, the Carthaginians, under Hannibal, ravaged Italy for sixteen years in succession, but the Romans, under the leadership of [Publius] Cornelius Scipio the elder, carried the war into Africa, crushed the Carthaginian power, took their ships and their elephants, and required them to pay tribute for a time. A second treaty was now made between the Romans and the Carthaginians which lasted fifty years, until, upon an infraction of it, the third and last war broke out between them, in which the Romans under [Publius Cornelius] Scipio the younger [Aemilianus] razed Carthage to the ground and forbade the rebuilding of it.

But another city was built subsequently by their own people, very near the former one, for convenience in governing Africa. . . .

About the beginning of the Sicilian war, the Romans sent 350 ships to Africa, captured a number of towns, and left in command of the army [consul Marcus] Atilius Regulus, who took some 200 more towns, which gave themselves up to him on account of their hatred of the Carthaginians; and continually advancing he ravaged the territory. Thereupon the Carthaginians, considering that their misfortunes were due to bad generalship, asked the Lacedaemonians to send them a commander. The Lacedaemonians sent them Xanthippus. . . .

Of the 30,000 men led by Regulus, only a few escaped with difficulty to the city of Aspis. All the rest were either killed or taken prisoners, and among the latter was the consul Regulus himself.

Not long afterward the Carthaginians, weary of fighting sent him, in company with their own ambassadors, to Rome to obtain peace or to return if it were not granted. Yet Regulus in private strongly urged the chief magistrates of Rome to continue the war, and then went back to certain torture, for the Carthaginians shut him up in a cage stuck full of spikes and thus put him to death. This success was the beginning of sorrows to Xanthippus, for the Carthaginians, in order that the credit might not seem to be due to the Lacedaemonians, pretended to honor him with splendid gifts, sent galleys to convey him back to Lacedaemon, but enjoined upon the captains of the ships to throw him and his Lacedaemonian comrades overboard. In this way he paid the penalty for his successes. Such were the results, good and bad, of the first war of the Romans in Africa, until the Carthaginians surrendered Sicily to them. . . .

After this there was peace between the Romans and the Carthaginians, but the Africans, who were subject to the latter and had served them as auxiliaries in the Sicilian war, and certain Celtic mercenaries who complained that their pay had been withheld and that the promises made to them had not been kept, made war against the Carthaginians in a very formidable manner. . . .

Then the Carthaginians blockaded the towns with a great fleet, and cut off their supplies from the sea, and as the land was untilled in consequence of the war they overcame the Africans by the famine, but were driven to supply their own wants by piracy, even taking some Roman ships, killing the crews, and throwing them overboard to conceal the crime. This escaped notice for a long time. When the facts became known and the Carthaginians were called to account, they put off the day of reckoning until the Romans voted to make war against them, when they surrendered Sardinia by way of compensation. And this clause was added to the former treaty of peace.

Source: Appian, *History of Rome: The Punic Wars*, in *The Roman History of Appian of Alexandria*, edited by Horace White (New York: Macmillan, 1899), http://www.livius.org/ap-ark/appian/appian_hannibal_00.html.

Further Reading

Clancy-Smith, Julia. *Mediterraneans: North Africa, and Europe in an Age of Migration, c. 1800–1900*. Berkeley: University of California Press, 2011.

Dossey, Leslie. *Peasant and Empire in Christian North Africa*. Berkeley: University of California Press, 2010.

Harris, W. V., ed. *Rethinking the Mediterranean*. Oxford: Oxford University Press, 2005.

King, Russell, Lindsay Proudfoot, and Bernard Smith, eds. *The Mediterranean: Environment and Society*. London: Arnold, 1997.

Lazenby, J. F. *The First Punic War*. Stanford, CA: Stanford University Press, 1996.

Memmi, Albert. *The Pillar of Salt*. Boston: Beacon Press, 1992.

Naylor, Phillip C. *North Africa: A History from Antiquity to the Present*. Austin: University of Texas Press, 2009.

Perkins, Kenneth J. *Tunisia: Crossroads of the Islamic and Mediterranean Worlds*. Boulder, CO: Westview Press, 1986.

Sebag, Paul. *Tunis: Histoire d'une ville*. Paris: Harmattan, 1998.

Web Resources

Ancient Tunisia: Ancient Punic and Carthiginian Empires, Ancient Web, www.theancientweb.com/explore/content.aspx?content_id=28.

Carthaginians, http://nethelper.com/article/Carthaginians.

Stuckey, Johanna. "Tanit of Carthage," *MatriFocus: Cross-Quarterly for the Goddess Woman Lammas* 8, no. 4 (2009), http://www.matrifocus.com/LAM09/spotlight.htm.

Vincenzo Salerno, "Sicilian Peoples: The Carthaginians," *Best of Sicily* (2005), www.bestofsicily.com/mag/art156.htm.

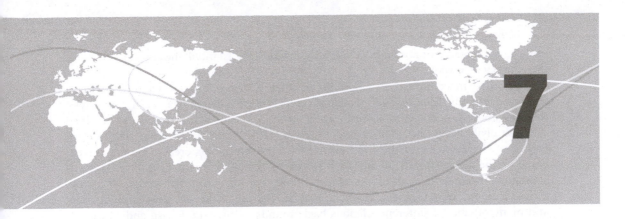

Constantinople/ Istanbul

A Vortex of Peoples and Cultures

(324–1500)

NINA ERGIN

IT HAS BECOME A WELL-WORN—IF NOT UNJUSTIFIED—CLICHÉ TO REFER TO ISTANBUL as a bridge between Asia and Europe, East and West, "Orient and Occident." After all, the enormous city, which due primarily to rural-to-urban migration now counts more than fifteen million inhabitants, straddles the nineteen-odd-mile-long Bosphorus Strait that connects the Black Sea and the Sea of Marmara (which in turn is connected to the Mediterranean by the Dardanelles Strait), each with its own climate and vegetation. The Bosphorus Bridge (built 1973) and the Mehmed the Conqueror Bridge (built 1989) enable trucks to transport goods between the two continents easily and swiftly as well as many residents to drive back and forth between the Asian and European parts daily on their way to and from work. Every year the greater municipality organizes the world's only marathon race that takes runners from one continent to another via the Bosphorus Bridge. The city's topographical characteristic and the resulting geopolitical importance have become significant identity markers for Istanbul and, by extension, for the country as a whole.

The bridge metaphor, however, also implies that the two sides on which the structure's feet rest are firmly delineated and remain two separate, distinct entities. A different way of thinking about how the city has historically attracted, brought together, and combined different civilizations and cultures into a unique mixture may derive from another geographical characteristic of the Bosphorus Strait: the whirlpools created by the current based on the density flow from the Black Sea to the Sea of Marmara. Like a vortex, Constantinople/Istanbul has sucked in and thrown together many different peoples—ancient Greek, Roman, Arab, Genoese, Venetian, Turkish, Persian, Albanian, Russian, Bulgarian, and many others—of different religious backgrounds—Christian, Jewish and Muslim—and then disgorged new civilizations—the Byzantine and Ottoman empires—thereby creating further currents and whirlpools downstream.

Many of those sucked into this vortex at first did not necessarily come to stay but arrived instead with the intention to trade or conquer and then return to their point of departure or move on. I also first experienced Istanbul as a tourist, as a child, arriving from my native Austria in the early 1980s for a three-day sightseeing trip with my family. We stayed in the Pera Palace Hotel, built in 1892 by the Franco-Turkish architect Alexandre Vallaury. Located in the most European-looking quarter of the city, it once accommodated wealthy European travelers who had arrived on the Orient Express railway line originating in Paris. The hotel's interior decoration and furnishings still seemed to date from the previous century, such as the creaking wood-and-wrought-iron elevator operated by a liveried liftboy. While the rest of our tourist group took part in impersonal tours, we had our own personal guide in my mother's high school friend, who had lived with her Turkish husband in Istanbul since the 1960s. Our visits to the many different mosques, the Basilica Cistern, the bazaars, and the Topkapı Palace are now a blur to me, but I vividly remember my wonderment at the fact that we were setting foot onto the Asian continent (even if only onto Asia Minor) to drink tea in a seaside café in Üsküdar: "Are we really in Asia now?"

Many years later I returned, equipped with Turkish language skills and conducting research on Ottoman architecture. Like so many previous travelers, I had no intent to stay at first, but then I happily became a permanent resident. Where in past centuries the vortex had drawn in, for instance, Turkish-speaking horsemen from Anatolia, Genoese and Venetian cloth merchants, and Sephardic Jews expelled from *reconquista* Spain, it now attracts rural migrants from Eastern Turkey, university students from provincial towns, and businesspeople from Europe and the United States, among many others. Whereas in past centuries the whirlpool created from different groups' customs and traditions Byzantine and Ottoman imperial culture and architecture, it has now created a globalized culture of universities teaching their curricula in English and of much-frequented shopping malls with popular US chain coffee shops selling *simit* (doughnut-shaped sesame rolls) sandwiches and tiny cups of thick Turkish coffee.

Following a description of the geographical setting and early settlement history of the area, this chapter will proceed chronologically through the city's changes—and continuities—from Byzantine to Ottoman imperial capital, from the fourth to fifteenth centuries. I pay attention to the link between the built environment and politics as well as to how the city attracted people from diverse cultures and religions, thereby making it into a true place of encounters. Because this chapter will cover the city both under Byzantine rule, when its official name was Constantinople, and under Ottoman rule, when its popular name was Istanbul, the chapter title refers to both names, as befitting to the city as a unique case not only in the context of this book but also in world history.

CONSTANTINOPLE AND THE WORLD: *The Lure of an Imperial Capital*

The Bosphorus Strait was formed in prehistoric times when the region's tectonic plates shifted and allowed the waters of the Black Sea basin to flow into the Marmara Sea, originally a freshwater lake much smaller than today. As archaeological evidence in the form of tools of the East African Olduvai type embedded in the eight-hundred-thousand–year-old Middle Pleistocene layers of the Yarımburgaz Cave west of the city demonstrates, even before the formation of the strait the region constituted an important land bridge facilitating human movement between the African, Asian, and European land masses. By the time ancient Greek settlers from the Attic city of Megara arrived and set up a colony on the Asian shore of the Bosphorus in the eighth or seventh century BCE, the landscape had largely taken its present shape. In addition to the waterway linking the Black Sea and the Mediterranean, the area boasts a large and well-protected inlet called the Golden Horn. This inlet branches from the southern end of the strait toward the northwest, creating a triangular peninsula. Legend has it that a second group of Megarans under the leadership of Byzas (from whose name "Byzantion" is derived) quickly realized the value of the peninsula and settled there around 660 BCE.

The promontory's value lies not only in the natural harbor that facilitated communication and trade as much as in the available fresh fish; it is also in its strategically advantageous location. This made it relatively easy to defend against intruders. Bordered by the Golden Horn to the north and the Marmara Sea to the south, the peninsula stretches its tip eastward, forming the end point of the Bosphorus. Although the peninsula is often described as having seven hills—obviously, in reference to Rome—it has in fact only one hill and a long ridge with several fingers jutting out toward the Golden Horn, separated by a valley. The ridge extends all the way to the peninsula's tip, creating an excellent vantage point to view the spectacular scenery of the confluence of the Golden Horn, the Bosphorus, and the Marmara Sea, thereby making it possible to survey and control the European and Asian shores as well as any maritime traffic.

This is where the beginnings of the ancient city lie, as the first acropolis was constructed here. Hence, a settlement with all the necessary urban amenities—temples, altars, a marketplace, city walls—began to grow westward. Following Byzantion's integration into Roman territory in the second century BCE, it became involved in a succession struggle among the Roman leadership and sided with the opponent of Septimius Severus (145–211 CE), who eventually became emperor. As punishment, Septimius razed the city and reduced its administrative status, but later on he rebuilt it and laid the foundation to many monuments that Constantine the Great would complete or extensively renovate in the fourth century CE.

From Byzantium to Constantinople (324–1453)

When Constantine came to power in 324 CE after defeating the other three emperors of the Roman tetrarchy ("leadership of four"), he was already familiar with the city of Byzantium and its strategic advantages for politics, trade, and commerce. He chose to make it into a new Rome (Roma Nova), a center from which to make an imperial presence felt in the eastern provinces. Constantine initiated a vigorous building campaign to give the city the splendor befitting an imperial capital. Most of the monuments he renovated or built catered to the needs of the urban residents and those he hoped to attract from elsewhere: the Augustaeum, a public square with a senate house; the *mese*, a colonnade-lined main traffic artery starting west of the Augustaeum and eventually linking the city to the overall road system of the Roman Empire; and the foundations of the Church of the Holy Apostles, through which Constantine openly showed that he favored Christianity in spite of his continued use of pagan symbols of power and legitimacy. He also divided the city into fourteen regions, taking Rome's administration as a model and establishing a system that endured beyond the Byzantine period. Constantinopolis, literally the city of Constantine, was consecrated on May 11, 330, and its founding was commemorated with especially minted coins. Still, initially it must have appeared rather underpopulated, as the emperor offered land gifts and free food to attract residents.

Constantine's strategies proved successful and the city grew quickly, remarkably so when considering that in Late Antiquity most cities either stagnated or contracted in size and population. Even the ecumenical council of bishops' meeting in Constantinople in 381 proclaimed it the center of religious and political authority within Christendom, second only to Rome. Claiming the title of ecumenical patriarch, the bishop of Constantinople wielded religious and moral authority over the Christian community from his seat in the Church of Hagia Sophia ("Holy Wisdom"), also called the Great Church (originally built in 360, its present shape dates to 537; see *Descriptio S. Sophiae* and *Tarih-i Ebü'l-Feth*, referenced at the end of the chapter). By the eighth century the "Great Church" had come to stand for the patriarchate itself and the Orthodox Church as a whole, figuratively uniting millions of Christians under its roof. Although further patriarchates were created in Eastern Europe as Christianity spread throughout the centuries, Constantinople's did not lose its power, even after the Ottoman conquest of 1453, and continues to provide spiritual leadership for the Orthodox Church today.

As seat of political and religious power, the city needed to be able to defend itself against any potential invaders motivated by the geopolitical ambition to obtain the key point between Europe and Asia or the riches that the Byzantines accumulated through the extensive trade networks reaching eventually as far as Scandinavia and China. To this end, Theodosius II (r. 408–450) completed new city walls in 413 CE. Stretching about 4 miles (6.5 kilometers) from the Sea of Marmara to the Golden Horn, the impressive engineering achievement consisted of inner and outer walls with ninety-six towers as well as a deep moat, each separated by terraces facilitating the movement of troops. This effective defense system allowed Constantinople to withstand for more than a millennium the many different peoples who hoped to conquer it: the Avars, Slavs and Persians as a combined force, the Arabs, the Bulgarians, the Rus', the soldiers of the Fourth Crusade (who managed to sack the city in 1204 only because they had already been permitted to enter), and, finally, the Ottomans.

In the seventh century a new religion emerged in the region bordering the Byzantine Empire to the east, on the Arabian Peninsula, where the well-established monotheistic religions of Judaism and Christianity met the polytheist and animist Bedouin tribes who were in constant conflict with each other. Based on the revelations of the Prophet Muhammad (ca. 570–632), which later became codified in the Qur'an, Islam offered a monotheistic belief even stricter than that of the Jews and Christians in that it negated any intermediaries between individual believers and God ("Allah"). Based on the practice of the "five pillars of Islam"—the confession of faith, prayer, fasting, charity, and pilgrimage—this new belief provided a strong ethical framework and created a politically and spiritually unified community of believers.

Decisive military victories against Persia and the Byzantine Empire demonstrated the cohesion and strength of this newly emerging community. They resulted in the Muslim conquest of Roman Syria by 638 and North Africa by 709, the latter occurring under the Umayyad Dynasty (r. 661–750), who assumed the political and religious leadership

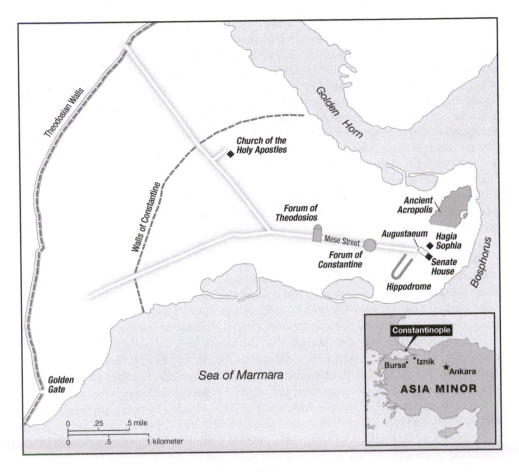

Map 7.1. Byzantine Constantinople, ca. 600

As a transit point between Europe and Asia, Constantinople held great strategic and economic importance and, therefore, attracted many people. Its status as the Byzantine imperial capital was reflected in its monuments and urban amenities: the Churches of Hagia Sophia and the Holy Apostles served worshippers; the forum of Constantine was an administrative center and the forum of Theodosius a marketplace; the hippodrome provided entertainment; and the Theodosian walls protected the city from armies hoping to conquer the wealthy city.

("caliphate") over all Muslims after a period of internal upheaval. The loss of Syria and Egypt, particularly wealthy and productive provinces, was a major blow to the Byzantine Empire, and the Arabs pressed on still. The two Arab sieges of Constantinople in 674–678 and 717–718 can be considered an extension of the wars between the Byzantines and the Umayyads on the empire's eastern frontier. Already by the lifetime of the Prophet Muhammad, Constantinople was so famed for its wealth and splendor that the Prophet proclaimed the greatness of the Muslim commander who was to conquer it. However, the harsh winter climate and Byzantine use of an incendiary weapon called Greek Fire averted conquest and halted Arab expansion into Anatolia.

Only much later, when the Seljuk Dynasty arrived from Persia and penetrated Eastern Anatolia in 1071, could Islamic civilization gain a permanent foothold in Asia Minor. Like the many other small principalities that Turcoman generals with origins in Central

Asia established, the Seljuks brought to the region a new religion and culture quite different from Eastern Roman civilization: a lifestyle that was based on pastoral nomadism and raiding; Persian language, literature, and political practices; and artistic and architectural styles based on that of Iran's heritage. The Seljuks' arrival has to be seen in the context of a larger Eurasian history, shaped by not only the requirements of a nomadic and warlike lifestyle as well as the history of the medieval Middle East but also power struggles among the many minor Islamic dynasties. To secure revenues the Seljuk Dynasty enhanced trade throughout their territory by constructing inns (caravanserais) for travelers and merchants, located apart from each other at a distance that could be covered in a single-day journey, and entertained good relations with Genoese merchants. While bringing with them typically Persian building types and styles, they also integrated ancient Greek and Roman statuary in the city walls of their capital Konya, for example. Like Constantinople, Anatolia was a place of encounters, a whirlpool that caught the Seljuks, mixed them with the local populace of Byzantine Anatolia, and turned them into the Seljuks of Rum ("Rome" in Arabic), as they called themselves.

In the late thirteenth century one particularly ambitious dynasty emerged in western Anatolia from among the different Muslim principalities. Named after their leader Osman, the Ottomans conquered from the Byzantines Bursa (1326) and Nicaea (1331) and soon pushed their territory's boundary to the Asian shore of the Bosphorus. By that time the Byzantine Empire had been severely weakened. Neither capital nor empire ever really recovered from the extensive damage that the Crusaders had inflicted on population, economy, and monuments when they conquered the city in 1204 and subsequently ruled until 1261. Thus, by 1361 the Ottomans were able to take the European hinterlands of Constantinople, effectively enveloping the city and reducing the empire to its capital and a few scattered territories in Asia Minor and today's Greece. In doing so, they received assistance from several Christian warrior families who had converted to Islam. It is important to note that religious identity and cultural boundaries in medieval Anatolia were fluid and often determined by pragmatic considerations. For example, Ottoman rulers entered alliances with the Genoese merchant colony of Galata in Constantinople, fought against other Muslim principalities in Asia Minor, and married Byzantine princesses for political purposes. Also, the practices and techniques of Byzantine craftsmen very much shaped early Ottoman architecture, so determining whether a structure was built for Ottoman or Byzantine patrons can be difficult. Constantinople contained an Ottoman quarter before the conquest, complete with a mosque, and the emperor Manuel II allowed Sultan Bayezid I (r. 1389–1402) to erect a castle, Anadolu Hisarı, about midway on the Asian shore of the Bosphorus, where the strait is at its narrowest.

Understanding the city's strategic importance for military, political, and economic purposes, the Ottomans now more firmly set their eyes on its conquest but were diverted when Tamerlane took Sultan Bayezid I prisoner in the Battle of Ankara (1402). With Bayezid I's death, Constantinople remained safe for a while longer. However, to think of the struggle between the Byzantines and the Ottomans for the imperial capital as nothing more than a clearly delineated conflict between Christianity and Islam would be misleading. Not only did much exchange occur, as mentioned above, but until the sixteenth century, the Ottomans also ruled over a territory in Anatolia and on the Balkans that was inhabited by many more non-Muslims than Muslims. In exchange for a head tax quite lucrative for the Ottomans, non-Muslims could practice their religion generally undisturbed. Mehmed II (r. 1444–1446, 1451–1481) did use religious rhetoric and symbols on many occasions, but more importantly, he saw possession of Constantinople as a necessity to establish himself as Roman emperor. After the conquest on May 29, 1453, he took the title *Kayser-i Rum* (Caesar of Rome), although this was not recognized by Europe, which was reeling from the shock that the Eastern Roman Empire was no longer in Christian hands and could therefore no longer be imagined as a "bulwark against Islam."

From Constantinople to Istanbul (after 1453)

Immediately after the conquest Mehmed II wanted to return the devastated city to its former glory with the help of activities and strategies that combined economic, social, political, and architectural elements. These strategies included a blend of Byzantine, earlier Ottoman, and Islamic (and in some cases also western European) practices and traditions that once again suggest the image of a vortex drawing in separate currents, combining and disgorging them in the form of another current. For himself, Mehmed II built the Topkapı Palace on the peninsula's tip, over the ruins of the ancient acropolis. By choosing this site, he also communicated his new image as *Kayser-i Rum* and as "Sultan of the two seas and two continents"—another title he now assumed. The palace consists of structures in a variety of styles, built by craftsmen brought from all over the empire and beyond: the second gate with its crenellations and towers reminds of a medieval European castle, the Tower of Justice over the imperial council hall is strongly reminiscent of a church tower, and Persian craftsmen constructed one of the pleasure pavilions in the outer palace grounds. The Seven Towers (Yedikule) Citadel built around the Golden Gate in the Theodosian city walls near the Marmara Sea reflected current fortification building practices west of the Aegean.

The Hagia Sophia, which had dominated the urban skyline since the sixth century, was one of the first sites that Mehmed II visited with a few of his viziers and courtiers immediately after the conquest. More than any other site, it had figured in the imagination of Muslims who aspired to conquer Byzantium for many centuries and therefore embodied the locus of imperial power of the vanquished state. The sultan had the Muslim confession of faith recited and the afternoon prayer read, thereby transforming the church into a mosque. Later, there were added a prayer niche orienting the worshippers toward Mecca, minarets for the call to prayer, and a pulpit for the Friday sermon. Mehmed II also established an endowment that would ensure its upkeep, but its name remained unchanged: Ayasofya Camii, or Hagia Sophia Mosque. During the fifteenth and sixteenth centuries even most of its mosaics with Christian imagery remained visible, contrary to the notion that Islamic worship spaces do not contain figures because of the prohibition against worshipping idols. However, by the seventeenth century the figural images had been covered, and over time the Ottomans constructed many myths and legends in order to retroactively "Islamicize" the monument. Among these, one tells of the collapse of the half-dome over the apse on the night of the Prophet Muhammad's birth; the collapsed part could be repaired only with a mixture of sand from Mecca, water from a holy well at the Ka'ba, and the saliva of the Prophet.

In contrast to his care for the Hagia Sophia, Mehmed II destroyed the remainders of the Church of the Holy Apostles, which had been begun by Constantine the Great and had included the founder's tomb. Instead, he erected an enormous mosque complex over the site. The symmetrical plan of the mosque and its ancillary structures (schools for primary and secondary education, a library, hospital, soup kitchen, caravanserai, hostel, and bath) may have been inspired by contemporaneous Italian urban design practices. That the domed mosque at the same time engaged in a rivalry with the Hagia Sophia and its famous dome was not lost on fifteenth-century observers. In order to revive trade and secure the upkeep of the Hagia Sophia through the above-mentioned endowment's income,

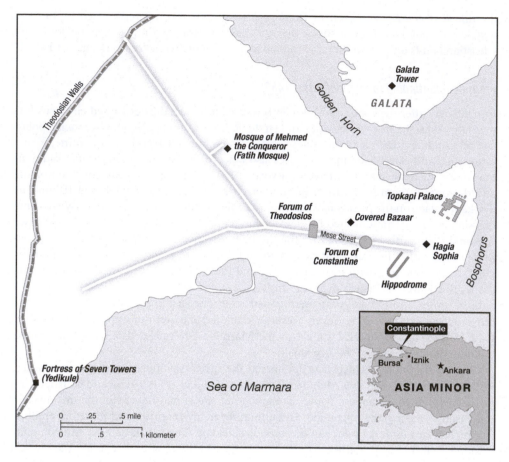

Map 7.2. Istanbul Under Mehmed the Conqueror, 1453–1481

Following the conquest Mehmed II consciously preserved great continuity in the urban fabric. He turned the Hagia Sophia into a mosque, built his own mosque over the Church of the Holy Apostles, and erected the Topkapı Palace over the ancient acropolis. The Covered Bazaar was constructed in the market area, close to the fora that remained open space. The hippodrome served as plaza for festivities. The Theodosian walls, with the addition of Yedikule Fortress, continued to protect the city.

the sultan commissioned two domed masonry buildings for the safe storage and sale of luxury goods; together with the vaulted commercial streets that immediately sprung up around them, these form the core of the Covered Bazaar. This bazaar and many other markets, together with the infrastructures necessary for trade and travel, as they were established and protected by Mehmed II and successive sultans, would ensure the city's continued economic prosperity throughout the Ottoman centuries.

Following the Islamic practice of dividing responsibility for major building projects among the ruler's officials, Mehmed II ordered his viziers to contribute actively to the construction of the new capital in the form of houses, baths, inns, markets, and places of worship. As Constantine the Great had done more than a millenium before him, the Ottoman sultan divided the urban area into about a dozen districts. The sultan's Greek court historian, Kritovoulos, recorded how he assigned each district to an official who then was requested to construct the necessary infrastructure there. They each commissioned a mosque complex—smaller in scale than the sultan's and with a variety of ancillary structures—and financed its upkeep with endowments that drew funds from urban real estate and landholdings from as far away as the outmost Balkan and Anatolian provinces. These complexes formed the core of each district and—by providing employment opportunities as well as amenities such as worship spaces, fountains, educational institutions, bathhouses, food markets, and health services—were meant to attract residents.

Mehmed II promised to the future residents houses, gardens, tax-exempt status, and religious freedom. He installed an Orthodox patriarch, made sure that not all churches were converted into mosques, and also gave to the Genoese merchant colony of Galata an imperial decree allowing them to continue worshipping in their usual manner, except for the ringing of church bells. These policies allowed, if not for a free intermingling of, at least an exposure to and relatively close contact with and relations between different faiths and cultures. In spite of Mehmed II's measures, the city's population at first did not increase as much as he desired. Therefore, a policy of forced settlement was instituted, bringing especially skilled craftsmen from various provinces of the empire. Postconquest resettlement, whether in the era of Constantine the Great's or Mehmed II's, was one of the few instances when the whirlpool lost its strength and needed to be stirred in a deliberate manner. By 1500 Konstantiniyye—"Constantine's city," as it was called in official Ottoman documents in contrast to the more popularly used "Istanbul" that was derived from the Greek *eis ton polis* ("from the city")—was home to Turks from Anatolia; the descendants of the Byzantine aristocracy who had remained in the city; Genoese and Venetian merchants; an Armenian community with its own patriarchate; Romaniot Jews whose ancestry dated to Late Antiquity; Sephardic Jews who settled in the city following the Christian reconquest of the Iberian peninsula; and an untold number of traders and travelers from both East and West. Although these diverse groups did not always live together entirely peacefully over the centuries, they all contributed to the emergence of a distinct cosmopolitan culture, architecture, music, and cuisine.

Mehmed II's aspirations to take over what was once the Roman Empire led him to mount a successful campaign to Otranto on the southernmost tip of Italy in 1480, but following his death in 1481 Papal Forces were able to retake the town. His son, Bayezid II (r. 1481–1512), did not share his imperial vision, but his grandson, Sultan Selim I (r. 1512–1520), added to the Ottoman territories by conquering from the Mamluk Dynasty (r. 1250–1517) Eastern Anatolia, Egypt, and the holy cities of Mecca and Medina. By doing so, Selim I changed the demographic makeup of the empire to a majority-Muslim one and assumed the role of caliph, the successor of the Prophet Muhammad and leader of the Islamic community. The addition of the universal rulership over all Muslims now enhanced the imperial image for which Mehmed II had laid the groundwork, even though this role was not always emphasized with equal strength throughout the centuries until it was abolished in 1924 after the Republic of Turkey was established. With the conquest of Mecca and Medina, the city of Istanbul became the seat of two major religious leaders, the Orthodox patriarch and the caliph, whose followers were found not only around the Mediterranean and in southeast Europe but also as far as sub-Saharan Africa and Southeast Asia.

GLOBAL ENCOUNTERS AND CONNECTIONS:
Istanbul's Enduring Global Network and Community

Because of its location at the point where Eurasia, the Black Sea, and the Mediterranean world intersect, Constantinople held great advantages in terms of geopolitics as well as for commerce and trade. The network of Roman roads continued to serve the people of

Byzantium; however, transporting goods was more easily accomplished by sea, even if navigation was not without dangers and afforded little profit. A dynamic interregional trade existed, and this is known thanks to the finds of Early Byzantine amphorae (serving as transportation containers for oil, wine, honey, and the like) throughout the entire Mediterranean and as far as Britain and the Arabian Seas. In the Middle Ages Constantinople became particularly renowned for its trade in luxury items, such as decorated metal objects, spices, ivory, and silk. Ivory was obtained from India and Africa, carved into caskets and other small objects, and then exported. Until the sixth century, when they began to produce their own silkworms, Byzantines imported raw silk from East Asia and wove it into beautiful cloth that was then sold to western Europe and the Arab world. The Byzantines therefore maintained the connections to the Silk Road that had already been established during Antiquity and that would continue to play an important economic role under the Ottomans.

Another phenomenon that spanned both Byzantine and Ottoman Empires was the presence of traders from Italian city-states. Venice and Amalfi had sent merchants to the city by the tenth century, and in 1082, in exchange for military aid against the Normans and the Crusaders, the Byzantine emperor Alexios I Komnenos granted the Venetians generous concessions, such as tax exemptions and a quarter of their own, which led to an increased number of Italians in the empire and a lively trade in textiles over the next few centuries. The Ottomans already entertained good relations with Genoese traders in the fourteenth century, frequently exchanging envoys between the Ottoman court and the *podestà* (ruling body) of Galata. Very much aware of their territory's advantageous location within the silk and spice trade networks, the Ottomans controlled the overland trade routes between Asia and Europe and dominated trade in the Eastern Mediterranean and the Black Sea, maintaining supremacy for four centuries. In spite of the close commercial relations between the Ottomans and European merchants, Ottoman trade policies were conservative in that they focused on ensuring self-sufficiency and favored imports over exports. Istanbul's markets, as they had been developed by Mehmed II, played a significant role in the commercial system, both in the quest for self-sufficiency as they provisioned the palace and the army and for distributing raw material to the capital's artisans.

Regardless of the strict state control, much cultural exchange occurred in parallel to commercial transactions. For instance, a number of Venetians converted to Islam and entered the Ottoman ruling elite in important positions; the ambassadorial reports written by Venetian envoys developed into a literary genre of their own; figures in turbans and caftans became a fixture in Venetian paintings; and many place names in Venice still give witness to the past Ottoman presence. Such close encounters of cultures and religions were not necessarily particular to Venice or Istanbul, but they were common to most major trade cities of the early modern world.

During its largest expansion in the sixteenth century the Ottoman Empire stretched almost to the western edge of the Mediterranean and therefore tied provinces as far away as Algeria to the capital of Istanbul; however, its ambitions to expand eastward into maritime Asia have received relatively less scholarly attention until recently. With the help of corsair attacks, diplomatic maneuvers, trade connections, and religious ideology, for a few short decades the Ottomans managed to challenge the Portuguese Empire in the Indian Ocean and wrest the lucrative Indian Ocean trade from them. Istanbul's power struggle with Lisbon was carried out as far east as Portuguese Malacca, which the Sultan of Aceh, together with Ottoman auxiliary forces, besieged several times during the sixteenth century, albeit unsuccessfully. Moreover, by turning his attention to Asia, the sultan in Istanbul also extended his authority as caliph over the global community of Muslims eastward, kept direct relations with Central Asian Sunni Muslim states and India, and even managed to have the Friday prayer read in his name on the Maldives, Ceylon, and Sumatra. As caliph, he was also responsible for the safety of *all* pilgrims who wanted to complete the *hajj* and therefore presided over a strong religiopolitical link between Istanbul and Mecca.

In spite of global economic and political shifts over the centuries, such as the European colonization of the Americas and the rise of alternative trade routes, Istanbul retained its significance as a commercial and imperial center until the early twentieth century. Shortly before World War I it was a lively metropolis of approximately one million, with about 130,000 foreigners taking advantage of its many trade and investment opportunities. After the establishment of the Republic of Turkey in 1923 the (at that time globally favored) nationalist ideal of an ethnically homogeneous population led to an "unmixing" of the previously multiethnic city, depriving it of most of the non-Muslim merchants and businessmen over the twentieth century. However, economic liberalization since the 1980s has ushered Turkey into a postnational era, and full membership negotiations with the European Union have been taking place since 2005. Once more, Istanbul has become a powerful vortex and major point of attraction for investment, both domestic and foreign; a center of commerce, trade, and banking; a logistical node in the global network of travel due to its two airports; and a magnet for tourists and travelers.

ENCOUNTERS AS TOLD: PRIMARY SOURCES

A great number of travelers and merchants drawn from all over the world into the vortex of Constantinople/Istanbul have penned accounts about what they saw there. The documents excerpted here present a traveler's view of Constantinople from the mid- to late twelfth century, when the city was part of the Byzantine Empire; a sixth-century Byzantine court member's impressions of the famed Hagia Sophia; and an Ottoman historian's account of Sultan Mehmed II's first visit to the Hagia Sophia in the mid-fifteenth century.

Letter on Constantinople, by Benjamin of Tudela

Because of their vivid and, according to some modern scholars, accurate descriptions of daily life, the writings of Benjamin of Tudela (1130–1173) are of particular interest here, especially in reference to the Byzantine trade that made the imperial capital into such a vibrant place of encounters. Setting out from his native northeast Spain around 1165, Benjamin probably traveled for both commercial and religious purposes, intending to visit the Holy Land as a pilgrim and showing great interest in the customs and conditions of the Jewish communities in the more than three hundred cities he visited along the route. As you read the excerpt from Benjamin's letter on Constantinople below, consider the following questions:

- Why were Jews "naturally very active" in Byzantine commerce?

- What limitations did the Byzantines impose on foreigners and why?

- Based on the information given in the narrative section above, what changes and/or continuities can you detect between Byzantine and Ottoman attitudes toward foreign merchants as well as commerce and trade in general?

Great stir and bustle prevail at Constantinople in consequence of the conflux of many merchants who resort hither, both by land and by sea, from all parts of the world, for purposes of trade. Merchants from Babylon and from Mesopotamia, from Media and Persia, from Egypt and Palestine, as well as from Russia, Hungary, Patzinakia to the north of the Khazar Kingdom, Budia of the Bulgars, and from Lombardy and Spain, are met with here, and in this respect the city is equaled only by Baghdad, metropolis of the Muhammedans. In all this commerce Jews are naturally very active. Jewish traders follow the silk route east to Damascus and Baghdad, some as far as India and China, to buy spices and raw silk, and they go west to Italy and France to sell them. They cross the Russian Sea [Black Sea] and go north into the kingdom of Kiev to buy furs and amber from further north and salt from the Azov region; and to sell spices from the east as well as Byzantine manufacturers like soap made from olive oil, and jewelry and wine. . . .

The law requires an arriving foreigner to go to register with the prefect, who grants him permission to reside in the city for a limited time (never more than three months). There are strict limits on the amount of silk which a foreign trader might buy: . . . Silk trading is confined to special houses; foreigners, throughout their sojourn, are closely watched—non-Jews, that is. Jewish traders are not limited in the time they may spend in the city or in the empire: and despite the laws against their exporting silk, they are under no surveillance.

In fact it is only Jews who can travel freely between Greek, Roman and Moslem lands. The Byzantines discourage their own Christian merchants from going abroad . . . they say that the city of Constantinople alone receives some twenty thousand florins every day; this revenue arises from rent of hostelries and bazaars and from the duties paid by merchants who arrive by sea and land.

Source: Sandra Benjamin, ed., *The World of Benjamin of Tudela* (Madison, NJ: Fairleigh Dickinson University Press, 1995), 129–132.

Descriptio S. Sophiae, by Paul the Silentiary

Just as Constantinople can be seen as a vortex that pulled in people from everywhere, so the Hagia Sophia is a legendary monument that has attracted everyone coming to the city—travelers (including the above-mentioned Benjamin of Tudela), ambassadors, conquerors, or tourists today. As a public monument carrying religious as well as political meanings in the Byzantine and Ottoman periods, it constituted a place of encounter between ruler and ruled, clergy and lay people, residents of the city and visitors. If the city itself reminds of a whirlpool, then the Hagia Sophia might be considered its center where everything stands still: once people arrive at this monument, they pause in wonder in view of its impressive size and towering dome. The Hagia Sophia added an imperial mark to the city's skyline, visible from the Sea of Marmara, the Golden Horn, the southern end of the Bosphorus, and from Europe and Asia alike; its shape was to determine how the urban silhouette would further develop over the centuries because it served as a source of inspiration for many Ottoman architects.

The building as it exists today was built following the 523 destruction of the previous church and seat of the Orthodox Patriarchate—a wooden-roofed basilica dedicated in 415, which in turn had been constructed over the first church dedicated in 360. Justinian I (r. 527–565), who commissioned Isodorus of Miletus and Anthemius of Thralles to plan the new Hagia Sophia, inaugurated the basilica together with the patriarch on December 27, 537. After the dome collapsed in 558 due to an earthquake and was rebuilt with a higher elevation to make it more stable, the superstructure took on its present appearance.

Paul the Silentiary, a writer and officer of the imperial court under Justinian I, described in a famous hymn of praise (encomium) the architecture and decoration of the church after the new dome had been completed in 562. In reading this passage you can learn about the appearance of the church as perceived by a sixth-century Byzantine court member and the sense of awe that it inspired.

- What are the architectural features that impressed Paul the Silentiary the most?

- What can you infer about the writer's mental map as he describes the monument's position within his geographical as well as spiritual world?

Rising . . . into the immeasurable air is a helmet rounded on all sides like a sphere and, radiant as the heavens, it bestrides the roof of the church. At its very summit art has depicted a cross, protector of the city. It is a wonder to see how [the dome], wide below, gradually grows less at the top as it rises. It does not, however, form a sharp pinnacle, but is like the firmament which rests on air. . . .

Upon the carved stone wall curious designs glitter everywhere. These have been produced by the quarries of sea-girt Proconnesus [an island in the Sea of Mamara, famous for its marble]. The joining of the cut marbles resembles the art of painting for you may see the veins of the square and octagonal stones meeting so as to form devices: connected in this way, the stones imitate the glories of painting. And outside the divine church you may see everywhere, along its flanks and boundaries, many open courts. These have been fashioned with cunning skill about the holy building that it may appear bathed all round by the bright light of day. . . .

Countless . . . other lights, hanging on twisted chains, does the church of ever-changing aspect contain within itself; some illumine the aisles, others the centre or the east and west, others shed their bright flame at the summit. Thus the bright night smiles like the day and appears herself to be rosy-ankled. . . .

The clear sky of gladness is thrown open to all, driving away the soul's dark-veiled mist. The holy brightness shines on all. And indeed the sailor travelling on the sea lanes—whether on leaving the hostile currents of the angry Pontus [the Black Sea], he weaves past the squeezing bends between the watch towers [the Bosphorus], or whether, after the Aegean, he steers his ship against the eddying current in the waters of the Hellespont [the Dardanelles Strait], receiving on his halyards the rush of the Libyan whirlwind—even if he directs his life-saving ship, looking not on the Great Bear or the Little Bear, but upon the divine light of the church, as the leading star of his bold cargo, [which guides] not only by the beams it cast at night—for the Pharos on the edge of Libya also does this—but also by the bounteous favors of the living God.

Source: Cyril Mango, ed., *The Art of the Byzantine Empire, 312–1453* (Englewood Cliffs, NJ: Medieval Academy of America, 1986), 83, 85, 91; "The clear sky . . . the living God," English translation by Paul Magdalino.

Tarih-i Ebü'l-Feth, by Tursun Beg

Tursun Beg, a noted Ottoman historian who was present at the siege, served as secretary while the conquered city was surveyed, and having authored the *History of Mehmed the Conqueror*, he wrote in great detail about the Hagia Sophia and

Mehmed II's first visit to the church. The verses that the sultan utters at the end of this extract are a couplet by the Persian poet Sa'di and refer to the desolate state of a famous ancient Iranian palace that all sorts of critters had taken over after its abandonment. It was quite typical of the Ottomans, with their multicultural background derived of elements both Eastern and Western, that they would have responded to the experience of a beautiful but ruined Byzantine church with a Persian literary reference.

• As you read the excerpt, compare the ways in which Paul the Silentiary and Tursun Beg describe and contextualize the monument—how are their frames of reference similar or different?

• Can you think of other ways in which the Ottomans, as conquerors, could have responded to—and subsequently treated—the Byzantine monuments they encountered?

And this is such a solid building and strong edifice that, when looking at the boundaries of its fundament—so heaven-like; even though having fallen into disrepair and abandoned, its likes are impossible to attain—one has to say: "The like of which were not produced in all the lands" [Qur'an 89:8, originally referring to the lofty architecture of the ancient South Arabian capital city of Iram]; however, because of the occurring circumstances, over the course of time its dependencies and outbuildings fell into a ruined state. . . .

And there is no architect left who could put stones into its cracks, and not enough of its body [i.e., its structure] is left that could be drawn with the help of a compass; only one dome remains. And what a dome it is, it equals the nine celestial spheres! A perfect master demonstrated all [aspects] of the science of engineering in this work; he enlarged its interior with half-domes stacked on top of each other and with acute and obtuse angles and with unique arches like the captivating arched eyebrows [of a lover] and with colorful decorations, in such a way that it is wide enough for 50,000 persons. And the elegant wall-covering they embellished with colorful tiny pieces of golden glass, as if the tiny pieces were indivisible—the skill of the artist who made this is incomprehensible—and they laid the floor with

colorful speckled marble slabs; it is such that, when looking from the ground to the ceiling, one sees the star-studded firmament and, when looking from the ceiling to the ground, one observes the wavy sea. And they clad the lower parts of the solid walls with thin and delicate slices of colorful speckled marble; this is done in such a way that whoever walks about to look at them will be amazed by this wondrous artistry. These masters gave such value and respect to the art of stone-cutting that one cannot find any two human or lifeless figures which are alike each other. And in the dome that corresponds to the middle [of the church] a skillful artist has depicted with golden glass pieces and colorful tesserae the figure of a venerable man [i.e., Jesus Christ] in such a way that, from wherever one looks at him, he turns his face in that direction.

The ruler of the world [Mehmed II] contemplated the marvelous works and figures inside the dome and then deigned to mount the outside of the dome. He mounted as the spirit of God [i.e., Jesus] mounted to the fourth story of the heavens. From the galleries of the intervening stories, he viewed the sea waves of the floor and then mounted the dome. When he saw that the dependencies and outbuildings of this imposing structure lay in ruins, he reflected that the world is transitory and unstable and would ultimately perish; of the sugar-sweet words which he uttered, deploring [this state of affairs], the following verse reached the ear of this poor man and engraved themselves on the tablet of his heart:

The spider serves as the gatekeeper in the halls of Khosrau's dome

The owl plays martial music in the palace of Afrasiyab.

Source: Tursun Beg, *Tarih-i Ebü'l-Feth*, edited by A. Mertol Tulum (Istanbul: Baha Matbaası, 1977), 63–64 (translation by Nina Ergin); Franz Babinger, *Mehmed the Conqueror and His Time* (Princeton, NJ: Princeton University Press, 1978), 96.

Further Reading

Babinger, Franz. *Mehmed the Conqueror and His Time*. Princeton, NJ: Princeton University Press, 1978.

Boyar, Ebru, and Kate Fleet. *A Social History of Ottoman Istanbul*. Cambridge: Cambridge University Press, 2010.

Casale, Giancarlo. *The Ottoman Age of Exploration*. Oxford: Oxford University Press, 2010.

Findley, Carter V. *The Turks in World History*. New York: Oxford University Press, 2005.

Finkel, Caroline. *Osman's Dream: The Story of the Ottoman Empire, 1300–1923*. London: John Murray, 2005.

Kafesçioğlu, Çiğdem. *Constantinopolis/Istanbul Cultural Encounter, Imperial Vision, and the Construction of the Ottoman Capital*. University Park: Pennsylvania State University Press, 2009.

Keyder, Çağlar, ed. *Istanbul between the Global and the Local*. Lanham, MD: Rowman & Littlefield, 1999.

Magdalino, Paul. *Studies on the History and Topography of Byzantine Constantinople*. Aldershot, UK: Ashgate, 1997.

Mango, Cyril. *The Art of the Byzantine Empire, 312–1453: Sources and Documents*. Englewood Cliffs, NJ: Medieval Academy of America, 1986.

Mark, Robert, and Ahmet Çakmak, eds. *Hagia Sophia from the Age of Justinian to the Present*. Cambridge: Cambridge University Press, 1992.

Web Resources

Byzantium 1200, www.byzantium1200.com.

Digital Library: Istanbul, Turkey, ArchNet, https://archnet.org/library/places/one-place.jsp?place_id=1754.

Historic Areas of Istanbul, UNESCO World Heritage Convention, http://whc.unesco.org/en/list/356.

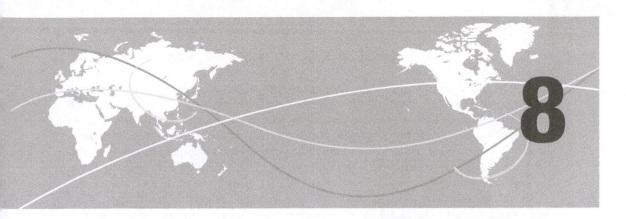

Mecca

Pilgrimage and the Making of the Islamic World

(400–1500)

Michael Christopher Low

As Islam's holiest city and the birthplace of the Prophet Muhammad (570–632 CE), Mecca's world-historical significance is almost self-evident. It is both the historical cradle of the faith and the global Islamic community's spiritual center of gravity. When Muslims kneel to perform their five daily prayers, it is toward Mecca that they must face. It is also the site of the annual pilgrimage, the hajj.

All great cities conjure certain images in our minds. When one thinks of New York, one inevitably imagines the Statue of Liberty set against the city's jagged skyline. Likewise, the Eiffel Tower is synonymous with Paris. When one imagines Mecca, the image that invariably comes to mind is an aerial panorama of the Grand Mosque (Masjid al-Haram). The massive mosque's nine minarets towering over the Ka'ba and its great open-air courtyard, overflowing with a sea of pilgrims hailing from every corner of the globe, is among the most awe-inspiring displays of man's shared humanity. Dressed in their simple white garments, pilgrims proclaim the equality of all believers in the eyes of God, regardless of their age, class, gender, language, nationality, or race. Standing shoulder to shoulder, circling around the black and gold cloth of the Ka'ba, and performing their prayers in unison, these markers of difference melt away as the pilgrims affirm their collective identity as Muslims.

As one of the five pillars of Islam, the performance of this ritual is an obligation for all Muslims at least once in their life, so long as they are physically and financially able. Each year nearly three million Muslims descend upon Mecca and its environs to participate in a series of sacred reenactments, physically and spiritually linking them to their forbearers. In addition to marking the personal zenith of Muslim spiritual life, these rituals also reinforce the individual's connection to the approximately 1.5 billion believers who make up the global Islamic community.

Despite its centrality to Islam, historians have shown a remarkable indifference to the hajj. Owing in part to its global nature, historians have struggled to capture the dynamic encounters between the local and regional authorities governing Mecca and its surrounding region, the Hijaz, and the diverse populations of pilgrims they host. However, Mecca's sacred status has often led scholars to treat it as almost beyond the bounds of the mundane politics that constitute the history of ordinary cities. Although many would point to the challenges of conducting research in Saudi Arabia or the fact that non-Muslims are prohibited from entering the Holy Places in Mecca and Medina as the greatest hindrances to Western academics, I would argue that these are actually not the biggest obstacles facing scholars. When we think of Mecca as the center of the Islamic world, we are implying a relationship between the local and the global. However, these questions cannot be adequately handled only by experts of Saudi Arabia or the Arab world. Some of the most penetrating explorations of Mecca's global significance have come from scholars of non-Arab societies such as Indonesia, India, Turkey, and West Africa. Thus, rather than thinking of Mecca's history only as Arab history, we must begin to take more seriously the cross-cutting webs of exchanges connecting Mecca to the rest of the Islamic world.

These tangled webs were precisely what first sparked my own interest in Mecca. When I began my graduate studies, I initially planned to study India. When asked to explain how my interests migrated from India to Arabia, I have often joked that I followed the pilgrims. What started as an essay on cholera outbreaks among India's pilgrims has become a career-long obsession with sketching Mecca's global tentacles. This project has led me to destinations as diverse as Britain, Egypt, India, Turkey, and Yemen. To the casual observer these locations might appear completely unrelated; however, even the most obscure routes to Mecca are littered with traces of the cross-cultural encounters the hajj generates.

I vividly remember visiting a tiny, barren island located just off the coast of Yemen. By most measures Kamaran Island is the definition of insignificance. However, a brief survey of the island's history reveals its position as a strategic gateway to the Red Sea. It was here that Afonso de Albuquerque, Viceroy of the Estado da Índia, anchored the Portuguese fleet in 1513 in preparation for an offensive against the Hijaz. De Albuquerque's grandiose scheme included plans to attack the Hijazi ports of Jidda and Yanbuʻ, destroy Mecca, and steal Muhammad's body from its tomb in Medina in the hope of ransoming it for the return of Jerusalem's Temple Mount to Christian hands. Later, in 1882, Kamaran served as a fortification of different kind. In an often losing battle to halt the spread of deadly outbreaks of cholera carried aboard steamships from India, Ottoman and European statesmen established an international quarantine station to prevent infected pilgrims from reaching Mecca. While on Kamaran I was fortunate enough to interview several elderly men who recalled the bustling steamship traffic arriving from India and Indonesia prior to the station's closure in 1952. As we talked, I began to better understand how those pilgrims, having braved long and arduous voyages across the Indian Ocean in overcrowded, often unsanitary vessels, must have been disheartened by the suffocating heat and invasive medical inspections that awaited them upon their arrival on this windswept desert island. I cannot help but marvel at the bravery and solemn piety that drove pilgrims to endure discomfort and even face death to reach their sacred destination as well as how Kamaran and thousands of other long-forgotten places bear witness to the centripetal forces that pull and connect every corner of the Islamic world to Mecca.

MECCA AND THE WORLD:
From the Age of Ignorance to the Dawn of Islam

Mecca is located approximately forty-five miles (seventy-two kilometers) west of the Red Sea port of Jidda in the Hijaz region of present-day Saudi Arabia. Founded around 400 CE, it sits in a barren valley situated between two ranges of steep hills. Like much of the Arabian Peninsula, rainfall is scant and irregular. However, when it does come, it often causes violent floods. Mecca is also plagued by extreme heat, with summer temperatures often soaring above 40° C (104° F). As the medieval Arab geographer al-Maqaddisi bluntly put it, Mecca's climate is characterized by "suffocating heat, deadly winds, and clouds of flies."

Due to its inhospitable climate, the Hijaz was a land of scarcity and deprivation compared to the climates of the Fertile Crescent to its north and Yemen to its south. In contrast to these agriculture-rich cradles of civilization, the Arabian interior could only support nomadic pastoralism. Farming was limited to scattered oases. Thus, unlike the complex societies of the Fertile Crescent, Arabian pastoralism produced a tribal culture of considerably less material sophistication. Although less hierarchical than the powerful states to the north, these more egalitarian tribal societies were chronically anarchic, as they were plagued by blood feuds and warfare.

This did not mean that the Arabian Peninsula was isolated from the outside world. In the sixth century Arabia had substantial contacts with Byzantine Syria as well as the Persian Sassanids, who dominated Mesopotamia and the Arabian coasts of the Persian Gulf. Although the golden age of the Arabian incense trade had long since passed with the collapse of its Roman markets, the contraction of the Byzantine and Sassanid frontiers to their north reinvigorated the Arabian caravan trade. Operating within this modest trading zone, Meccan merchants exchanged leather, raisins, and dates for items like textiles and oil more readily available in Palestine, Syria, Mesopotamia, and Yemen. Owing to these contacts, Meccans were well acquainted with Byzantine and Persian affairs.

Like most of their fellow Arabs, Meccans were polytheists. Indeed, prior to the Islamic era Mecca was an important pagan pilgrimage center. Because pre-Islamic Arabia was plagued with tribal conflict, religious mechanisms were developed to ensure periods of truce, during which pilgrimages and commercial activities could be conducted without the threat of violence. According to this system, Mecca was defined as a *haram* (sacred space) where bloodshed was strictly prohibited. The haram contained a cubical shrine, called the Ka'ba, which housed the sacred idols of the surrounding tribes of the region. This attraction positioned Mecca as a nexus of intertribal trade and diplomacy.

The Prophet's Mecca: Muhammad and the Birth of Islam

To understand Mecca and its global connections, it is important to understand Islam's development and relationship to the city. By the sixth century outside influences had begun to challenge the region's pagan traditions. There were well-established Jewish populations in the Hijaz and Yemen. In Syria and among the Arab tribes of the northern desert the prevailing Christian doctrine from the fifth century onward was Monophysitism, a theological position espousing that Jesus Christ's human and divine natures are unified. Monophysitism had also gained importance in both the Axumite Empire in Ethiopia and across the Red Sea in Yemen.

In the decades preceding Muhammad's birth, conflict between Monophysites and Jews in Yemen sparked an interimperial rivalry among the Byzantines, Axumites, and Persians. In 525 the Byzantine Emperor Justinian backed an Axumite invasion of Yemen to avenge the slaughter of the Christian community in Najran at the hands of the Jewish king of Yemen. Following the conquest of Yemen, the Ethiopian viceroy Abraha had a magnificent church built in Sana'a' in an attempt to divert Mecca's lucrative pilgrimage trade to Yemen. Not satisfied with this, Abraha's army marched on Mecca in 570, intent on destroying the Ka'ba. Abraha's forces included one of the ancient world's greatest psychological weapons, the elephant. This episode is remembered in *Sura al-Fil* (The Elephant, Qur'an 105):

> Has thou not seen how thy Lord did with the Men of the Elephant?
> Did He not make their guile to go astray?
> And He loosed upon them birds in flights,
> Hurling against them stones of baked clay
> And He made them like green blades devoured.

According to the great Muslim historian Ibn Ishaq, Abraha's army was likely the victim of an outbreak of measles or smallpox rather than divine intervention. However, the result was the same. Abraha retreated and was soon ousted from Yemen by the Persians.

According to Islamic tradition, the Year of the Elephant coincided with Muhammad's birth, illustrating the degree to which, even before Muhammad's prophetic career, monotheism had already begun to encroach on Mecca's pagan traditions. This episode also underscores the privileged status of Muhammad's Quraysh tribe as the guardians of the Ka'ba. After all, it was Muhammad's grandfather, 'Abd al-Muttalib ibn Hashim (d. ca. 578), who led the effort to defend Mecca against Abraha's army. Five generations before Muhammad, the Quraysh were united by Qusayy ibn Kilab. Around 400, Qusayy gathered his scattered tribesmen, settled them in Mecca, and built the city's first permanent habitations. Under Qusayy's leadership, the Quraysh also established themselves as the guardians of the Meccan sanctuary. Qusayy's grandson, Hashim ibn 'Abd Manaf, is credited with having obtained edicts of protection from the Byzantine Emperor, thereby allowing Quraysh caravans to operate unmolested in Byzantine lands; his brothers negotiated similar concessions with Persia, Yemen, and Ethiopia. These alliances shaped the Mecca into which Muhammad was born. Despite his tribe's prominence, however, Muhammad's position was by no means secure. He was an orphan in a society dominated by kinship ties. Having lost his father, mother, and grandfather by age eight, he was eventually taken in by his uncle. While the Qur'an says little about Muhammad's life before his prophetic mission, biographies (*sira*) and reports of Muhammad's sayings and deeds (*hadith*), provide a fuller picture. A wealthy widow named Khadija hired Muhammad at age twenty-five to oversee her caravan trade with Syria. Muhammad performed well and, in time, Khadija married him. At this stage Muhammad remained a somewhat marginal figure, owing much to his wife's wealth and status. Although Muhammad's life up to this point offered few hints of his eventual importance, numerous hagiographical sources report miraculous signs of his future prophecy. For example, on one occasion when Muhammad accompanied his uncle on the caravan to Syria, he was recognized by a Christian monk who is reported to have foretold the boy's role as God's messenger.

In 610, at age forty, Muhammad's prophetic career began on nearby Jabal al-Nur. Following pagan tradition, Muhammad was in the habit of withdrawing to the mountain cave of Hira' to meditate. One night while Muhammad was sleeping in the cave, the angel Gabriel (Jibril) appeared before him and commanded him to "recite!" Over time Gabriel's visits revealed the scriptures we now know as the Qur'an. For twelve years between this initial revelation and Muhammad's departure from Mecca in 622, Gabriel introduced Muhammad to the new moral code and system of ritual, which we now know as Islam.

Above all else Muhammad's message was one of strict monotheism. At its heart was the concept of *tawhid,* which declares the absolute oneness, unity, and uniqueness of God as the creator and sustainer of the universe. This was a rebuke of both Arabian idolatry and the Christian Trinity. The strongest statement of this critique was revealed in *Sura al-Ikhlas* (the Purity, Qur'an 112), which declares that, unlike Christian conceptions of God as both father and son, Allah neither "begets nor is He begotten; and none is like Him."

Despite critical differences between Islam and its monotheistic relatives, Islamic traditions go to great pains to connect Muhammad and Mecca with the biblical history of monotheism. This revision of biblical genealogy takes the story of Abraham (Ibrahim) as its point of departure. According to the Book of Genesis, Abraham's wife Sarah was able to bear him a son, Isaac (Ishaq), only extremely late in life, by which time he already had a son, Ishmael (Isma'il), by his Egyptian concubine Hagar. This led to bitterness between the two women, and upon Isaac's birth, Hagar and Ishmael were sent away. During her flight into the wilderness Hagar ran out of water. Ishmael was on the verge of dying of thirst when again an angel came to their rescue, miraculously revealing a well. The angel promised Hagar that Ishmael would father a great nation. Although the Bible records that Ishmael did indeed have twelve sons, giving rise to the twelve Ishmaelite tribes, Abraham's heir was Isaac. Thus, it was with Isaac and his Israelite descendents that God made His everlasting covenant. From this perspective, the Ishmaelite lines seemed to dead-end.

However, Islam reopened the Ishmaelite line as an alternative Arabian branch in the history of monotheism. According to Islamic tradition, in the wake of the quarrel between Sarah and Hagar, Abraham took Hagar and Ishmael to an uninhabited location and left them there. As in the Bible, Hagar and Ishmael ran out of water and an angel intervened. In the Islamic version, however, Gabriel appears, striking the ground with his foot, from which a spring bursts forth. As it turns out, the spring was the holy Well of Zamzam, marking the site of the Meccan sanctuary. The Qur'an then takes this connection a step further. In *Sura al-Baqara* (The Cow, Qur'an 2:125–127), Allah commands Abraham and Ishmael to build a sanctuary and establish the rites of pilgrimage to it. Thus, Muslims claim Abraham and Ishmael as the architects of the Ka'ba.

In addition to tying Abraham to Mecca, the Qur'an also emphasizes that Abraham's monotheism predates the advent of either Judaism or Christianity. Abraham is described as a believer in the true faith (*hanif*) and one who submits to God (*muslim*). By describing Abraham as a Muslim, Muhammad's prophecy is framed not as a heretical offshoot of Judaism or Christianity but rather as a reassertion of the "pristine" monotheism that the Arabs had inherited from Abraham and Ishmael. Just as the Israelites had periodically fallen away from God's message and figures like Moses and Jesus had warned them of their errors, the Arabs had likewise fallen into what Muslims call "the age of ignorance."

From an Islamic perspective, however, unlike previous prophets, Muhammad was not merely warning a particular people or nation; as the "Seal of the Prophets," Muhammad was God's final messenger to all mankind before the end of the world and Judgment Day.

Islam Challenges Mecca's Social Order

For three years Muhammad's message remained private. His first converts were confined to his immediate family. However, Allah eventually commanded him to make his revelations public. Although the initial reaction was relatively tolerant, he endured much mockery and cynicism. Although Meccans were accustomed to accommodating a variety of belief systems, as it became clear Muhammad's message was in fact a direct challenge to Mecca's entire social order, the opposition stiffened. The nascent Muslim community represented a grave threat to the values of tribal tradition and loyalty to clan kinship. Meccans also feared that Islam's militant opposition to polytheism and idol worship would ruin the city's lucrative pilgrimage trade and unravel the region's delicate system of intertribal politics. As the rift between Muhammad and the rest of Meccan society grew wider, an economic boycott against the Muslims prevented them from purchasing food in the markets.

As the harassment grew, a group of Muhammad's followers sought refuge in Ethiopia in 615. Muhammad appealed to the Christian king of Ethiopia to shelter his followers. Muhammad reasoned that it was preferable for his fledgling community to seek shelter among fellow monotheists and "People of the Book" than to risk its destruction at the hands of the pagan Arabs. This was a prelude to the migration (*hijra*) of the entire Muslim community to Medina in 622, marking the first year of the Islamic calendar. The move marked a critical transition from a pagan society based on kinship ties to a Muslim one bound together by common faith. During this period Muhammad was able to consolidate the Muslim community and forge a confederation of tribes strong enough to challenge his Meccan rivals. After weathering eight years of Meccan attacks, in 630 the Muslims finally recaptured Mecca. Upon entering the city, Muhammad granted amnesty to almost everyone and offered generous gifts to the Quraysh, paving the way for his tribe's absorption into the Islamic community. He also destroyed the idols housed in the Ka'ba. Rather than ending Mecca's pilgrimage tradition, however, Muhammad reinterpreted it both as a key symbol of Islamic unity and of Islam's connection to earlier traditions of Abrahamic monotheism. Shortly before his death in 632, Muhammad made his "Farewell Pilgrimage," which still serves as the model for the rituals performed today. This ensured that Mecca would remain the geographical center of the new globalizing faith.

The Spread of Islam and the Marginalization of Mecca

The unification of the once-fractious Arab tribes under the banner of Islam was a decisive turning point in Middle Eastern and world history. Within a decade of Muhammad's death the Arabs swept through Egypt, Syria, and Palestine, forcing the Byzantines to retreat to Anatolia. To the east the Arab onslaught in Iraq and Persia completely shattered the Sassanid Empire. By 750 Arab-controlled territories stretched from Spain and North Africa to the frontiers of India in the East. These rapid victories carved out a new geographical space for a massive Arab migration, spawning a wave of urbanization, economic expansion, and the organization of a dynamic new Islamic empire, laying the foundation for the eventual conversion of much of Afro-Eurasia to Islam.

The Caliphate Moves North: The Sunni-Shi'a Rift

Despite the breathtaking expansion of these conquests, this did not guarantee that Mecca would continue to play a leading role in the new Islamic order. Following Muhammad's death in 632 the Prophet's companions elected a successor, or Caliph (*khalifa*), who functioned as both the spiritual and political leader of the Islamic community. By virtue of their close personal connection to the Prophet and their loyalty to Islam, the first four Caliphs (Abu Bakr, 'Umar, 'Uthman, and 'Ali), the so-called Rashidun or "Rightly Guided Caliphs," were accepted as Muhammad's successors and God's earthly deputies. However, infighting over the rightful succession of the Caliphate sparked the first Muslim civil war (656–661), spawning a schism that would ultimately split the faith into Sunni and Shi'a sects. The supporters of the Prophet's cousin and son-in-law 'Ali (d. 660), eventually identified as Shi'is, believed that only 'Ali and his descendents were the legitimate heirs of Muhammad's spiritual legacy. Conversely, according to the Sunni position, the Caliph needed not be a member of the Prophet's blood line; only the consensus of the Muslim community was necessary to claim the title. Thus, they accepted the Caliphal claim of the civil war's eventual victor, Mu'awiya ibn Abi Sufyan (r. 661–680).

Mu'awiya transferred the Caliphate and imperial capital away from Arabia to Damascus, where he had served in the early Muslim campaigns against the Byzantines prior to his appointment as governor of Syria. This northward shift proved permanent. Even when the 'Abbasids toppled the Umayyad dynasty in 750, the Caliphate moved to Baghdad, not Mecca. As a result, both Mecca and Medina slid from the center of the Islamic world to a distant, unruly periphery. Mu'awiya's reign is generally regarded as a transition from the more religiously legitimate Rashidun era to a new imperial age in which the military and political realities of ruling the expanding Muslim domains decisively eclipsed the Caliphate's religious aspects. (See Map 8.1.) Under the Umayyad dynasty (661–750) the Caliphate morphed into a hereditary monarchy, blending Islamic ideals with Arab tribal institutions and administrative, economic, and military methods borrowed from the Byzantines and Sassanids.

Although most people assume that Mecca has always been an important Islamic cultural, political, and religious center, by almost every measure it played little role in the flowering of Islam's cosmopolitan culture. By contrast, Damascus and Baghdad emerged as the urban engines of Islamic civilization's "golden age." In these cities Arab-Muslim culture incorporated Hellenistic, Roman, Byzantine, and Sassanid influences into its art, architecture, literature, science, philosophy, and theology. Perhaps the greatest expression of this dynamic fusion of civilizations came under 'Abbasid Caliph Ma'mun (r. 813–833), who established the famous Bayt al-Hikma ("House of Wisdom"). Scholars at this academy translated into Arabic political treatises, great works of folklore and literature, and the best of mathematic, philosophical, and scientific thought from Greek, Syriac, Persian, and Sanskrit.

Another indication of Mecca's marginalization was its comparatively anemic population growth. In the eleventh century the Iranian pilgrim Nasir-i Khusrau estimated that the permanent population of Mecca was no more than two thousand and that there were no more than five hundred foreign sojourners present during his visit. Even as late as the beginning of the twentieth century, Mecca's permanent population was only around eighty thousand. By contrast, ninth-century Baghdad boasted a population of between three hundred and five hundred thousand, making it the largest city in the world outside of China.

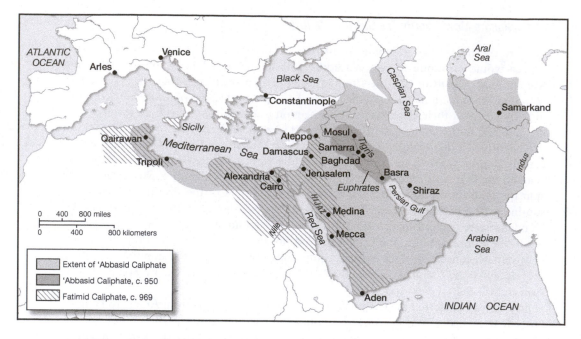

Map 8.1. ‘Abbasid Caliphate

Though the ‘Abbasid Caliphs survived until the Mongols devastated Baghdad in 1258, in reality, ‘Abbasid decline had been evident since the second half of the ninth century. By the tenth century, the ‘Abbasid state was conquered by the Shi‘i Buyid dynasty of northern Iran. Reduced to little more than a figurehead, the authority and prestige of the ‘Abbasid Caliphate was irrevocably damaged. This point is underscored by the Fatimid dynasty's rival claim to the Caliphate and their administration of the Hijaz.

However, Islam's imperial capitals could not afford to neglect Mecca entirely. Beginning with the Umayyad but especially during the ‘Abbasid period, it became customary for the Caliphs to make major investments in the Hijaz in order to demonstrate their piety and legitimate their political power. The Caliphs organized the pilgrimage caravans to Mecca. Each year they appointed an official, known as the *Amir al-Hajj*, to lead the pilgrimage. They took responsibility for maintaining the roads connecting the Hijaz and Syria and Iraq, and they protected them from Bedouin raids. They repaired the Ka‘ba, expanded the Meccan sanctuary, and made improvements to the Prophet's Mosque in Medina. Even more critical than the upkeep of Mecca's monuments was the need to maintain constantly the network of springs and aqueducts that supplied the city with a reliable source of fresh drinking water and to provision the region with grain transfers from Egypt.

Despite this patronage, from the seventh through the tenth century Mecca remained an unstable frontier, ripe for various forms of anti-Caliphal Shi‘i resistance and insurrection. During the Caliphal succession crisis that sparked the second Muslim civil war (680–692), the Umayyads found themselves completely cut off from the Hijaz when ‘Abd Allah ibn Zubayr claimed the title of Caliph for himself. Although the Zubayrids were eventually crushed in 692, the revolt is thought to have prompted Caliph ‘Abd al-Malik ibn Marwan (r. 685–705) to construct the Dome of the Rock in Jerusalem in hopes of building up an Umayyad-dominated shrine to rival Mecca.

In the early tenth century Mecca was once again a major site of Shi'i resistance. Around 900, the radical Qaramatian movement led a series of anti-'Abbasid revolts across Syria, Iraq, and northeastern Arabia, culminating in a bloody campaign against 'Abbasid pilgrimage caravans. The Qaramatian reign of terror climaxed in 930 when they attacked Mecca itself, slaughtering thousands of pilgrims, desecrating the well of Zamzam with the corpses, and stealing the Ka'ba's sacred Black Stone in an ill-fated attempt to redirect the pilgrimage away from Mecca.

Caliphs, Sultans, and Sharifs: Servants of the Two Holy Places

Although the Mongol destruction of Baghdad and the execution of the last 'Abbasid Caliph in 1258 is generally accepted as the effective death of the Caliphate, in reality this merely confirmed nearly three centuries of decline. Rival claims to the Caliphate by the Shi'i Fatimids (909–1171) of North Africa and Egypt had already begun to undermine the prestige and universality of the Caliphate. Although the infamous Ottoman ruler Abdülhamid II (r. 1876–1909) successfully revived the title during the late nineteenth century, for most of the last millennium the Caliphate has ceased to function as the center of Islamic authority. Despite this, Middle East historians have tended to lavish attention on the Caliphate and the numerous Muslim rulers who subsequently attempted resurrect it. By contrast, Mecca is curiously absent from the main narrative of Islamic history after the transfer of the Caliphate to Damascus in 661.

With the decay of 'Abbasid power, by the tenth century Mecca was increasingly left to its own devices. This paved the way for the growth of what has been called the Hijaz's "national dynasty," the Sharifs of Mecca. Although the Sharifs would eventually embrace Sunni Islam, in many respects their claims to nobility based on Qurayshi descent from 'Ali suggest that their origins were closely related to the anti-Caliphal Shi'i sentiments of the period. Between the ninth and eleventh centuries the formal title of Sharif evolved into a form of kingship over Mecca and the Hijaz. Although the Sharifs never achieved total independence from the militarily superior Fatimid (909–1171), Ayyubid (1169–1250), and Mamluk (1250–1517) Dynasties of Egypt or the later Ottoman Empire (ca. 1300–1923), the Sharifs largely maintained their autonomy by acknowledging the sovereignty of their imperial masters and pledging their cooperation in ensuring an orderly and stable pilgrimage. This tradition of semi-autonomous compromise with the great Muslim dynasties sustained Sharifal leadership in Mecca until 'Abd al-'Aziz ibn Sa'ud conquered the Hijaz in 1924, incorporating it into what is now the Kingdom of Saudi Arabia.

By the thirteenth century Mecca and the pilgrimage once again regained prominence as a source of political legitimacy. Because the title of Caliph had become so debased, however, a new claim to Islamic leadership emerged. Gradually the term *Khadim al-Haramayn al-Sharifayn* ("Servant of the Two Holy Places") gained currency. Curiously, no Caliph had used the title, presumably because protecting the Holy Places had always been considered an inherent duty of the office. The appearance of this novel method of claiming Islamic leadership is likely related to the fact that the leaders of the Ayyubid, Mamluk, and Ottoman Dynasties were all of Kurdish or Turkic origins. In other words, none of them could legitimately adopt the Caliphal title because they were not of Arab or Qurayshi descent.

The title first appears in a twelfth-century inscription associated with Saladin (d. 1193), the famous defender of Muslim lands against the Crusades and founder of the Ayyubid dynasty. The importance of the title continued to grow under the Mamluk sultans who took control of Egypt and Syria in 1250, and the Ottomans subsequently adopted it following their conquest of Egypt in 1517. In essence, the title came to function as a de facto claim to political leadership of the global Islamic community. Even today the title lives on: mired in a propaganda war with Ayatollah Khomeini's revolutionary Iran, the Saudi monarchy resurrected the title in 1986 in an attempt to bolster its sagging credibility.

The Rise of the Hajjis

Although the title Khadim al-Haramayn was naturally part political theater, it does appear that the duties the title implies were taken seriously. Each of the dynasties that adopted it took a lively interest in both the pageantry of the hajj and the efficient administration of the Hijaz. Taken together, these shifts of title and administrative functions signal both a usurpation of the duties previously reserved for the Caliph and the growing importance of the hajj. Particularly under the Ayyubids and the Mamluks, this meant a greater emphasis on securing the caravan routes. A judicious mixture of financial and food aid along with military threats, usually in the form of troops deployed alongside the annual pilgrimage caravans, was generally enough to secure the Sharifs' cooperation. For the Ayyubids and Mamluks, investing in the hajj was certainly good politics, but it was also economically lucrative. The hajj route from Cairo and Damascus was also the main artery of trade connecting Egypt and the Hijaz with the spice trade from India and Southeast Asia. Especially under the Mamluks, the port of Jidda blossomed into a flourishing Indian Ocean economic hub.

As Islamic societies from East Africa to China gradually took root, from the eleventh century until well into the age of European imperialism Muslim trade in the Indian Ocean expanded. (See Map 8.2.) Although historians have long understood the important role that seafaring merchants and colonists from Yemen and Oman played in the spread of Islam to parts of India, Indonesia, Malaysia, Kenya, and Zanzibar, less attention has been paid to the role that hajj-related travel and commerce played in integrating the Indian Ocean's economic system or the role that this increasing traffic played in diffusing civilizational norms and intellectual trends from Islamic heartlands of the eastern Mediterranean and the Arabian Peninsula to the farthest reaches of the expanding Islamic world.

Owing to the increased security and economic potential of pilgrimage-related trade, we see both an increase in the popularity of the hajj and the reemergence of Mecca and Medina as centers of Muslim intellectual life. During this period the hajj appears to have taken on a new importance at the individual level. Prior to 1200, surveys of Arabic biographical dictionaries of important Muslim personalities reveal no evidence of returning pilgrims adopting the title of *hajji* or *al-hajj*. By the early 1300s, however, the title had become fairly common. The growing popularity and respect for these titles was likely related to the increasing stability of the Hijaz during the Ayyubid and Mamluk periods.

The increasing popularity of the hajj likely stems from an overall rise in the number of converts to Islam. Despite the rapid conquest of North Africa, the Middle East, and Iran, as late as two centuries after this military expansion Muslims remained an elite minority. Substantial Christian populations remained in Iraq, Syria, and Egypt. Likewise, Iran continued to be home to large Zoroastrian populations. From the available evidence, it is unlikely that Iran and Iraq gained Muslim majorities until the eleventh century. However, in northern Mesopotamia and Syria conversion proceeded much slower, and the population

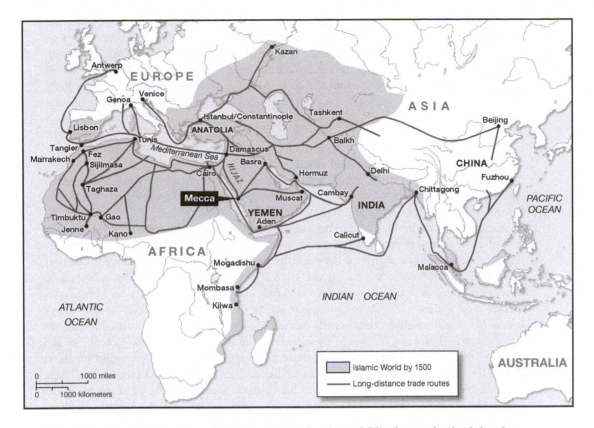

Map 8.2. Principal Routes of Long-Distance Trade and Pilgrimage in the Islamic World, ca. 1500

By the dawn of the sixteenth century, Islam had spread well beyond its original Arab heartland. Across the caravan routes of West Africa and the sea lanes of the Indian Ocean, Muslim merchant, pilgrimage, and missionary networks forged an increasingly cosmopolitan Islamic civilization. Despite the increasing diversity of the global Islamic community, however, the annual pilgrimage to Mecca helped to ensure that Islamic cultural norms diffused widely across vast distances.

retained a Christian majority until perhaps as late as the latter half of the thirteenth century. Taking into consideration the lag between Muslim conquests and the slow process of mass conversion helps explain why it took several centuries for the hajj to achieve its mass cultural appeal.

A closely related clue concerning the hajj's increased accessibility and popularity, particularly among non-Arabs, was the emergence of the powerful guilds of pilgrimage guides (*mutawwifin*) during the Mamluk period. At the most basic level they were responsible for guiding non-Arabic-speaking foreigners through the required prayers and rituals of the hajj. However, in time they became highly specialized, full-service guides and brokers, acting as interpreters; securing camel transport, lodgings, and food; and overseeing virtually every aspect of their customer's stay in the Hijaz. The mere existence of a demand for these services indicates that by at least the fifteenth century Muslims from Africa, Central Asia, India, and Southeast Asia were beginning to represent a larger portion of the pilgrimage traffic. Another indication of the growing security of the

Hijaz was that prior to this period lengthy sojourns in the Hijaz were much less common than they were in subsequent years. This was most likely due to the unreliability of food supplies needed to support a large year-round urban population. Both a lack of security and inadequate provisioning may also explain why institutions of higher learning (*madrasas*) were not established in Mecca or Medina prior to the late twelfth century. With the establishment of generous *waqf* funds (pious endowments) for these institutions, in later centuries pilgrims often combined the hajj with extended periods of study. The growth of these schools also provides important evidence of the Islamic world's increasing orientation to the Indian Ocean. Of the twenty-three madrasas founded prior to 1517, six were founded by Yemeni rulers and officials and three by Indian rulers. As these schools took root they became increasingly popular among non-Arab Muslims, attracting large numbers of students and permanent settlers from across the Indian Ocean, especially from India and Indonesia.

Another sign of the increasing importance of the hajj is the emergence of pilgrimage narratives as a distinct genre of Islamic literature. This genre was especially prominent in Islamic Spain and North Africa between the twelfth and fifteenth centuries, but they eventually became common across the Islamic world. Though normally centered on Mecca and the hajj, these accounts provided rich descriptions of the famous personages, shrines, and academic institutions across much of the Islamic world. Not unlike today's *Lonely Planet* guides, these manuscripts created popular itineraries and warned of hazards along the way. The most famous of these works is undoubtedly the *Rihla* (travels) of Ibn Battuta (1304–1368). As his travels illustrate, particularly for the Islamic world's learned classes the comingling of the pilgrimage with higher learning provided access to far-flung professional and commercial contacts. This fostered a high degree of social mobility, which in turn facilitated the flow of intellectual trends, goods, and technologies between the Muslim heartland and the frontiers of Islamic civilization.

GLOBAL ENCOUNTERS AND CONNECTIONS:
A Coveted City in the Colonial Crossfire

In many respects Ibn Battuta's travels belong to a lost age of Muslim dominance. Virtually everywhere he roamed between Morocco and China was under some form of Muslim rule. Despite crossing numerous cultural and linguistic boundaries, his writings exude the cosmopolitan confidence of a man whose Islamic learning and legal skills were marketable across much of the known world. Unlike European travel narratives, which emphasize the author's "discovery" or "exploration" of exotic locales, the unity of Islamic civilization almost always mitigated Ibn Battuta's experience of difference.

After 1500 that Islamic world began to unravel. In coming centuries European maritime exploration and expansion would bring conflict and exploitation to most of the Islamic world. Neither Mecca's remote location nor its sacred status completely shielded it from the changes that Europe's expansion wrought. The first harbinger of this global power shift came when Portuguese explorer Vasco da Gama rounded the Cape of Good Hope in 1498. In a matter of a few years the Portuguese established themselves as the preeminent naval power in the Indian Ocean. Until then internal Muslim rivalries had posed the greatest danger to Mecca's security; the closest that a European military force had come to Mecca was during the famous Crusader Reynaud de Chatillon's surprise attack on the Hijaz's Red Sea ports in 1181. Although Crusader piracy in the Red Sea had been a nuisance, it never posed a sustained threat to Mecca.

The Portuguese threat, however, was of an entirely different order. As the Portuguese seized control of Indian Ocean commerce they began to systematically strangle the Mamluks' lucrative spice trade by blockading the Red Sea. In addition to gravely undermining the Mamluk economy, Portuguese naval superiority left Mecca painfully vulnerable. Fearing an attack, the Mamluks (and later the Ottomans) worked feverishly to fortify Jidda. Although the attack never materialized, Mecca was in fact in grave danger. As the Portuguese admiral Afonso de Albuquerque made clear in a letter to his king, he intended nothing short of the destruction of Mecca and the conquest of the spice trade.

Although the Mamluks and their Ottoman successors were able to fend off the immediate Portuguese threat, in the long run European supremacy was inescapable. By the nineteenth century the British, Dutch, French, and Russians had all seized sizable colonial possessions in Muslim lands. Especially as Britain's power in India grew, so too did its naval supremacy in the Indian Ocean and Red Sea. The development of steamship routes between the Mediterranean and India and the opening of the Suez Canal in 1869 further intensified British interest in the Red Sea. These transportation advances put the once-peripheral Ottoman Hijaz alongside the main artery of trade between the Indian Ocean and Europe. As a result, the region became an object of British strategic interest. British influence on the Hijaz ultimately culminated in an alliance with Sharif Husayn during World War I, leading to the 1916 Arab Revolt that overturned four centuries of Ottoman rule and completely redrew the map of the Arab Middle East. However, Sharif Husayn's British-backed rule proved exceedingly short. In 1924 Saudi expansion from the east overran Mecca. With the Saudi conquest came a stricter, more puritanical version of Islam known as Wahhabism; to this day Wahhabism is the official religious doctrine of the Saudi state. Through a combination of its petroleum-based economic might and control of Mecca and Medina, the monarchy has successfully exported its extreme brand of Islamic thought across much of the Muslim world.

The advent of steamship travel and colonial-era interventions also had other unforeseen consequences. The steamship led to a dramatic increase in the number of ordinary Muslims who could afford to make the pilgrimage to Mecca. Owing to the rising numbers of pilgrims crowding aboard steamships, the hajj became a conduit for the globalization of epidemic cholera and plague. As Europe and the Ottoman Empire struggled to prevent further outbreaks, the pilgrimage became a constant subject of international scrutiny. For the first time ever non-Muslims would regulate pilgrimage transportation, require passports, and enforce public health controls. Thus, although Mecca itself never came under direct colonial control, virtually every aspect of the hajj did come under European administration.

With the rise of air travel most twenty-first-century pilgrims no longer endure tortuous camel caravans or dangerous oceanic passages. Today pilgrims arrive at Jidda's state-of-the-art hajj air terminal and are whisked away by the brand-new Mecca Metro system. Indeed, pilgrims arriving at the Grand Mosque, now ringed by gaudy skyscrapers, would scarcely recognize the tiny Ottoman town of a century ago. Yet in many respects the Kingdom of Saudi Arabia's bureaucratization of the hajj is in fact a continuation of the policies hammered out between the Ottomans and their European counterparts over a century ago. The Saudi oil wealth that has funded Mecca's redevelopment and modernization is likewise an echo of the Arabian Peninsula's absorption into the European-dominated world economy of the nineteenth century.

ENCOUNTERS AS TOLD: PRIMARY SOURCES

The primary sources below represent two very different eras of Meccan history. The first comes from *The Travels of Ibn Battuta* and reflects his experience of the fourteenth-century overland pilgrimage caravan. The second comes from a late nineteenth-century Ottoman physician's observations of the biological and political hazards facing pilgrims of the steamship era.

The Travels of Ibn Battuta

Often dubbed the Islamic Marco Polo, Ibn Battuta left his native Morocco to perform the hajj in 1324. Though he initially planned to make the hajj and study Islamic law, instead he embarked on a twenty-nine-year odyssey taking him across much of North and West Africa, Arabia, Central Asia, the Indian Ocean, and even to China. Here, Ibn Battuta describes his experience of the camel caravan between Damascus and Mecca in 1326.

- What are Ibn Battuta's primary concerns in this text?

- What does Ibn Battuta's account tell us about the nature of travel in the fourteenth century?

- What is the importance of water for the overland pilgrimage?

The enormous caravan camps near the spring, and everybody satisfies his thirst. The pilgrims stay here for four days to refresh themselves, water their camels, and stock up on water for the even more fearsome emptiness between Tabuk and Ula. The water bearers set up buffalo-hide tanks beside the spring, filling them up like reservoirs. They water the camels and also fill water bags for the caravan and smaller skins for individuals. Each amir and person of rank has a private tank; the rest of the pilgrims make arrangements with the bearers for a fixed amount of money. Then the whole caravan leaves Tabuk and pushes on with haste, traveling night and day without stopping, for the wilderness is at its worst here. Halfway through lies the valley of Ukhaidar, which might be more aptly named Valley of Hell. One year the hajjis suffered terribly in this place, for the *samoom* [poison wind] began blowing, their waterskins dried up, and the price of a drink rose to a thousand dinars. Both seller and buyer perished. The story is inscribed on one of the rocks as you pass through the valley. . . .

Five days beyond Tabuk the pilgrims reach the well of Thamud, which is full of water. In spite of their violent thirst, however, nobody draws a single bucket from this well, for the Prophet, when he passed there, told his people not to drink from it. (A few had already used the water to make dough; they subsequently fed it to their camels.) Here the dwellings of ancient Thamud stand carved into the hills, hewn out of reddish rock with elaborately decorated thresholds that look quite modern. Their builders' bones lie turning to dust inside them, "a real sign for those with eyes to see."

From Thamud to Ula is about a half-day journey. It is a large, pleasant village with palm groves and springs. Here the pilgrims stop for four nights to re-provision and to wash their clothes. The local people are honest and many pilgrims leave surplus provisions on deposit with them for the return journey, taking along only what they may need to reach Medina. Ula marks a boundary line, south of which the Syrian Christian merchants may not go. These people trade in provisions and goods with the pilgrims.

The day after the caravan leaves this town, the pilgrims camp in the valley of Itas. The heat here is killing and the fatal *samoom* is common. The last time it blew in this season, only a few pilgrims escaped with their lives. Past Itas they camp at Hadiyya, a place with underground water in a valley, where they dig shallow pits and water magically appears, but it is brackish. On the third day out we caught sight of the sanctified city of Medina, the City of the Prophet. . . .

When it came time to leave Medina and head for Mecca, we halted near Dhu al-Hulayfa mosque, where the Prophet himself put on his pilgrim clothes for the Farewell Hajj. The mosque is five miles from Medina near the stream of Aqiq. It marks the limit of Medina's sacred territory. Here, I put away my tailored clothes, bathed, put on my consecrated lengths of unstitched cotton, and performed the customary prayers. I entered the life of a pilgrim at this stage, stating my intention to perform the Hajj as a rite separate from the Umra. I felt such enthusiasm then that I took up the chant of the caravan and went on with it through every hill and valley until we reached the pass of Ali, where we stopped for the night.

Source: *The Travels of Ibn Battuta*, in *One Thousand Roads to Mecca: Ten Centuries of Travelers Writing about the Muslim Pilgrimage*, edited by Michael Wolfe (New York: Grove Press, 1997), 62–63.

"Interview with an Indian Muslim Doctor, the English Vice-Consul," from Dr. M. Şakir Bey's *Memoirs of the Hijaz*

The second excerpt comes from the recollections of an Ottoman physician, Mehmed Şakir Bey, who was dispatched from Istanbul to report on the public health conditions of the Hijaz and Yemen in 1890. His account demonstrates just how much the administration of Mecca and the hajj evolved over time. By the late nineteenth century the Ottomans could no longer attend to the affairs of the Hijaz without consulting the European colonial powers. His report also underscores how the personal experience of pilgrimage had changed. The hazards and obstacles facing pilgrims had been transformed from the foreboding desert expanses Ibn Battuta described into a deadly gauntlet of poverty, lethal epidemics, quarantines, and international border controls.

- How has transportation technology evolved between Ibn Battuta's and Mehmed Şakir Bey's accounts?

- How does Mehmed Şakir Bey's perspective on the hajj differ from Ibn Battuta's because he is a government official and a doctor as opposed to a pilgrim?

- What does Mehmed Şakir Bey's description of the administration of the hajj tell us about European influence over Mecca and the rest of the Islamic world?

England's Acting Consul in Jidda, named Doctor 'Abd al-Razzaq, an Indian Muslim doctor, is an individual of medium height and build and very heavily deaf. When we went to visit him with another Indian man, he respectfully welcomed us at the door. After shaking hands and having coffee with this very deaf disabled physician, first I wanted to check his opinion concerning how this terrible cholera epidemic came to the Hijaz. His translator, a young teen-ager from Jidda, yelled loudly into his left ear so that he could hear our reply.

After collecting himself for a moment, he answered our question in the following way:

"[Cholera] came by sea from Kamaran [Island]. It was brought by the steamship, the

Deccan. The *Deccan's* 1,200 passengers, consisting of pilgrims, waited on Kamaran for 70 days. I received news that approximately 50 pilgrims from among them died as a result of spending the hajj period at the Kamaran Island quarantine station. Prior to that cholera was not present at Mecca.

Later, they loaded 1,200 Indian pilgrims onto an English steamship called the "Hive." However, the capacity of this steamship was only 900. I received news that between Jidda and Aden 300 Indian pilgrims were thrown overboard into the sea because they overloaded the steamship with 400 more pilgrims than the ship's capacity. Even though I have not actually gone on the hajj this year, in years past I have seen that if the rains come at Mina it causes cholera to appear immediately afterwards."

[Doctor 'Abd al-Razzaq says], according to his research: "Cholera first originated from a few of your naval troops on the corvette, the *Muzaffer.*" Upon Doctor 'Abd al-Razzaq saying that, signaling with my hand to the translator, [Mehmed Şakir Bey says], "I have something to tell the Consul. Please speak into his ear. My statement is this: Thank you for saying that cholera first appeared in Kamaran with the *Deccan* steamship. With his permission I would also like to say that this year in Mina cholera was first seen among the elderly Indians. Since the outbreak could not be put under observation, when the Indian pilgrimage guides came to the health administration to apply for the death certificates of those poor Indians who died in the tents in order to bury them in the cemetery of Masjid al-Khayf in Mina they were officially asked the cause of death. To which they replied: 'yâ efendim miskîn vecâ'ân mine'z-zaman! Yemşi batnî.'*

That is to say, the corpse was that of a very poor man who had been suffering from this illness for a long time and whose stomach was distended. In the beginning they could not diagnose cholera on the corpses of the Indians. By confessing that he died from this they were claiming that this situation was a deadly illness which is specific to the Hijaz and which causes many deaths, such as either a chronic diarrhea or a severe case of bloody hemorrhoids.

Many times I saw that they were brought to the basement of the Mina hospital in a state in which their skins clung to their bones specifically because people who are extremely thin like the Indian poor become twice as emaciated under the effects of cholera. However, two soldiers from the navy were extremely sick in their tents and had to be brought to the hospital. Even those with light cases had to be brought to the hospital. However, those two who were very ill had to be carried on their friends' backs.

When they entered the hospital cholera was officially announced. Since within a few hours Mina's hospital was filled with poor Indians and in Mecca and other places most deaths were among the Indian poor and destitute I thought that it would not leave any room for objection. However, the translator said, "Sir, since it would take a long time to explain all these things and, in any case, the disease has already subsided in Jidda. If there is any other important question that you would like to ask I would be happy to translate it." In response to this, [I asked the following question.] "Well, as for India's poor, by coming to make the hajj without enough money for shelter, by begging they act in a manner that is discouraged in Islamic law (*shari'a*) and [socially] inappropriate. They wander the streets until dawn crying out '*yâ Rab, yâ Kerîm*' [oh Lord, oh Most Generous]. Later many pass away and one witnesses that those who come after [the completion of] the

---

*The phrase "*Yemşi batnî*" is an Ottoman Turkish corruption of the Arabic phrase "*Yamshi alá batnihi.*" By comparing the poor to those who creep upon their bellies, the speaker is referring to the following passage from *Sura al-Nur*: "And Allah has created every animal of the water. So of them is that which crawls upon its belly, and of them is that which walks upon two feet, and of them is that which walks upon four. Allah creates what He pleases. Surely Allah is Possessor of power over all things." See Qur'an 24:45.

hajj experience many hardships and difficulties. What is your opinion of not allowing those thousands of poor and beggars to come to the Hijaz?"

Answer: For the last four years I have been writing to the Governor of India about poor Indians not coming to the hajj. The answer that I received, which I still have, roughly states: 'Since there is freedom of religion among the English, I can never be in a position to prevent the poor from coming to the hajj.'

The Governor of India's position was motivated by his fear of provoking a great disturbance and a revolt. Owing to this fear he could not find any other solution. Thus, they offer every form of social assistance to intending pilgrims.

In short, the reports that I submitted four or five times concerning this important issue were left unanswered. Recently, I received news that my dear friend Doctor Dickson, the Embassy's doctor in Istanbul, wanted to raise this matter with the Board of Health. However, the Vice President of the Board of Health would not grant permission and immediately responded by saying "this is a matter of religion. This is not the appropriate place to discuss it." There is only one way for the extremely poor people of India to be prohibited from going on hajj. This can only be accomplished by the central government's Minister of Foreign Affairs sending a memorandum to the embassies in Istanbul. Future Indians intending on making the hajj should have to show their passports to the Ottoman *şehbender* [Ottoman commercial representative or Consul in a foreign port] in Bombay. The Ottoman Consulate should be able to examine whether or not Indians intending on making the hajj have enough money for the journey to Mecca and back. Those without money should not have their passports approved. . . .

Primary source title: Hicaz'ın Ahval-ı Ummumiye-i Sıhhiye ve Islahât-ı Esâsiye-i Hâzırasına Dair Bazı Müşahedat ve Mülahazât-ı Bendegânemi Hâvî Bir Lâyiha-i Tıbbiye (A Medical Memorandum Concerning Some of My Observations and Thoughts on the Current Public Health Conditions and Fundamental Reforms of the Hijaz).

Source: Gülden Sarıyıldız and Ayşe Kavak, eds., Halife II. Abdülhamid'in Hac Siyaseti: Dr. M.Şakir Bey'in Hicaz Hatıraları (The Caliph Abdülhamid II's Politics of Hajj: Dr. M.Şakir Bey's Memoirs of the Hijaz) (Istanbul: Timaş, 2009), 297–300. **English translation by Michael Christopher Low and Züleyha Çolak.**

Further Reading

Bianchi, Robert. *Guests of God: Pilgrimage and Politics in the Islamic World.* Oxford: Oxford University Press, 2004.

Bulliet, Richard. "The History of the Muslim South." *Al-'Usur al-Wusta: The Bulletin of Middle East Medievalists* 20, no. 2 (2008): 59–64.

Cook, Michael. *Muhammad.* Oxford: Oxford University Press, 1983.

deGaury, Gerald. *Rulers of Mecca.* New York: Dorset Press, 1991.

Dunn, Ross. *The Adventures of Ibn Battuta: A Muslim Traveler of the Fourteenth Century,* 2nd ed. Berkeley and Los Angeles: University of California Press, 2004.

Low, Michael Christopher. "Empire and the Hajj: Pilgrims, Plagues, and Pan-Islam under British Surveillance, 1865–1908." *International Journal of Middle East Studies* 40, no. 2 (2008): 269–290.

Mortel, Richard. "Madrasas in Mecca during the Medieval Period: A Descriptive Study Based on Literary Sources." *Bulletin of the School of Oriental and African Studies* 60, no. 2 (1997): 236–252.

Ochsenwald, William. *Religion, Society, and the State in Arabia: The Hijaz under Ottoman Control, 1840–1908.* Columbus: Ohio State University Press, 1984.

Peters, F. E. *The Hajj: The Muslim Pilgrimage to Mecca and the Holy Places.* Princeton, NJ: Princeton University Press, 1994.

———. *Mecca: A Literary History of the Muslim Holy Land.* Princeton, NJ: Princeton University Press, 1994.

Wolfe, Michael, ed. *One Thousand Roads to Mecca: Ten Centuries of Travelers Writing about the Muslim Pilgrimage.* New York: Grove Press, 1997.

Yamani, Mai. *Cradle of Islam: The Hijaz and the Quest for Identity in Saudi Arabia.* London: I. B. Tauris, 2004.

Web Resources

The Ministry of Hajj, Kingdom of Saudi Arabia, www.hajinformation.com/index.htm.

Nicolai Ourousoff, "New Look for Mecca: Gaudy and Gargantuan," *The New York Times,* December 29, 2010, www.nytimes.com/2010/12/30/arts/design/30mecca.html.

The Rituals of Hajj and Umrah and the Virtual Hajj, www.princeton.edu/~humcomp/vhajj.html.

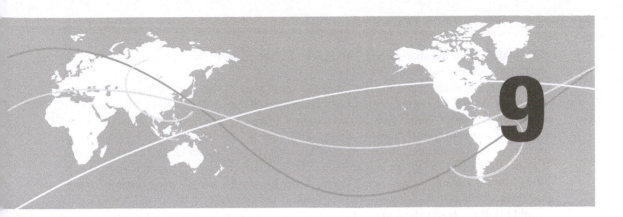

Kilwa

A Commercial City in the Economic and Cultural Cross-Currents

(1000–1500)

ERIK GILBERT

MANY PEOPLE VISIT THE SITES OF SWAHILI CITIES. ON KENYA'S NORTH COAST Lamu is an essential stop for backpackers, fashion photographers, and the European jet set. Gedi, a couple of hundred miles south of Lamu, is billed as the Pompeii of East Africa and is a regular feature on the tourist route. Visitors come to Mombasa because it is the most important port city in East Africa and to Malindi because it has a thriving beach (and sex) tourism industry. Just to the south in Tanzania tourists flock to the island of Zanzibar, some to visit the beaches and others to see the historic Stone Town with its narrow streets and romantic decrepitude. On the mainland the Kunduchi ruins just outside the city of Dar es Salaam are a frequent stop on the way to the beach hotels north of the city. Kilwa, however, is visited by only the most committed Swahili ruins enthusiasts. To get there one must make a fairly arduous overland journey from Dar es Salaam and then go by boat to the island, where the ruins of the city lie. Though there is now a town on the mainland called Kilwa, the original site was on the island, abandoned since the sixteenth century. Kilwa's isolation today means that one really has to want to visit the place to end up there. I have made

145

it to all the sites listed above along with dozens of more obscure sites on Zanzibar, Pemba, and Mafia islands, but Kilwa has thus far eluded me.

I first became interested in Kilwa and the other cites of the East African coast as an undergraduate. I had spent most of my childhood living in West Africa, moving from Ghana to Nigeria to Cameroun. In each of these places we lived in cities, although in the course of our travels we saw many villages and, very occasionally, wildlife. Thus, my experience of Africa was essentially urban. When we were back in the United States on leave I realized that cities were not something that my American peers associated with Africa. Kids I met would ask if I saw lions. This is rather like an African meeting someone from, say, Philadelphia, and asking if he worries about the grizzly bear menace. Other people would ask if my family lived in a hut—we did not. Through these kinds of questions, I realized that cities were not the first thing that came to people's minds when they thought of Africa; instead, they thought of villages and wilderness. But my Africa, the Africa of my memories, was one of cars, buses, crowds, noise, and buildings. It was all about the city.

Likewise, my scholarly interest in Africa has always been about cities. I took my first African history class in college at a time when my parents were living in Dar es Salaam, Tanzania. During a visit on summer break, while on our way to the beach, we stopped to visit a small group of ruins. I had seen ruins before in Africa—slave trade castles in Ghana, some pre–World War I German plantations in Cameroun, and the abandoned Safari Club, a colonial-era nightclub on a mountaintop outside of Yaoundé, Cameroun, that looked like a place where Humphrey Bogart's Rick might have set up shop after giving up the lease on his café in *Casablanca*. But these ruins were different. They predated the colonial period by a good three hundred years and it was obvious that what we were looking at was not a village—it was a small city. It was a bit of the African past that resonated with my experience of the African present. Those ruins stuck with me, and when I went to graduate school, it was the Swahili coast and its cities that I studied. I wrote my dissertation and first book about Zanzibar, but I always remained interested in the once-bustling, now-abandoned and isolated Kilwa, which to me embodied the Swahili world at its peak.

Kilwa served as a major trade center that effectively monopolized the East African gold trade, reaching the height of its cultural and commercial success from the thirteenth to fifteenth centuries. When the Portuguese arrived in Kilwa shortly after 1500, they were awestruck by the built environment of the city and determined to take advantage of the rich resources and trade on the Swahili coast. Kilwa, a commercial city, was unprepared for military assault and quickly fell. This chapter will review Kilwa's rise and fall as well as the legacy left behind through historical records and its modern-day ruins.

KILWA AND THE WORLD:
A City in the Cross-Currents of Indian Ocean Trade

Kilwa is on a small island about 90 miles (145 kilometers) south of Dar es Salaam, the capital of the modern nation of Tanzania. (See Map 9.1.) It is near the Rufiji Delta, where Tanzania's biggest river enters the Indian Ocean. The channel that separates the island from the coast is shallow and not very wide. Like many Swahili cities, Kilwa is situated in a place where land and sea intermingle. The island is part of a complex estuary with many small inlets and islands. (See Map 9.2.) Kilwa was among the most important of the Swahili cities, and its location serves as a sort of metaphor of the nature of Swahili society. The Swahili occupy the narrow coastal strip from southern Somalia to northern Mozambique, with the majority of the Swahili people living in Kenya and Tanzania. On the most basic level, to be Swahili is to be Muslim, to speak the Swahili language, and to be urban

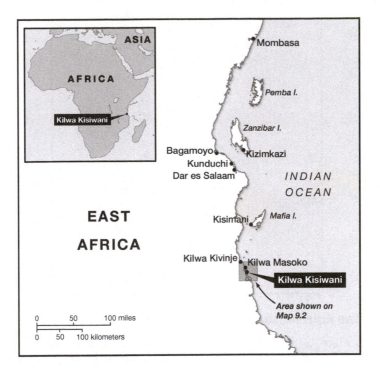

Map 9.1. East African Coast, ca. 1450

Kilwa was one of many city states on the East African coast. During the period between 1200 and 1500, Kilwa in the south and Mombasa in the north were the largest and commercially dominant towns in the region.

(or at least to be in the political or economic shadow of a city). But there is more to it than that. Just as the estuarine site of the city of Kilwa blurs the line between land and sea, the Swahili world is rooted on the land but strongly influenced by the sea. What distinguished the Swahili from the people of the interior, whom they dismissively referred to as *Washenzi*, or savages, was their access to the trading world of the Indian Ocean. Islam, luxury items like cloth and ceramics, and various foods that were unique to the coast, all came to the Swahili world courtesy of the trade networks that linked towns like Kilwa into a system that stretched from the Mediterranean to the South China Sea.

In the fourteenth century when the Indian Ocean trade was booming, Kilwa was anything but a backwater. Its sultans, who sometimes claimed origins in the Persian city of Shiraz and at others in the Hadhramaut region of Yemen, minted their own coins, built a mosque that is believed to have been the largest enclosed space in sub-Saharan Africa, and hosted visitors and merchants from around the Indian Ocean. When the Swahili coast was at its cultural and economic height from the thirteenth through the fifteenth centuries, Kilwa's only real regional rival was Mogadishu, located in present-day Somalia. When the Portuguese arrived in Kilwa shortly after 1500, they were awestruck by the built environment of the city. An early Portuguese account of the Southeast Asian city of Malacca (near modern Singapore) mentioned the presence of merchants from Kilwa, a sign of the city's far-reaching engagement with Indian Ocean trade, though it appears that the Swahili hosted merchants in their cities more often than they ventured as far afield as Malacca.

147

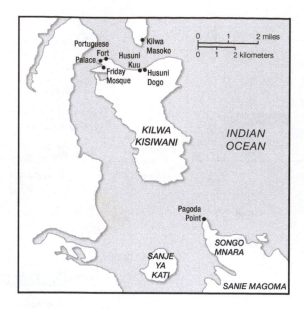

Map 9.2. Kilwa Kisiwani, ca. 1400–1600

This map shows a detailed view of the site of Kilwa Kisiwani (Kilwa on the Island). The city's island location offered access to the sea and the coast, while making the city difficult to invade from the mainland.

Kilwa's history can open a number of windows for us. As the archetypical city of the Swahili coast when it was at its maximum, it offers us a view of the rise of the Swahili in the context of the Indian Ocean world. From 1000 to 1500 the Indian Ocean was the economic center of gravity for most of Eurasia and Africa, and the rise of the Swahili sites occurred in the economic and cultural cross-currents of the Indian Ocean. As a place that was urban—even urbane—Kilwa's story also challenges some of our deeply held ideas about Africa's past. Kilwa has also been at the center of one of the great debates among African historians: the argument over the role of non-Africans in the development of states and other institutions in the continent and the opposing view that sees Africans as the primary forces in their own history. Finally, Kilwa's decline is as historically interesting as is its rise. Its transformation from major commercial center and thriving port to isolated ruins brings into view major shifts in the economic and political geography of the Indian Ocean that took place shortly after 1500.

The World of the Swahili

From very early times the east coast of Africa has been in contact with the other lands of the Indian Ocean rim. The evidence for the earliest of these contacts is indirect. A cluster of food crops of Asian origin, including a type of banana as well as other less familiar crops, appeared in West and Central Africa in the first millennium and presumably passed through East Africa to get there, although no evidence of that passage has been found. The first documentary evidence that mentions the world of the Swahili comes to us in the form of a merchant's guide to the Indian Ocean. Dating from the early part of the first millennium, the *Periplus of the Erythrean Sea* was written in Greek, probably by a

Greco-Roman merchant from Egypt. It describes the routes that merchants should follow to get to the various trading ports of the Indian Ocean and what to expect when they arrive. The portions that deal with East Africa indicate that trade to East Africa was in the hands of Arab merchants, who sailed down the coast to a place called Rhapta, where they bought ivory, tortoise shell, beeswax, and slaves in exchange for cloth, grain, wine, and iron. Archaeologists remain uncertain where Rhapta was or even whether it was a permanent settlement or only occupied seasonally during the trading season. Most readings of the distances indicated in the *Periplus* suggest that Rhapta was somewhere in either modern Tanzania or Kenya. A prominent Tanzanian archaeologist, Felix Chami, considers the most likely location to be near the mouth of the Rufigi River in Tanzania—right in the heart of the region where the Swahili civilization would eventually take shape and very close to the eventual location of Kilwa.

The *Periplus* does not say much about the people with whom these Arab merchants traded, only that they built sewn boats and fished with a type of fish weir still in use in East Africa today. The name *Rhapta* may derive from the Arabic word for bound or sewn, and as such it may refer to the boats these people made. The consensus now is that by 100 to 300 CE, shortly after the time of the *Periplus*, Bantu-speaking farmers inhabited the coast. Prior to their arrival the coast was occupied by foragers and herders who did not disappear with the arrival of farming; herders in particular seem to have been in fairly close contact with the emerging farming communities on the coast.

By the middle of the first millennium a society that we might describe as proto-Swahili, in that they lived on the coast (the term *Swahili* means "people of the coast" in Arabic) but had not yet accepted Islam or begun to build cities, emerged on the East African coast. Small communities that not only farmed but also exploited the area's resources dotted the coast, but there is little evidence of maritime trade. Between 800 and 900 CE, however, pottery from the Middle East, beads, and other items become increasingly common in Swahili communities, suggesting that they were engaged in long-distance trade with other regions of the Indian Ocean.

The increasing tempo of Indian Ocean trade and its growing importance in coastal communities had a transformative effect on the towns of the Swahili coast. Some of them grew in scale, becoming cities rather than towns. They became much more hierarchical and were dominated by a merchant elite, conventionally called "patricians," who used imported goods and foods as markers of their social status. Between 800 and 1000 their inhabitants accepted Islam, making them members of a vast religious, intellectual, and cultural community that not only reached across the ocean to Asia and North Africa but also distinguished them from their non-Muslim neighbors on the coast and in the interior. In time they began to build public buildings, like mosques, in stone. Later the homes of the wealthy came to also be built in stone, though common people continued to live in mud-and-coral rag houses. They also began to use a language that is clearly ancestral to the modern language of Swahili. By 1000 the coast had become Swahili, and Kilwa was growing into one of the new cities that characterized the Swahili coast.

Kilwa's Origin Myths

Because most sub-Saharan African societies were nonliterate, historians of Africa have few internally generated written documents to work with, especially for the earlier periods of the continent's history. The Swahili coast is an exception. The Swahili embrace of Islam brought with it the religious obligation to read the Quran, which led to the spread of literacy in Arabic, at least among religious scholars and leaders, and eventually to the use of Arabic script to write both Swahili and Arabic. Although there is not the wealth of written documentation that one would find in European or Chinese archives, the city of Kilwa has two written histories. The first and oldest is known as the "Arabic History of Kilwa," and the second and probably more recent is the "Swahili History," both named as such because the former was written in Arabic and the latter in Swahili. The Arabic history came from the papers of an Islamic scholar, and though the only surviving manuscript dates from 1867, the original text is thought to date from the early 1500s. A German linguist collected the Swahili history in 1889. It was mostly likely an oral history that he had someone recite to him and then transcribed. Although the outline of both texts is similar, there are some differences in the names given to sultans and the details of events. It is also worth noting that any histories or chronicles composed during the period we are examining (900–1500) have been lost; a tropical environment does not favor the preservation of paper or parchment. There are, however, many brief dated inscriptions on tombs and mosques that help historians to flesh out the chronology of the various towns. The Swahili were also among a very small group of sub-Saharan Africans who produced coins. Because Islam discourages the representation of humans or animals, these coins have the names of the rulers who struck them and the dates of their production inscribed on them. The rulers of Kilwa were particularly prolific coin makers, so the names and reign dates of Kilwa's kings are well established.

Both contain a story about the origins of Kilwa, but because the Arabic history is more detailed, we will use its version. The story begins in the Persian city of Shiraz in the ninth century. Interestingly Shiraz is quite far inland, so it's hard to imagine that it ever had direct trade contacts with East Africa; here it seems to be representing Persia in a sort of generic sense. According to the Arabic History the sultan of Shiraz had a dream that foretold the collapse of his kingdom. In response, Sultan Husein and his six sons took to the sea, each in his own ship. Each ship stopped at different places on the East African coast, and the ship that came to Kilwa was the vessel of Ali ibn Husein (Ali son of Husein).

When Ali arrived at the island of Kilwa, he met a man named Muriri wa Bari. Muriri was a Muslim, and Kilwa already had a mosque. However, it was by a non-Muslim (an "infidel" in the text) from the mainland ruled Kilwa. The king was away on the mainland hunting but was expected back soon. When the king returned, Ali asked him if he could buy the island and settle on it. The king agreed and asked that, as payment, the island be encircled in cloth. This he collected and took with him to the mainland. In the Swahili version Ali actually covers the area between the island and mainland with cloth, allowing the king to walk to the mainland on a cloth causeway. That Ali had access to so much cloth earned him the epithet *Nguo Nyingi*, which is Swahili for "many clothes." Apparently, however, the king was not satisfied even with this vast quantity of cloth and decided to retake the island by force. Muriri wa Bari suspected the king might do something like this and warned Ali of the danger. In the Arabic history Ali responds by having his followers dig out the channel between the island and the mainland, making it too deep for the king and his army to cross. The Swahili history depicts Ali using a much more interesting and symbolic defense: instead of digging out the channel, Ali reads from the Quran and offers sacrifices to make the channel impassible to the king, in effect using the power of religion rather than shovels to protect the island from threats from the mainland. Also noteworthy in the Swahili history is that when he first arrives, Ali marries one of the infidel king's daughters.

These are stories that tell us more about how the Swahili saw their place in the world than they do about the origins of Swahili towns. However, there is much that is historically interesting about these stories, and archaeology can corroborate some of the material in them. First, a major aspect of Swahili identity concerns the idea of foreign origins. Elite families all over the coast claim either Arab or Persian origins. In fact, many of the people whom scholars (and books like the one you are reading) designate as Swahili refer to themselves as "Shirazi." Although there has certainly been migration to East Africa from the Arab and Persian worlds, most of the coastal population is of local, African origin. What defines them as a people, however, is their cultural and commercial connections to places on the other side of the Indian Ocean. Thus, the cloth that Ali brought with him and used to purchase his new home is imported cloth, a mainstay of Indian Ocean trade and an important marker of social status for Swahili elites. But it is not simply cloth that distinguishes Ali from the king. Islam—especially in the Swahili history—another defining quality of Swahili identity, completes the separation of Ali's island realm from the non-Muslim mainland. Thus, the importance of things foreign—people, objects, and religion—to the Swahili is established in these two histories.

At the same time, it is worth noting that when Ali, Kilwa's "founder," shows up, there is already a community of some sort on the island, including a Muslim population. Muriri wa Bari's name suggests that he was not an Arab or Persian but rather a Swahili Muslim. That the Kilwa chronicle has Ali marry the king's daughter suggests that the social distance between the Muslim people of the island and the non-Muslim people of the coast was not that great. Even Ali's epithet, Nguo Nyingi, is telling in that though it refers to his access to foreign trade goods, it is also in the local language, Swahili, not in Persian or Arabic. Ali may have been from Persia, but the histories are quick to embed him in local culture. The society that developed in Kilwa and on the rest of the Swahili coast reflected the mixing that is apparent in the two histories. The Swahili towns were neither African (in the usual essentialized sense of the term) nor were they Arab or Persian colonies; rather, they are probably best described as part of the Indian Ocean world.

Kilwa's Transformation

According to the Arabic history the founding of Kilwa occurred in the middle of the third century of the Islamic calendar, which would be roughly 875 CE. This date matches up with the archaeological record in an interesting way. Kilwa and the region surrounding it were certainly settled prior to the late ninth century. Kilwa itself was one of a number of small villages in the region, many of which appear to have been repeatedly occupied and abandoned, perhaps because their inhabitants practiced shifting cultivation. But between 750 and 1200 Kilwa, like many other sites on the Swahili coast, experienced a transformation. It grew in size relative to its neighbors, an elite class emerged, and some of its buildings began to be made of stone rather than mud. In short, it became a city.

How this process occurred is not entirely clear, but both written and archaeological records suggest that Kilwa's connection to the commercial and cultural world of the Indian Ocean triggered the change. The written record speaks of the importance of imported cloth probably from Gujarat in India and of Islam as defining qualities of the Swahili cities. The archaeological record indicates that during this time imported pottery became available in places like Kilwa that were emerging as cities but not in the surrounding communities. Combined, these suggest the centrality of Indian Ocean trade to the development of Kilwa and the other Swahili towns.

Around 900 CE the Indian Ocean as a whole was experiencing a maritime revolution. In the western Indian Ocean this meant the development of new types of sails and the replacement of fragile steering oars with much more effective and sturdy rudders. The type of vessel that emerged as the characteristic ship in the region is called a *dhow*, and these vessels served to integrate the world of the Swahili into the broader Indian Ocean region. Dhows carried trade goods and passengers within the western Indian Ocean. Dhow captains used their knowledge of the Indian Ocean wind system to make long-distance voyages of a type that would be almost unthinkable for their contemporaries in the Atlantic and Pacific Oceans: both the Atlantic and Pacific are much bigger than the Indian Ocean, and because their "tops"—the northern land or island bridges that allowed early sailors to first cross these oceans—are at much higher and colder latitudes, they were more challenging to sailors wishing to stay near land while making their voyages. Chinese trade goods made it across the Indian Ocean long before they reached the Americas.

By contrast the Indian Ocean's winds and weather were much better suited to early navigators. Because the Indian Ocean has monsoon winds that blow one way for part of the year and another way for the rest of year, it is possible to make long-distance voyages in the Indian Ocean and to have a tailwind going both ways, provided you have the patience to wait a couple of months for the winds to change directions. For ships coming from the Persian Gulf or India to East Africa, Kilwa is the southernmost point one can sail to with reasonable confidence of making it home on the next monsoon. If one goes further south, there is the possibility that the return voyage will take two monsoon seasons rather than one. So the area around Kilwa represented a sort of pivot point in Indian Ocean trade patterns. In the same way that straits in the entrance to the Red Sea or the Persian Gulf helped make Aden and Hurmuz important trading cities during the same period, the wind patterns that drove Indian Ocean trade helped make Kilwa an important trade center. They also enforced long layovers for ships' crews who were waiting for the winds to turn. The result was a pattern in which sailors and merchants often maintained long-term social relationships in the ports they visited, and in many cases had wives and families in them too. At first Kilwa, like most Swahili cities, acted mostly as an intermediary between the people of the interior, who provided ivory, beeswax, slaves, and other goods, and the visiting merchants, who sought these goods. However, when gold from Zimbabwe began to reach the southern Indian Ocean port of Sofala, Kilwa emerged as the port where that gold was concentrated for shipment to the Middle East and India.

Thus, there were two phases in the growth and expansion of Kilwa. The first, which was associated with the emergence of an elite class through trade, took place between 800 and 1200 and occurred at numerous sites along the coast. During this time Kilwa grew from a village to a trading town as a result of its role as an intermediary with the interior. The second phase of growth occurred after 1200, when Kilwa became one of the dominant trading ports of the East African coast, a process that happened to only a few of the cities that had gone through the first phase of transformation. Its growth into the biggest and richest city on the Swahili coast likely stems from Kilwa's role as an intermediary in the gold trade. Although the gold trade from Sofala, a city on the coast of modern Mozambique that was linked to the gold-producing areas of south central Africa, was originally dominated by the city of Mombasa, Kilwa wrested control of the trade from its rival sometime early in the thirteenth century. The result was Kilwa's growth into one of the dominant cities of the East African coast.

The First Phase

Stephanie Wynne-Jones, an archaeologist who has worked in and around Kilwa, has taken a particular interest in Kilwa's first transformation (though she does not make so sharp a distinction between the two periods as I do). Her work has shown that Kilwa was pretty much like any other small coastal settlement until 800, when new types of pottery, imported ceramics from the Middle East and China, appear in Kilwa's archaeological record but not in the hinterlands. Chinese ceramics in particular came to East Africa though an interlocking system of trade circuits across the Indian Ocean. They would have changed hands many times before they arrived in places like Kilwa and, as a result, would be quite valuable after all the middle men took their cut. They seem to have functioned as markers of elite status, a sort of visual representation of their owners' connection to the commercial world of the Indian Ocean. Thus, the trade connections that made the emerging elite wealthy also gave them access to the symbols of wealth and status. Bowls and plates were displayed in the public parts of merchants' homes, the *mihrabs* (the niche that indicates which wall of a mosque faces toward Mecca) of Swahili mosques often had imported bowls set into the mortar around them, and the tombs of Muslim holy men had bowls set into their surfaces as well. This seems to speak eloquently of the value that the Swahili placed on these items, though it can be jarring to the modern observer to see ceramics with Chinese characters on them set into the tombs of Muslim holy men.

Another interesting observation made about the changing nature of ceramics in Kilwa and other sites is that bowls become more common, meaning they may have been associated with new dietary habits, possibly public feasting. Food and how one eats it is always a major marker of status, and as a new elite class emerged in Kilwa, they appear to have changed the way people ate. It is also possible that what they ate changed as well. Excavations at Swahili sites on the island of Pemba indicate that right around 1000, elites in Pemba began to consume a new staple food—rice. Commoners, however, continued to eat sorghum and millet, grains that are African domesticates consumed all over the continent. Sativa rice (the variety cultivated and eaten in East Africa) is not native to the African continent and presumably came to East Africa from Asia, most likely from the Indian subcontinent. Few aspects of human culture are more class and culture bound than what we eat, how we eat it, and with whom we eat. Thus, the appearance of new foods, along with new dishes from which to serve them, appears to mark the emergence of a new elite class even before this new class began to build new types of houses for themselves. It's also worth noting that this new elite culture was not a package imported wholesale from across the ocean; rather, Kilwa's emerging elites combined imported goods and foods from several regions of the western Indian Ocean as markers of their status. There is nothing in the record that would suggest that this new elite culture was transplanted to the coast from elsewhere.

The Second Phase

Kilwa's role in the gold trade allowed for further expansion and elaboration of the elite culture that had emerged. Not until the thirteenth century did Kilwa come to have a significant number of stone buildings. Even after its rise to prominence the city continued to have more mud houses and fewer stone houses than those of the northern Swahili coast, though no one has a compelling explanation for this difference.

When Kilwa was at its peak, prominent merchants built their houses in stone. Sometimes these were two-story houses, but more often they were single story. Swahili patrician houses were elaborate affairs meant to house the merchant and his family as well as to contain areas where trade goods could be stored and processed. They also had apartments in them that appear to have been used to house visiting merchants and their goods.

These houses were as comfortable and well designed as any in the world. Houses at Gedi, which is much better preserved than Kilwa, had toilets in them, something few houses in the world could claim in 1300. They also had systems for channeling water from nearby wells to cisterns in the houses. Set into the bottoms of these cisterns were Chinese ceramic bowls, often with the Chinese character for "long life" inscribed on them.

In addition to these domestic structures there were a number of prominent public buildings in Kilwa. The most famous of these were the Husuni Kubwa and the Great Mosque. Every Swahili city had a congregational mosque where the city's Muslims could all pray together on Fridays, but none could claim anything on the scale of Kilwa's Great Mosque. Constructed in the twelfth century, Kilwa's Great Mosque went through a major expansion in the reign of Sultan Hasan bin Sulaiman in the 1330s. It had a barrel-vaulted ceiling and a dome—probably the first true dome constructed in East Africa—which remained the coast's largest until the nineteenth century. It also had an enclosure used exclusively by the sultan called a *maqsura*, allowing him to pray in kingly privacy. When the mosque was completed, it was the largest enclosed space south of the Sahara. Unfortunately, shortly after this expansion parts of the roof collapsed and were not fully repaired until the fifteenth century.

Hasan bin Sulaiman also constructed the Husuni Kubwa. Although the Great Mosque is a larger and grander version of a type of building found in any Swahili city, the Husuni Kubwa has no real parallels in other cities. It is a royal palace, built on a staggering scale, with multiple levels, courtyards, a water basin large enough that some archaeologists call it the swimming pool, vast storage areas, and a complex of apartments that all surround a large courtyard. It appears that Hasan bin Sulaiman was building a royal palace to be not only a visible symbol of his wealth and power but also as a place that might house many visiting merchants and their trade goods. The word *husn* from which Husuni derives is an Arabic word that refers to storage; Kubwa is Swahili for big. Thus, the Husuni Kubwa was the big storehouse. The courtyard surrounded by apartments seems to have been intended as a place where visiting merchants could live and trade as guests of the sultan. Its scale suggests that Hasan may have intended to dominate some part of the city's trade. If that was his intention, however, he failed; the building was never finished. The usual interpretation of this is that the city's patrician class was not pleased with this effort to infringe on their rights, so they put a stop to it. It is noteworthy, however, that Hasan's failed bid for greatness took the form of a vast warehouse and self-contained market. Hasan was as much a merchant as a king, aspiring more to the status of a Venetian Doge than a Louis XIV.

That Hasan bin Sulaiman attempted to build so grand a palace was quite out of the ordinary in Swahili towns. In the ruins of many Swahili archaeologists have difficulty determining which house belonged to the ruler, and often they end up designating a house that is slightly larger than the others as a "palace." Some Swahili towns treated their rulers with elaborate deference: some of these rulers were carried by slaves in a bed when they left their homes and proceeded by men playing *siwas*, side-blown horns made from elephant tusks. The last Swahili ruler of Zanzibar, the Mwinyi Mkuu, was approached by his subjects on their hands and knees. Some Swahili rulers were also seen as sources of magical power. When the Omani Arabs who took over Zanzibar in the nineteenth century imprisoned the Mwinyi Mkuu, it did not rain until he was released, a fact attributed to the Mwinyi Mkuu's power. However, the Mwinyi Mkuu's palace, though structurally different from other houses in that it had an audience chamber, is hardly vast. It's only slightly larger than the typical merchant's house. Even in places where kings were treated with great deference, they were usually selected by their peers rather than inheriting the office on strictly hereditary terms. Other Swahili towns, like those on the north coast of Kenya, have no tradition of kingship at all; they were oligarchies ruled by their patrician families. Similar patterns of oligarchic rule are found in other trade-oriented societies. For instance, merchant families dominated many Italian city-states as well as the Netherlands at its seventeenth-century peak. Intriguingly, there are also a few references to Swahili queens. When the Portuguese arrived in Zanzibar, the island was purportedly ruled by a queen, but it is not clear how common female rulers were, nor is much known about the general status of women on the coast during this period, though at least in historical times Swahili women had valued privacy but were not in any sense isolated or marginal members of society.

Kilwa, by contrast, had kings, but such evidence as there is suggests that they were not treated much differently from other patricians. The Arab traveler Ibn Battuta visited Kilwa in 1331 and reported having a conversation with the sultan (Hasan bin Sulaiman) in the street. A beggar, who asked the sultan for his clothes, interrupted their conversation. These the sultan handed over, earning him the respect of the crowd of onlookers as well as Ibn Battuta. This suggests that Kilwa's rulers, even an exceptional character like Hasan bin Sulaiman, did not cultivate much of an air of mystery about themselves and instead seem to have been intent on using their wealth to curry favor in their subjects. If anything, Kilwa's rulers—and most Swahili rulers for that matter—seem to have been first among equals in a ruling class rather than hereditary royalty.

Although the various cities of the coast were rivals and fought occasional wars with each other, they don't seem to have been a terribly warlike people. Some accounts mention a holy war being waged against the peoples of the interior, and the cities and island, as was the case with Kilwa, were usually walled, presumably for defensive reasons. In general little is known about the relationship between the Swahili towns and the people of the interior. Some scholars see the Swahili as having very limited contact with the interior, mediated through nearby allies, whereas others think there may have been more extensive contact between the coast and interior. Major conflicts with the peoples of the interior occurred when drought and famine triggered movements of people that threatened coastal cities. The best known example of this occurred in the sixteenth century when the arrival of ten thousand marauding Zimba from the interior interrupted the struggle between Ottoman Turks and the Portuguese over the Swahili town of Mombasa. The Zimba, who had menaced many other cities on their way north to Mombasa, were most likely refugees from drought who had taken to raiding in an effort to obtain food. Believing that the Zimba were cannibals, the Turks fled the city in the only direction they could—toward the ships of the Portuguese—leaving the inhabitants of the city to face the Zimba on their own.

The town chronicles say little about the military exploits of towns and their rulers, though vicious intrigue and conspiracy seem to have been the norm. These were merchant princes, not war leaders. There was never a Swahili empire, and any effort from one town to dominate another was usually short lived. The coastal cities saw occasional military threats from the interior, but these cities usually depended on their walls, location, and allies in the hinterland to protect them. Occasionally threats appeared from the sea. In one case, during the thirteenth century, Sakalava raiders from Madagascar attacked the city and carried off a number of people. Later they made a second attack and were repelled.

GLOBAL ENCOUNTERS AND CONNECTIONS:
Kilwa's Place within the Indian Ocean Trading Network

In 1498 raiders who could not be so easily repelled slipped by Kilwa without stopping. During the sixteenth century, as part of a broader expansion that included the discovery of the Americas, Iberian sailors entered the Indian Ocean by sailing around the southern tip of Africa. They brought with them maritime technology in the form of ships built to carry cannons and ideas about the use of naval power to control sea trade that, though common in the Atlantic and Mediterranean, were novel in the Indian Ocean. The first Portuguese navigator to reach the Swahili coast, Vasco da Gama, passed close enough to see Kilwa on his way north toward India. He had entered the Indian Ocean by sailing around the southern tip of Africa and was on his way to complete the first roundtrip voyage from Europe to India. The next Portuguese expedition into the Indian Ocean, led by Pedro Cabral in 1500, did stop briefly in Kilwa, but after a nervous and inconclusive meeting between Cabral and the sultan in their respective boats, Cabral went on his way. Da Gama returned in 1502 and forced the sultan to become a tributary of the king of the Portugal. In 1505 Francisco d'Almeida sacked the city, installed a new king, and built a fortress, leaving a small garrison behind to protect his puppet ruler. Perhaps most devastating to Kilwa, the Portuguese seized Sofala and took over that city's gold trade. Portuguese power on the Swahili coast never reached much farther inland than the range of their ships' guns, but Kilwa and other Swahili cities had no prior experience of naval bombardment, and the Portuguese, despite their small number, were formidable and determined soldiers.

Kilwa might have bounced back from this, but the Portuguese also seized Sofala, the source of the gold that had made Kilwa so rich. The Portuguese made a serious effort to control the trading system of the Indian Ocean, a policy that no Indian Ocean power had ever tried to implement on so grand a scale. By 1550 they had captured the most strategically placed trading cities of the Indian Ocean, save for Aden, and required that any ship sailing on the Indian Ocean purchase a *cartaz,* a sort of passport, or face attack from Portuguese ships. It was, in effect, a region-wide extortion scheme.

Most scholars think that the overall effects of the Portuguese effort to reshape the economy of the Indian Ocean were fairly small. There were never enough ships to enforce the rules about the cartaz, and merchants simply added the cost of dealing with the Portuguese to the expense side of the ledger and carried on with businesses. Although this may have been true of the broader region, the Portuguese did have a more profound effect on the Swahili coast than they did elsewhere. They were able to control the southern reaches of the Zambezi River and actually had territorial possessions in Mozambique. With their relatively poor hinterlands, Swahili cities were more dependent on sea trade than on the trading port of Malabar, so the diminution of their sea trade had larger effects for a place like Kilwa than it did for Cambay or Calicut.

In the seventeenth century Omani Arabs drove out the Portuguese. The Omanis had been building a trading state based in the port city of Muscat, and their influence reached from East Africa to India. Swahili elites were pleased at first but soon realized that the Omanis had come to stay. Under Omani control, Swahili cities were able to retain various levels of autonomy, but most had Omani governors imposed on them, and in the nineteenth century there was significant migration from Oman to the Swahili coast. Swahili elites became increasingly impoverished, and despite cultivating a strong sense of cultural superiority to the new arrivals from Oman, the elites were steadily marginalized.

The Omanis occupied the same fort in Kilwa that the Portuguese had used to dominate the town. By the eighteenth century the city, for reasons unknown, had been abandoned and a new town, Kilwa Kivinje, had emerged on the coast. Kilwa Kivinje, however, never rivaled its namesake for size, wealth, or power, though it had a brief boom as a slaving port late in the eighteenth century, supplying slaves to the Omani capital in Zanzibar and to the French sugar islands of Reunion and Mauritius.

Kilwa's vulnerability to the Portuguese and the Omanis tells us something about both the benefits and risks of trade. Kilwa depended on its access to Indian Ocean trade networks for income as well as maintenance of its unique social order. Kilwa's merchants traded African gold for the cloth and ceramics that not only distinguished the merchants from their social inferiors within the Swahili world but also distinguished the Swahili as a group from their non-Swahili neighbors. Although there are passing references to Kilwa merchants turning up in other parts of the Indian Ocean, they seem to have specialized in one small branch of the Indian Ocean trade—their control of the gold trade from Sofala. When the Portuguese, global leaders in naval warfare at the time, severed that link, Kilwa was dealt a fatal blow.

Unlike other Indian Ocean ports such as Aden or Malacca, Kilwa, with its dependence on the gold trade, was a one-trick pony. Aden, which was, if anything, less connected to its hinterlands than Kilwa, survived the Portuguese incursion easily. Aden sat at the entrance to the Red Sea and was a transit point for trade among the Mediterranean, the Persian Gulf, India, and East Africa. Severing a link in that system would be a problem, but not a fatal one. Other Swahili cities like Mombasa proved much more resilient than Kilwa. Mombasa had connections to the interior as well as to the islands of Pemba and Zanzibar, and it likewise fared much better under the Portuguese.

Seeing the Swahili as highly receptive to cultural influences from people with whom they came into contact is tempting. After all, one thousand years ago they became Muslim due to the influences of their engagement with the largely Muslim trading world of the Indian Ocean, adopted the Arabic script, and showed a real enthusiasm for the material goods of the Indian Ocean; however, their experience of the next five hundred years tempers that fact. Between 1500 and the present the Swahili have been exposed to Portuguese, German, and British rulers and missionaries espousing many different types of Christianity. Yet people on the coast, the Swahili, have remained resolutely Muslim. In the nineteenth century the British Empire's expansion to include both East Africa and India encouraged large numbers of Indians to migrate to East Africa. There are now Hindu temples in almost every coastal city, but the Swahili have shown no interest in Hinduism. Although the Swahili language has absorbed some vocabulary from Gujarati and Urdu, it is East African Indians who have adopted Swahili as their mother tongue, not the reverse.

Unlike Kilwa, many other Swahili cities survived into the present day. Mombasa is Kenya's second largest city and East Africa's busiest port, but the Swahili are a minority, overwhelmed in a population swollen by migrants from the interior. Lamu lives on as a sort of Swahili version of Colonial Williamsburg, Virginia, but its elites are poor and much of the prime property belongs to Europeans. In the nearby town of Siyu Swahili patricians have not had the wherewithal to maintain their stone houses and have instead moved into mud houses; however, the status of owning a stone house remains, even when it has not been occupied for a century. The crumbling structures still stand in Siyu, and everyone knows which houses belong to which families. Swahili wealth and political power have vanished, but Swahili culture survives.

Kilwa's status as a busy trading port with commercial connections that stretched across the western Indian Ocean meant it had many visitors. Few, however, put pen to paper to describe the city. An exception was Ibn Battuta (1304–1377), who was one of the world's great travelers.

"A Visit to Zeila, Mogadishu, Mombasa, and Kilwa Kisiwani," by Ibn Battuta

Originally from Morocco, Ibn Battuta spent much of his adult life on the road. He completed the *haj*, or Muslim pilgrimage to Mecca, as a young man and served as a *qadi*, or Islamic judge, first in Delhi and then in the Maldives Islands. He went to China, crossed the Sahara to visit Mali in West Africa, and made a voyage down the coast of East Africa to the Swahili coast, where he stopped in Kilwa.

Certain themes run through Ibn Battuta's work. He tends to be interested in the way Islam is practiced in the places he visits, approving of practices that he deems orthodox while noting his disapproval of those he thinks contrary to proper Islamic practice. His other recurring interest is the generosity or lack thereof that his hosts show to him. He expected to be given lavish gifts and became a bit tetchy if the gifts received were not quite up to snuff. His memoirs make him sound like a fairly unpleasant person, but they are an invaluable resource for understanding the world of the Indian Ocean in the centuries before the Portuguese arrived. The following excerpt is from his description of East Africa, which he visited in 1331.

- Does Ibn Battuta seem surprised by anything he finds in Kilwa? Is he in an exotic foreign land, or is this familiar territory for him? What does this tell you about the world of Islam in fourteenth century?

- Ibn Battuta lists the names of a cluster of Islamic scholars who are in residence in Kilwa. Where do these people come from? What does this tell you about Kilwa's oceanic connections? Why do you suppose they came all the way to Kilwa?

Then I set off by sea from the town of Mogadishu for the land of the Swahili and the town of Kilwa, which is in the land of the Zanj. . . .

We spent a night on the island and then set sail for Kilwa, the principal town of the coast, the greater part of whose inhabitants are Zanj of very black complexion. Their faces are scarred, like the Limiin at Janada. A merchant told me Sofala is half a month march from Kilwa, and that between Sofala and Yufi in the country of the Limiin is a month's march. Powdered gold is brought from Yufi to Sofala.

Kilwa is one of the most beautiful and well-constructed towns in the world. The whole of it is elegantly built. The roofs are built with mangrove poles. There is much rain. The people are engaged in holy war, for their country lies beside that of the pagan Zanj. The chief qualities are devotion and piety: they follow the Shafi'i rite.

When I arrived, the Sultan was Abu al-Muzaffar Hasan surnamed Abu al-Mawahib [father of gifts] on account of his numerous charitable gifts. He frequently makes raids into the Zanj country, attacks them and carries off the booty, of which he reserves a fifth, using it in the manner prescribed by the Quran. That reserved for the kinfolk of the Prophet is kept separate in the treasury, and, when the Sharifs come to visit him, he gives it them. They come from Iraq, the Hijaz, and other countries. I found several Sharifs from the Hijaz at his court, among them Muhammad ibn Jammaz, Mansur ibn Labida ibn Abi Nami and Muhamma ibn Shumaila ibn Abi Nami. At Mogadishu I saw Tabl ibn Kubaish ibn Jammaz, who also wished to visit him. This Sultan is very humble: he sits and eats with beggars, and venerates holy men and descendants of the Prophet.

I found myself near him one Friday as he was coming away from prayer and returning to his house. A faqir from Yemen stopped him and said: "O Abu al Mawahib." He replied: "Here I am, O beggar! What do you want?" "Give me the clothes you are wearing!" And he said: "Certainly you can have them." "At once?" he asked. "Yes, immediately!"

He returned to the mosque and entered the preacher's house, took off his clothes and put on others. Then he said to the faqir: "Come in, and take these." The beggar entered and took them, wrapped them in a cloth and put them on his head. Then he went away. Those who stood by thanked the Sultan most warmly for the humility and generosity he had displayed.

His son and successor designate took back the clothes from the faqir and gave him ten slaves in exchange. When the Sultan learnt how much his subjects praised his son's action, he ordered that the beggar should be given ten more slaves and two loads of ivory. In this country the majority of gifts are ivory: gold is very seldom given. . . .

Source: Ibn Battuta, "A Visit to Zeila, Mogadishu, Mombasa, and Kilwa Kisiwani," in *The East African Coast: Select Documents from the First to the Earlier Nineteenth Century,* edited by G. S. P Freeman-Grenville, 31–32 (Oxford: Clarendon Press: 1962).

Further Reading

Chittick, Neville. *Kilwa: An Islamic Trading City on the East African Coast* Nairobi, Kenya: British Institute in Eastern Africa, 1974.

Freeman-Grenville, G. S. P. *The East African Coast: Select Documents from the First to the Earlier Nineteenth Century.* Oxford: Clarendon Press, 1962.

Gilbert, Erik, and Jonathan Reynolds. *Africa in World History,* 2nd ed. Upper Saddle River, NJ: Prentice Hall, 2008, ch. 7.

Horton, Mark, and John Middleton. *The Swahili.* Oxford: Blackwell, 2000.

Kusimba, Chapurukha. *The Rise and Fall of the Swahili States.* Walnut Creek, CA: Altamira Press, 1999.

Spear, Thomas. "Early Swahili History Reconsidered." *International Journal of African Historical Studies* 33, no. 2 (2000): 257–290.

Web Resources

Ruins of Kilwa Kisiwani and Songo Mnara, UNESCO, http://whc.unesco.org/en/list/144.
World Heritage Site: Ruins of Kilwa Kisiwani and Songo Mnara, www.worldheritagesite.org/sites/kilwakisiwanisongomnara.html.

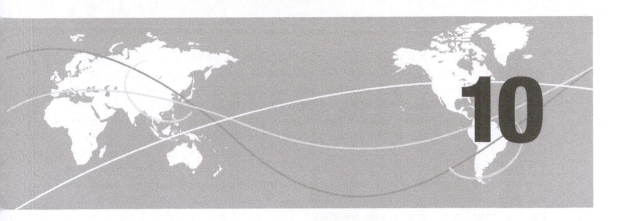

10

Varanasi

The Microcosm of India and Exemplar of Balance

(ca. 1200–1600 CE)

NITA KUMAR

Personal Prologue

EVEN A FIRST-TIME VISITOR TO VARANASI WILL SEE THIS ANCIENT CITY'S multifaceted history—the structure of a wealthy commercial and manufacturing center (that Hindus call *artha*), the trappings of lifetimes spent enjoying leisure (*kama*), the accumulated traditions of many religions (*dharma*), and the devotion to the ultimate goal of individual enlightenment (*moksha*). And a frequent visitor will recognize even greater complexity of global influences.

"There are many European-style cafés in Varanasi now," I was told as I got ready to visit favorite haunts on my last visit to this ancient city in India. Varanasi, also known as Banaras, is a city of narrow lanes with wandering cows and cow dung, tall houses with overhanging balconies, steep riverside steps called *ghats,* and prehistoric occupations—weaver, stone carver, boatman—and an aura of ancient history over everything. Modern cafés? A purist might think that nothing could be more incongruous.

But I was familiar with the city. I added the new cafés to my list of old haunts. Varanasi is one of the oldest living cities in the world—older than other civilizing and religious centers such as Mecca, Athens, Jerusalem, and Beijing. As ancient as the city is, however, it has longevity *because* it is ever changing. The new cafés today are only one symptom of the city's dynamism. I chose to study Varanasi because it was the best example of an ancient Indian, pre-colonial city I could find, and I fell in love with my subject as it revealed itself as the ultimate statement of the traditional Hindu values of a *balanced* life. I want to share this philosophy with readers, of balance among the economic, or *artha*; the pleasurable, or *kama*; the righteous, or *dharma*; and pursuit of the ultimate truth, or *moksha*, by weaving that balance into the continuous history of Varanasi as a vibrant urban center.

I headed to Flavours Café, located strategically at Lanka crossing, a stone's throw from the university. Right below it are traditional restaurants that serve filling Indian dishes at half the price of the modern café above. But you come to Flavours for the café-style seating, the leisure of hanging around, the choice of teas and coffees, and the power of experimenting with date nut muffins and banana bread. The café's menu has no recognizable Indian dishes, but foreign items have been adapted to suit the Indian palate, such as "panir roll" and "chicken tikka masala sandwich." Flavours is teaching Varanasi residents how to regard a café, and these residents are curious and interested. They are becoming global citizens by the day by learning Western-style café culture.

This is not the first time Varanasi has transformed itself. Although we do not have the social history that tells us what people drank on the streets in the thirteenth to the seventeenth centuries, we do know it was neither tea nor coffee. Tea shops, for instance, are ubiquitous in Banaras today, even something as simple as a roadside bench with a counter and improvised stove, serving clay cups of tea popularized in the West as "chai." Tea is so quintessentially Indian that it makes the city traditional, one may think. Yet tea, though familiar in northeast India, was introduced into Varanasi less than a hundred years ago, and tea companies had to work very hard to popularize it because it was culturally unfamiliar and inferior to established drinks like milk. Yet tea shops did gradually catch on, and tea became a popular drink in Varanasi, though many decades passed before people began making it at home, showing us that radical change and innovation is a way of life in Varanasi. Varanasi is not a city of contradictions; rather, it is a city of flexibility and movement.

Seen through the lens of the four aims of life—*artha* (prosperity), *kama* (pleasure), *dharma* (duty), and *moksha* (salvation)—this chapter will focus on Varanasi in the thirteenth to seventeenth centuries. We will see that Varanasi has been and remains today not simply a holy city that draws thousands of pilgrims daily to its shores but rather a center of commerce and a beacon of intellectual and artistic achievement. We will see that the biggest message of the city has been one of tolerance, balance, and holism.

VARANASI AND THE WORLD:
A Vital City of Learning and Religion

Prior to even the Buddhist period beginning in the sixth century BCE Varanasi has been a vital hub for commerce, learning, and religion. It is one of the key South Asian cities whose reputation contributed to the image of India as a culturally and economically rich civilization, one that the Europeans "discovered" in the fifteenth and sixteenth centuries, thereby setting the wheels of global trade and colonization in motion.

Beyond its status as a commercial center and the capital of a rich and prosperous kingdom, however, Varanasi emerged as early as 800 BCE as an important center first for the earliest South Asian religions. These consist of early folk cults, followed by the religion we know from the books called the Vedas, sometimes known as "Vedism." Furthermore, it is an important center for other religions that originated in South Asia, such as Buddhism and Jainism (ca. sixth century BCE), Hinduism (ca. third century CE), and Sikhism (ca. sixteenth century CE). Islam, originating in West Asia, also played a major role beginning with the Delhi Sultanate in the thirteenth century. Although economic and political stability and patronage are necessary prerequisites for culture and religion to flower, these alone do not explain Varanasi's predominance as a cultural and religious center. South Asia has had many important pilgrimage centers, so Varanasi's emergence as the predominant one merits enquiry.

In the seventh century CE the Chinese traveler Hiuen Tsang visited Varanasi and wrote about its enduring importance as a Buddhist center, with scores of monasteries and thousands of monks. Furthermore, Varanasi had long attracted Hindu philosophers and teachers to its *ashrams*, or retreats of learning, including the grammarian Patanjali in the second century BCE, the philosopher Shankara in the eighth and ninth centuries CE, and the theologian Ramanuja in the eleventh century CE (to mention only the most notable). Even to this day all the principal Hindu sects have their monastic centers in Varanasi.

What's more, by the thirteenth to the seventeenth centuries CE, the term *Banarasi*—related to the other name of Varanasi, Banaras—came to denote high quality, whether that be a school of literature, philosophy, or art, or even a type of cloth or a kind of sweet. For example, Banarasi silk fabric, made by Muslim weavers beginning during this time, is to this day considered a highly desirable commodity in Hindu weddings all over the world because it is intricately woven with unmatched skill and is also considered to be benign and auspicious. Furthermore, of all pilgrimage centers, Varanasi was the only one that Hindus came to believe would guarantee release from the heaviest burden of all, the cycles of life and their suffering, merely by being present in the city at the time of death.

Artha: The Political Economy of Varanasi

Artha is the action that results in profit, either of money or power, and Hindus understand such action to be a part of the correctly lived life. Varanasi was called the "Forest of Artha," where Hindus believed every person could make their fortune and attain their desired power. As such, Varanasi's history is a small part of the history of northern India, and, therefore, to narrate the former in part narrates the latter. The history begins with the Indus Valley Civilization, the first excavated civilization in South Asia. Located in northwest India, it existed from around 3000 BCE to about 1500 BCE. Scholars believe that there were many settlements as old or older along the Ganges as well, perhaps even in the Varanasi region, but no excavations have yet taken place.

After the Indus Valley civilization ended, groups of nomad herdsmen who called themselves Aryans entered India from the northwest. As they expanded into the Gangetic Valley between 1200 and 700 BCE, the Aryans encountered settled cultures and, in time, adopted their practices. Varanasi, then known as Kashi, was one of these places. As the Aryans developed civilization, partly from the earlier civilized cultures there, Varanasi became a center of Vedic learning, the Sanskrit language, of the study of mathematics, astronomy, logic, grammar, and literature. During this time it also maintained its pre-Vedic worship of the sun as well as tree and water cults.

Buddhist sources that refer back to Varanasi around 800 BCE refer to it as an important manufacturing and commercial center, mentioning its merchant guilds, the use of money, and trade along the river. The city used the Ganges as a waterway to trade goods from as far away as China, and this became the backbone of the city's *artha*, or economy, by encouraging craftsmen to create goods and merchants to sell them.

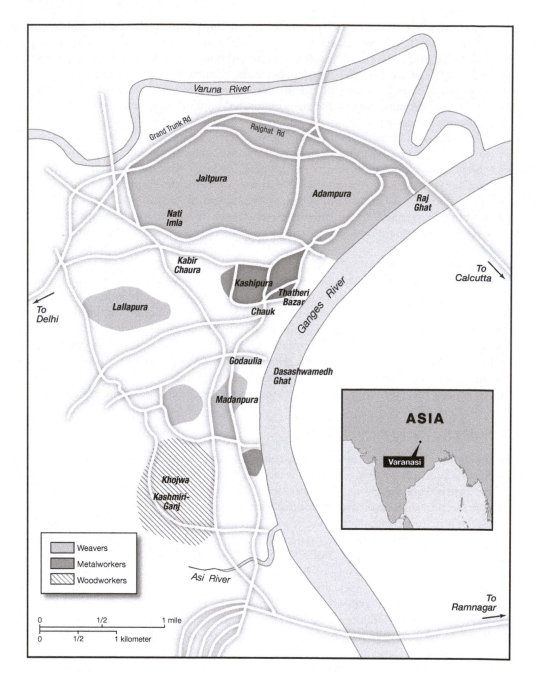

Map 10.1. Varanasi: Artisans

In the thirteenth to the seventeenth centuries, artisan groups were probably clustered in certain parts of the city, as today, reflecting the urban preference for spatial specialization. Metalworkers lived in the heart of the city, Kashipura and Thatheri Bazar. They were Hindus who manufactured ritual and worship items and images. The weavers of Madanpura lived in the second circle, and were well-integrated Muslims manufacturing precious silk. The weavers of the northern neighborhoods of Jaitpura and Adampura, in the third tier of the city, were later converts to Islam and were poorer. Woodworkers lived outside the city proper, in Khojwa and Kashmiriganj. They were Hindu, low caste like the metalworkers, but far less unified as a group.

Not only did Varanasi's political economy benefit from its location at the confluence of the Ganges, the holiest river in Hindu mythology, and its two minor tributaries, the Varuna and the Assi (its very name combines the names of these two rivers), but Varanasi also benefitted from its strategic location on a ridge that rendered it immune to floods but still provided it needed water. Its access to the river and natural ponds as well as its salubrious climate made the city a desirable place to live. In the earliest times wealthy merchants flocked to Varanasi, and later, pilgrims and scholars also followed to be a part of the city's hermitages and schools. Even the Buddha is said to have been a citizen of Varanasi in some of his past lives.

In fact, Siddhartha Gautama, the Buddha, did come to Varanasi in the sixth century BCE, delivering his first sermon after his enlightenment to five disciples in nearby Sarnath, and after this his influence expanded quickly during the time of the Mauryan Empire, around 322 to 183 BCE. Buddhism became the dominant religion in South Asia for over a millennium, and the religion was carried to China, Sri Lanka, and East and Southeast Asia. By the seventh century CE Buddhism had become the largest religion in the world.

These powerful Mauryans came to unify India into one vast empire, and as a result, the Ganges Valley became the home of Indian civilization. Ashoka, the most important of the Mauryan emperors, built outside Varanasi a polished, stand-alone sandstone pillar with a four-headed lion capital that today is the official national emblem of India.

The opportunity to sell to foreign traders created a market for faraway consumers eager for Varanasi's fine luxury goods. Early references to Varanasi's woven goods, brass, copper and silver crafts, and jewelry are abundant, but actual histories of these early industries have not yet been written. In the thirteenth to seventeenth centuries the most popular items for trade included finely woven silk and gold brocade, as fabric as well as turbans, scarves, and other finished goods; metal products such as swords, trays, and utensils; and statues of Hindu deities and ritual objects. Furthermore, records from Indian and foreign travelers during this period attest to the city's magnificence. In the 1330s, for instance, Jinprabh Suri, a Jain monk, called it "a city studded with many-colored jewels, surrounded by the north-flowing Ganga River, in which lived remarkable people." Ralph Fitch, an Englishman who visited Varanasi in the 1580s, testified that its textile trade made it the biggest center of commerce in north India and that visitors came to the city from both near and far. Finally, in the late eighteenth century Thomas Macaulay described Varanasi as though it remained the city it had been hundreds of years earlier:

> Commerce has as many pilgrims as religion. All along the shores of the
> venerable stream lay great fleets of vessels laden with rich merchandise.
> From the looms of Benares went forth the most delicate silks that
> adorned the balls of St James's and of Versailles; and in the bazaars, the
> muslins of Bengal and the sabres of Oude were mingled with the jewels
> of Golconda and the shawls of Cashmere. (Eck 1983, 311)

The best description of Varanasi's prosperity, however, is found in the literary work *Kashi Khand*, written down first perhaps in the fourteenth century but composed much earlier in the oral tradition. In it Himalaya, the Hindu deity that personifies the mountains of that name, traveled to Varanasi to visit his daughter Parvati, the wife of Shiva. Although Himalaya's own home contained the richest of jewels, when he saw the city, he was awestruck:

> Its very earth was completely studded with a multitude of different kinds of jewels, and the brilliance of the rubies of its many palaces filled the sky. . . . The city illumined the four directions with the many golden pinnacles that topped its mansions. It surpassed even the paradise of the gods with its profusion of flying banners. Marvelous was the pleasure palace of the eight perfections, with its forests which bore all fruits, surpassing even the wishing-trees of heaven. (Eck 1983, 312)

The available records demonstrate that for about two millennia the city thrived with artha, or material success. As such, when Varanasi came under the control of the Delhi Sultans at the beginning of the thirteenth century, the city's life was hardly disrupted: commerce drove the city more than empire.

The Delhi Sultans were Muslims. Previously, in the seventh and eighth centuries, Muslim-Arab traders had come to the Indian subcontinent peacefully. In the tenth century, however, Muslim kingdoms were established after rulers such as Mahmud of Ghazni in Afghanistan conducted violent raids into India. The first Muslim army, directed by the governor Qutb-uddin Aibak, reached Varanasi in the 1190s CE. Varanasi, previously governed by pre-Vedic, Vedic, Buddhist, and Hindu rulers, came under Muslim control and remained that way for the next five and a half centuries, along with much of the rest of India.

Because India was so large that mass conversion to Islam would have been impossible, the Delhi Sultans, many of whom were Turks, would need to consolidate their power and establish legitimacy for their rule. Instead, however, the Delhi Sultans and their local governors adopted a variety of policies to maintain power. They destroyed the symbols of previous rulers' legacy, particularly the temples and shrines to Hindu gods and goddesses. In their place, they constructed mosques, usually from the very materials of the temples or on the sites of destroyed temples and built by the same artisans who had built the temples. They built these mosques in order to proclaim themselves the all-powerful and righteous rulers who had taken over from the deposed kings. The architectural styles blended those of Hinduism and Islam, of India, Turkey, Afghanistan, and Iran, thereby creating a new Indo-Islamic synthesis. Even today, for some, remnants of temple carvings in some mosques are a painful reminder of the temples' destruction from the thirteenth to seventeenth centuries. Varanasi in particular has scores of such reminders; for instance, the oldest mosque of the city, Arhai Kangura ("two and a half domes"), built around the end of the twelfth century or the beginning of the thirteenth, has Hindu temple foundations.

In addition, the Delhi Sultans permitted decentralized rule as another method of governance. As a result, during the three centuries of Sultanate rule the capital, Delhi, fluctuated between tighter and looser control of Varanasi, depending on the local governor's inclinations. Many governors, such as Syed Jamaluddin during the twelfth to thirteenth centuries, seem to have been popular; neighborhoods in the city bear their names, such as Jamaluddinpura ("the quarter of Jamaluddin").

There were five important Sultanate dynasties. The first, the Slave Dynasty (1194–1290) established the new rule and asserted its imperial right by destroying temples and erecting mosques in Varanasi. But as temples were destroyed, others were also built anew, typically by patrons from distant Indian provinces. The next dynasty, the Khalji (1290–1320) had a Sultan, Ala-uddin, who was equally determined to destroy Hindu temples in Varanasi, but once again, construction of new temples continued. The Tughlak Dynasty's

(1320–1414) Mohammad and Firoze Shah were both stern taskmasters who would not exempt Hindu Brahmans from the *jiziya*, a tax on non-Muslim infidels, or *kafirs*. Then, in 1394, Varanasi came under the control of the neighboring kingdom, Jaunpur, a town some fifty miles away. Its rulers broke from the Tughlaks in Delhi and ruled directly over Varanasi. In the style of previous dynasties, they destroyed the temple of Varanasi's reigning god, Shiva, also known as Vishwanath ("Lord of the World"). Although rebuilt soon after, for some Hindus today the temple and its adjoining mosque with Hindu pillars stands as the most dramatic evidence of Muslim aggression in the past. Then, when Varanasi returned to Delhi control during the Lodi Dynasty, its chief ruler Sikandar Lodi (1489–1517) likewise proved to be, as Muslim chroniclers describe him, a *gazi*, or warrior for the faith.

All this destruction of Hindu temples must be understood as part of royal politics. It affected professional priests, the Brahmans, most of all, though craftsmen and manufacturers continued their work undisturbed, with some shift in patrons at the top. The characteristic description of Varanasi during this period demonstrates that everyday life continued peacefully: "Banaras [Varanasi] had the quality of being able to retain its old character, and the thousands of oppressive acts of the Sultanate period were powerless to destroy the city . . . the Brahmans lost their spiritual authority and almost all Hindu temples were razed to the ground. But Banaras showed its trait of returning again and again to its previous state" (Motichandra 2003, 155).

Finally, in 1529 Babur, the first of the Mughal emperors, came from Samarkand to defeat the last Sultan of Delhi, staking a claim on Varanasi as well as other parts of North India. Babar was himself the descendant of Chingiz Khan (also known as Genghis Khan), a pagan Mongol, and Timur Lane (known in the West as Tamerlane), a Muslim Turk, and thus embodied the melting pot found in so much of Varanasi's history. In his autobiographical writings Babur confessed to having difficulty keeping all the prescriptions of Islam, but he did have artistic sympathies; scholars see his reign as having ushered in a flourishing of the arts, especially those influenced by Persian literary and architectural traditions.

Each of the next five important Mughal emperors, reigning from 1526 to 1707, had their own methods of rule that led to further amalgamation of cultures. For instance, Emperor Akbar's reign from 1556 to 1605 saw the patronage of Hindu learning and temple building. His minister, Todar Mall, along with Todar Mall's son Govardhan paid particular attention to Varanasi, helping to rebuild the important temple of Vishwanath. Because Akbar experimented with a new religion, Din-i-ilahi, both Hindus and Muslims in Varanasi experienced less authoritarian control. We have records of some conversions to the new religion as well as a liberalization of religious practice. Din-i-ilahi did not become a popular religion and is now considered simply a testimony to Akbar's eclecticism. Conversely, Shah Jahan (1627–1658) and Aurangzeb (1658–1707) focused on patronizing Islamic learning and mosque building at the expense of Hinduism and other religions. Furthermore, we know a little about ordinary people's experiences during this period from *Ain-e-Akbari*, the chronicle of Akbar's reign. For example, their production of goods and crafts in Varanasi continued to expand. In 1665 Jean-Baptiste Tavernier, a French traveler to India, described Varanasi as a city of many caravansaries and as having the tallest buildings and narrowest lanes he had ever seen. He also explained how weavers sold silk and cotton fabric in a Varanasi market directly after having it stamped by the Mughal Crown's insignia. Tavernier attested to the significance of Varanasi as a trade center, with roads and routes radiating in all directions.

Kama: The Pursuit of Pleasure

In the Hindu imagination there is no strict separation between the religious-spiritual and the worldly-material. *Kama* is pleasure, and it is as important to experience and pursue as is worldly success (artha) or spiritual duty (dharma, discussed below). In Varanasi people have always understood how to work and play hard, how to live and die well. This is not limited to Hindus; ordinary Muslims also do not fear living well. Hindus' and Muslims' religious fairs—such as the homecoming of the goddess Durga, the awakening of the god Jagannath, the breaking of the Ramadan fast at Id, and the birthday of the Prophet Mohammad—are not only sacred but also fun occasions, with food and rides, poetry and performance, and lights, tents, and entertainment stalls. Images of Hindu gods are regularly honored with music and dance alongside solemn worship, and the musicians are sometimes Muslim. Poetry competitions and public singing mark the birthday of the Prophet and the martyrdom of his son-in-law, and the composers are sometimes Hindu. Hindus and Muslims can sometimes share in each other's festivals and, at other times, perform them in similar ways because they enjoy the same pleasures: poetry, music, night lights, feasts, and parades.

There are portrayals of life from the sixth century BCE in Classical literature and paintings. A ninth-century CE narrative, *Kuttanimtam* by Damodar Gupta, gives a detailed picture of the elite social life of Varanasi. In it an upper-class male is dressed in silk, with a light shawl and polished leather shoes. His body and hair are perfumed in oils, and his forehead sports a bright yellow mark. His ears, neck, and arms are tastefully decked out in beautifully crafted jewels. He carries a walking stick and has a sword in his belt. He twirls his moustache, walks with a swagger, and is full of passion for all of life's pleasures. At a moment's notice he is ready to take a barge ride down the river, visit a Shiva temple, attend a theater performance, or pay a call to a courtesan's boudoir. His body language, especially the style of reclining in sheer enjoyment when watching a performance, is an iconic representation of leisure and hedonism of the time.

Pleasure for men, however, could be work for women. Courtesans were renowned in India for their skills in acting, dancing, singing, and lovemaking, and the lore of the powerful courtesan inhabits Indian pleasure narratives from the third century BCE in Buddhist narratives continuing even to Bollywood films of today. Whenever an Indian courtesan was depicted as having especially excellent skills and appearance, she was from Varanasi.

As with much of Varanasi's culture, the arts have evolved as an amalgamation of many traditions. Almost all the music, dance, painting, sculpture, and poetry that comprise the canon of classical arts in India today originate from the synthesis that the patronage of the Islamic courts in the thirteenth to the sixteenth centuries produced. Artistic styles from Turkey, Iran, and Afghanistan were brought to India, where it was applied and adapted, leading to a kind of "cultural renaissance." Although Varanasi boasts fewer examples in architecture than it does in music, dance, and religion, it nonetheless shares in the larger syncretic Indo-Islamic culture of Northern India. During this time Urdu (Urdu meaning "camp" in Turkish) arose as a common people's language, a result of the intermingling of the speakers of Sanskrit and Prakrits (local Indian languages) with those of Turkish, Arabic, and Persian. Urdu has been spoken in Varanasi since the language first developed.

Vedic chants, the oldest forms of music that exist in India, are sung in styles that many claim derives from the authentic styles from three millennia ago through a process of oral teaching. During the Sultanate and Mughal periods the Dhrupad style of singing emerged, based on Vedic chanting and incorporating new Islamic influences. Tansen (ca. 1506–1586), a court musician of the Emperor Akbar, was one of the most influential musicians in the North Indian classical canon and an exponent of dhrupad singing. As the legend goes, his father lived in Varanasi. Hindus consider the solemn sonority of dhrupad to be spiritual, and many of its best practitioners have been—and are today—Muslim musicians who sang to Allah, thereby making it an excellent example of the Hindu-Muslim synthesis that characterized the thirteenth to seventeenth centuries. (See Map 10.2.) Its accompanying instrument, a drum called the *pakhawaj*, is heard relatively rarely today but has nonetheless influenced the Banaras style played on the more popular drum, the *tabla*. Following dhrupad, vocal music forms called *thumri* and *khayal* emerged as similar instances of Indo-Islamic synthesis. They are today regarded as some of the most popular and evolved vocal genres of North Indian classical music, and one of the most important musical *gharana,* or school for these genres, is Varanasi.

Two important pursuits of kama that exist today in Varanasi are also further instances of cultural synthesis as a result of the Sultanate and Mughal periods. Varanasi takes pride in its wrestling and bodybuilding, and it has had *akharas,* or schools and clubs, of wrestlers that are written and sung about. The styles of wrestling and bodybuilding are themselves partially derived from the styles brought to India from Turkey, Iran, and Afghanistan.

Similarly, the Muslim ascetic *sufi* saints, discussed in the next section, are worshipped in shrines around the city. There are similar shrines to scores of Hindu saints and heroes. Together, these individualized Hindu and Muslim shrines, which are not part of their respective classical religions, offer locations for their followers to interact socially, hold weekly fairs, and attend popular music performances. The boundary between religion and pleasure, therefore, has not existed for ordinary people in Varanasi, both Hindus and Muslims, and the everyday life of the city exemplifies this lack of division.

Dharma: The Pursuit of Righteous Conduct

Dharma means obligation or duty, and it has many nuances, including the pursuit of understanding through debate and discussion, practicing spirituality and religion, and living a life aligned with other human beings and nature. Dharma is a complex idea, and in this section we will simplify it and look at its religious aspects: ritual, popular gods, abstract worship, devotion, and religious synthesis.

We have already seen that when the Aryans spread into the Gangetic Valley, Varanasi became a center of Vedic learning and Sanskrit studies. As such, the city became an important Vedic ritual center to which pilgrims came specifically in search of the correct shrines to visit as well as specialists to conduct their rituals. Varanasi even gained a certain notoriety for its emphasis on sacred sites, bathing in the river, mantras, and rituals. When Buddhism challenged the dominance of the Vedic religion, however, Varanasi was at the hub of the change. Centuries later Buddhism came to be transcended or included within the emerging Hinduism. Hinduism's expansion, from the third to the tenth centuries, resulted from inclusion rather than proselytization. Rather than trying to fight reformers or eradicate indigenous beliefs, instead the new mainstream religion incorporated both the new and old traditions. Hinduism's mythology and ritualism came to include the local practices of ancient places like Varanasi, new and old gods, and a new pacifist worship.

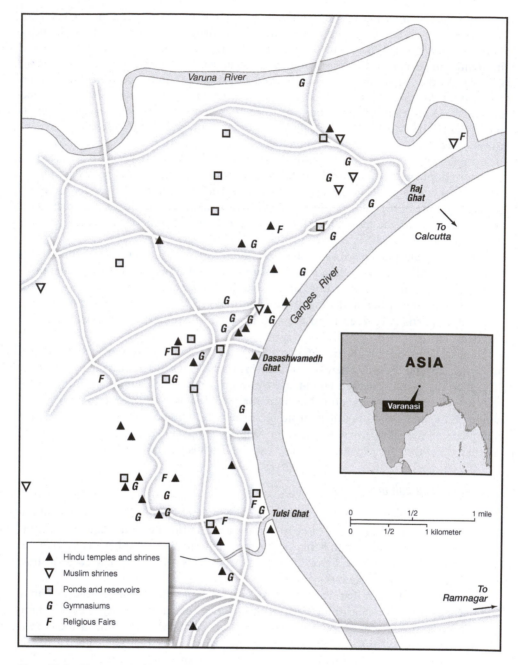

Map 10.2. Varanasi: City of the Good Life

Hindu and Muslim temples and shrines are distributed all over the city. Together with ponds and reservoirs, religious fairs, and gymnasiums, these were all places where ordinary Hindus and Muslims spent leisure time. This partial mapping of leisure activities today gives us an idea of how kama often mingles with dharma, and of the synthetic nature of popular culture in Varanasi, mixing other traditions with the dominant Hindu culture.

River worship may have been one old practice that was taken over. Myths describe the goddess Ganges as dangerous but tamed by Shiva, as he caught her in the matted locks of his hair and domesticated her into a nurturing mother who loved and protected her children. In the eleventh and twelfth centuries, then, the Ganges became a central site of pilgrimage, and Varanasi was confirmed as the holiest city in this Hindu tradition. Visiting pilgrims traveled to Varanasi to cleanse themselves with a ritual bath in the Ganges, and at her banks the dead and dying were guaranteed *moksha,* or release from the cycle of life, death, and rebirth. Visitors carried away the water from the sacred river at Varanasi to keep at their homes, wherever those may be.

Scholars conjecture that over several centuries in the late Vedic period (roughly 500 BCE to 500 CE), as Vishnu, Shiva, and Devi emerged as the major gods of Hinduism, other local gods and heroes were progressively adopted as family members and subsidiary deities. In fact, the term Hindu is a modern term used to categorize a diverse group of sects, such as Shaiva (the worshippers of Shiva) and Vaishnava (the devotees of Vishnu). In Banaras the terms Hindu and Hinduism were not used until well into the twentieth century.

Shiva emerged as the patron lord of Varanasi. He is also called the "Lord of Creatures" or "Lord of the Universe," thus encompassing all the creatures and deities that had previously been worshipped locally. By the Gupta period (320–550 CE), Shiva worship had developed as an offering—of flowers, water, and hymns—and circumambulation of Siva's image, a *linga,* or phallus symbol. This form of Shiva is found all over Varanasi, and his devotees began to donate lingas to temples and install them out in the open and under trees. The male citizens of Varanasi have adopted Shiva's spirit of eccentricity as well as his multiple roles as Lord of Dance, Lord of Destruction, the Supreme Yogi, the Lord of Meditation, and many others as role models. These men have an explicit ideology of *mauj* and *masti,* best translated as craziness and living in the moment, that they claim is the practice of their lord Shiva. They claim that, like him, they can reconcile opposites—dance and destruction, meditation and eroticism.

Even as Shiva became the most popular deity, the *avatars,* or incarnations, of Vishnu, chiefly Rama and Krishna, and the goddess Devi also emerged as important figures in Varanasi. The mythology and forms of worship of Rama and Krishna have been steady from the Gupta period onward. In fact, their stories inspire much of what may be classified as kama, or pleasure, when discussing the life of the city. Paintings, sculptures, and performances made the gods come alive for people, and in the fifteenth and sixteenth centuries *bhaktas,* or "poet-saints," rendered these gods' stories into popular poetry, thereby further popularizing them.

Meanwhile, Islam had also come to Varanasi. With the beginning of the Delhi Sultanate in the thirteenth century followed by each ruler's different approach to religious and cultural tolerance, two results emerged. First, during times of Islamic rulers' religious intolerance, Hindu sectarian worship went underground but nevertheless continued, as beloved images were hidden away. Second, during times of tolerance Hindu sectarian practices flourished, and temple and shrine building resumed. The most outstanding figure among tolerant political leaders was the Emperor Akbar (1556–1605), who took pride in an intellectual engagement with different religions in his realm, discriminating against none. In Varanasi, as elsewhere in North and Central India, there was a burgeoning of Hindu art and literature.

An important indirect development of Islamic political rule was the popularization of *bhakti,* or a personal road to salvation that influences the egalitarian teachings of Islam.

The teachers of this new approach, called *bhaktas*, were so-called poet-saints who came from all over India. Quite a few were either born in Varanasi or went there to write. Tulsi Das, who lived sometime during the sixteenth and seventeenth centuries, was the author of the *Ramcharitmanas*, which retold in the local language the story of the ideal King Rama, adding many beloved discourses and tales to the classic myth. In writing this, Tulsi Das built a bridge between the Brahmin-dominated Hinduism that existed and a popular devotional religion that made everyone equal in their love of Rama. Similarly, he furthered the eclecticism of the city by bridging the worship of Shiva, who figures in Tulsi's life of Rama, and the supreme god who, for Tulsi, was Rama. Today there are annual street pageants in September and October that enact the story of Rama, and Tulsi Das himself purportedly started this tradition.

Other important poet-saints were Ravidas, a cobbler by profession, and Kabir, a weaver. We do not know their exact dates, but they both lived in Varanasi sometime in the fifteenth or sixteenth centuries. All of their poetry was composed orally, and later others wrote their work down, as schools of followers developed who called themselves Ravidasis or Kabirpanthis. Different from the Rama devotee Tulsi Das, Ravidas and Kabir preached *nirguna bhakti,* or devotion to an abstract god who is beyond all description and has no form or characteristics. Similar to Tulsi Das, however, they were against established high religion and were radical enough to declare that all people are born and destined to be equal. Kabir was most probably a Muslim, though he attacked established Islam and its sacred places and rituals as much as he attacked Hinduism.

Devi, or the goddess, was also worshipped in many different forms, each of which encompassed one or more local goddesses. In various myths Devi is either married to an established god, such as Parvati to Shiva, or is an independent force that can slay a demon and lead an army to victory over foes, such as Durga. Locally produced artifacts as well as the music and performance associated with the goddess—just as that for Shiva, Rama, and Krishna—have been found from the fifth century onward.

Religion changed in Varanasi in other ways as well. During the period of Muslim coercive rule, the state may have forced followers of other religions to convert to Islam. Muslims in Varanasi today are divided into a minority who claim lineage from immigrants from West Asia and a majority who trace themselves back to their ancestors' conversion from Hinduism to Islam. However, the majority of conversions to Islam were not by force but instead were the result of charismatic sufi saint-leaders called *pir.* To be a sufi is to subscribe to one of four schools of Sufi philosophy, with a common practice of asceticism and love. The sufi saints were teachers, social activists, counselors, and mentors. Studies of their activities in other parts of India give us a clue as to what they must have done for ordinary people in the city: they were the doctors and psychiatrists, the guides in troubled times, and the everyday practical guides in domestic peacekeeping and social interaction. What we know for certain is that all classes of people came to revere these Muslim pirs. Upon their deaths, shrines were erected on their tombs, and their funerals were marked by rituals of prayers, cleaning and decorating the grave, offering incense and flowers, reading the Qu'ran, or keeping of vows, or supplicating the dead saint through vows and devotion for whatever one wishes. Such shrines have proliferated in Varanasi since Islam came to the city, providing another powerful testimony to the power of Hindu-Muslim synthesis for everyday people.

Varanasi had always been a Hindu city because of the enduring importance of pilgrimage, and during the Sultanate-Mughal period it also became a dynamic center of Muslim celebrations and popular culture. Parades marked the martyrdom of Shahs

Hasan and Hussain as well as the birthday of the Prophet; fairs were held at the end of the holy month of Ramadan; and feasts were the order of the day at Id-ul Zuha, the festival of the sacrifice of animals. Scores of other, more everyday practices began to distinguish Varanasi as an Islamic city alongside a Hindu one. During their reigns, the more dogmatic rulers, such as Shah Jahan and Aurangzeb, sought to reform some of these practices because, the rulers claimed, they demonstrated Hinduism's influence. During others' reigns, such as Akbar, the practices were left alone, respected as the choices made by ordinary people. Thus, by and large Varanasi has a remarkable history of interfaith tolerance not because people did not have strong convictions but rather because they imagined and lived out innovative new paths and syntheses.

Moksha: The Pursuit of Final Truth

The three values of artha, kama, and dharma are superseded by the fourth value, that of *moksha*. Moksha means, literally, release. It implies the pursuit and ultimate understanding of truth. Moksha is only for those who have lived their lives to the fullest and experienced artha, kama, and dharma. It completes the four ends of life. To pursue moksha is to become an ascetic; to be henceforth uninterested in wealth, pleasure, or popular worship; and to live solely for self-discovery. Because it is the final and supreme aim of life, Hindus revere asceticism as its highest ideal because they give up everything and have no more care for society.

Emphasis on the importance of supreme knowledge of the self emerged in the late Vedic period and is called the Vedanta, or the "end of the Vedas." It is laid out in the teachings of the Upanishads, texts that date from around 500 BCE to 500 CE. The Upanishads consist of lessons, the essence of which is to lead the student to realize that true knowledge lies in looking past the superficial disputes and desires of the mundane world to the deeper realities beyond.

Study of the Upanishads took place in ashrams, where gurus (teachers) and students lived and studied together. In their ashrams the gurus taught students for no charge, as patrons or benefactors covered all expenses. Every Hindu text of the period mentions Varanasi's ashrams, where ascetics migrated to teach, study, or meditate, and patrons earned merit and status by funding the life of study and devotion. During Islamic dynastic rule ashram teaching was partly supplanted by the more popular devotional teaching, which taught that every single individual could aspire to oneness with the Supreme simply through love and devotion. But the more extreme practice of asceticism survived well through the thirteenth to eighteenth centuries because the practice was essentially an individualistic one and did not rely on patronage except that which could be provided from ordinary households in the course of an ascetic's wanderings.

Throughout Varanasi's history these ascetics, who pursue this fourth, final aim of life by renouncing everything worldly, would have been seen regularly, and they are still present today. They wore saffron and sometimes distinguished themselves in their appearance according to the school of ascetics to which they belonged. They let their hair grow, wore beads or even snakes, carried sticks or tridents, wore wooden clogs, and were free of all attachment to house, family, possessions, or occupation. They spent their time in discourse and meditation. Just as the population of Varanasi included people from all over India, the ascetics likewise came from every part of India. By virtue of their very identity, they must have played a major role in disseminating the values of Hinduism and keeping it alive through the centuries of Islamic rule.

Finally, moksha in Varanasi presents a paradox. Because the city gives liberation, or moksha, to one and all, Varanasi, beyond everything else, is famous for being the site where death means immediate release. Its famous cremation places and rituals of death, along with the liberation that accompanies them, have been known and celebrated since before 1200 CE.

GLOBAL ENCOUNTERS AND CONNECTIONS:
A Synthesis of Cultures

Varanasi has been and continues to be a global city. Its history is told by the texts of the Aryans, who originally came from central Eurasia; of Buddhists who came from elsewhere; of Jain monks; and of travelers, such as the Chinese traveler Hiuen Tsiang in the seventh century. The writing on the city is prolific and creates a consistent picture. The texts include the *Puranas,* Hindu histories of fifth to fifteenth centuries CE, with their evocation of a "Forest of Bliss." Hiuen Tsiang also described this utopia of temples by pool sides, monasteries and schools in groves, elite houses and gardens, and public streams, parks, and markets for all.

Although almost no architectural remains survive from before the Mughals in the sixteenth century, we know from sculptures and texts that Varanasi was already a commercial center for a few centuries before it became one of Vedic worship and then of Hinduism beginning in the fifth century CE. As an intellectual-philosophical center, then, Varanasi has been a destination for leaders of other religions as well as reformers and critics, including the Buddha in the fifth century BCE, the South Indian philosopher Shankara in the ninth century CE, Nanak and Mirabai in the fifteenth century CE, and Christian missionaries and orientalists in the centuries following. When François Bernier, a French scholar and doctor, visited Varanasi in the middle of the seventeenth century, his descriptions of Varanasi were typical:

> The town contains no colleges or regular classes, as in our universities, but resembles rather the schools of the ancestors, the masters being dispersed over different parts of the town in private houses, and principally in the gardens of the suburbs, which the rich merchants permit them to occupy. Some of these masters have four disciples, others six or seven, and the most eminent may have twelve or fifteen. (Eck 1983, 84)

Trade and manufacture always lay at the heart of this internationalism. The silks woven in Varanasi were already exported everywhere in the known world—Europe and East and West Asia—beginning in the Buddhist period in the fifth century BCE. The actual products—first silk yarn, then wraps, turbans, suit pieces, and, most recently, saris—changed over the centuries, as weavers took notice of market demand. But "Banarasi silk" was a powerful brand throughout the world and remains so even today. Ritual and religious items such as containers for holy Ganges water, vermilion dye for married women to indicate their status, and images of gods and goddesses also provided manufacturing and export opportunity. The images of deities were made from copper, bronze, silver, wood, clay, and stone, and they were sold both locally and globally. When the thousands of pilgrims who visited Varanasi returned home, they brought these products back with them along with powerful confirmations of rituals and sacraments. They even brought back Ganges water, of which a few drops would be used in any important ritual and put in the mouth of a dying person.

Our history above traces how this global identity is reciprocal: just as Varanasi's products and intellectual influences have traveled all over the world, what is called Banarasi for short—that is, "*of* Varanasi"—is a synthesis of the many practices of people from all corners of India and beyond.

ENCOUNTERS AS TOLD: PRIMARY SOURCES

The two excerpts below give a firsthand account of the plural values of artha, kama, dharma, and moksha. The first is an excerpt that tells of the gods' visit to Varanasi. It is taken from the *Kashi Khand*, a part of the *Skanda Purana*, one of the sacred *Puranas*, whose authorship is imputed to Vyasa, author of *Mahabharata*. The dates of the text are not exactly known; it was composed orally around 300 BCE and first written down much later. This excerpt is one of many that testifies to the glories of the city of Varanasi, or, as it is called below, Kashi.

Kashikhanda of Mahrshi Vyasa

What is important about Varanasi, called Kashi in this excerpt *Kashikhanda* from the Mahrshi Vyasa, is that it does not derive its importance from a particular god or event or practice but instead truly seems to have been "already there." Shiva, one of the three gods of the Hindu pantheon, for instance, is the Lord of Kashi and resides in the city. But the city predated him. Indeed, because of its beauty and luminosity, he *chose* the city as his new home when he married Parvati, daughter of the Himalayas. Varanasi radiated with the presence of innumerable gardens, retreats, temples, and palaces.

- If a city is to be celebrated as a religious center, as Varanasi is, how does a description, like the one below, serve this purpose?

- Why do you think people would actually believe this exaggerated description? Were there other facets to Varanasi's existence that might have already made people like it?

- How do the four goals of artha, kama, dharma, and moksha describe the life of the city?

[Brahma said to the gods] Where the Lord Shiva himself resides, that place that guarantees release to all as no other place does, it is there that the austere sage Agastya is immersed in a profound penance. Go there and put your cause to him. He will see your work through.

Brahma vanished. The gods were pleased and said to each other, "We are blessed! In this way we will get to have *darshan* [sight] of Kashi, the Lord of Kashi, and Parvati. . . . Because only those steps are blessed, that lead to Kashi. Today we listened to Brahma, and as the blessed result of that, we are en route to Kashi." In this way, the beautiful, well-speaking, well-intentioned gods, conversing among themselves on the matter, reached Kashi.

All around Shiva's ashram even the animals forgot their characteristic animosity and seemed full of peace. . . .

The gods on seeing the animals, began to criticize the heavens that were so full of troubles. In comparison to the gods, they said, the animals, birds, and deer who live in Kashi are very well off. They are not born again, whereas the gods have to suffer the pains of rebirth.

"Even though we live in the heavens, we cannot compare with the fallen of Kashi. In fact, there is no danger of suffering in Kashi, but in heaven there can be many troubles.

Living in Kashi, even while keeping a fast for a full month, is better than living elsewhere, sitting under a fine umbrella, eating a grand feast.

The happiness from living in Kashi cannot be matched by living anywhere in the whole world. Now, if people were aware of this, would they not all wish to live in Kashi? But it is after thousands of lifetimes of creating merit that one gets to live in Kashi.

Dharma, artha, kama and moksha—these four ends of life can be found in Kashi in a complete way, such that they cannot be found anywhere else. . . . In Kashi, dharma stands on all four feet, artha is present in various ways, and kama is the sole refuge of innumerable people. Indeed, what is that excellent thing that is not present in Kashi?

After all, where the Lord Shiva is himself present to give dharma, artha, kama and moksha, why should one be surprised that the three worlds are nowhere equal to Kashi?"

Source: Kashikhanda (Part one) of Mahrshi Vyasa, foreword by Ashok Kumar Kalia, edited by Acarya Sri karunapai Tripathi (Varanasi, India: Sampurnanand Sanskrit University, 2008), 69–94. Translated by Nita Kumar.

Poems of Kabir and Tulsi

The second document consists of poems by Kabir and Tulsi. Kabir (ca. 1440–1518) was a weaver who lived in Varanasi and is regarded as a *sant,* or saint. Through his verses and aphorisms he challenged the ritualism of both Hinduism and Islam, the dominance of *pundits,* or Hindu priests, and *qazis,* Muslim preachers, and the divisions into high and low. His followers grouped themselves into what is sometimes described as a new religion, Kabirpanth, or "the way of Kabir." He is important in the history of Varanasi, India, and the world, because he was a popular poet and teacher whose message of egalitarianism recurs time and again. As a Muslim, he is also a representative of the many-faceted Hindu-Muslim synthesis that characterizes popular religion and everyday life in India.

Tulsi Das (ca. 1532–1623) is as unknown as Kabir as a historical person but is even more popular for his writings. He too lived in Varanasi and suffered adverse circumstances in his childhood, though he rose to fame quickly as a poet and a bhakta, or mystic. He composed many poems and is most famous for his epic about Rama, based on the Sanskrit original but composed in local Hindi and embellished with many original poetic touches. Tulsi Das is extremely important because his *Ramcharitmanas,* or story of Rama, is one of the most popular books in the world, read by millions of Hindus wherever. It is excerpted for music, dance, and performance, is taught and recited, and is memorized for its beauty and simplicity. Because he provided a new direction for Hindu worship, that of loving devotion to Rama, he can also be credited with historically having helped the religion to withstand Islamic onslaught that might have reduced its importance. Finally, his imaginative rendering of worship made it all the stronger.

- Do Kabir and Tulsi have an identical perspective on god, as shown in poems two and three? What is the difference? How may it be reconciled within Hinduism?

- There was obviously a sharp class difference in the city between the poor and the privileged. Does it surprise you that two such important religious leaders came from the poorest classes?

- Kabir's is the only mention of women, apart from just a couple in the whole discussion of Varanasi. Can you recollect what these other two mentions are? What do you think of the fact that real women (apart from Kabir's mention of them) are absent but are present as Parvati, wife of Shiva; Devi, the goddess; and courtesans? (These are the other two mentions—of goddesses and courtesans.)

FROM *KABIR GRANTHAVALI*, VERSE 178

Hey Qazi,
    what's that book you're preaching from?
And reading, reading—how many days?
    Still you haven't mastered one word.
Drunk with power, you want to grab me;
    then comes the circumcision.
    Brother, what can I say?—
If God had wanted to make me a Muslim,
    Why didn't he make the incision?
You cut away the foreskin, and then you have a
        Muslim;
    so what about your women?
    What are they?

Women, so they say, are only half-formed men:
    I guess they must stay Hindus to the end.
Hindus, Muslims—where did they come from?
    Who got them started down this road?
Search inside, search your heart and look:
    Who made heaven come to be?
Fool,
    Throw away that book, and sing of Ram.
    What you're doing has nothing to do with
        him.
Kabir has caught hold of Ram for his refrain,
    And the Qazi?
    He spends his life in vain.

FROM *KABIR GRANTHAVALI*, VERSE 46

Tell me, Ram: what will happen to me?
I haven't shown much wit: I've abandoned
    Benares

Like a fish who leaves the water and finds
    himself outside,
I'm stripped of any merit earned in former lives.

I squandered a life spent in Siva's city:
moved to Magahar when my time was ripe—

Penance in Kashi year after year
And here I am in Magahar to die.

Kashi, Magahar: they seem the same.
Which can rectify a life of little faith?

In Kashi, they say, you can cry to Siva when you
    die.
And Kabir? Dead already.
    He's enjoying life with Ram.

FROM TULSI DAS' *KAVITAVALI*, VERSE 7.73

I was born in a beggar family
And, hearing the sounds of celebration,
My mother and father felt anguish,
    felt pain.

From childhood on, poor thing that I was,
I went weeping, begging from door to door.
To me the four great goals of life
    were four little grains of food.

And that is the Tulsi who has become
The good servant of that worthy Lord:
When Fate, the great astrologer, hears,
    how cheated it feels.

Your name, O Ram:
Is it wise or mad?
It makes a weighty mountain
    from a tiny scrap of straw.

Source: Paras Nath Tivari, *Kabir Granthavali*, and Ramcandra Sukla et al., eds., *Tulsi-Granthavali*, both quoted in *Songs of the Saints of India*, edited by John Stratton Hawley and Mark Juergensmayer (New Delhi, India: Oxford University Press, 2004).

Further Reading

Chandra, Moti. *Kashi ka Itihas (The History of Kashi*, in Hindi). Varanasi, India: Vishwavidyalaya Publishers, 2003; 1st pub. 1962.

Eck, Diana. *Banaras: City of Light.* New York: Penguin Books, 1983.

Freitag, Sandria, ed. *Culture and Power in Banaras: Community, Performance, and Environment, 1800–1980.* Berkeley: University of California Press, 1989.

Hawley, John Stratton, and Mark Juergensmeyer. *Songs of the Saints of India.* New Delhi, India: Oxford University Press, 2004.

Hertel, Bradley, and Cynthia Humes, eds. *Living Banaras: Hindu Religion in Cultural Context.* Albany: State University of New York Press, 1993.

Kumar, Nita, *The Artisans of Banaras.* Princeton, NJ: Princeton University Press, 1988.

———. "Work and Leisure in the Formation of Identity: Muslim Weavers in a Hindu City." In *Culture and Power in Banaras: Community, Performance, and Environment, 1800–1980.* Edited by Sandra Freitag. Berkeley: University of California Press, 1989.

———. *Lessons from Schools: The History of Education in Banaras.* New Delhi, India: Sage Publications, 2000.

Parry, Jonathan. *Death in Banaras.* Cambridge: Cambridge University Press, 1994.

Singh, R. L. *Banaras: A Study in Urban Geography.* Banaras, India: Nand Kishore & Bros, 1955.

Web Resources

The Holy City of Varanasi, Ganga and Ghats, http://varanasi.nic.in/ghat/ghat.htm.

The Story of India: Varanasi, PBS, http://www.pbs.org/thestoryofindia/gallery/photos/9.html.

Varanasi City, http://www.varanasicity.com/history-of-varanasi.html.

A Sampling of the Music of Banaras (cassettes)

Bismillah Khan. *Shehnai: Puriya Dhanashree and Bhairavi.* RPG Enterprises STCS 850089.

Channulal Mishra. *Thumri, dadra.* Music Today B01004.

Channulal Mishra. *Tulsidas Ramcharitmanas.* Music Today D02101A and D02101B.

Rajan and Sajan Mishra. *Lalit, Puriya.* Music Today A92030.

Rajan and Sajan Mishra. *Tirth: Kashi.* Music Today D96001.

NIRMAN. *Children Playing Gods* (a documentary about NGO work in Banaras using Tulsi's story of Rama), www.nirman.info.

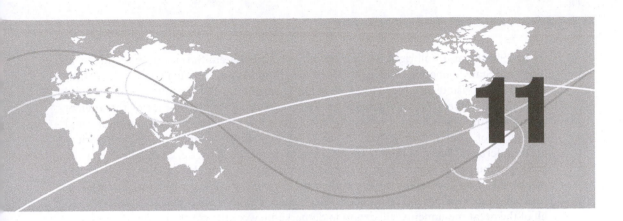

Samarkand

Political and Economic Hub Connecting East and West

(1220–1660)

REUEL R. HANKS

We travel not for trafficking alone,
By hotter winds, our fiery hearts are fanned,
For lust of knowing what should not be known,
We take the Golden Road to Samarkand.

THE BRITISH POET AND PLAYWRIGHT JAMES ELROY FLECKER'S FAMOUS STANZAS evoke a sense of place both mystic and exotic, an ancient city of conquerors and commerce, marked by grandeur and intrigue. Samarkand, in present-day Uzbekistan, is all that and more, as I found when I visited the city. There is compelling evidence that Samarkand is one of the oldest settlements in the world, with excavations showing that irrigation works supported a small sedentary population in the prehistoric era. By 700 BCE the city was an influential city-state and had emerged as a key trading hub along the ancient Silk Road, its economic success bestowed by advantages of its geographic location. Today Samarkand is home to approximately six hundred thousand inhabitants and is one of Uzbekistan's major cities.

In 1995 I was a Fulbright Scholar teaching in Uzbekistan. Several of my students at Tashkent State Economics University were from Samarkand, and on a long weekend they invited me to visit their fabled city. Arriving by car from the east, we left the highway and crossed the defile of a large irrigation canal when suddenly the domes of the ancient necropolis, the Shahi Zinda, broke into view. After a few more moments the antiquity and past glory of Central Asia spilled out before me in a startling panorama of both ancient and modern. Hulking, pollution-spewing trucks from the Soviet era lumbered past the edifice of the Bibi Khanym mosque, a massive structure built in the 1300s that was nearly destroyed in an earthquake at the end of the nineteenth century but was undergoing restoration funded by UNESCO when I first saw it. The Bibi Khanym, along with almost all of the great monuments still extant in Samarkand, were the contributions of Timur, or Tamerlane (1370–1405) along with several generations of his successors, typically referred to as the Timurids. It was this dynasty that made Samarkand, at least for much of the fourteenth and fifteenth centuries, arguably the most important city in Asia. Six hundred years later the urban landscape of modern Samarkand still reflects the passions and ambitions of Timur and his successors. The mystery and allure I encountered on my first visit there has continued to draw me back, and each journey has only deepened my attraction for this magnificent city.

That first encounter with Samarkand only served to make me crave additional opportunities to explore and learn about the city. Several years later I returned to teach at Samarkand State Institute of Foreign Languages, and I was reminded of both the geographical and historical reach of the Timurids. The shadow of Timur, both literally and figuratively, may be found throughout the old city. At the intersection adjacent to the institute an enormous bronze statue of a seated Timur, built since Uzbekistan's independence in 1991, glares out over the landscape, while just three hundred yards away, directly in view from the classrooms filled with students, Timur himself lies interred under the Gur-i-Amir, a mausoleum crowned by a magnificent turquoise dome. Legend holds that an inscription at the entrance to the crypt warned of misfortune, death, and destruction to any who disturbed the great warlord's eternal slumber. Local guides are quick to point out that on June 22, 1941, the day after Soviet scholars opened the sarcophagus that holds the conqueror's remains, Germany attacked the USSR, ultimately resulting in twenty million deaths in the Soviet Union. Despite his curse, the new Uzbek regime has adopted Timur as a national icon and Samarkand as a showcase city, reminding all of a glorious heritage that heralds an equally glorious future, at least according to the current governmental slogans. If past is indeed prologue, then Samarkand stands to take its place in the ranks of the world's great urban places once again.

Samarkand was almost completely destroyed in the 1200s, but within 150 years would not only recover but would emerge as the capital of one of history's greatest conquerors and his descendants. This rebirth made the city into a political center and commercial magnet that influenced the history and development of Central Asia as well as that of Russia, the Middle East, and South Asia. Samarkand was the hub connecting East and West, a conduit for the transfer of goods, ideas and people.

SAMARKAND AND THE WORLD:
A Magnet for Merchants and Conquerors

The American communist and journalist Anna Louise Strong, a visitor to Soviet Central Asia in the 1920s, accurately noted that "it is the geography of Samarkand that has fixed her destiny." Samarkand, both ancient and modern, has been given life by the waters of the Zeravshan River, a stream that begins in the mountains lying to the east. For centuries the river has provided the basis for agriculture, and the region near Samarkand long has enjoyed a reputation for verdant orchards, vineyards, and wheat fields. A second gift of geography was the city's position astride trade routes running between China and the Middle East, servicing caravans bound to both the East and the West. Attracting merchants, traders, and pilgrims from every corner of Eurasia, Samarkand was a cosmopolitan, sophisticated "global city" long before the full extent of the globe was known. A magnet for world conquerors, including the likes of Alexander and Genghis Khan, Samarkand's greatest glory was achieved as the capital of the empire of Amir Timur, or Tamerlane as he is more commonly known in the English-speaking world.

At the start of the thirteenth century the cities lying along the ancient Silk Road in Central Asia were thriving. The caravan traffic and the business it generated had made Samarkand, Bukhara, and other oasis settlements prosperous in Transoxiana, a Greek name meaning the "land beyond the Oxus River" (a stream known today as the Amu Darya).

Samarkand's Destruction and Rebirth (1220–1660)

By 1220 these cities and others would be smoldering ruins, devastated by history's most prolific conqueror, the leader of the Mongol hordes, Genghis Khan. The Mongol army arrived from the east, where it had already subdued two Chinese states and the Khitan Empire as it expanded along the Silk Road, a trading route that had linked China to the West for centuries. The fury of the great Khan was ignited in 1218 by the miscalculation of Ala al-Din Muhammad, the ruler of the Khwarazm empire, an oasis state lying to the west of Samarkand. That year one of Ala al-Din's governors, ruling the eastern city of Otrar, executed the members of a caravan sent by the Mongol leader. The response was fast and furious: Mongol armies swept across the region, laying siege to the major cities and destroying all in their path. After capturing its sister-city of Bukhara, the Mongols surrounded Samarkand. For almost a week the city resisted the attack, but eventually the defenders capitulated, and the Mongol warriors were turned loose on both the inhabitants and the city itself, pillaging and burning for days.

The destruction had lasting effect. More than a century later the great Muslim traveler Ibn Batutta would pass through the city, as he also did the cities of Mecca and Kilwa, and though he found much to admire, he also noted the many ruined buildings that remained from the Mongol horde's devastation. Ironically, only a few decades after Batutta's visit another great conqueror and a descendant of Genghis Khan would remake Samarkand into not only the greatest city in Central Asia but also arguably one of the most impressive urban places in the entire world.

The City of Timur

The small city of Shahrisabz, once known as Kesh, today lies about two hours' journey by car from Samarkand. There, only three years after Ibn Battuta visited Samarkand in 1333, a boy was born into the Barlas clan, the family of local rulers who claimed to be related to Genghis Khan's second son Chagatay. Called "Timur," a name meaning "iron" in the local Turkic dialect, the lad grew into a formidable soldier and was battle hardened by his early twenties. Wounded by an arrow in the right leg early in his career, he walked with a pronounced limp and acquired in some quarters the less-than-flattering nickname "Timur the Lame," which became corrupted into Tamerlane, the name he is still commonly known by in Western sources. Gradually gaining experience and building up his forces, by about the age of thirty-three Amir ("Prince") Timur, as he is known to-day in Uzbekistan, had amassed a sizable realm covering much of Transoxiana. A de-vout Muslim, he set about building an empire that incorporated lands from both the Islamic and non-Islamic realms. Conquest and expansion were the hallmarks of Timur's ambition, and he spent his adult life pushing the boundaries of his dominion toward the four points of the compass. In fact, when almost seventy years of age, Timur mounted a campaign against China, determined to join the western lands of the Ming Dynasty (1368–1644) to his already-massive imperial state, but he died of a fever be-fore reaching Chinese territory. Timur made Samarkand the capital of his budding em-pire, determined to make the city the centerpiece of a vast realm that, at its greatest height, stretched from Baghdad to India and from the Persian Gulf to the steppes of Russia.

Not only did Samarkand function as the political capital of Timur's vast empire, but its location astraddle major trade routes connecting China to the Middle East meant that the city once again became a bustling hub of commerce, with goods from every corner of China, India, Persia, and Russia filling the markets. Spices, silk, musk, glass, slaves, and other rare and expensive goods might all be found in the bazaars of the city. The Spanish ambassador Ruy González de Clavijo, upon his arrival in Samarkand in 1404, estimated that the city exceeded Seville's in population, which at that time was one of the most populous cities in Spain. The best estimates of historians put Samarkand's popula-tion at about 150,000 in 1400, meaning the city was more populous than London at the time and contained only a slightly smaller number of inhabitants than contemporary Paris. Samarkand had become the center of the unified economic space represented by Timur's empire, and the city's status from several centuries earlier as one of the leading trade centers on the Silk Road was reestablished and, indeed, greatly enhanced. (See Map 11.1.)

But the greatest impact on Samarkand of the Timurids, as historians have dubbed the dynasty Amir Timur established, was the complete remaking of the urban profile of the city. Samarkand had not recovered from the destruction the Mongols wrought in the pre-vious century, and there were few large structures remaining. The dynasty accomplished remaking the city by commissioning grand structures that surpassed any previously seen in Central Asia. Timur considered himself a patron of the arts, and his conquests pro-vided two essential factors that enabled him to recast the city: wealth and skilled artisans. As Timur's holdings expanded into India, Persia, and the Ottoman Empire, he typically looted the wealth from other cities or demanded tribute in the form of precious jewels, gold, or other valuable commodities. With his coffers filled with this booty, the emperor could then engage in spectacular building projects not only in Samarkand but also in many cities throughout the region.

One of Timur's first projects was to rebuild and extend the walls of the city, which had not been completely restored since the Mongols' siege more than a century and a half earlier. But Timur was also fond of open spaces and nature, so he built spacious, verdant gardens around the city in which he often held festivals and entertained visitors. There he held court under enormous tents that could contain his entire retinue of several thousand people, including numerous wives, and surrounded by groves of fruit and nut trees. Many of these retreats were enclosed by gates and walls and were given specific names such as the "Enchanting Garden," and scholars have established that a considerable por-tion of the city's landscape consisted of such green space, making Samarkand famous as a city of orchards and gardens.

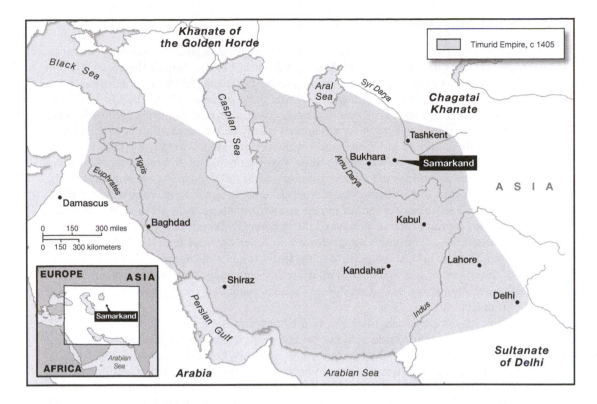

Map 11.1. Timurid Empire, ca. 1405

Amir Timur's empire stretched from Delhi to Baghdad, and from the Caucasus Mountains to the Indian Ocean. This realm, lying at the crossroads of Asia, the Middle East, and Europe, provided the stage for cultural and economic exchange between all these regions. The legacy of this interaction remains evident in India, Russia, and Central Asia, where examples of Timurid architecture continue to astonish visitors six centuries later.

Timur also orchestrated the construction of monumental edifices and structures, many of which have survived the ensuing six centuries, to some extent or another, and were worked on by a veritable army of skilled workers, architects, and artisans from every corner of Eurasia. By the late 1300s there were thousands of such men in Samarkand who had been brought from Damascus, Baghdad, Shiraz, and other locations across western Asia. These immigrants possessed abilities, techniques, and artistic secrets that heretofore had not been prominently featured in Central Asia architecture. The art of glazing tiles, for example, was imported to Central Asia along with construction techniques and architectural skill that allowed enormous free-standing domes to be built. Such knowledge had been perfected in the Middle East but now contributed to the urban spaces of Central Asia.

Timur also gathered hundreds of scholars and artists, offering them financial support and access to his growing libraries, or *kitabkhanas*, institutions of learning and art that he had borrowed from the Persian Empire. Collectively, the scholars and craftsmen would transform urban landscapes across much of the continent, and the forms and styles they introduced are still followed today in the states of Central Asia.

Timur's Lasting Legacy

In 1398 Timur set out on an expedition to conquer India, a land that not only held great riches but was also populated by large numbers of Hindus, whom the pious Muslim Timur considered infidels. Hinduism, an ancient faith, had held sway in northern India for over one thousand years, although the Delhi Sultanate, a state ruled by Muslims, controlled the region. Timur crushed the armies sent against him, capturing Delhi and other cities, and amassed an enormous amount of booty, including thousands of gemstones. Many of these rubies, sapphires, and other precious stones were transported back to Samarkand to embellish a massive mosque, Bibi Khanym, built to honor one of his wives while he was away from the city. As the story goes, the builder was so smitten with the beautiful woman that he demanded a kiss before he completed the construction, and his peck was so ardent that it left an impression on her cheek. When Timur returned and found the offending mark, he executed the impetuous admirer and thereafter ordered all the women of his empire to adopt the veil in order to avoid tempting men with their charms. There is not a shred of truth to the story, as it is well known the mosque was built over the course of five years, and Timur himself personally oversaw at least some of the construction, but the legend reinforces the almost-mythological status that Timur still holds in Central Asia.

After its completion in 1404, the Bibi Khanym mosque stood as one of the world's largest mosques. The façade marking the entryway, a huge portal containing an arched gateway called an *iwan* in the Muslim world, reached a height of approximately 100 feet. Inside was a large courtyard leading to another enormous edifice that contained the entrance to the mosque itself. Minarets and domes surrounded the courtyard, along with a ribbed dome in blue tiles that would closely resemble the dome on the Gur-i-Amir, Timur's final resting place, located about a mile away. The mosque itself featured a larger, brilliant blue dome rising to almost 120 feet. The walls of the mosque and most of the other structures were adorned with quotations from the Quran, Islam's most important scripture, in the stylized Arabic script known as geometric Kufic, presented using glazed bricks and tiles.

In the decades immediately after its completion the Bibi Khanym was a dazzling and incomparable sight and an apt representation of Amir Timur's ambition and ego. Yet few builders in Central Asia had experience erecting a structure so immense, and unfortunately the techniques employed to set the foundations of the massive walls were flawed. These shortcomings in the construction resulted in a deterioration of parts of the mosque in only a couple centuries, a process aided and accelerated by the region's frequent earthquakes. In the late nineteenth century a powerful quake brought most of the main mosque down as well as the surrounding minarets and smaller domes. For almost a century the Bibi Khanym crumbled until an effort at reclamation was initiated during the late Soviet period. In the 1990s UNESCO, the United Nations Educational, Scientific, and Cultural Organization, in conjunction with the government of Uzbekistan, began funding the restoration of the mosque, and today the magnificent building has regained its former grandeur.

Before the rise of Timur the art of making majolica tiles was apparently unknown in Central Asia. These ceramic tiles are manufactured by applying a glaze to a ceramic tile, painting or coloring the tile, and then firing it, thereby fixing the glaze and color onto the tile. Carried from the Middle East by Timur's captives, the skill of manufacturing turquoise and blue tiles enabled craftsmen to cover the massive domes that were raised over many structures Timur commissioned, including the Bibi Khanym and Timur's own resting place, the Gur-i-Amir. The art was used not only in Samarkand but also across Timur's realm in Central Asia.

In Samarkand Timur also expanded the Shahi Zinda, a necropolis that legend claims holds the remains of a cousin of the Prophet Muhammed, Qusim ibn Abbas, one of the Arab leaders who brought Islam to Central Asia in the eighth century. The name of the cemetery may be translated as "Tomb of the Living King," a reference to the legend surrounding the crypt of Qusim. According to the story, Qusim was praying when he was attacked and beheaded. But, miraculously, he simply picked up his head and jumped down a well, over which his mausoleum was built, centuries before Timur was born. Ibn Battuta described how the local Muslims venerated the location, and certainly, by Timur's reign the tomb had become a place of pilgrimage for local believers.

Timur's place of burial, the Gur-i-Amir, became a family crypt, coming to house the remains of the first three Timurid rulers, his son and immediate successor, Shahrukh, and another grandson, Ulug Beg, as well as another son and two of Timur's teachers. The interior of the classic ribbed dome, a style unknown in Central Asia before the rise of Timur, was originally covered in hammered gold leaf. The Gur-i-Amir not only stands as one of the most beautiful and important mausoleums in Central Asia, but it is also considered the model for many of the structures built by the Mogul rulers of India (who were descendants of Timur), including what is arguably the world's most famous building, the Taj Mahal (completed in 1648). The classic "onion dome" architecture may be observed in both structures along with other similarities regarding the design and function of the buildings. Some scholars contend that the domes of St. Basil's Cathedral in Moscow, a Christian church built in the 1500s, were also derived from Islamic architectural styles borrowed from Central Asia.

Ulug Beg: Scholar and Builder

Timur was succeeded by his son, Shahrukh, who, perhaps, to escape the shadow of his father, moved the capital of the empire to the city of Herat, now located in northwestern Afghanistan. Although Shahrukh is buried in the Gur-i-Amir with his father, he spent little time in Samarkand, and early in his reign commissioned his young son Ulug Beg to rule the province of Transoxiana from the former capital. Shahrukh therefore had little direct impact on Samarkand, but his decision to award the city to his son had important consequences for the city as well as for the scientific and intellectual world of the Middle Ages.

Ulug Beg, the third of the Timurid line to rule Samarkand, had a far different character from that of his father and certainly from his grandfather. He ruled the entire Timurid Empire for only two years, but under his father he served as governor of Samarkand for nearly forty years, from 1411 to 1447. Much more a scholar than a general, Ulug Beg changed the urban landscape of his capital city almost to the same degree that his grandfather Timur had, but the buildings and structures he constructed were not monuments and mausoleums. Instead, his focus was on education and learning, and his legacy in the urban development of Samarkand mirrors these interests. Ulug Beg began the construction of Samarkand's most famous landmark, the Registan. A square bordered on three sides by medressehs, or Islamic schools, "Registan" means "place of sand." At one time the square may have been covered in sand, as it was the location for public executions, which were usually performed by beheading the condemned. Ulug Beg had the first medresseh built there in 1420, and a number of historians believe that he himself taught mathematics at the school.

Flanked by two towering minarets, the façade of the medresseh is inlaid with Arabic calligraphy and the colorful tiles his grandfather made famous. An inscription on the building reads, "It is the responsibility of every believer to seek knowledge." Ulug Beg attracted numerous mathematicians and other scholars from Perisa and other corners of the Middle East to train and study at his school in Samarkand. The structure would withstand dozens of earthquakes over the centuries without collapsing. During the lifetime of Ulug Beg, only his medresseh would grace the Registan, but his successors over the next two centuries would build two more magnificent edifices to enclose the square on three sides. In the interim Ulug Beg's medresseh would train hundreds of scholars from across the Islamic world for the next four centuries, a fitting monument to a ruler who valued knowledge more than power and wealth. Ali Kushji, perhaps Ulug Beg's most accomplished student, had a major impact on the study of astronomy in both the Muslim world as well as Europe.

However, Ulug Beg's greatest scholarly contribution remained underground and out of sight for almost four hundred years. Ulug Beg was not only a mathematician but also one of the most accomplished astronomers of the Middle Ages. His observatory, situated on the outskirts of Samarkand, was the most advanced facility of its day and eclipsed the technology available to European astronomers. Ulug Beg's observatory contained a gigantic sextant nearly two hundred feet long, which had an astrolabe mounted on it, allowing the astronomer to slide along the curve of the sextant, taking observations. His measurements of the positions of many celestial bodies, including many stars, the moon, and the sun, were amazingly accurate and more precise than those taken by European astronomers at the time. His data contributed to the study of the stars for centuries.

Ulug Beg made Samarkand not just a city of conquerors but also a center of scholarship and learning. Alas, he was a better scholar than administrator, so he failed to discover a plot his own son organized. Toppled from power in 1449, Ulug Beg was executed by his son, who seized the throne, though the Timurid Dynasty would soon end.

The last of the Timurid Dynasty to rule from Samarkand was Babur, a prince who came to power in 1495. Babur was ambitious and sought to recreate the glory of the early Timurid period, but he faced a capable and shrewd rival, Shabany Khan, the leader of a seminomadic tribe called the Uzbeks. By 1510 Babur's dream of resurrecting the empire of his great-grandfather Timur had been dashed. Forced further southward into modern Afghanistan, Babur turned his imperial ambitions toward the lands of India, which was laden with resources and treasure. There he founded the Mogul Dynasty, an imperial epoch that would rival that of his great forebear. But Samarkand and much of Central Asia now belonged to a new ruling elite, who later historians would identify as the Shaybanids after the warlord who closed the door on Babur's efforts to reclaim the grandeur of his ancestors. By 1600 Shaybanid control of the region had been replaced by the Ashtarkhanids, who ruled primarily from Bukhara, an ancient Silk Road city lying to the west of Samarkand, and Samarkand's political influence waned.

Some Ashtarkhanid rulers followed in the path of their Timurid predecessors and glorified the city by adding still more spectacular buildings to its skyline and embellishing the existing architecture. In the early 1600s, almost a century and a half after Ulug Beg had erected the medresseh that bears his name, the khan Alchin Yalantush Bahadir ordered the construction of two medressehs to enclose the open space of the Registan. The first, Sher Dor ("With Lions") differed radically from Ulug Beh's medresseh in that it featured two stylized lions above the front portal, accompanied by two suns with human faces. The structure openly ignores the Islamic prohibition against the depiction of animate figures. Some scholars claim that the suns represent Zoroastrian symbols, which, if true, would certainly indicate the persistence of a faith largely eliminated in Central Asia more than six hundred years before. The second, Tilla Kari ("Gold Covered") contains a huge domed mosque featuring an interior ceiling covered in hammered gold leaf. A stunning kaleidoscope of color and pattern, the Tilla Kari was the last great addition to the urban landscape of premodern Samarkand, and its construction marked the end of four hundred years of expansion and spectacular building on a scale that has seldom been equaled and never surpassed in any other city.

GLOBAL ENCOUNTERS AND CONNECTIONS:
Samarkand's Confluence of Cultures

The Timurids built Samarkand into one of the great cosmopolitan centers of the medieval period by bringing people, goods, and ideas from abroad and incorporating these influences into the profile of the city. The designers and builders who were brought by force from Damascus, Shiraz, and other cities of the Middle East quickly transformed Samarkand into a city of glorious, towering Islamic architecture. Their influence may be found elsewhere in the region as well, such as in the spectacular mausoleum Timur had built at Turkistan, today in southern Kazakhstan.

Commerce also thrived in the city because of Samarkand's traditional position as a major Silk Road center, an advantage enhanced by its role as an imperial capital for much of the Timurid period. Located in the heart of Asia along numerous established trade routes, commodities from every corner of the Eurasian land mass flowed to the city's markets. The city attracted traders from as far away as Russia, China, and India. These visitors not only engaged in business but also exchanged information and world views. From the middle of the fourteenth century to the early decades of the fifteenth century no other city in the world drew a greater variety of visitors from so many corners of the globe.

By 1700 Central Asia was politically fragmented and economically adrift, as the importance of the Silk Road trade had sharply declined. The region's great cities—Samarkand among them—lost both their economic relevance and cosmopolitan nature as global trade that now traveled via the world's oceans bypassed them. Europe had arisen as the global center of trade and technology, and Samarkand and its environs were too distant and inaccessible to attract European traders and settlers. For several centuries the rest of the world almost forgot Timur's incomparable city.

Modern Samarkand has recovered much of its past glory. After suffering numerous earthquakes and almost total abandonment in the early 1800s, the city began to recover in the late nineteenth century, and for a few years in the early twentieth century even served as the capital of the Uzbek Soviet Socialist Republic. During the Soviet period there was limited interest in restoring the city's great monuments, but since the collapse of the Soviet Union the government of Uzbekistan has devoted considerable resources to reconstructing the architecture of the Timurids and their successors. Samarkand now finds itself at a curious crossroads of rebuilding its past in an effort to secure its future. The potential for tourism to drive economic development in the city and its region remains largely unfulfilled, due in no small part to its distance from Europe, North America, and Japan; its lack of infrastructure and adequate facilities; and its poor management and advertising in the tourism sector. But these challenges are gradually being overcome, and those who take the golden road to Samarkand today will be rewarded with a vision of exotic grandeur that cannot be encountered anywhere else. Six hundred years ago Amir Timur and those who followed him built a city like no other in the world. Their matchless achievements continue to awe and inspire those who "travel not for trafficking alone."

ENCOUNTERS AS TOLD: PRIMARY SOURCES

Although records exist from throughout Samarkand's history, little is available in English, particularly for the time period this chapter covers. The following presents a diplomat's firsthand impressions of the city in the early fifteenth century.

Narrative of the Embassy of Ruy González de Clavijo to the Court of Timour, at Samarcand, A.D. 1403–6, by Ruy González de Clavijo

Ruy Gonzáles de Clavijo was a Spanish diplomat sent by King Henry III of Sevilla (Spain) to the court of Amir Timur in 1403. It took more than a year before Clavijo and his entourage arrived in Samarkand, and they stayed in the capital for only about three months. Even in this short period, however, Clavijo and his companions were able to observe a great deal about life in Timur's city. The following passages are from a diary Clavijo kept while traveling, but it was not published for over a century and a half after his death in 1412. His observations provide a unique window into life in Samarkand as well as the personality of Timur.

- What aspects of Samarkand appear to impress de Clavijo the most? Why does he find these qualities so admirable?

- De Clavijo finds some similarities between Samarkand and his home region of central Spain. What are these, and why does he take pains to mention them in his narrative?

Now that I have related those things which befell the ambassadors in this city of Samarcand, I will give an account of that city and its territory, and of the things which the lord has done to ennoble it.

The city of Samarcand is situated in a plain, and surrounded by an earthen wall. It is a little larger than the city of Seville, but, outside the city, there are a great number of houses, joined together in many parts, so as to form suburbs. The city is surrounded on all sides by many gardens and vineyards, which extend in some directions a league and a half, in others two leagues, the city being in the middle. In these houses and gardens there is a large population, and there are people selling bread, meat, and many other things; so that the suburbs are much more thickly inhabited than the city within the walls. Amongst these gardens, which are outside the city, there are great and noble houses, and here the lord has several palaces. The nobles of the city have their houses amongst these gardens, and they are so extensive that, when a man approaches the city, he sees nothing but a mass of very high trees. Many streams of water flow through the city, and through these gardens, and among these gardens there are many cotton plantations, and melon grounds, and the melons of this land are good and plentiful; and at Christmas time there is a wonderful quantity of melons and grapes. Every day so many camels come in, laden with melons, that it is a wonder how the people can eat them all. They preserve them from year to year in the villages, in the same way as figs, taking off their skins, cutting them in large slices, and drying them in the sun.

Outside the city there are great plains, which are covered with populous villages, peopled by the captives which the lord caused to be taken from the countries which he conquered. The land is very plentiful in all things, as well as bread and wine, fruit, meat, and birds; and the sheep are very large, and have long tails, some weighing twenty pounds, and they are so abundant in the market that, even when the lord was there with all his host, a pair was worth only a ducat. Other things are so plentiful, that for a *meri*, which is half a rial, they sell a *fanega* and half of barley, and the quantity of bread and rice is infinite.

The city is so large, and so abundantly supplied, that it is wonderful; and the name of Samarcand or Cimes-quinte is derived from the two words *cimes* (great), and *quinte* (a town). The Supplies of this city do not consist of food alone, but of silks, satins, gauzes, taffetas, velvets, and other things. The lord had so strong a desire to ennoble this city, that he brought captives to increase its population, from every land which he conquered, especially all those who were skillful in any art. From Damascus, he brought weavers of silk, and men who made bows, glass, and earthenware, so that, of those articles, Samarcand produces the best in the world. From Turkey he brought archers, masons, and silversmiths. He also brought men skilled in making engines of war: and he sowed hemp and flax, which had never before been seen in the land.

There was so great a number of people brought to this city, from all parts, both men and women, that they are said to have amounted to one hundred and fifty thousand persons, of many nations, Turks, Arabs, and Moors, Christian Armenians, Greek Catholics, and Jacobites, and those who baptize with fire in the face, who are Christians with peculiar opinions. There was such a multitude of these people that the city was not large enough to hold them, and it was wonderful what a number lived under the trees, and in caves outside.

The city is also very rich in merchandize which comes from other parts. Russia and Tartary send linen and skins; China sends silks, which are the best in the world, (more especially the satins), and musk, which is found in no other part of the world, rubies and diamonds, pearls and rhubarb, and many other things. The merchandize which comes from China is the best and most precious which comes to this city, and they say that the people of China are the most skilful [sic] workmen in the world. They say themselves that they have two eyes, the Franks one, and that the Moors are blind, so that they have the advantage of every other nation in the world. From India come spices, such as nutmegs, cloves, mace, cinnamon, ginger, and many others which do not reach Alexandria.

Source: Ruy González de Clavijo, *Narrative of the Embassy of Ruy González de Clavijo to the Court of Timour, at Samarcand, A.D. 1403–6* (London: Printed for the Hakluyt Society, 1859), 169–171.

Further Reading

Blunt, Wilfrid. *The Golden Road to Samarkand*. New York: Viking Press, 1975.

Liu, Xinru. *The Silk Road in World History*. New York: Oxford University Press, 2010.

Manz, Beatrice Forbes. *The Rise and Rule of Tamerlane*. New York: Cambridge University Press, 1999.

Marozzi, Justin. *Tamerlane: Sword of Islam, Conqueror of the World*. Cambridge, MA: Da Capo Press, 2006.

Moorhouse, Geoffrey. *Apples in the Snow: A Journey to Samarkand*. New York: Faber and Faber, 2009.

Soucek, Svat. *A History of Inner Asia*. Cambridge: Cambridge University Press, 2000.

Web Resources

Samarkand—Crossroads of Culture, UNESCO World Heritage Convention, http://whc.unesco.org/en/list/603.

Samarkand: History and the Registan, http://romeartlover.tripod.com/Samarcanda.html.

Zaimeche, Salah. "Samarkand," Foundation for Science, Technology, and Civilisation, 2005, www.muslimheritage.com/uploads/Samarkand.pdf.

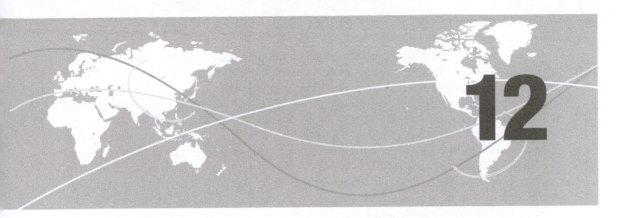

12

Venice

A Center of International Exchange in the Renaissance World

(1350–1550)

MARITERE LÓPEZ

I FIRST VISITED VENICE AS A NEW GRADUATE STUDENT, WHEN IT OCCURRED TO ME THAT in order to really understand the history of Italy, I needed to experience the place firsthand. I signed up for a summer study-abroad program in Rome and planned a weekend side trip to Venice with friends. I felt a strange urgency to experience this city in particular, as its history had loomed large in my studies of art. I also feared I might miss the opportunity altogether, for I had heard repeatedly the saying that Venice is, quite literally, sinking. Built on small islands on the shores of a lagoon on the Adriatic Sea—and buttressed over time with added sand, wood, and stones—Venice was originally the refuge of immigrants fleeing from "barbarians" who invaded the Italian peninsula in late Antiquity, such as the Huns in the fifth century and the Lombards in the sixth. Seemingly floating on water, the city has always been at the mercy of floods, as the Adriatic has risen over time and the islands have settled deeper into the seabed. In summer the risk of flood is less likely, however, so my fears that Venice would sink before my very eyes were dispelled. Still, captivated by the city, I came to feel that if Venice were to sink, to paraphrase a song, I would gladly go under too.

From the very moment I exited the train station and walked out into this resplendent place, I was struck by the fact that, interconnected by bridges built at odd angles, the islands that make up Venice, over one hundred in total, have no streets and consequently no car traffic. Rather, locals and visitors alike move about by foot or boat, meandering along sidewalks and canals, crossing over bridges, and following signs that direct one to the city's major sites. The lack of streets lends Venice a unique sound, at the core of which is an ensemble of human voices, thousands of them during high tourist season. This sound is uniquely Venetian because the noise of cars often muffles this human hum in other cities. I was also struck by Venice's radiance. Called by many "the City of Light," Venice is characterized by the sunshine's reflection on both water and buildings, many of which are richly adorned with marble and painted in luminous colors. Walking along the major artery of the city, the Grand Canal, I was amazed by the size and beauty of the houses, palaces, and warehouses, which are unique in their combination of Western and Byzantine looks. Venetian architecture is also distinctive in its historicity, for Venetians have purposely focused their attention on preservation rather than modernization, thereby maintaining the organic, haphazard planning of its urban spaces and keeping the design introduced during the city's golden age. In its aesthetic and very layout as well as in its sense of historical significance, Venice remains at heart a city of the Renaissance.

This period, dated roughly from 1350 to 1550 CE, was characterized by a degree of prosperity and cultural interaction, particularly with the Near East, unknown in Europe since the fall of the Western Roman Empire in the sixth century. Also characteristic of this period was the development of a new philosophy of life—known as humanism—which celebrated human potential and greatness as God's ultimate creation. Many contemporaries saw this excellence reflected in the innovative character of the Venetian people and in the rich urban spaces of the city itself. Highlighting the geographical layout of Venice's neighborhoods and major sites, in this chapter we trace the history of the city during the period, concentrating first on Venice's role as a global center of commerce. We then move on to a discussion of the Venetians' part in the development of the intellectual and artistic innovations that defined the Renaissance and deeply influenced how both contemporaries and later peoples, particularly in the West, came to understand, envision, and represent mankind and its place in the cosmos.

VENICE AND THE WORLD: A Global Center of Trade

The term "Renaissance" has come to denote the period of transition between the European Middle Ages and the modern age, which began in Italy in the fourteenth century. Literally meaning "rebirth," the term was coined in the nineteenth century to refer to the resurgence of classical literature that characterized the period's intellectual pursuits. Although Renaissance people did not use the term, they did recognize their age as different from previous ones. Importantly, they saw the population's resurgence after the Great Plague of the fourteenth century as well as a reduction in political unrest and economic hardship across Europe. Re-energized and with new hope, contemporary thinkers like Leonardo Bruni (1370–1444) came to call the period "the modern age," differentiating it from the "dark ages" that had preceded it. At the core of this modern age was the embrace of ancient Greek and Roman ideals celebrating man's abilities, particularly his potential to improve his life and that of others. Although the period's focus on the individual's worth has led scholars to argue that the rise of individualism characterized the Renaissance, each person's merit was measured also by his loyalty and service to the community, whether that be family, state, or church.

Although not thought of as the "birth place" of the Renaissance (an honor commonly given to Florence), Venice's history between the fourteenth and sixteenth centuries makes it a perfect window into the period. Located roughly in the middle of the Mediterranean's northern basin and with easy access to major waterways, Venice was uniquely placed to capitalize on its strategic location along major medieval trade routes (both maritime and over land), thereby ultimately dominating international trade. As a result, the city came to link Europe to the rest of the world, particularly to Byzantium and the Arab lands, in both commercial and cultural terms. Venetians traded from East to West not only material goods, such as Chinese silk and South East Asian spices, which enriched Westerners' sensory experiences, but also intellectual products such as treatises on science and philosophy, which expanded Europeans' understandings of the world. Venetians also traded from West to the East, perhaps most importantly introducing the peoples of Constantinople to the printed book.

Their singular position prompted Venetians to embrace commercial and industrial innovations, and this led to unprecedented economic prosperity and, in turn, a renewed faith in human ability. Encapsulated in the intellectual movement known as humanism, the Renaissance worldview challenged medieval conceptions of life as a mere way station to Salvation, arguing instead for man's continued involvement and investment in the here and now. The importance of man as God's greatest creation was also embodied by the new art styles developed during the period, particularly in Florence and Venice, which concentrated on realistic representations of man and his surroundings. Venice also exemplified, perhaps more so than any other Renaissance state, Italy's greater involvement in global developments as well as its cosmopolitanization, as Italians came into greater contact with peoples from around the globe, particularly North Africa and the Near East.

The Venetians' growing participation in global events was tightly linked to the city's extensive commercial interests. The protection of their trade empire required the city to scrutinize carefully and become involved strategically in the affairs not only of neighboring European countries but also of states around the eastern and southern Mediterranean basin, including the Byzantine Empire and Islamic sultanates. Venetian global interactions, significant since the ninth century, became of greater importance after the Fourth Crusade in the early twelfth century. Venetians, the main transporters of crusaders to the Holy Land, not only richly profited directly from their participation in the crusades but also subsequently formalized trading partnerships with Byzantium and several major Islamic powers. The Venetians' trade hegemony, although also reliant on the conquest of strategic ports such as the island of Cyprus, depended above all on the commercial privileges the city gained from its trading partners. Therefore, Venetian success required smooth relationships with Byzantium and the Islamic sultanates, relations often complicated by religious tensions, as Roman Latin Christianity, Greek Orthodox Christianity, and Islam vied for the souls—and lands—of the peoples of Europe, North Africa, and the Near East.

The inexorable advance of the Ottomans, a Turkish tribe originally from Anatolia, further complicated the situation. By the late fifteenth century the Ottomans had taken Constantinople, ending the Byzantine Empire and establishing the Ottoman Empire in its place. They had also gained control of almost all ports on the eastern and southern Mediterranean. Decidedly a direct threat to the Venetian empire—and, therefore, to the city's survival—the Ottomans further involved Venice in global affairs, as Venetians sought both to defend old commercial privileges and gain new ones. All the while Venetian interactions with the peoples of Byzantium, the Islamic sultanates, and the Ottoman Empire fostered a two-way exchange of commodities and ideas that changed the ways in which all of these peoples experienced everyday life.

The Most Serene Republic's Growth and Social Structure

Merely a collection of small, isolated islands in the sixth century, by the thirteenth century Venice was the most prosperous European city and, by the sixteenth, the third most populous in the world (after Constantinople and Tenochtitlan), with approximately 180,000 inhabitants. Furthering its commercial dominance by creating a powerful navy, Venice made itself into the world's *entrepôt*, a port of exchange through which all the world's goods flowed. To buttress the city's supremacy, Venetians also expanded its territory, creating an empire reaching into the Italian mainland to the west and as far as Cyprus in the east. The uniqueness of Venice's economic and political standing led contemporaries to call it *La Serenissima*, or the "Most Serene Republic." The term was part of a "Myth of Venice" that described the city as a peaceful haven in which civic harmony reigned supreme. This harmony, proponents of the myth asserted, was reflected in the city's splendor and based on freedom from outside domination, equal justice assured by the government, and an abiding Christian faith reflected in Venetians' charity to the less fortunate.

The first component of Venice's serenity was its unique longevity, as the city had, by the fifteenth century, enjoyed over seven hundred years of self-government. Although under Byzantine protection and nominal domination from its foundation in 421, by 697 Venetians began to assert their autonomy by electing a *doge*, or duke, to lead them. Between 807 and 814 the establishment of the Dogado, or Duchy of Venice, solidified their political independence. The final break from the Byzantine Empire was a symbolic one, denoted by the city's rejection of their Greek patron saint in favor of the patronage of St. Mark the Evangelist who, as legend had it, stopped in the islands when he was on his way to Rome. To solidify his patronage, St. Mark's bones were stolen from Alexandria, Egypt, and brought to Venice in 828. These relics also came to represent Venice's pious devotion. The city's sustained freedom and safety was surprising to many, particularly because Venice lacked defensive walls, a fact remarkable to visitors accustomed to their own cities' thick protecting ramparts. The city was easily defended because, until the nineteenth century, it was approachable only by water. The city's layout further protected it, dividing it into six unequal neighborhoods, known as *sestieri*, that extended over 117 tiny islands. The islands are irregular in shape and linked by small bridges, features that would make any attack easily repelled. (See Map 12.1.)

Venice's security, as well as its ascendancy, was ensured also by political and social structures that, though not quite granting equal rights and justice to all, did guarantee an uncommon degree of internal stability. From 1032 onward Venice's Dogado was no longer a monarchy, replaced instead by an unusual "mixed form" that was mainly oligarchic yet also included attributes of monarchy and democracy. Based on republican representation, the General Assembly was at the base of government. Made up of male citizens whose right to political action depended on either birth or success in business, the Assembly ratified basic legislation and elected the doges. From the Assembly were elected the 480 members of the Great Council, who made judicial decisions, passed legislation, and elected members to the various other councils in charge of domestic and foreign policy. Above the Great Council were The Forty, the committee tasked with the preparation of legislation, and the Senate, a deliberative body. Finally, at the very top of power lay the doge himself and the Ducal Council, six councilors whose main responsibility was simultaneously to advise the doge and curtail his power. In 1297 the oligarchic nature of Venetian government was cemented by the *Serrata*, or the closing of the Great Council. In effect creating a hereditary nobility, this drastically reduced the political power of the

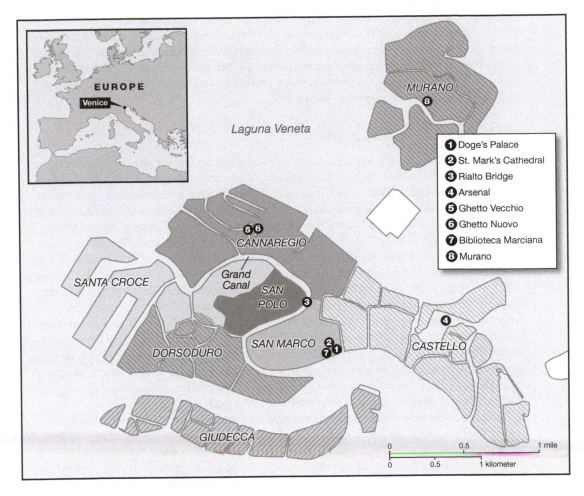

Map 12.1. Venice's Sestieri

Divided into six major neighborhoods, native Venetians and immigrants coexisted and worked in relative peace. However, immigrants and temporary workers were closely monitored, often living in specially designed areas.

popolani, or lower classes, by limiting membership on the Council to male descendants of members active in the Council at the time.

Comprising about 5 percent of the population, the members of the new nobility enjoyed the privileges of power, as they had direct say in the running of the state. Though equal in rights, they were unequal in wealth, as noble affluence depended on individual success in commerce. In this, the Venetian nobility differed greatly from its Northern European counterparts, who viewed any type of labor as beneath their station. Nobles had common economic interests with members of Venice's lower two social groups, the *cittadini* and the *popolani*, so policies guided by noble interest also benefitted a broader sector of the population and limited social unrest. The cittadini, or citizens, made up 5 to 8 percent of the population and were the middle tier of Venice's social hierarchy. Including wealthy and middling merchants as well as a professional class of permanent salaried bureaucrats, the cittadini enjoyed certain rights, including zealously guarded access to government posts. At the bottom of the Republic's social hierarchy were the popolani, composing between 85 and 90 percent of the population. The popolani included a wide range of people, most without political voice. At the top were artisans, skilled craftsmen, shopkeepers, and wealthy foreigners; at the bottom were unskilled laborers, mariners, and shipyard workers. All, however, benefitted to one degree or another from Venice's prosperity and were encouraged to work together for the glory—and serenity—of the city.

Immigration, Inclusion, and Exclusion

During the Renaissance Venice's large population was one of the most diverse in Europe—and the world—making the Republic highly cosmopolitan both in terms of its internationality and sophistication. Due to the great number of immigrants who moved there each year, Venice came to be known as a "city of immigrants," leading visitors such as French envoy Philippe de Commynes to comment that "most of their people are foreigners." Coming from far-off places such as Byzantium, Greece, and Albania, as well as from cities across mainland Italy and Europe, artisans, laborers, traders, and soldiers flocked to Venice. For its part, the city depended on immigration to sustain its population and, therefore, its tax base and workforce. Venice, like most other cities of the period, was susceptible particularly to high infant mortality and disease. For example, in the first wave of the bubonic plague, which struck the Republic in late 1347, three out of five inhabitants perished. So important was the influx of newcomers to the city that Venetian officials set immigration quotas, recruiting especially professionals such as physicians and jurists as well as skilled artisans like silk weavers and printers so as to buttress the city's success. Venetians also welcomed the chance, even if most often unsuccessful, to convert to Catholicism those immigrants who were not of the faith.

Some newcomers settled permanently while others remained only temporarily. For many the main attraction of migration to Venice was the riches to be gained, particularly in trade monopolies the city granted; others found the civil privileges that the city offered appealing—civic rights not commonly granted elsewhere in the world. At a time when both in Europe and around the globe the state enforced religious orthodoxy, immigrants to Venice were instead given the right to practice their religion (except Protestantism) in specially appointed areas. Likewise, although elsewhere citizenship was tightly limited, Venice offered newcomers the possibility of gaining citizenship after fifteen years of living in—and paying taxes to—the city. Still, the majority of immigrants were never fully assimilated into the Republic's politics or culture, instead creating insular communities and carving out for themselves part of the urban space. A perfect example is the many Greeks who came to conduct business in the city or join the crews of trading galleys, and who mostly lived in the *sestier* of Castello. In the early sixteenth century Venetians granted the Greek community permission to build their own church there, which remains a main tourist attraction to this day, and Greek immigrants created their own confraternity (a lay religious association), so, to them, the area seemed like another Byzantium.

In part because of many immigrants' refusal to assimilate but also due to what Venetians saw as the dangers foreigners posed, the city's relationship with newcomers remained ambivalent at best. Although aware of the city's dependence on immigration, the government nevertheless kept a close watch and placed tight restrictions on foreigners' movements, behaviors, and practices. These restraints, including where people could live or practice their religion, aimed principally to reduce competition against Venetian commerce and protect Christians by preventing their completely free association with "pagans" (like Protestants and Jews). Perhaps the most dramatic example of Venetians' ambivalent attitude was their interactions with Jews, whose status had rapidly declined during the late imperial period as a result of the rise of Christianity as the one religion of Rome. Antipathy against Jews reached unprecedented heights during the Middle Ages and Renaissance when, at the behest of several popes, Jews were forced to convert to Christianity. Those who refused to do so were expelled as a group from many European states, most famously from England (1290) and Spain (1492) but also from Italian city-states like Naples (1540) and Rome (1556). Although systematic persecution of Jews remained a mostly European phenomenon during this period, Jews also faced severe antagonism elsewhere in the world and at other times, particularly in Muslim lands like Persia, where, in the eighteenth century, the leaders ordered mass forced conversions.

Venice's treatment of Jews was somewhat milder. Although originally prohibited from staying in the city proper for more than fifteen days a year and constrained to live in the mainland and wear a yellow beret as a sign of their difference, Jewish immigrants from across Europe and Italy were nevertheless essential to the city, particularly as money lenders and sellers of secondhand goods to the lower classes. Equally important, many of the Republic's physicians, indispensable to the city, were Jews. Recognizing in 1503 that the city had important needs that Jews could help fulfill, the Senate allowed them to move into the city and granted them conditional freedoms such as the right to carry arms and complete freedom of movement. Many Venetians, however, still viewed the Jewish presence as dangerous, particularly in the threat of interactions that could lead to the corruption of Christians, either through conversion to Judaism or through inappropriate sexual relations between Jewish men and Christian women. In order to discourage these behaviors, in 1516 the Senate passed a historic decree that constrained Jews to live in an area of the sestier of Cannaregio known as the *Ghetto*. The decree also forbade Jews from moving around the city at night and ruled that new walls were to be erected around the area and guarded at night. Those found breaking curfew without permission, even physicians tending to the sick, were to be heavily fined or even exiled. The creation of the first ghetto in world history is a stark example of the city's complex relationship with foreigners and immigrants, a tenuous and conflicted interdependence that survived well after the sixteenth century. Although no longer forced to live there, modern Jewish life in Venice is still centered around the Ghetto, where a small but lively community still eat, pray, and study in the neighborhood's five active synagogues, community center, archives and museum.

Venice and the Commercial Revolution

The Renaissance was characterized in part by an unprecedented increase in the amount and fluidity of wealth, and by the consequent creation in Europe as well as exportation throughout European empires of a consumerist culture focused on the acquisition of material goods. Between the thirteenth and fifteenth centuries Italians in particular became more affluent, a prosperity that a greater segment of the population enjoyed more than ever before. Due in great part to their role in worldwide trade, Italians honed the economic innovations collectively known as the first Commercial Revolution (roughly 1475–1550). Leading to radical changes in the scope and nature of trade, the Commercial Revolution ushered a full-scale system of capitalism by developing the basic techniques that facilitated the accumulation and investment of large amounts of capital. First introduced in the twelfth century, these practices included banking, the large-scale minting of coins, double-entry bookkeeping, contracts, and insurance. The true economic genius of Renaissance Italians, however, lay not just in perfecting these innovations but also in developing capitalist techniques focused specifically on making long-distance trade profitable. Italians became international bankers, introducing lucrative practices, such as money exchange and credit lines, that, for a fee, simplified trade across international boundaries. Italians also developed crucial nautical innovations that shortened the time it took to complete long voyages as well as a series of investment opportunities, such as the sea loan and the selling of shares, each allowing for a different degree of opportunity and risk and therefore open to a greater number of investors across the economic spectrum.

Renaissance Venetians implemented and perfected many of these early developments, as the very topography of Venice, devoid of arable land except that added through mainland conquests, made the city intrinsically dependent on trade. From their earliest history Venetians traded commodities such as fish and salt to the mainland in exchange for basic staples like grain and wine. Venetian trade expanded exponentially in subsequent centuries, and by the ninth century Venetian merchants bought and sold goods in places as far away as Byzantium and the Arab world. By the twelve century Venice had become a bustling commercial port, directing the loading and unloading of hundreds of vessels from all over the Mediterranean. The city's most significant coup was perhaps the defeat of its greatest commercial rival, the Italian city-state of Genoa. With a flourishing commercial network of their own, the Genoese became bitter enemies of the Venetians, fighting particularly over control of trade ports in the Greek islands and the Black Sea. Engaged for over a century in a series of wars known as the Venetian-Genoese Wars (1255–1381), in the decisive last stage of the conflict, the War of Chioggia (1378–1381), Venice emerged triumphant. Although not gaining any Genoese monopolies or territories, from that point onward Genoa continued to decline while Venice gained increasing control of commerce along the eastern Mediterranean. Ultimately, the city came to be hailed as the unchallenged "Queen of the Sea."

At the height of the city's power, Venetian ships traded along the Adriatic, Mediterranean, and Aegean Seas. Western maritime trade routes took them as far as London and Bruges, and eastern routes led them to major cities such as Constantinople, Alexandria, and Cairo. From such ports Venetian businessmen traveled inland, going as far as Persia, Armenia, and the Caucasus, from where they imported both local merchandise and goods coming from as far as China and the so-called Spice Islands. (See Map 12.2.) Venice's main commercial partner until the fourteenth century was the Byzantine Empire, from which it secured favorable trading agreements and unique privileges within Byzantine cities, like the right for Venetian merchants to live and trade anywhere in the city. In contrast, other foreign merchants were instead constrained to live and do business within designated neighborhoods. The Ottomans' relentless expansion into Byzantine lands, however, led Venetians to seek other equally profitable markets. Perhaps the most important and lucrative of Venice's new trading partners were the rulers of the Mamluk Dynasty, who came to control Syria, Palestine, and Egypt in the late thirteenth century after they expelled the last crusaders from the Holy Land. In 1415 the Mamluks granted Venetian merchants special trading rights, thereby making Venice the Mamluk's main supplier of manufactured goods from around the world, including textiles and paper from northern Europe, ceramics and silk from the Far East, and luxury textiles, glassware, and hats from Venice itself. By the end of the fifteenth century trade with the Mamluk sultanate made up a full 45 percent of Venetian investments in overseas commerce.

Overland trade also bolstered the city's commercial supremacy. Venetian merchants traveled both to northern Europe through the Alpine passes, reaching major trading

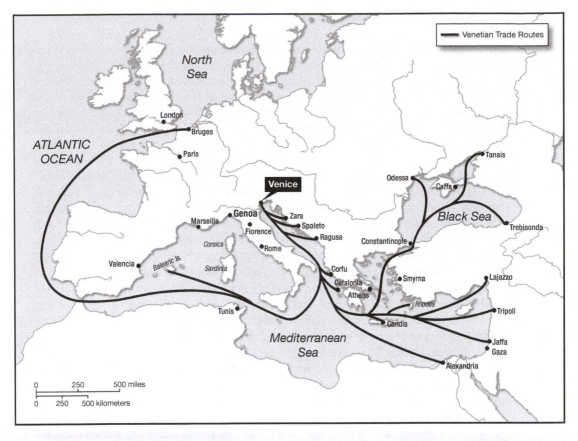

Map 12.2. Venice's Empire and Trade

Venice's prosperity and cosmopolitan nature were due mainly to its extensive network of trading routes. Linking the city to places as far east as Byzantium and the Arab world, sea trade brought to Venice both goods and peoples, making it a hub of global contact during the Renaissance.

cities in Germany and France, and to the Italian mainland, following roads and rivers to cities such as Florence and Rome. The extent of their trade networks meant that Venetians were in a unique position to move all sorts of goods, including grain and wines from the Italian mainland, wood and slaves from Dalmatia, raw metals and metal products from Germany, woolen cloth from Flanders, as well as alum, silk, and spices from Constantinople.

All the ordinary and exotic merchandise that flowed through Venice to the rest of the world could be found in the warehouses and shops lining the commercial center of the city, the Rialto. Part of the sestier of San Polo on the left bank of the Grand Canal, the Rialto became an important district in the late eleventh century, when the city moved its main market there. As Venice's commercial networks expanded and the city became a major port, the Rialto grew in importance, becoming also the home of Venice's banks and insurance agencies. Across the Rialto Bridge from the political center of the city was the sestier of San Marco, the commercial district and a regular gathering place for merchants and politicians. Across the water, on the right bank of the Grand Canal, wealthy Venetians and foreign traders built, only with the Senate's written consent, great warehouses and exchange buildings to accommodate both merchandise as well as the foreigners whose livelihood depended on its trade.

Although trading foreign goods comprised a significant part of Venice's revenue, Venetians were more than middlemen. Rather, over time locals developed sizeable industries, producing widely sought-after goods such as ships, glass, and printed books. Perhaps most significant among these industries was shipbuilding. In effect, the single-most important enterprise in Venice was the state-run Arsenal, a series of armories and a public shipyard founded in 1104. Located in the Castello neighborhood, the Arsenal dominated that section of Venice's cityscape, occupying around sixty acres of land surrounded by two and a half miles of walls and moats. These not only protected Venice's weapons and vessels but also guarded the shipbuilding tradition that the workers of the Arsenal (*arsenalotti*, or "sons of the Arsenal") passed down from generation to generation. Employed by the thousands year round, the arsenalotti were a community within a community, building and maintaining the fleets, both merchant and military, that made Venetian dominance feasible. At its zenith in the fifteenth century the Arsenal produced up to one hundred ships in fifty days, dividing the work into three stages (framing, planking and cabins, and final assembly). The speed with which the Arsenal built ships was due in great part to the implementation of the first moving assembly line in world history, a system not employed again until the early twentieth century. Moving the galley along an inner canal, the system brought the ship to the materials and workers at each stage of construction, saving the time it would take to move materials and workers to the galley instead. Also crucial to Venice's unique shipbuilding success was the fact that the city's naval architects standardized both war and trading ships, building them out of precut parts and to the same specifications. Such standardization allowed for not only faster assembly but also the possibility of holding up to one hundred galleys in reserve at any one time, thus making Venice an unrivaled naval power.

Technological innovations were also at the heart of Venice's thriving glassmaking industry, which was first developed in the tenth century and reached unprecedented heights in the fifteenth. Producing a wide range of glasses, goblets, and bottles as well as jewelry and beads, Venetians improved upon techniques learned from Byzantine immigrants to the city. Particularly, Venetian glassmakers perfected in the mid-fifteenth century the process for making crystal, glass of unrivaled clarity and transparency. Venetians also developed special techniques for the decoration of glass, including engraving, enameling, and gold-leafing, all of which made Venetian products highly desired luxury goods. Venetian glassmakers were also famous for more practical products such as timekeeping sandglasses, invented in the thirteenth century, and spectacles, introduced in the fourteenth. Moved from the main islands to the outlying island of Murano in the late thirteenth century, the glassblowing industry became one of Venice's main sources of income. Consequently, it came under tight scrutiny and control by the Senate, both to assure quality and to minimize the threat of technological espionage. In fact, their trade was so important that Murano glassmakers, although not among the city's nobles, gained special privileges, including immunity from state prosecution. However, with their movements closely watched, glassmakers were proscribed from leaving the city for fear that they would sell the secrets of Venetian glass to the Republic's competitors.

The Senate also enforced tight controls over Venice's book trade. First brought to Venice by Johannes von Speyer, a German immigrant in 1469, printing developed into another of the city's top money makers. More importantly, it made Venice both a center of intellectual ferment and a source from which knowledge flowed to the rest of Europe. The movable-type printing press, invented in China in the tenth century, was perfected in the 1440s in Germany by Johannes Gutenberg, who in the process revolutionized printing in the West. Gutenberg introduced three core innovations that led to an exceptional mechanical system allowing books to be mass produced: first, Gutenberg proved the practicality of using separate pieces of type, or plates each with a particular letter or symbol, to replace single plates in which a full page had been cast; second, he cast type in metal rather than wood, and this made the plates more durable; and third, he repurposed the design of existing screw presses, thereby producing a better ink imprint than traditional hand presses did. Thanks to these time-saving and cost-effective innovations, a single press in the sixteenth century could produce over thirty-five hundred printed pages a day, compared to fewer than fifty hand-pressed and no more than a few hand-copied ones.

Venetians were quick to capitalize on Gutenberg's printing press. To attract knowledgeable printers to the city, from whom the trade could be learned and the industry developed, the Senate granted early monopolies to immigrants like Speyer, whose sole rights to print books in Venice were protected by stiff penalties, exacted by the State on anyone who printed or imported books into the city. Such protections drew both locals and foreigners to the trade, hoping to gain similar monopolies and thus making Venice, by the late fifteenth century, one of the leading typographical centers worldwide. Because Venice fostered these new technologies, coupled with the intellectual atmosphere that Renaissance humanism promoted, books became a main Venetian export. Representing a wide range of subjects, Venetian editions included maps, medical books, translations of ancient Greek works, and music scores, numbering around twenty thousand by the mid-sixteenth century. These works were published not only in Latin, the language of educated Europeans, but also in Italian, Greek, Hebrew, and Arabic, reflecting the ever-more cosmopolitan nature of Venice and the city's attractiveness to people from around the world.

Humanism and the Venetian Experience

Modern scholars have characterized the Renaissance as a secular age because, during this period, the Church increasingly lost both its monopoly on education and much of its influence in politics. Nevertheless, Renaissance peoples remained deeply pious, a devoutness that colored almost all of their interactions. As Italians came increasingly to dominate trade, a greater segment of society than ever before enjoyed unprecedented prosperity. The enjoyment of this new affluence, however, conflicted in crucial ways with the predominant Christian view of morality, upon which medieval ideas of a life worthy of Salvation were predicated. Confronting biblical denunciations of wealth as ultimately inimical to Christians because it distracted from God, Renaissance Italians developed a new philosophy of life, encapsulated in the ideal of "living well and holy," which attempted to reconcile the Christian life with both the enjoyment of wealth and the acceptance of man's God-given ability to produce it.

This ideology was at the core of a new intellectual movement known as humanism, which was first fully developed in Florence in the fourteenth century. Finding in classical literature both guidelines and models for living a full and worthy life, the proponents of humanism, known as *umanisti,* or humanists, created a new educational curriculum, the *studia humanitatis.* Including five core subjects—grammar, rhetoric, moral philosophy, history, and poetry—the studia differed from the medieval liberal arts that, although also emphasizing grammar and rhetoric, prioritized mathematics and astronomy. Humanists concentrated instead on the full development and useful application of human virtue, to be achieved through the study of ancient works on moral philosophy, such as those by the Roman philosopher Seneca, and histories from which to learn by example, such as those written by Livy and Tacitus. The knowledge gained was not to benefit only the individual; humanists were charged with leading others to live worthy lives as well, a task for which the study of rhetoric, or eloquent speech, was crucial. Only through mastering this art, humanists believed, could they move others toward virtuous action.

Although no longer defined solely in religious terms, humanists' ideas of "the good" remained deeply linked to Christian morality. The Florentine Francesco Petrarca (aka, Petrarch, 1304–1374), the father of humanism, advocated man's full development of his potential in the here and now while also pointing out that worldly success did not necessarily prevent one from having a faithful relationship with God. Petrarch's Italian successors, such as Giannozzo Manetti (1396–1459), further argued that man is not a fallen, unworthy being but rather God's greatest creation, given by Him incalculable intellectual and creative potential as well as common sense. These attributes, humanists believed, should be used to the fullest and in the service of both God and our fellow men. It was this aspect of the ideology as well as its later focus on civil service that made humanism attractive to Renaissance Venetians.

Tuned in to important developments both in Italy and beyond, Venetians soon recognized the potential of humanist ideas to ease their conflict between worldly success and concerns over Salvation. The Republic even invited Petrarch to live and teach in Venice at the city's expense. Many of the city's noblemen found Petrarch's ideas incompatible with what they saw as their high standards for civic discipline and service; therefore, Venetians adopted humanism only cautiously. It was not until the early fifteenth century that humanism flourished in the Republic, thanks to the Florentine development of civic humanism. Arguing that the attainment of virtue through classical studies was not an end in itself but only the foundation for public service, civic humanists called for a type of responsible republicanism in which individuals all worked together for the glory of the city. Such an ideology was sure to find support among Venetians, particularly members of the upper class, whose very identity was fundamentally tied to *La Serenissima*'s success. Not surprisingly, roughly two-thirds of Venetian humanists were patricians, a fact that slanted their works toward the defense of the city's nobility, government, and values.

Their civic responsibilities, however, limited Venetian humanists' scholarly productivity, and as a consequence they are not as well known as their Florentine counterparts. Francesco Barbaro (1390–1454), a patrician politician and diplomat, translated two of the biographies of notable Greeks and Romans written by Plutarch in the second century CE. Barbaro focused on the lives of Aristides, renowned in ancient Greece for his fairness, and Cato, famous to the Romans for his wisdom, and he commented on them as models of civic virtue. Bernardo Giustiniani (1408–1489) also embodied the values and approaches of Venetian humanism. His most important work, *Origins of the City of Venice*, is simultaneously a history and a panegyric, or praising celebration, of the city, aimed exclusively at bolstering the Republic's reputation at home and abroad, even at the cost of historical accuracy.

In the sixteenth century humanism in Venice developed even further, bolstered by both an influx of newcomers to the cultural scene and an expansion in the range of topics covered. Attracted by the availability of high-quality printed works as well as the opportunity to have their own works published, intellectuals flocked to the city, many to end up as "hired pens." A number of women and many more patricians also joined the ranks of Venetian writers during this period.

Renaissance Ideals and Venetian Art

The humanist celebration of human abilities and potential was reflected in the period's art, particularly painting. Man's dignity, as Manetti called it, made him and his world worthy of artistic depiction and commemoration. Artists' goal became to represent realistically the natural world and reflect the range and depth of human personality. Their ambition required new techniques so as to allow the faithful depiction of three-dimensional objects, such as men, in a two-dimensional plane like a panel or canvas. Based on creating the illusion of recession from the front to the back of the panel by presenting objects in proportion to one another, all in relation to a middle point in the backdrop, the first crucial innovation was the development of linear perspective. To add to the realism, Renaissance artists also developed *chiaroscuro* (literally, "light-dark"), a modeling technique that, by making the lighter parts seem to protrude from the darker areas, gave bulk to the figures, thereby producing the illusion of volume. These revolutionary artistic techniques deeply influenced Western art, making Renaissance artists some of the most influential men of their age. Examples of their innovative work can be seen today in any number of museums around the world, highlighting their place of honor in the history of art.

Elide Florentines first introduced many of these advances that were readily adopted in Venice, where, up to the fifteenth century, the greatest artistic influences had come from Byzantium. Hearing of the high quality and beauty of the new art, the Senate invited renowned painters and sculptors, such as Paolo Uccello (1397–1475) and Donatello (1386–1466), to work in the city. Venetians came to master the new art forms, developing their own techniques and style in the process. The most famous of the early Renaissance Venetian painters were Jacopo Bellini (ca. 1430–c. 1470) and his sons, Gentile (ca. 1429–1507) and Giovanni (ca. 1430–1516). Giovanni came to be known as the "father of Venetian painting" for perfecting his father's perspective technique and introducing the coloristic style, which used deep, rich colors to give paintings a sensuous and lustrous quality. He also was among the first to use oil paints, adopted from Northern European artists, that not only made paintings glow but also withstood Venice's usual humidity.

Other Venetian innovations in painting include the use of color to recreate the soft, reflected light characteristic of the city, the use of smooth brushwork to produce a rich velvet-like surface texture, and the introduction of new subjects besides religious ones. Titian (Tiziano Vecellio, ca. 1487–1576), for example, is best known for painting beautiful nude women in lusciously decorated rooms as well as for his portraits of the rich and powerful. Usually depicted in sumptuous clothes in deep but muted colors, Titian's sitters personify the complex interplay between wealth and virtue that characterized the city's history. As patrons of secular art for private consumption, Venetians advertised their status and influence, whereas as sponsors of religious art for public viewing they charitably shared their bounty. The government also capitalized in the patronage of art, proclaiming the Republic's own wealth and power by sponsoring the grandiose public statuary and stunning civic buildings that to this day adorn the city.

GLOBAL ENCOUNTERS AND CONNECTIONS:
Venice as an Influential Nexus for East and West

Venice's Renaissance came inevitably to an end, ushered by the slow but inexorable decline of the city's commercial dominance. The first blow was the fall of Constantinople in 1453 to the Turks, who eventually seized Venice's eastern territories, effectively crippling the Republic's trade networks to the Levant. Further decline followed the Portuguese rounding of the Cape of Good Hope, which opened a new trading route to the East and negated the centrality of Venice's geographical location. The Spanish colonization of the New World also weakened Venetian commerce, as it made available new goods and opened rival markets in Europe and beyond, to which Venetian merchants had little access and from which, therefore, Venice could not benefit. Although partially successful in shifting their focus to improving and increasing their production of manufactured goods, the city's position and international significance would not be the same after the late sixteenth century.

Venice's decline, however, cannot detract from its historical significance as one of the best connected and most influential cities of the Renaissance world. The city was more than a producer and purveyor of goods; it was, above all, a center of international exchange wherein the cultures of East and West met and came to influence each other. Most obviously, the city's dependence on and interactions with the peoples of Byzantium and the Islamic sultanates shaped in great part Venetian politics, society, and culture. The city's commercial interests almost always dictated government decisions, and the need to secure its empire determined questions of war and peace. The city's topography echoed the diversity of its population, as immigrants came together in neighborhoods that visually resembled the countries from which they had migrated and reflected the city's cosmopolitanism, as Venetians and foreigners alike crowded the city's streets and marketplaces. Both techniques that Venetian craftsmen learned from abroad and ornate motifs borrowed from Eastern art enriched Venetian manufactured goods such as glass and luxury textiles. Its architecture also reflected Eastern influence because Venetians not only copied Byzantine domes and arches but also imported columns, marbles, and sculptures from Egypt and Constantinople. Even the Venetian dialect showed the impact of the city's global connections, as Greek and Arabic words were added to its vocabulary.

Because the city was a major conduit for Eastern goods, customs, and ideas during the Renaissance, through Venice the Byzantine and Islamic cultures also influenced the rest of Europe. Commodities that Venice imported affected, in both minor and major ways, Westerners' everyday, practical experiences. Goods such as furniture, carpets, and decorative artifacts transformed the interiors of both private homes and public spaces, introducing colors and shapes previously unknown in the West. Silks reshaped Europe's fashions and spices revolutionized its cuisine, forever changing the diet and tastes of peoples across the continent.

Venice's role as cultural transmitter was not one way; rather, as Venetians traveled to ports around the Mediterranean, they introduced the peoples of the Near East to innovations developed in Europe and perfected in Venice. Venetian innovations invigorated the pictorial arts in the Byzantine and Ottoman empires, as many artists abandoned traditional approaches to art, adopting instead the advanced use of oil paints. The introduction of deeply saturated colors developed in Venice, like Titian red (named after the famous Venetian Renaissance artist), further influenced Eastern art, adding to both its intensity and drama. Venetian art further changed the visual world of the Ottomans through architecture, as rulers hired Venetian architects and craftsmen to design and build their palaces. The introduction of textiles and ready-made clothing and accessories as well as the importation of mirrors also influenced everyday life in the East, and all of these altered fashion and the way in which peoples in the Near East presented—and, literally, saw—themselves. Finally, Venetians introduced their non-European partners to the printed book and the humanist ideas first developed in Italy, thus opening new intellectual horizons and fostering further cultural interaction between East and West.

The city's place in the history of the Renaissance world was, therefore, vital, for the city was a place of encounters where diverse peoples met and cultures intertwined. Thanks in great part to its Renaissance greatness, Venice remains to this day one of the most visited cities in the world, attracting millions from around the globe to its canals, palaces, and marketplaces. Today, those who wish to experience the Renaissance as lived in Venice may walk along its narrow streets at night, visit a traditional glass-blowing workshop, or tour the great rooms of the doge's Palace. Closer to home, one may simply visit any of the major world-class museums around the world, almost all of which count among their treasures the paintings of Venetian masters like the Bellini father and sons, Titian, and Tintoretto.

ENCOUNTERS AS TOLD: PRIMARY SOURCES

Countless visitors, including pilgrims, ambassadors, and merchants, commented on the wonders of Venice. Adding to a growing genre of travel writing, many such travelers recorded in journals, both private and for publication, their impressions of the city. The excerpts below are typical examples of the genre, highlighting many of the themes discussed in this chapter. The writers echo the myth of Venice's long-lasting serenity and freedom, comment on the cosmopolitanism of the population, highlight the city's unique topography, and marvel at the riches to be found there.

Canon Pietro Casola's Pilgrimage to Jerusalem in the Year 1494, by Pietro Casola

The first excerpt comes from Pietro Casola's account of his pilgrimage to Jerusalem in 1494, two years after Christopher Columbus's first voyage seeking new passage to the East. A Milanese priest and former ambassador to Rome, Casola journeyed overland from Milan to Venice, where he joined a group of pilgrims traveling across the Mediterranean on a Venetian ship. He was welcomed to Venice by the Milanese ambassador and was hosted by merchants for whom he brought letters from home. Casola begins his description of Venice with short reports on its foundations, palaces, and government. He then spends significant time describing the goods to be found in the city's many markets.

- As you read his description below, consider the kinds of goods Casola encountered. From where is this merchandise brought? Of what quality and in what quantity are they available?

- How do the city's wares compare with those Casola had encountered in other major markets?

Something may be said about the quantity of merchandise in the said city, although not nearly the whole truth, because it is inestimable. Indeed it seems as if all the world flocks there, and that human beings have concentrated there all their force for trading. I was taken to see various warehouses, beginning with that of the Germans—which it appears to me would suffice alone to supply all Italy with the goods that come and go—and so many others that it can be said they are innumerable. I see that the special products for which other cities are famous are all to be found there, and that what is sold elsewhere by the pound and the ounce is sold there by *canthari* and sacks of a *moggio* each. And who could count the many shops so well furnished that they also seem warehouses, with so many cloths of every make—tapestry, brocades and hangings of every design, carpets of every sort, camlets of every color and texture, silks of every kind; and so many warehouses full of spices, groceries and drugs, and so much beautiful white wax! These things stupefy the beholder, and cannot be fully described to those who have not seen them. Though I wished to see everything, I saw only a part, and even that by forcing myself to see all I could.

As to the abundance of the victuals, I can testify that I do not believe there is a city in Italy better supplied than this with every kind of victuals. This time my own city, which I used to think the most abundant, must forgive me, and so too all the other cities in Italy and also abroad where I have been, because, whether it is due to the good order or other cause I do not know, but I never saw such a quantity of provisions elsewhere.

I went to the place where the flour is sold wholesale; the world at present does not contain such a remarkable thing. When I saw such abundance and beauty around me I was confused. The bakers' shops, which are to be found in one place specially, namely, the piazza of St. Mark, and also throughout the city, are countless and of incredible beauty; there is bread the sight of which tempts even a man who is surfeited to eat again. In my judgment Venice has not its equal for this.

With the meat they give a great piece of bone. When I saw the place where the meat is sold, I thought I had never seen such a miserable place in any city, or more wretched meat to look at. It drives away the wish to buy. I do not know the reason for this, unless it be that the Venetians are so occupied with their merchandise, that, they do not trouble much about what they eat. It is enough to say that in that place you could not have a good and fine-looking piece of meat whatever you were willing to pay, or at least in the quantity to be had at Milan.

For the time of year I was there, there seemed to be a great abundance of fowls and other kinds of eatable birds, though they were somewhat dear. There was a great abundance of cheese or caxi, and butter—more, I can assure you, than at Milan, which ought to be the great centre for these things, and which used to be.

It is superfluous to try and recount the daily abundance of fish, especially in two places—at St. Mark's and at the Rialto, as it is commonly called. There is never a dearth of fish, though in truth, as to the excellence of the quality, it is not on a level with that of certain other cities. All the time I was there I never saw a fine fish and never ate a good one, although my hosts took great trouble to procure good fish.

As to the fruit. During the time I was awaiting the departure of the galley—not having anything else to do—I went several times very early in the morning to St. Mark's, and also to the Rialto, to watch the unloading of the boats which arrived from time to time. There were so many boats full of big beans, peas and cherries—not indeed of every kind as at Milan, but every day in such quantity, that it seemed as if all the gardens of the world must be there. The number was so great that I declare that after seeing them, when I turned my back I hardly believed my eyes. There is an abundant supply of good vegetables of every kind—*verdure*, as we say—and they are cheaper than in any place I ever visited. I heard that they come from a distance of twenty-five miles. I went several times in the morning to watch the unloading of the boats, and the vegetables looked as if just taken from the gardens and very fresh. I know it is difficult for anyone who has not seen these things to believe what I say, because I have fallen into the same error myself—that is, I used not to believe what was told me about them.

I may recount the abundance of wine of every sort—so much malmsey, so many muscatel wines, Greek wines, white wines of every kind and also red wines,—but it is almost incredible. Although they are not so perfect as ours, nevertheless they are good—I speak of the red wines—and owing to the heavy duties they are dear. I wanted to count the wine shops of every kind, but the more I counted the more I became confused, for they are indeed innumerable.

Source: *Canon Pietro Casola's Pilgrimage to Jerusalem in the Year 1494*, translated by Mary Margaret Newett (Manchester, UK: The University Press, 1907).

Coryat's Crudities: Hastily Gobbled Up in Five Months Travels in France, Savoy, Italy, Rhetia Commonly Called the Grisons Country, Helvetia Alias Switzerland, Some Parts of High Germany and the Netherlands, by Thomas Coryat

In the late fifteenth century a new kind of traveler also came into the scene: the tourist. This second excerpt comes from the travel diary of Thomas Coryat, who in 1608 embarked on a five-month-long walking tour of Europe, including a lengthy stay in Venice. His observations of the city and its people are extremely rich, highlighting the city's cosmopolitanism and diversity. Seventeenth-century spellings from the document have been modernized for easy comprehension, though capitalizations have been retained. As you read the excerpt, consider how Coryat describes the city itself as well as its people and goods.

- What makes Venice so unique?

- What sort of interactions did Venetians and foreigners enjoy?

- What does Coryat have to say about the goods traded in Venice?

My Observations of the most glorious, peerless, and maiden City of Venice: I call it maiden, because it was never conquered.

IN PRAISE OF VENICE

I ingenuously confess mine own insufficiency and unworthiness . . . to describe so beautiful, so renowned, so glorious a Virgin (for by that title does the world most deservedly style her) because my rude and unpolished pen may rather stain. . . . Such is the rareness of the situation of Venice, that it does even amaze and drive into admiration all strangers that upon their first arrival behold the same. For it is built altogether upon the water in the innermost gulf of the Adriatic Sea which is commonly called Gulfo di Venetia, and is distant from the main Sea about the space of 3 miles.

450 BRIDGES IN VENICE AND LAND STREETS

Each street has many several bridges, some more, some less, of which most are stony, and those vaulted bridges in with one Arch. The whole number of them is said to be four hundred and fifty. Almost every channel (whereof there are about seventy two, even as many as doe [sic] answer the number of the Islands whereon the city is built) has his land street joining to it, which is fairly pitched or paved with brick, and of so convenient a breadth some few of them are, that five or six persons may walk together there side by side, and some are so narrow, that but two can walk together, in some but one. Also in many places those land streets are in both sides of the channel, in some in one side only, in some few in neither. Moreover there are other little streets called Calli, which we may more properly call land streets then [sic] Land streets. . . . Many of them are much narrower than those by the channels. For I have passed through divers of them which were so narrow, that two men could not without some difficulty walk together in one of them side by side.

CONCOURSE OF THE NATIONS

This part of the Piazza is worthy to be celebrated for that famous concourse and meeting of so many distinct and sundry nations twice a day, between six and eleven o'clock in the morning, and between five in the afternoon and eight, as I have before mentioned, where also the Venetian long gowned Gentlemen do meet together in great troupes. . . . There you may see many Polonians, Slavonians, Persians, Grecians, Turks, Jews, Christians of all the famous regions of Christendom, and each nation distinguished from another by their proper and peculiar habits. A singular show. . . .

THE JEWS' GHETTO

I was at a place where the whole fraternity of the Jews dwelled together, which is called the Ghetto, being an Island: for it is enclosed round about with water. It is thought there are of them in all between five and six thousand. They are distinguished and discerned from the Christians by their habits on their heads. . . .

They have diverse Synagogues in their Ghetto, at the least seven, where all of them, both men, women and children do meet together upon their Sabbath, which is Saturday, to the end to do their devotion, and serve God in their kind, each company having a several Synagogue. . . . I observed some few of those Jews especially some of the Levantines to be such goodly and proper men, that then I said to myself our English proverb: To look like a Jew (whereby is meant sometimes a weather beaten warp-faced fellow, sometimes a frantic and lunatic person, sometimes one discontented) is not true. For indeed I noted some of them to be most elegant and sweet featured persons, which gave me occasion [all] the more to lament their religion. . . .

[It is] pitiful . . . to see that few of them living in Italy are converted to the Christian religion. For this I understand is the main impediment to their conversion: All their goods are confiscated as soon as they embrace Christianity. . . . Seeing then when their goods are taken from them at their conversion, they are left even naked, and destitute of their means of maintenance, there are fewer Jews converted to Christianity in Italy, than in any country of Christendom.

VENETIAN GLASS

I passed in a Gondola to pleasant Murano, distant about a little mile from the city, where they make their delicate Venice glasses, so famous over all Christendom for the incomparable fineness thereof, and in one of their working houses made a glass myself. Most of their principal matter of which they make their glasses is a kind of earth which is brought there by Sea from Drepanum a goodly haven town of Sicily. . . .

Source: Thomas Coryat, *Coryat's Crudities: Hastily Gobled Up in Five Moneths Travells in France, Savoy, Italy, Rhetia Commonly Called the Grisons Country, Helvetia alias Switzerland, Some Parts of High Germany and the Netherlands* (Glasgow: J. MacLehose and Sons, 1905), 301–428.

Relations of the Most Famous Kingdoms and Commonwealths Through the World, Discoursing of Their Situations, Manners, Customs, Strengths and Policies, by Giovanni Botero and Robert Johnson

The last excerpt comes from a 1591 scholarly essay written by Giovanni Botero, an Italian diplomat, political philosopher, and early demographer. Published in four volumes, Botero's work was one of the earliest anthropological studies systematically detailing and comparing the lands and customs of peoples around the world. The work was translated into English and expanded by Robert Johnson in 1603 and again in 1611. Copying Botero's style and focus, Johnson included in his edition of the work a lengthy consideration of Venice's wealth and its sources.

- What does Johnson have to say about the Venetian's wealth?
- What were its major sources?
- Which markets and trading partners does Johnson mention?
- Finally, according to Johnson, how does Venice compare to other cities in terms of its commercial reach and significance?

Fame reports the Venetians to be exceedingly rich. But, besides opinion, there is great reason why they should be so indeed. First, they are lords of a large territory, both by land and sea. . . . Another reason is the great advantage which the Venetian has for traffic, both in drawing unto himself other men's commodities and inventing his own. . . . The flower of gain, and emolument to the state, is the traffic of the great Sea of Syria and Egypt, which the Venetian has altogether in his hand, especially the ancient traffic for spice, which has always been, and yet is, of great consequence to them. In sum, all the trade of cloves, nutmegs, cinnamon, pepper, wax, sugars, tapestries, clothes, silks, and leather . . . all the commodities of the East to pass this way, and are uttered from hence into the greater part of Italy, and a good part of Germany. The greatness of this trade may the better be perceived by the greatness and multitude of private shipping, belonging to citizens and other strangers, merchants of Venice and other towns belonging to the state—as also by the multitude and wealth of said merchants, and by the great stirring and bartering that is there every day. In which kind the merchants only of the Dutch Nation, in Venice do dispatch as much, as were thought sufficient to furnish a whole world. To which purpose I may not omit to note that cities of traffic have three degrees of difference, for either the trade lies by the warehouse that dispatches by the gross or by open shops that do retail, or by both. Of the first sort are Lisbon, Antwerp, Amsterdam . . . and in Italy, Naples, Florence, and Genoa. Of the second sort are all the other cities of France and Germany. And among the cities of Italy, Milan is herein the chiefest, where there are to be seen shops of all wares so rich and well furnished. . . . In both sorts, Venice goes beyond all the cities of Italy. For there are open shops of infinite number, and the warehouses there do far pass all others in Italy. So that this city does traffic by way of shop as much as any other city, and by warehouses, more. And to conclude, putting both together, it is the city of greatest traffic in Europe, and perhaps of the world. . . . Venice is, as it were, the center of the East and West, the storehouse of everything that is produced by sea or land, and in sum, the receipt of the whole wealth of Asia and Europe.

Source: Giovanni Botero and Robert Johnson, *Relations of the most famous kingdoms and commonwealths thorough the world, Discoursing of their situations, manners, customs, strengths and policies. Translated into English and enlarged, with an addition of the estates of Venice, Saxony, Geneva, Hungary, and the East-Indies, in any language never before imprinted.* (London, 1611), 234–236.

Further Reading

Brotton, Jerry. *The Renaissance Bazaar: From the Silk Road to Michelangelo*. New York: Oxford University Press, 2002.

Carboni, Stefano. *Venice and the Islamic World, 828–1797*. New Haven, CT: Yale University Press, 2007.

Coggins, Jay S., and C. Federico Perali. "64% Majority Rule in Ducal Venice: Voting for the Doge." *Public Choice* 97, no. 4 (1998): 709–723.

Davis, Robert C. *Shipbuilders of the Venetian Arsenal: Workers and Workplace in the Preindustrial City*. Baltimore, MD: The Johns Hopkins University Press, 2007.

Fortini Brown, Patricia. *Art and Life in Renaissance Venice*. New York: Harry N. Abrams, Inc., 1997.

———. *Private Lives in Renaissance Venice*. New Haven, CT: Yale University Press, 2004.

Hibbert, Christopher. *Venice: The Biography of a City*. New York: Norton, 1989.

Hopkins, T. C. F. *Confrontation at Lepanto: Christendom vs. Islam*. New York: Forge Books, 2006.

Johnson, Paul. *The Renaissance: A Short History*. New York: Modern Library, 2002.

King, Margaret L. *The Renaissance in Europe*. Boston: McGraw-Hill, 2005.

Ludivine, Julie Olard. "Venice-Babylon: Foreigners and Citizens in the Renaissance Period (14th–16th Centuries)." In *Imaging Frontiers, Contesting Identities*. Edited by Steven G. Ellis and Lud'a Klusakova. Pisa, Italy: Pisa University Press, 2007.

Martines, Lauro. *Power and Imagination: City-States in Renaissance Italy*. Baltimore, MD: The Johns Hopkins University Press, 1988.

Muir, Edward. "The Myth of Venice." In *Civic Ritual in Renaissance Venice*. Princeton, NJ: Princeton University Press, 1981.

Norwich, John Julius. *A History of Venice*. New York: Alfred A. Knopf, 1982.

Romano, Dennis. *Patricians and Popolani: The Social Foundations of the Venetian Renaissance State*. Baltimore, MD: The Johns Hopkins University Press, 1987.

Web Resources

Core Documents for Italy, Primary Sources on Copyright (1450–1900), www.copyrighthistory.org/database/identityhtml/static_link_core_i.html.

The Jewish Virtual Library's Tour: Venice, www.jewishvirtuallibrary.org/jsource/vjw/Venice.html.

Venice versus the Sea, National Geographic, http://ngm.nationalgeographic.com/2009/08/venice/venice-animation.

Venice Walking Tour: Rialto, National Geographic, http://travel.nationalgeographic.com/city-guides/venice-walking-tour-1/.

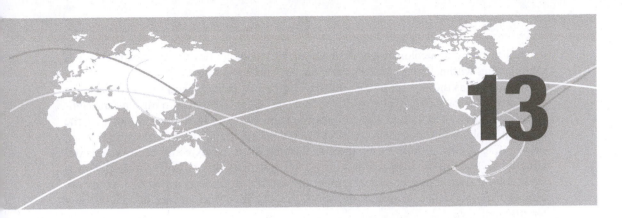

13

Potosí

A Motor of Global Change

(1545–1600s)

Jane E. Mangan

THE CITY OF POTOSÍ IN SOUTH AMERICA WAS SO RICH IN SILVER THAT THE early-modern world came to use its name as a synonym of wealth, regardless that few people ever even visited the region. During a break from my research on a June afternoon in the 1990s I walked from the archive at the Casa de la Moneda, a building that used to be the Spanish colonial mint, and returned to my apartment to eat lunch and do laundry. The Cerro Rico, the "rich hill" and ubiquitous symbol of this southwestern Bolivian city, stood tall in the distance. The midday sun beamed down on the city from a bright, blue Andean sky. Yet even on the sunniest day Potosí is a cold place to be, and its barren landscape and high altitude can make it feel like it is in the middle of nowhere. Potosí sits at thirteen thousand feet above sea level and is far from any major rivers or bodies of water. As I scrubbed my clothes in the freezing water I wondered—and not for the first time—how did more than one hundred thousand people create a thriving city . . . here . . . in this location high in the Andean altiplano during the 1500s?

The significance of Potosí and its mines shows up in archives throughout South America and Spain. I learned early in my career as a historian that a visit to an archive in Lima or Quito, among others, would produce documents that mentioned connections to Potosí, but the archives of the city itself provided the richest trove to explore, as they offered the view of a colonial city in creation, with as many ties to the outside world as complexities within. Potosí's history drew me back time and again.

As isolated as the city felt in the 1990s, its economic, political, and social connections to South America and the wider world loomed large from the sixteenth through the eighteenth centuries. The Potosí silver mines were the single-richest silver mines that the Spanish exploited in their entire period of colonial rule, and the influx of silver from those mines is cited as influencing the global economy of the sixteenth century. Asia desired its silver coins, English colonies hoped to emulate its riches, and Spanish peninsular literature used it as a common symbol of wealth ("it is worth a Potosí"). However, although Potosí's silver traveled the world, the city was hidden, reachable only by a lengthy journey.

Many first-time visitors to Potosí will ask—as I have—how in the world did the largest sixteenth-century metropole emerge at this spot thirteen thousand feet above sea level, where the sky is a brilliant blue, the mountains a dusty brown, and nothing is green save for some patches of grass and a few trees in the town's main square? The city is not a ghost town, properly defined. Its current population hovers around 150,000, much smaller than cities like La Paz, Cochabamba, or Santa Cruz, and it is decidedly no longer the largest in the region as it was in the sixteenth century. Yet Potosí and its surroundings suggest a weathered present descended from a gilded past. That past is present in the city's architecture. The building most associated with Potosí's silver past, its mint, or Casa de la Moneda, once housed the riches from the city's silver mines and today serves as a museum and archive. The Catholic church of San Lorenzo, another city-center jewel, is famous for its intricate bas-relief sculptures that were fashioned by the hands of indigenous artisans in the colonial era. The city's structure reflects imperial power by showcasing dominance and wealth in its downtown buildings and rigid control in its outskirts. From the private residences at the town center, one can walk in the direction of the mines and encounter the famous *rancherías*, which provided segregated housing for indigenous mine workers and their families, coming ever closer to the Rich Hill, the silver-laden reason for Potosí's existence.

In 1987 UNESCO declared Potosí a Cultural World Heritage Site, recognizing the city's significance as a center of silver production and a sophisticated early-modern example of an industrial complex. Even before UNESCO's designation, however, Potosí used mining as a way to promote tourism. Visitors can tour the mines and see workers toiling away inside the earth. This tourism industry has a slow pulse and is fed mostly by visitors using Potosí as a stepping-off point for the Salar de Uyuni salt flats, a marvel of the natural world. In the 1500s and 1600s not a soul would have imagined using Potosí as a stepping-off point to anywhere—not the the fortune seekers from Europe and elsewhere in the Andes, the forced indigenous workers, the African slaves, the priests, the missionaries, the merchants, or the viceroy. In this era Potosí *was* the destination.

To study Potosí in the early-modern era is to encounter the forces of colonialism and early globalization. The silver deposits spawned a mining industry. The mining industry drew record numbers of people to the Bolivia high plains. These residents created an urban culture that combined traditional indigenous practices with the increased economic and social opportunities of the city, all under the concerned eye of Spanish royal officials. The ripple effects of these developments in South America's interior made their way to Europe, Asia, and Africa through economic developments related to the silver bullion and human trafficking. Despite the conical shape of Potosí's mountain of silver, this seat of riches was one of the early examples of how flat the world might become through the processes of globalization.

POTOSÍ AND THE WORLD: Silver Links to Global Trade

The Spanish landed in the Americas in 1492, and within a few decades they had moved from the Caribbean Islands to the mainland, through Mexico and Central America, reaching the Andes by 1532. During this time the Spanish gained political power and territorial control by both waging war against native peoples and creating alliances with them. Spanish explorers had the backing of Spain's king and queen as well as approval from the pope to acquire land and resources from any non-Christian they encountered. The ramifications of this unfolded in a lengthy process of discovery, battle, negotiation, and rule. Spain used the Indies, as the American territories were known, to harvest natural resources, create trade links, and institute elements of Iberian culture, namely through evangelization. The process of colonial expansion was never one-sided, however, and native peoples responded in many ways, ranging from outright resistance to negotiation for self-benefit. The importation of slaves to the region began in earnest in the late sixteenth century and altered dynamics of labor and cultural change in important ways during a later stage of change.

Potosí's dynamism comes from the magnitude of its silver deposits as well as its sizeable population, estimated at 160,000 in 1620. For comparison's sake, London had some 350,000 residents in 1650, whereas Boston had around 2,000. People—thousands of them and from many places—moved in and out of Potosí on a regular basis. Native Andeans migrated from around the region for labor in the mines or to earn money in the city's thriving economy. Spaniards traveled from cities throughout the Indies as well as from Iberia with the hope of striking it rich in the silver mines. Other Europeans also made the trek to find riches, and the arrival of slaves connected Potosí's sphere of influence to Africa.

Silver moved around within Potosí, circulating through markets and corners of the city dominated by native Andean trading networks. Yet mainly silver flowed *out* of Potosí, to Arica and on to Spain via Panama or onto the Philippines via Acapulco, Mexico. Galleons returned from the Philippines laden with silks, porcelain, and spices from China, India, Persia, and Java, all purchased with Potosí silver. One scholar estimated that a third of all Spanish American silver, much of it from Potosí, made its way to China. Silver also left Potosí in contraband style to travel to Buenos Aires and the Río de la Plata region, where French, Dutch, Portuguese, and Spanish traders offered European textiles, swords, and other luxury items.

Imperial City, ca. 1600

Founded in 1545 after the discovery of silver mines, Potosí (located in the colonial viceroyalty of Peru and in modern-day Bolivia) quickly became a heavily populated urban center. By 1550 as many as 25,000 native Andean men and women trekked along Inca roads to Potosí, and the city grew to an estimated 160,000 by the early seventeenth century. It functioned as a source of silver for the Spanish Crown and others around the globe for much of the sixteenth and seventeenth centuries.

During this era of its global significance Potosí served as a flash point for debates about expanding empire and exploiting native peoples. Its location on a high-altitude plain reveals the critical links of place and environment to understanding Potosí's history as well as its image in history. The city and its mines are not located at a natural crossroads; in its heyday it was located in the middle of nowhere, yet despite its isolation, it was also the pride of an empire. Moreover, given its altitude, it is not particularly easy for newcomers to adjust to life in Potosí. The city offers a lesson in what humans will do to adapt when there is a valuable resource to be exploited. It further shows how a region can mount an economy oriented toward a profitable center even when that center is a challenging—if not completely inhospitable—locale.

Currents of early-modern expansion and empire created Potosí (the locale) and then spawned linkages between Potosí and the larger world (with particular focus on Europe and, by the late sixteenth century, Africa). Spain had already conquered the Inca Empire by 1545 when silver was found in the Potosí region. Spaniards used Iberian law and ideas of property in conjunction with forced labor of indigenous people to exploit the mines. The mines' isolated location sparked new economic circuits for luxury goods within the Andean region and eventually in Europe, and the mines brought governmental interest, European explorers, and mine technology to the region. Although Potosí demands attention for the silver that made it world famous, it is equally instructive from the perspective of the human interactions and practices that emerged as a result of the thriving economy in this high-Andean metropole. Potosí's reputation was full of contradiction, as it garnered awe in some circles over its great wealth and horror in others for its forced labor. It is necessary to consider both faces of the fabled city as we peer over our shoulders in history to understand processes of globalization. In particular, Potosí intensified economic activity and cultural exchange *and* inspired global expansion through its connections to the Andean region, the African slave trade, and European imagination. Ultimately, the high-density population and high-level productivity of this site propelled its impact across the globe through personal experiences as well as "pieces of eight."

Potosí as a Local and Regional Motor of Change

With silver as fuel, Potosí was a motor that sped native Andean encounters with Spanish culture and, in particular, Spanish economy. The foundation of the city led to dual forces of labor exploitation and economic motivation as Spain built its empire. These patterns created an impact on the economy in the hinterland; they forced native Andean peoples, mainly Quechua- and Aymara-speaking, to adapt to urban colonial life; and brought about practices that were unique to the city.

The particulars of Potosí's founding reveal how it became a dynamic place. The region was home to ancient Aymara kingdoms invaded by Inca expansionists during the fifteenth-century reigns of Tupac Inca Yupanqui and Pachakuti. Potosí lies close to the southeastern frontier of the Inca Empire. Unlike Cuzco, for example, the city that served as the heart of the Inca Empire, Potosí was a newly created urban center. In the 1540s the Cerro Rico drew the attention of Spaniards, who founded an official mining town on the site in 1545. Massive indigenous migration to Potosí, unswayed by cold temperatures and high altitude, began in 1549. The silver shone as a beacon for potential earnings for indigenous commoners who had to pay tribute to Spanish rulers. A small stratum of the early indigenous residents had relative economic success that afforded them status in the city during its first century. Spanish masters, the *encomenderos*, sent other indigenous workers from the valley of Cuzco and other agricultural zones to work the mines for them. Many indigenous workers kept some profits for themselves. Male workers dominated the waves of migrants, but some families arrived as well. Women soon dominated urban markets as vendors.

The Spanish sector of Potosí diversified with the arrival of women as well as non-Spanish Europeans in the second half of the sixteenth century. In addition to an increase in people of Spanish descent born in Peru, European migration swelled in response to transatlantic tales of silver riches. Spaniards and other Europeans, such as Italians and Portuguese, tried their hands at the business of mining. For instance, Nicolás del Benino was a Florentine miner who oversaw the construction of the first mine tunnel and stayed in Potosí for decades. Like other mining boom towns, people continued to arrive even after the biggest shares of the mine had been distributed. Spaniards owned most of the mine shares, though Europeans from other locations and some indigenous people owned shares as well. The late arrivals created tension for economic resources and concern for political rulers. The Spanish Crown repeatedly warned local leaders to exile vagabonds from the city.

Lazy inhabitants would have been easy to identify because most descriptions of the town suggest a beehive of activity, especially surrounding trade. Silver drove commerce in the early days of the Potosí market. Among the more remarkable qualities of this great market was indigenous vendors' as well as Spaniards' participation. Although indigenous people, especially women, were a fixture in markets of urban centers of the colonial Americas, their presence in Potosí is of particular interest because we are used to hearing about Potosí only as site of labor exploitation and not of the potential economic activities of indigenous peoples. Estimates from the era suggest that there was twenty-five to thirty thousand pesos' worth of trade per day. This amount caught the eye of Spanish officials because a basic house and small plot of land in Potosí would sell for a few hundred pesos.

Of particular interest in this trade was the coca leaf. Indigenous women were primary vendors of the leaves, which they transported in large baskets and traded for ore or silver. The great market for coca shows the transformation of a product with highly ritual significance in the pre-Columbian era into one with commercial purpose. Coca leaves grow well in the highland valleys of the Andes, though not in the immediate vicinity of Potosí. Indigenous Potosinos chewed coca to bring out juices that offer nutrients and chemicals to help the body function at high altitudes. In the preconquest era native Andeans made ritual offerings of coca leaves to deities. After conquest production rose to meet consumption demands from natives and Europeans in Potosí.

The path of this coca to Potosí highlights economic circuits *within* the Andes. Even given its isolated location, Potosí stimulated the regional economy. Foodstuffs came from Cuzco, Arequipa, Tarija, Tomina, Arica, and Cochabamba. Cloth came from textile workshops throughout the Andes. Native Andeans transported the merchandise to the high-altitude markets on the backs of llamas, a domesticated pack animal used prior to Spanish arrival. As Potosí became a hub for regional economy, its population became a blend of those who hoped to profit from the boomtown and those who labored in the mines.

The silver mines themselves functioned as the result of a complex industrial process that developed over the course of the sixteenth century and drew on local resources, indigenous knowledge, and European technology. The Spanish ordered the construction of twenty-two reservoirs of water and then used that waterpower to fuel some 140 mills to grind the silver ore. Workers mixed the ore with mercury to refine it, and the refined silver was then molded into bars, which received the stamp of the Casa de la Moneda before being moved into production.

Under Spanish rule, adult indigenous males throughout the Spanish Americas had to pay a tribute to the Crown. The Spanish system relied heavily on the Inca system of labor expectations, *mita* (rotating labor draft), which required all males to work for the good of the community and the empire in order to carry out their system of tribute. In some areas this tribute labor was used for textile production, building, or farming, but in the region of Potosí their tribute took the form of mine labor. This labor draft was dramatically changed by the Spanish viceroy, Francisco Toledo, in 1572. His version of the mita called on ninety-five hundred men from a total of sixteen provinces between Potosí and Cuzco and as far away as Guamanga to engage in forced labor in the mines. Absenteeism was a problem; the Spanish collaborated with native Andean chieftains in order to gather the laborers. These men collected workers in their regions, presented them to the *corregidor* (magistrate) of the indigenous at a roll call, and sent them to Potosí. The laborers, known as *mitayos*, used age-old customs to prepare for the journey. They loaded llama caravans with preserved food such as *chuño* (preserved potato) and *charqui* (dried llama meat) to sustain themselves for the one- to two-month trip.

Gathering men to take on the onerous mita duty was not easy. They typically worked from Monday to Saturday, during which time they ate and slept in the mines. In addition to the onerous schedule, the work was dangerous. Unstable mine conditions, on-the-job accidents, and long-term illnesses, such as lung afflictions brought on by breathing the unhealthy air inside the mines, contributed to a high volume of worker injuries and death. Miners routinely made offerings, including llama sacrifices, to Andean deities to ask for protection. Because of the mines' unrelenting labor needs, Potosí's impact through the mita spread region-wide and depleted each community's labor resources, political structures, and overall viability. As Spanish demands intensified, Potosí's mines came to stand as a symbol of the dark exploitative heart of the colonial endeavor; the quest for mineral riches existed hand in hand with disregard for indigenous life and community.

Once in Potosí, mitayos and their family members entered a new world. They lived in the rancherías on the outskirts of the city. Men and women settled near others from their home regions in modest adobe and straw homes and with a few material belongings, such as textiles woven of llama or alpaca and clay pots or jugs. The urban concentration also brought change for mitayos and their kin. Native Andean chieftains charged that once in the city, the natives changed their dress, spoke in Spanish, and apprenticed their sons to tradesman. For some native leaders this bespoke the undesirable consequences of colonial cities, where many people—too many different kinds of people—interacted at both work and play. As indigenous men and women began to engage in the urban economy for their own benefit, this created a pull away from indigenous traditions that ultimately threatened the Andean community.

Many of these new workers faced a difficult transition to Potosí's urban economy. The area's concentration of mita laborers and proximity to silver created an accelerated transition from a barter-based to cash-based colonial economy. Wage labor emerged earlier in Potosí than it did in other Andean cities. Viceroy Toledo pushed for cash wages—3.5 reales daily wage in coin for mita workers—which moved the ranchería population toward more cash-based transactions. In addition, costs were high because the city experienced inflation. Average food expenses for a mitayo in 1596 totaled more than the salary Spanish royal ordinances set. What emerged, then, was the use of credit to buy staples. Vendors also provided small peso loans in this era. These practices coexisted with barter exchanges of, for instance, coca leaves for potatoes, textiles, or even a house. The overlap of petty credit, barter, and use of silver pesos represents the transition of economic exchange from pre-Columbian to colonial during the sixteenth century. Similar overlap of practices occurred in other urban centers of the Spanish Americas.

Material Culture in Places of Encounter: Corn Beer as an Urban Commodity

As we have seen with coca leaves, new urban practices had a direct effect on Potosí's economic impact on the Andes. Whereas coca was essential, other changes were equally telling about cultural and economic transitions in the midst of a heavily populated town. Native corn beer, known as *chicha*, became a micro-industry for Potosí between the 1560s and the early seventeenth century. Native Andeans had brewed chicha for centuries, with the select women (*aclla*) of the Inca king brewing the finest-quality chicha. It was used in rituals that intertwined political and spiritual significance and as offerings for deities. Even objects had evolved in the region to suit the corn beer: *keros* were specialized vessels produced in pairs (always) and used solely for consuming beer. Further, chicha's history did not disappear after the discovery of silver at Potosí. Instead, Spanish hacienda owners and millers smelled the potential for profit, so production (and probably the taste of the drink itself) and consumption (who drank it, where they drank it, and the significance attached to drinking it) of the brew changed radically.

Consumption of chicha rocketed skyward with the growth of Potosí, illustrating economic differentiation among those people involved in producing and selling it. In the sixteenth century mill owners in nearby (yet lower-altitude) regions began to grind corn flour, and the ancient task of brewing chicha changed. Female brewers no longer waited days for grains of corn to soak in water, nor did they then grind them by hand or chew them in their mouths to form the paste known as *muk'u*. Corn flour shortened the production process by taking away the need for the extensive grinding stage.

Spanish officials linked the corn flour to a dangerous increase in chicha consumption. If producing the brew now took less time, officials assumed that the city's growing colonial population would be more prone to drinking binges and illicit sexual activity, which they reasoned made controlling the laboring population for the job of mining more difficult. Potosí's main officials lobbied for a prohibition of the corn flour so as to save Potosí's mine laborers from themselves and keep them fit for mine labor. Despite these efforts, chicha evolved into an important colonial business. By 1600 sources observed hundreds of thousands of corn-flour sacks en route to Potosí in order to make chicha. Chicha consumption, like credit practices, also underwent a change during this era. Although Spanish warnings were exaggerated concerns about cultural differences and potential disorder in the mining city, it is also important to acknowledge that the context in which people consumed chicha had changed. It could now be consumed less inside of ritual context and more in a colonial social context.

In 1603 vendors sold more chicha than wine (the drink identified with Spanish culture). In fact, in the Andes during the sixteenth and seventeenth centuries Africans, *mulatos*, *mestizos*, indigenous people, and Spaniards—a more diverse group of people than at any other time in Potosí's history—made, drank, and sold chicha. Most significantly, between the 1560s and the 1620s chicha shed its label as an indigenous product to emerge as a distinctly colonial product, becoming a unique cross-cultural item of consumption. As with coca, Potosí's massive demand for chicha sent ripples into the circuits of trade in the Andean region. Simultaneously, it sent Spanish officials into bouts of anxiety about social control of the laboring population as well as the city's increasing mixed-race population. It is a prime example of how the creation of a large urban center like Potosí, whose primary reason for existence was silver, set into motion numerous other changes as well. Indigenous families traveled to the city for forced labor or economic activity and had their children there even as they maintained ties to ancestral regions in the Andes. Many stayed in Potosí after completing their labor obligations because of the strong colonial economy. They lived in the large mining town, spoke native languages even as they learned Spanish, wore traditional dress even if they might use European fabric to fashion it, and went to Catholic church while keeping native Andean objects like *cocos*, silver drinking cups, in their homes.

GLOBAL ENCOUNTERS AND CONNECTIONS:
The Atlantic on the Pacific, Incorporating Africans into Potosí

We see in this era how outside forces, namely the rise of the Atlantic slave trade, affected Potosí's population in ways both economic and cultural. The opening of a Buenos Aires trade route was significant for reasons beyond the slave trade: it gave many European merchants concrete ideas about how to pursue Potosí silver by trading goods from the Atlantic coast as it also led to increased economic exchange along a new axis.

When colonial chroniclers described Potosí, all noted the variety of its population. Notwithstanding its inland location and lack of proximity to plantations, the city had an important Afro-Peruvian population. And, indeed, an early seventeenth-century census (1611) recorded 120,000 inhabitants and showed the diversity of the city's population: 76,000 native Andeans; 43,000 Europeans; 35,000 creoles, including *mestizos*; and 6,000 inhabitants of African descent. The numbers reveal that some 5 percent of the population in Potosí was African or Afro-Peruvian. This minority was a noticeable one, as it was concentrated in the very center of town, making its impact on the urban center of social, economic, and governmental life all the more marked. Slaves worked not in the silver mines but as domestics and in the silver refineries in the city center.

Tension existed between Spanish officials and Spanish mine owners regarding the use of African slaves in the mines. The mine owners argued that Africans were incapable of mining silver because they could not survive at high altitude, their bodies were too large to fit in the mines easily, and they had no experience in mining silver. Regardless of the dubious nature of these arguments (e.g., with regard to the first, thousands of Africans lived in Potosí and other high-altitude Andean cities during this era), the racial divide held strong: indigenous men mined the silver and African men refined it (some nine hundred feet below the mines). How and why these slaves came to Potosí reveals important migration patterns for the late sixteenth century and rising merchant desires in the early seventeenth.

Through the late sixteenth century, when Spaniards, Portuguese, and *criollos* (persons of Spanish descent born in the New World) traveled to Potosí, they came with slaves in tow. Owners could sell slaves in urban markets, but as an indication of the relatively slow pace of trading slaves in the city and of the city's scant need for slave labor, the slaves were not sold in groups unless they were married or had children. Through the 1590s the African population was generally born in the Americas or Iberia and did not come directly from Africa.

By the early seventeenth century Potosí had become a jumping-off point for the transatlantic slave trade as it extended into the Andes through a more direct route. Criollo slaves came from New Spain, the island of Santo Domingo, and the isthmus of Panama as well as from locations within South America, including such cities as Arequipa, Cuzco, Santiago de Chile, and Trujillo. That the overwhelming majority of slaves in sixteenth-century Potosí were criollos should not obscure the fact that newly arrived Africans did indeed come to Potosí from places such as Wolof, Bran, Congo, Guinea, Biafra, and Mandingo.

These locations emphasize the transatlantic and regional migrations to Potosí during the silver-rush era that drew tens of thousands of people to the city. The development of multiple routes shows the impact of larger forces of Atlantic economy on Potosí. Moreover, it reminds us that newly arrived Africans had already been the subjects and actors in negotiation about trade, culture, and power long before they arrived at the

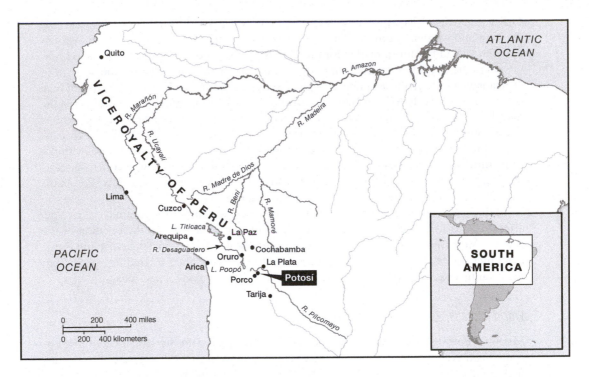

Map 13.1. Western South America

By the turn of the seventeenth century the Viceroyalty of Peru contained many established cities. Chief among them was Potosí, set inland, 13,000 feet above sea level and far from any major body of water. The city's Cerro Rico was mined for its silver, which brought great wealth to Spain. Potosí's silver made its way across the Atlantic to Europe and other locales, making the city influential to the global economy.

silver metropolis. The slave trade to Potosí in the sixteenth century was a drawn-out affair for African men and women, and it was inefficient and expensive for those who purchased the slaves. Slaves traveled from Africa or Spain to Nombre de Dios in Panama, where they crossed the Isthmus of Panama to the Pacific. They boarded ships anew to sail down to Callao (Lima's port) or Arica, where they would be sold for a land journey up the mountains and to Potosí. This official trade route had slaves pass through Crown-approved ports so as to pay the Crown its due taxes. It was a lengthy and often deadly journey.

By 1580 a new circuit of illicit trade between Potosí and the Atlantic coast changed slaves' journeys to Potosí and dramatically increased the number of African-born slaves. The founding of Buenos Aires in 1580 confirmed the persistence of this route, despite continuous denunciations from the Spanish crown, and several hundred slaves traveled through Buenos Aires to Potosí each year. Francisco de Vitoria, bishop of Tucuman and former trader, promoted the city of Tucuman as a bridge between the Atlantic and silver-rich Upper Peru. Brazilian merchants known as *peruleiros* traversed this path, where they hoped to offer Potosí residents all manner of saleables in exchange for silver. Silver then followed that same route back toward Buenos Aires.

In the seventeenth century the trade of African slaves to Potosí increased. Those who arrived to the area were overwhelmingly African-born, not criollo. In a change from earlier practices, sellers, probably slave merchants as opposed to individual owners, sold the men and women in groups. The change in tempo, place of origin, and sellers reveals how Potosí had become a market for the Atlantic slave trade and doubtless attracted new buyers to the city. Thus, by the turn of the century the notable increases in the amount of Africans began to make an impact on the city, its economy, and, ultimately, its colonial character. The largely African-born, specifically Angolan, slave population emerged in the decade of the 1590s. Potosí was not only, then, a location of strictly Spanish-indigenous relationships as it is often portrayed; it was also a city that was home to Africans. Africans worked in homes, sold food on the streets, healed sick people, refined silver, and, within a short time, appeared in all manner of judicial records and town council records, suggesting that they were fully engaged in Potosí society. A small group of free Afro-Peruvians also emerged in the city as property owners and merchants.

In this era, then, we see how outside forces, namely the rise of the Atlantic slave trade, affected Potosí's population in ways both economic and cultural. Yet the opening of the Buenos Aires route was significant for reasons beyond the slave trade: it gave many European merchants concrete ideas about how to pursue Potosí silver by trading goods from the Atlantic coast and led to increased economic exchange along a new axis.

World Famous: Potosí in European Imagination

Much of Potosi's fame stems from the role its silver played in the global economy. For some historians it is a root cause of the price revolution in Europe, a time of massive inflation linked in part to the influx of silver and gold from the New World. Even if someone had not seen Potosí silver, they might well have heard of the place. Potosí—the idea, the place, the riches—traveled across the globe in ways related to, yet distinct from, its bars of silver. The references to the city continued far from home and years after its peak silver production. Books, images, and word of mouth spread tales of Potosí far and wide. As a result, the city stirred imaginations and gained mythological status. Thus, it is worth analyzing Potosí's intellectual and ideological implications. How did stories about these locales serve as models for others engaged in the cycles of exploration, trade, and expansion in the early-modern world? Further, could these cities live up to their larger-than-life images?

The Portuguese, racing against the Spanish to expand their global influence, felt keen motivation to find an El Dorado, a legendary city of gold, especially after the concrete tales of silver came from Potosí. By the late 1530s Portugal learned of Spain's riches gleaned from the conquest of the Inca Empire. This fostered Portuguese desires to find great deposits of gold or silver in the interior. The Portuguese were at work on the Atlantic side of South America, where they made numerous trips into the continent's interior with the express goal of finding mineral wealth. (See Map 13.2.) Around the time when the Spanish "discovered" Potosí, a group of Portuguese soldiers was relatively close. Led by Domingo Martinez de Irala, the group arrived to the Andean foothills in 1547 and learned that the Spanish had beat them to the treasure, finding Potosí in 1545. Antonio Rodrigues and other foot soldiers from the expedition, however, were undeterred. Further expeditions to locate another Potosí took place through the 1500s and continued as late as 1694 through 1696 into the Brazilian interior.

The Portuguese not only held a monopoly on supplying slaves through 1640 but also controlled the sale of slaves from the port of Buenos Aires inland to Potosí.

Map 13.2. Spanish and Portuguese Territories in the Americas, ca.1600s

Early modern expansion and empire in the sixteenth and seventeenth centuries linked Potosi to the outside world. Spain conquered the Inca Empire by the mid-sixteenth century, and the Portuguese established themselves on the Atlantic side of Latin America. Both empires sought to mine their American holdings for their rich natural resources, like Potosi's silver mines, and, as this map shows, settlements grew both along the coast and in the interior.

Furthermore, they did not hesitate to traffic in a variety of other contraband trade items during that same era. Though Portugal never presided over their own Potosí in the Americas, many Portuguese merchants benefited from the economic repercussions of Potosi's existence.

Ideas of Potosí spread beyond the Americas to Africa. The Portuguese in Africa hoped to find gold in quantities similar to the Spaniards' find in Potosí. They left disappointed when they realized that gold mining was slower, being laborious in a different way, and they could not easily draw the quantities of mineral from the region as they had hoped. If the notion of finding another Potosí spread across the world in this sixteenth-century wave of global expansion, it was never satisfied.

The English also listened to tales of Potosí with great interest. Rich silver mines were an important tool in the recruitment kit for investors and settlers in the New World schemes. Silver riches from Spain's empire proved inspirational for pirates and privateers. Indeed, the English saw Virginia's coast as an ideal staging ground for the Spanish fleets returning to Spain laden with silver. Select members of Sir Walter Raleigh's expedition expected little work and lots of riches, as the English had notions based upon tales of silver and gold from the Spanish Americas. The English, for instance, imagined that mining the shores of Virginia would be as profitable as Potosí had been. Many New World chronicles of Spanish empire, such as Agustin de Zárate's 1581work, *The discovery and conquest of the province of Peru,* appeared. Over time, of course, English privateers did reap riches from Spanish ships, but settlers never found their "ritche mines."

As famous as Potosí was for its silver, it was equally infamous for the exploitation associated with the mita, the forced labor draft. It is well known that as much as English audiences hoped to find a Potosí in their New World territories, they also claimed they would never manage it as the Spaniards had. Englishmen consumed images of Potosí as a hell on earth for indigenous peoples. With the help of early-modern Dutch engraver Theodor de Bry, Europeans held an image of Potosí that has proved one of the most enduring visual images of the mine labor. In contrast to pictures showing the grand Cerro Rico from the outside, de Bry's engraving opened up the view to indigenous workers laboring inside, depicting them as being built in the same mold as the men native to Virginia. For those who know Potosí's grand, conical shape and the slope of the mine entrances, it would appear that de Bry, who had never seen Potosí, had it all wrong. His image became legendary, however, because it portrayed the Indians' victimization by the Spanish. In this aspect de Bry could not be accused of misrepresentation; the Spanish victimization of native Andeans through the mita is indisputable. De Bry's striking image of Potosí is still routinely used to illustrate the exploitation of native peoples at the hands of Spanish colonizers.

As the prime example for showing how Spaniards had ruined New World populations, Potosí's mita draft became a symbol in global battles over empire. Thus, whether it was the dream of a single adventurer, the model of other Europeans for the wealth they might earn through expansion, or an unconscionable example of exploitation, Potosí forged debates and plans about empire in the early-modern world.

Potosí's silver production reached its peak in the 1590s and remained a significant source of silver through the mid-1600s. After 1650, however, production declined precipitously. The War of Spanish Succession (1701–1713) meant that Spanish ships were occupied elsewhere. The chaos of this larger context allowed British and French ships to ply trade goods off the coast of Peru in exchange for Potosí silver, and as a result, the mines experienced a brief upswing in activity. When this flurry of activity slowed, however, Potosí trudged into its future. Modern Potosí is a large and complex city, far from a ghost town, but it has never regained the dynamism of its first century of existence. Although mining booms occurred in other regions of the Iberian empires, such as Guanajuato in Mexico or Minas Gerais in Brazil, none matched the intensity of Potosí's sixteenth-century boom, which left an early-modern watermark on colonial economic and labor relations for the rest of the world.

ENCOUNTERS AS TOLD: PRIMARY SOURCES

This section contains excerpts from three distinct primary sources. As a group the three reveal the complexity of changes that the growth of a major urban center put into motion. For both colonial and some indigenous rulers, the production of wealth through silver offered important material gains. These came with other changes that challenged old traditions and created new ones, especially for the native Andean population. These voices prompt students to consider how the growth of this city and its mines created change in economy, labor, local politics, culture, and society. As you read, be alert to those changes and consider how different sectors of the population experienced those changes in distinct ways.

Natural and Moral History of the Indies, by José de Acosta

José de Acosta, a famous Jesuit chronicler of Spain's American empire, provides a sixteenth-century description of Potosí.

- What does Acosta, the Spaniard, emphasize in his description?

- How does he attempt to relate this New World marvel to his mainly European audience?

- Can you find elements of environment and economy in his characterization of the city?

- Can you characterize his representation of the city?

The famous mountain of Potosí is located in the province of Los Charcas, in the kingdom of Peru; it is twenty-one and two-thirds degrees distant from the southern or Antarctic Pole, so that it lies within the Tropics near the edge of the Torrid Zone. And yet, it is extremely cold, more than Old Castile and more than Flanders. . . . What makes it cold is that it is so high and steep and all bathed in very cold and intemperate winds, especially the one they call tomahavi there, which is gusty and very cold and prevails in May, June, July, and August. Its surroundings are dry, cold, and very bleak and completely barren, for it neither engenders nor produces fruit or grain or grass and thus is by nature uninhabitable owing to the unfavorable weather and the great barrenness of the earth.

But the power of silver, desire for which draws all other things to itself, has populated that mountain with the largest number of inhabitants in all those realms; and silver has made it so rich in every sort of foodstuff and luxury that nothing can be desired that is not found there in abundance. And, although everything has to be brought in by wagon, its marketplaces are full of fruit, preserves, luxuries, marvelous wines, silks, and adornments, as much as in any other place. The color of this mountain is a sort of dark red; it is very beautiful to look upon, resembling a well-shaped tent in the form of a sugar-loaf. It rises above and dominates all the other mountains in its vicinity. To climb it is difficult even on horseback. It terminates in a round peak, its slopes measure a league in circumference, and from the peak of this mountain to its foot and base there are 1,624 yards of common measure, which, reduced to the measure and reckoning of Spanish leagues, is a quarter of a league. On the lower slope of this mountain is another, smaller one, which rises from it. . . .

On the slopes of this little mountain begins the town inhabited by Spaniards and Indians attracted by the riches and workings of Potosí. This town has a circumference of two leagues: it contains the largest population, and the most commerce, in all of Peru.

Source: José de Acosta, *Natural and Moral History of the Indies*, edited by Jane E. Mangan, introduction by Walter D. Mignolo, translated by Frances M. López Morillas (Durham, NC: Duke University Press, 2002), 172–173.

"Sobre la arina del maiz," by Gaspar de Saldana

The next excerpt comes from a local-level political document written in 1565 to address policing alcohol production in the city. When Spanish officials noted a rise in the production of chicha, or corn beer (described above), they plotted to end it. Interestingly, the document reveals changes at a bird's-eye view of the city.

- How does this description of the city differ from Acosta's?

- What does Saldana's (the *corregidor's*) concern suggest about Spanish rule in the city or about indigenous life in the rancherías?

- Finally, how does this document show the parallel economic changes the growth of Potosí wrought?

In the Villa Imperial of Potosí in the province of los Charcas of this kingdom of Peru on the tenth day of the month of March year of our lord of 1565 years in front of me, Melchior de Vitoria, public and town council scribe of this Villa, the very illustrious sir Gaspar de Saldana corregidor and chief justice of the Villa and province of Charcas by his majesty, said that as it is public and notorious and we have seen and see from experience that the invention of the flour that is made from corn has occasioned great drinking binges in the Indians and natives who reside in this Villa. [This is] because as they discover the ground corn from which they make the acua [chicha] that they drink, they brew much bigger quantities of it than they did previously, which occasions consuming much larger quantities than they used to . . . that [practice of drinking] is very rooted in them and they are drunk almost all week long during which time occur many acts of incest and other sins that they commit in offense of God, our Lord, and of your majesty and [is] the greatest impediment to their conversion and Christian doctrine that is preached to them, and [impediment] to the labor of the mines that was the reason that they were brought here. Because most of the time that they are supposed to work in the said labor they are occupied in the said drinking binges and even though the sheriffs continuously have tried to remedy this so there are fewer drinking orgies, it has been extremely difficult for them to be able to do this. The said corregidor [Saldana], to remedy this great universal danger, has spoken and conferred zealously with the leaders of this Villa and with many other persons. . . . And to everyone it seems that there can be no other remedy other than take away the cause, which is the said corn flour, because without it [they will have to] grind the corn to make the said acua [chicha] [and] they cannot grind more than that which is necessary and moderate like they did before the said flour was made.

Source: AGI Charcas 32, f. 92v (extant folio 1): Gaspar de Saldana, "sobre la arina del maiz," [partial ms.], March 10, 1565.

Petition Presented by Don Gabriel Fernandez Guarache to the Azogueros Guild

The final excerpt is a petition from a native Andean chieftain, or *kuraka*, named Don Gabriel Fernandez Guarache. He writes in 1663 about the challenges of providing indigenous laborers for the mita. This leader talks about the injustice of the mita, but he is perhaps more concerned with the disintegration of his *ayllu* (his community) and sees the mita draft as a primary cause. Guarache's voice is an indigenous one about Potosí as well as a voice that comes from the mid-seventeenth century.

- How does this different identity and chronology compare with the previous two excerpts?

- How does life in Potosí sound in 1663?

- Further, when you read this excerpt, look for the creative responses native people make to avoid the mita. What do these responses suggest about racial identity in a colonial city?

One cannot deny that this [forced mine labor] is an injustice that is carried out as if there were no King to whom these indefensible Indians could come, so exasperated and hurt they finish [their turn], and because of having to pay these expenses [of life in the city] and not having any other more respectable recourse, they sell or indenture their wives and children in private homes and in chicha taverns, thus denying themselves the consort and licit friendship of [their wives and children] as well as the love and natural proximity of their children who become separated from the nest and [the wife from the] union of holy matrimony. . . . And this is public and notorious and as such I allege it and their sons and daughters are lost with the lapse of time, being already young men and they lose themselves [their indigenous identity] and stray from the natural origin of where they are from. Others flee with their wives and children to very remote places at a distance of 200 to 300 leagues from this Villa taking advantage of the owners of the small farms [so their children can] contract marriage with women different from their nation and they become *yanaconas* [an indigenous person without a home community] changing their dress and last names constituting themselves as free and exempt from the mita. And the daughters with warning from their fathers [the farmers] marry men of different lineages so their children who are born are not subject to the obligations of the mita and other personal duties taking advantage of the insignia and coat of arms of the yanaconas of the owner of the chacara or of his Majesty. . . . The other that is no less malicious is that married Indian women, who actually live with their husbands, list their own legitimate children during the act of baptism (without warning their husbands) as children of unknown fathers to guarantee that at 15 or 16 years the child will be exempt from the mita.

Source: AGI Escribanía 868a, legajo 1, fols. 12r–16r: Petition presented by don Gabriel Fernandez Guarache to the azogueros guild, Potosí, 1663.

Further Reading

Bakewell, Peter. *Miners of the Red Mountain: Indian Labor in Potosí, 1545–1650.* Albuquerque: University of New Mexico Press, 1984.

Capoche, Luis. *Relación general de la Villa Imperial de Potosí.* In *Relaciones histórico-literarias de la América Meridional.* Vol. 122 of *Biblioteca de Autores Españoles desde la formación del lenguaje hasta nuestros días.* Madrid: Ediciones Atlas, 1959.

"Descripción de la villa y minas de Potosí. Año de 1603." In *Relaciones Geográficas, de indias: Peru.* Edited by Marcos Jiménez de la Espada. Vols. 183–185 of *Biblioteca de autores españoles desde la formación del lenguaje hasta nuestro días.* Madrid: Atlas, 1965.

Ferry, Stephen. *I Am Rich Potosí: The Mountain that Eats Men.* New York: The Monticelli Press, 1999.

Mangan, Jane. *Trading Roles: Gender, Ethnicity, and Urban Economy in Colonial Potosí.* Durham, NC: Duke University Press, 2005.

Padden, R. C., ed. *Tales of Potosí.* Translated by Frances M. López-Morillas. Providence, RI: Brown University Press, 1975.

Web Resources

City of Potosí, UNESCO World Heritage Centre, http://whc.unesco.org/en/list/420.

Common Place, John Demos, "The High Place: Potosi," www.common-place.org/vol-03/no-04/potosi/.

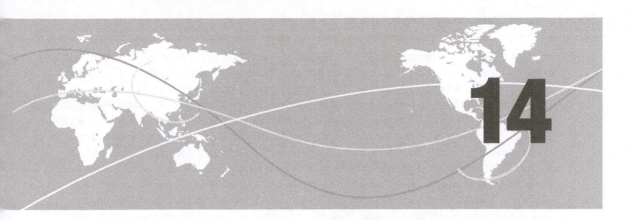

Malacca

Cosmopolitan Trading Port of the Early Modern World

(1400–1824)

BARBARA WATSON ANDAYA

AND LEONARD Y. ANDAYA

A S GRADUATE STUDENTS MAJORING IN SOUTHEAST ASIAN HISTORY, WE WERE introduced to Malacca (the Malaysian spelling is Melaka) through Malay and Portuguese chronicles that celebrated its golden age in the fifteenth century. During this time Malacca rose to become one of the great entrepôts (a place where goods can be exchanged with few or no import duties) of the early-modern world. From 1511, however, it fell under European control—first the Portuguese, then the Dutch, and finally the British—and this ended only when Malaysia gained its independence from Britain in 1957.

In 1970 both authors were writing our theses on Malay history, and we were therefore eager to see what remained of Malacca's historical heritage. The long bus ride from Singapore through seemingly endless rubber plantations brought us to a town that was much quieter than today's tourist hub but where the legacy of a multicultural past was everywhere apparent. For budding historians it was a heady experience actually to see the Dutch Town Hall (Stadhuys) and the remains of the Portuguese fortress that were familiar to us from written sources. We can still remember our excitement as we walked along "Jonkerstraat" and "Heerenstraat" (Dutch: "nobleman" and "gentlemen" streets, now Jalan Hang Jebat and Jalan Tun Tan Cheng Lock), which were once European enclaves but now the houses had long since been remodeled by later wealthy Chinese-Malay (*baba*) owners. What was especially impressive was the vibrancy of Malacca's places of worship, like the much-frequented Buddhist temple Cheng Hoon Teng ("Abode of the Green Merciful Clouds"). Founded in 1645 and constructed according to the Chinese principles of *feng shui* (literally "wind-water," the Chinese art of positioning objects in an auspicious manner), it houses a bronze statue of Guanyin, the goddess of mercy, said to have been brought from India in Victorian times. Equally distinctive was the eclectic Kampung Keling Mosque ("Keling" refers to south Indians) dating from 1748. Built in the Sumatran style, it is embellished with Chinese ceramic roof tiles but also displays European touches such as Corinthian columns and a Victorian chandelier. (See Map 14.1.)

Because eighteenth-century Malacca, then under the Protestant Dutch, was known for its religious tolerance, we were especially keen to see the Catholic Church of St. Peter, established in 1710. We recalled older connections, however, from the date of 1608 on the church bell, which had been imported a century earlier from the Portuguese-controlled city of Goa in India. Our visit coincided with Easter, and on Friday evening we joined the hundreds of devotees crowding St. Peter's churchyard to watch the dramatic enactment of the procession to Calvary. Though the absorbed spectators were only half-visible in the flickering candlelight, we could see that this was not an occasion for Christians alone. The presence of so many individuals of other faiths was a telling comment on Malacca's rich history as an international meeting place.

Today Malacca is no longer the provincial town we first encountered. From the 1970s, when the Malaysian government initiated new programs to attract visitors, it has been elevated to prominence as a tourist destination. Well positioned on the Asian tourist route, Malacca is an increasingly popular stop for cruise ships, disgorging visitors to shop at the handicraft boutiques, antique shops, and art galleries and to eat at the restaurants jostling for space along the major streets. Panoramic views, abundant shopping, an array of historical sites and museums, and, of course, the local cuisine, with its fusion of Chinese, Indian, and Malay tastes, make it an appealing destination. Yet our personal fascination with Malacca has deeper roots. Displaying a tangible past that is rare in the bustling urban centers of modern Asia, it remains an obligatory pilgrimage site for anyone interested in Southeast Asian history. Although the architectural heritage is the town's most striking feature, a visitor can also see signs of the human encounters that led UNESCO in 2008, upon designating Malacca a World Heritage Site, to speak of a "cultural townscape without parallel anywhere in East and Southeast Asia." On a recent visit this legacy was made memorably evident as we passed a small shop where an old man was skillfully fashioning paper images to be burned during a Chinese funeral. Among those already completed were a miniature baba woman wearing the distinctive *sarong kebaya* (sarong and embroidered overblouse) and a Sikh guard, both of whom would accompany the deceased into the next world.

This chapter will explain why Malacca emerged as one of Asia's most important ports and why it attracted such a cosmopolitan population during its heyday in the fifteenth century. Though the city's regional preeminence ended with European conquest, it has retained its significance in Malaysian history as a symbol of the global connections that underlay Malay prosperity in the past and continue to be valued today.

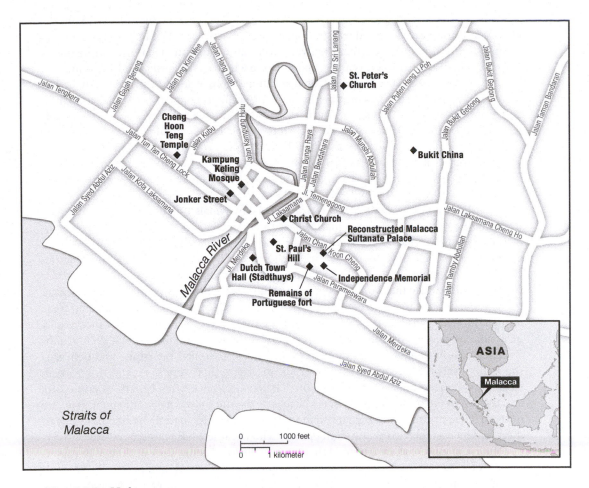

Map 14.1. Malacca

This map of modern Malacca helps explain why the city was selected for a Malay settlement in the early fifteenth century. The river gave easy access to the Straits and to the interior jungles, St. Paul's Hill provided a vantage point for the surrounding area, and a stream near Bukit China provided fresh water. The layers of history are evident in the reconstructed Malay palace, Chinese and Indian temples, Muslim mosques, the remains of the Portuguese fort, and Dutch administrative buildings. After independence most streets were renamed after Malaysian figures well known in history or legend.

MALACCA AND THE WORLD: A Fifteenth-Century Entrepôt

Like so many other "places of encounter," the global significance of Malacca stems from its geographical position on the straits that bear its name. The Straits of Malacca, one of the world's longest sea corridors, is bounded on one side by the Malay Peninsula and on the other by the island of Sumatra. Apart from a narrow opening between Java and Sumatra, the straits provide the only sea connection between China and India and are likened by an early Chinese source to a "gullet" through which all maritime traffic moving in either direction must pass. (See Map 14.2.) The importance of the straits in early Asian trade can also be attributed to the influence of the annual monsoon winds, which made the Straits of Malacca a natural meeting place. The northeast monsoon sweeps down across the South China Sea November to January, after which it gradually decreases in force and is followed by a transitional period April to May. The southwest monsoon is the dominating airstream between May and September; another transitional period occurs October to November, and then the whole cycle starts again. With increasing use of the all-sea route between China and India from around the fifth century, ports along the straits became exchange points for ships originating in Arabia, India, and China and sailing between eastern and western Asia. During the lull between the monsoons cargoes could be unloaded and sold while traders waited for the change in the direction of the wind that would enable them to return home. In the early sixteenth century, when the first Europeans arrived, it was this favorable location that led the Portuguese official Tomé Pires to assure his superiors that Malacca's importance "cannot depreciate, but must always grow" (Cortesão, 1: 228; 2: 251).

The Malay epic known as *Sejarah Melayu* (Malay Annals), Chinese records, and later Portuguese accounts all indicate that Malacca's emergence on the world stage was initiated in the late fourteenth century when a prince from Palembang in southeast Sumatra established a settlement. There are various stories explaining the choice of a name, including the proximity of the Malacca tree, but Pires was told that the word meant "hidden fugitive," referring to the founder's flight from Sumatra. This origin was highly significant because Palembang was the center of the Srivijaya kingdom, which once dominated trade in the region and left a well-established court culture and a style of authority that readily incorporated peoples of different ethnicities and lifestyles. Foremost among such groups were the sea-dwelling *orang laut* ("sea people"), who patrolled the straits and delivered the fish, corals, seaweeds, and other ocean products that were a magnet for foreign traders. Numerous orang laut followed the Palembang prince when he left his homeland, and they were the ones who proposed Malacca as the site for the new settlement. Because of these links, prominent orang laut were rewarded with titles, and the daughter of one of their leaders was married to the young prince who became Malacca's second ruler.

Other encounters characterize Malacca's early history, as the surrounding area was already home to various forest-dwelling groups or *orang asli* ("original people"), who collected the jungle rattans, resins, and aromatic woods that were so desired on the international market. Initially they kept their distance from the newcomers, but a shortage of women among the migrant community encouraged intermarriage. Successive rulers also made concerted efforts to encourage migrants from other parts of the archipelago, thereby contributing to Malacca's cosmopolitan urban environment.

A few years after its founding Malacca already boasted a population of around two thousand people, and its natural advantages enabled it to eclipse its neighbors quickly as the preferred port on the straits. The shoreline was sheltered and free of mangrove swamps, with approaches sufficiently deep so as to allow large vessels safe passage. Although it did not have a natural harbor, ships could shelter in the lee of the offshore islands, and from here smaller boats could carry the wares to be sold in various locations along the extended coastline.

A high hill behind the town (St. Paul's Hill) provided an advantageous point from which to survey surrounding waters and thus ensure the town's safety, whereas river connections and overland routes gave access to the interior and the peninsula's east coast. The reliable source of fresh water at the base of the nearby Bukit China (China Hill) and the availability of jungle trees for masts and spars meant that Malacca could provide the basic necessities for ship repairs and replenish supplies. Added to these advantages was

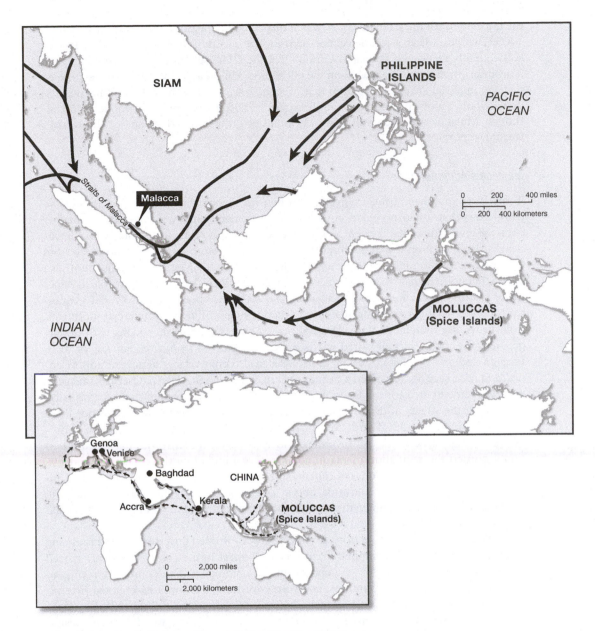

Map 14.2. Trade Routes Through the Straits of Malacca

Strategically located on the pathway of the annual monsoon winds cycle that governed Asia's maritime trade and dominating the Straits that connected eastern Asia and India, the fifteenth-century port of Malacca was renowned as a center for international trade, attracting merchants from all over Asia. Because its cosmopolitan population included many foreign and local Muslims, Malacca also became a dissemination point for Islam.

the imprimatur of the Chinese court, which dispatched a mission to the new settlement in 1403. Two years later a full delegation arrived, led by Admiral Zheng He, and Malacca subsequently received a special inscription that the Chinese emperor himself composed. This inscription was to be placed on the hill behind Malacca, and it carried the assurance that the imperial ancestors would watch over the town so that the ruler and his descendants would enjoy "great fortune and respect." These words proved prophetic, for although Malacca was then still relatively small, it grew to become one of the world's wealthiest ports.

Malacca's Administration

Tomé Pires may have been exaggerating when he alleged that Malacca's trade was so prosperous that it had no equal in the world, as similar claims were also made of other contemporary entrepôts like Venice. Pires emphasized, however, that Venice's wealth was heavily dependent on the trade in rare spices (especially nutmeg, cloves, and mace from eastern Indonesia), acquired through maritime links with Malacca. His account also shows that policies that Malacca's rulers adopted were critical in ensuring its role as Asia's major distribution center. First, their *orang laut* followers mounted patrols that guaranteed the safety of surrounding sea lanes. Second, rulers offered commercial incentives, even providing merchants who were waiting for the change in monsoons with underground warehouses so that stored goods could be protected from fire, damage, or theft. Foreign traders who took up residence in Malacca also enjoyed a reduction of import duties, and their security remained a prime concern. The *Sejarah Melayu* describes one ruler who was remembered for the favors he bestowed on foreign merchants and for his habit of roaming the streets in disguise in order to learn of any ill treatment or injustice these merchants might suffer. Third, Malacca's efficient legal machinery provided a predictability that was essential for incoming traders' long-term plans, with particular attention accorded the regulation of maritime commerce, including the collection of debts, shipboard crimes, and the duties of captain and crew. Finally, the special favor of the Chinese emperor was carefully cultivated, and in 1433, when Zheng He made his final visit, the Malacca ruler accompanied the expedition when it returned to China so that he could personally offer tribute.

Malacca's reputation for security, for having a well-ordered government, and for being a cosmopolitan and well-equipped marketplace all attest to the priority its rulers placed on creating the conditions for safe and profitable commerce. The combination of geographic location, natural advantages, and wise government ensured its regional preeminence as the major distribution point for Chinese porcelain and silks; Indian textiles from Gujarat, Coromandel, Malabar, and Bengal; and spices, aromatic woods, rattans, resins, sea products, and other exotic items from Southeast Asia's oceans and jungles.

Evidence that Malacca was specifically founded to exploit the flourishing trade environment is best demonstrated in its response to the needs of a multicultural trading community. The foreign population was divided into four groups according to their ethnic origin: Gujarat in northwest India; southern India and Bengal in northeast India, Burma (Myanmar), and northern Sumatra; Java, Maluku, Borneo, and the Philippines; and Champa (central Vietnam), China, and the Ryukyu Islands (probably including Japan). Each group was under the supervision of a *Syahbandar* (harbor master) who was responsible for overseeing its affairs, maintaining commercial standards, and adjudicating in any disputes. Whenever a ship arrived in port, the captain reported to his particular Syahbandar, who in turn referred him to Malacca's principal minister, the *Bendahara* (arbiter of quarrels among Malacca residents and between them and foreigners). The Syahbander then supplied elephants for the captain to transport his cargo to a warehouse assigned for the temporary storage of his goods. Before trading could be conducted, customs duties were paid in accordance with the value of the merchandise and the trader's place of origin. He was also expected to present gifts to the ruler, the Bendahara, and the *Temenggung* (the Malacca official principally involved in the collection of import and export duties) as well as to the appropriate Syahbandar.

A much simpler procedure was used for large ships. Import duties were regularized, with larger ships required to pay a flat 6 percent of the cargo's value, eliminating any necessity for giving separate gifts to officials. Following payment of duties, a group of Malacca merchants would negotiate a price with the ship's captain or the traders on board and then arrange for their distribution. This method disposed of a ship's merchandise quickly and efficiently, a highly desirable feature because merchants were often working against time, aiming to complete their business in order to catch the right monsoon back to their homelands. Malacca traders then sold the goods they had bought in local markets, in booths set up along the bridge, and in the streets in front of houses, or else they transported them to various parts of the archipelago to barter for other products. Listing the range of products that Malacca could supply, from textiles of silk and muslin to spices and rare jungle products, the Portuguese official Pires could only remark that this is a place "where you find what you want and sometimes more than you are looking for" (Cortesão, 1: 228).

Because so many traders were residents only part of the year, the actual number of inhabitants in Malacca fluctuated, but at the beginning of the sixteenth century the Portuguese estimated that the total population could range from forty to two hundred thousand. In this cosmopolitan environment even Pires claimed that in a single day he heard eighty-four different languages! Gujarati, Tamils, Javanese, and Chinese were demographically dominant in the trading population, but there were many smaller communities from places further afield, such as Japan and Armenia. Crews from ships loaded with rice from Java and Myanmar, cloth and ceramics from Siam, and spices from the eastern archipelago added to the town's ethnic diversity. Foreign merchants were grouped in a settlement known as Upeh, which comprised numerous semi-independent *kampung*, or villages, where each ethnic group congregated, each with its own jurisdiction and places of worship. Servicing all these activities required importing labor, and about 5 percent of Malacca's population were slaves, mostly from the Indonesian archipelago and India, who were employed in loading and unloading ships, as crew members, in construction, and as domestic help. Female slaves often became concubines for the wealthy or temporary "wives" for foreign traders, and children of these mixed unions could play an important role as interpreters or translators.

Kingship and Islam

The administrative stability that guaranteed a safe and profitable trading environment ultimately depended on general acceptance of a social hierarchy in which the ruler's authority was unquestioned. According to Malay tradition a compact between the ancestor of Malay commoners and the first ruler of Palembang laid down that his exalted position was no license for arbitrary government. Although subjects should render unquestioning loyalty, they should not be "bound or hanged or disgraced with evil words." Despite the ruler's great wealth and status, and despite deep-rooted beliefs that treason was a heinous crime, the notion of consensual government was central to Malay kingship, and the

Sejarah Melayu stresses the need for consultation, comparing the ruler to a fire and the ministers to the firewood that produces the flame. This collective decision-making process normally prevented arbitrary acts by a ruler and guaranteed that an agreed-upon resolution would be faithfully implemented.

In the fifteenth century increased revenue from trade transformed Malacca from a small fishing village into an international emporium. Smaller polities on the Malay Peninsula acknowledged its overlordship, and its political and cultural authority extended over much of east coast Sumatra and the islands of the South China Sea. For the most part these areas were willing to associate with Malacca because they gained access to trading privileges and basked in its prestige. A principal factor in Malacca's status was its adoption of Islam, generally ascribed to the 1430s, although the Malacca Straits area had been exposed to Muslim influence from various areas, including China and the Arab lands, since at least the thirteenth century. In Malacca the most important transmitters of the new faith were Muslim Indian traders from the Malabar and Coromandel coasts in south India, Bengal, and Gujarat. The type of teaching they brought is still a matter of speculation, although, as in other Islamizing areas such as the Swahili coast, there was considerable localization of Muslim teachings. Sufism, a stream of mystic Islam, probably played a significant role because of its readiness to incorporate indigenous pre-Islamic practices, such as meditation and communication with divinities through trance.

The *Sejarah Melayu* rightly sees the ruler's conversion as a watershed in Malacca's history, a miraculous event that confirmed the kingdom's superior status and divine favor. But although many aspects of Islamic doctrine were appealing, there were clear temporal benefits, as Muslim traders were more likely to frequent a port where the ruler was Muslim and where mosques and other facilities for worship were maintained. Indeed, Malacca's mosque was considered the finest in the region. Stories of powerful Muslim kingdoms such as the fabled "Rum" (Ottoman Turkey) must have helped reinforce the decision to embrace this new faith, especially after the capture of Constantinople in 1453. Adoption of Islam also strengthened the justification for kingship, for by the eleventh century Muslim kings elsewhere were styling themselves as the "Shadow of God upon Earth," and in Malacca Arabic words were adopted to reinforce much older beliefs that divine punishment would be visited on those who defied the ruler. In the 1470s there were even plans for the sultan to make the pilgrimage to Mecca. Malacca's dependencies in the straits region followed their overlord and accepted Islam, and Muslim traders and missionaries carried Islamic teachings from Malacca to distant parts of the archipelago. Because Malaccan Malay was well established as a trading lingua franca throughout the entire archipelago, it became a natural vehicle for imparting Muslim teachings and rendering Islamic texts.

Unfortunately, we know relatively little about the ways in which ordinary people actually practiced Islam, although it is evident that Malacca resembled many other newly converted areas in its retention of older customs. An Arab visitor, for example, condemned the extent to which Muslim men married non-Muslim women as well as their failure to observe Islamic prohibitions against certain foods, such as eating dog meat and drinking alcohol. Women retained a relatively independent position, and they continued to be highly visible as petty traders, even maintaining their own night market. The continuing tolerance of non-Islamic customs facilitated cross-cultural marriages and helps to explain the lack of hostility between ethnic communities.

In many ways local adaptation of a Muslim style of government heightened Malacca's attraction to both residents and traders. For example, Islam encouraged giving alms and maintaining charitable institutions, and taxes levied on stall holders and street sellers supported a hospital for poor people. Islamic law encouraged the development of a regulated court system and the codification of legal codes to settle disputes and provide judges with a manual for decision making. They devoted considerable attention to regulating commercial matters, property sales, and maritime trade, especially in regard to collecting debts. Muslim scholars from India and the Middle East who were sponsored by the ruler would have assisted in compiling these texts, but they also incorporated local customs that allowed for more lenient punishments than did "the law of God." This tolerant environment is reflected in the lack of discriminative taxation against non-Muslims, as was the practice in some Indian ports. Although Muslims were generally favored in Malacca's administration, capable individuals could assume influential positions regardless of religion or ethnic background. The *Sejarah Melayu* thus refers to a Hindu merchant who had come to Malacca, married the daughter of a nobleman, and was subsequently appointed to a high office. Intermarriage also linked non-Malays to the court aristocracy. Malacca's rulers set the style: taking wives of Chinese, Indian, and Javanese descent, whereas the daughters of Hindu and Parsi merchants were married to Malay nobles and customarily converted to Islam. Malacca thus remained a cosmopolitan town even as its style of government, courtly titles, literature, music, dance, dress, and amusements came to be regarded as distinctively "Malay."

By the beginning of the sixteenth century Malacca's wealth and reputation as a commercial and religious center had established a pattern of government and a lifestyle that other Malay-Muslim kingdoms, such as Brunei in northwest Borneo, emulated. In 1509 a group of Portuguese, the first Europeans to reach Malacca, were impressed by what they saw, commenting on the size of the population and the hundreds of boats moored offshore. Advocating a Portuguese conquest, Tomé Pires told his superiors that Malacca was so profitable that it was "made for merchandise." Its extraordinary commercial success, he said, had prompted the last ruler to claim that the world needed his port and to boast that Malacca was of such importance that it could even rival Mecca (Cortesão, 2: 253, 269, 286–287). Such overweening pride may well have aroused resentment among neighboring straits polities, for the Portuguese received assistance from a Sumatran prince when they attacked in July 1511, and it was the ruler's hubris, said some Muslims, that led to Malacca's unexpected and humiliating defeat.

Malacca Under Europeans (1511–1826)

The primary aim of Portuguese expansion into Asia was to dominate the spice trade, which was then largely in Muslim hands. The capture of Malacca was central to the plan to create a seaborne empire because of the city's role as a collection and distribution point. Afonso de Albuquerque (1453–1515), who had already led the forces that had taken Hormuz on the Persian Gulf and Goa in India, headed the expedition that captured the town in August 1511 after a month's siege. Determined to control maritime trade in the straits and throughout the Asian region, the Portuguese administration set about eliminating any possible rivals. In Malacca all Muslim traders were evicted, the great mosque was destroyed, and construction was begun on a fort, to be named A Famosa, "The Famous." The refugee sultan of Malacca fled to the southern part of the Malay Peninsula, followed by most of his subjects, including the orang laut.

Because the Portuguese never sought to extend their control beyond Malacca itself, the situation was very different from Cape Town in the same period, and the immediate concern was to strengthen the defenses in anticipation of attacks from hostile Muslim forces. Although many Chinese and Hindu Indians remained after the conquest, there was no standing army, and the numbers of Portuguese men overseas were never sufficient to fulfill the demand for soldiers and personnel. Albuquerque therefore promoted the idea of an interracial family, where the father was Portuguese and the mother a Christianized local woman. This, he hoped, would ensure an adequate supply of manpower by producing offspring who would feel "Portuguese" through a shared religion and language. Over the next hundred years Malacca's Christian population grew to seventy-four hundred people, comprising about three hundred married Portuguese men with their Asian wives and families as well as numerous "black Portuguese" (Portuguese-Asian mestizos and recent Christian converts, mostly Indians) as well as some Chinese. Because of this miscegenation, Portuguese joined Malay as a diplomatic and trading language, and a creole language, Kristang, still survives in Malacca today among descendants of Portuguese-Asian unions.

Although the Portuguese rebuilt Malacca to accommodate numerous convents, churches, and other religious establishments, Christians were always a minority in a multicultural population of around one hundred thousand people. Visiting priests often railed against the lack of piety among Malacca's Catholic population, and in many respects the city continued to operate very much as it had under Malay rule, with Portuguese officials becoming merely a new elite. Like their Malay predecessors, the Portuguese captains of Malacca offered privileges to Asian traders willing to settle in Malacca, and wealthy Hindus and Portuguese collaborated in commercial ventures. Chinese migration was welcomed, and Chinese graves on Bukit China testify to the presence of a large resident community who filled many of the city's needs for skilled artisans. Even Portuguese enmity toward Islam was laid aside in the interests of profit, and the Muslim Malay population began to increase. However, most foreign Muslim traders had become accustomed to alternative ports and had little inducement to accept invitations to return to Malacca.

Notwithstanding some continuities, the Portuguese conquest represents a new chapter in Malacca's history because without a ruler and court, Malacca could no longer stand as a guardian of Malay culture. Furthermore, economic rivalry fueled the European heritage of Muslim-Christian enmity that was so evident in Malacca's conquest, thereby injecting considerable hostility into Portuguese relationships with local states. Surrounding rulers, including the ousted dynasty, assaulted Malacca, thus invoking the idea of a holy war, while priests holding crucifixes urged on the defending Portuguese. Malacca's development into a missionary training center also confirmed its image as a Christian stronghold. When Dutch East India Company (VOC) forces attacked Malacca in 1641, they made specific reference to the wealth of the Catholic churches, libraries, and monasteries. This wealth reminds us that despite some commercial decline, Malacca remained one of the richest entrepôts in the East. As the foremost Portuguese possession after Goa and Hormuz, it was the key to trade with China, and European visitors continued to marvel at the amount and variety of wares brought from every corner of Asia.

Against this background it is not surprising that the directors of the Dutch East India Company, established in 1602, initially believed that the capture of Malacca would be a great prize. Although the establishment of the VOC capital at Batavia (modern Jakarta) in 1619 rendered Malacca less important for Dutch trade, in strategic terms conquest was considered essential. Though the Portuguese brought in Japanese and African mercenaries to strengthen the city's defenses, a prolonged VOC siege commenced in August 1640 and finally ended with the Portuguese capitulation in January 1641. Bombardments and extensive looting destroyed much of the town and surrounding suburbs, necessitating a substantial rebuilding program. The Dutch converted monasteries and churches for use as hospitals, schools, Protestant churches, or private homes. The Portuguese fort, extended through the construction of moats and the addition of bastions that followed designs favored by Dutch engineers, served as the center of VOC government, and its walls enclosed new administrative buildings that included the still-standing Stadhuys (Town Hall), built by Javanese and Chinese artisans. The main gate was adorned with Malacca's coat of arms, which incorporated a Chinese junk, a woman holding the palm of peace, and a soldier whose shield bore the letters VOC.

Because most European-born Portuguese merchants and church personnel were sent back to India, VOC officials initially believed that Malacca could be developed as a Dutch settlement that would promote Protestantism and the Dutch language. They soon found, however, that compromises were necessary, for VOC officials and Dutch *burghers* (free citizens) were never more than a few hundred souls, a steadily diminishing proportion of a population that rose from only two thousand in 1641 to six thousand in 1708 to about fourteen thousand in 1796. Because of the dearth of Dutch women, VOC officials often took Christian Eurasian women as brides, which helped maintain Portuguese and Malay as Malacca's lingua franca. Though VOC officials were reluctant to use non-Europeans in positions of responsibility, "black Portuguese" were frequently employed as intermediaries and envoys. Efforts to encourage conversion from Roman Catholicism were unsuccessful, and by the early eighteenth century the construction of a new Catholic Church, St. Peter's, acknowledged the popularity of the Catholic faith. However, the survival of mosques and Hindu and Chinese temples from this period demonstrates that Malacca remained a tolerant and multireligious society.

Dutch burghers, "black" Portuguese and Eurasians, Malays (including groups from elsewhere in Indonesia), Chinese, "Kelings" (southern Indians, mostly Hindu), and "Moors" (a general term used in Asia for Muslims, in this case mostly from India), and slaves of various African and Asian origins comprised this cosmopolitan population. Each ethnic group had its own captain, whose main task was to settle minor disputes and decide if cases should be brought before the VOC court. Over the years increased migration meant that the proportion of Asian residents rose. Malays remained a majority, but the number of Chinese grew from less than four hundred in 1641 to about two thousand in the mid-eighteenth century. As tax farmers, skilled artisans, shopkeepers, landowners, and traders, they made a significant contribution to Malacca's economy. Because migrant Chinese usually married local women, Malacca became known for its mixed baba culture, exemplified in cuisine, dress style, and language. The "nyonya" food, so popular in Malaysia today, takes its name from the term of address for Chinese-Malay women. Though less numerous than previously, there was a significant Indian population that included Gujaratis, Bengalis, and, especially, Hindu and Muslim Tamils from south India. As time passed, however, the older pattern of ethnic enclaves began to change because of intermarriage and because wealthier Asian citizens moved into areas such as Heerenstraat, previously a Dutch preserve.

Although VOC administrators bemoaned Malacca's commercial decline, the city was still a regular port of call for European and Asian traders, who frequently commented on the pleasant climate and its multiracial environment. Through the eighteenth century, however, the British advance in India and their superiority in navigation and cartography emphasized the VOC's financial difficulties. Following their victory in the fourth Anglo-Dutch war (1780–1784), the British gained the right of free trade in Asian waters previously controlled by the VOC. In 1786 the British East India Company established a free-trade port on the nearby island of Penang, drawing away much of Malacca's existing trade. In 1795, after Napoleon's conquest of the Netherlands, the Dutch were further humiliated when Britain occupied Malacca to prevent it falling into French hands. The

Dutch briefly returned in 1818, but hopes of economic recovery faded the following year when Thomas Stamford Raffles founded another free trade port on the island of Singapore. Many Chinese, the backbone of Malacca's economy, relocated to this new entrepôt, so the town was already a commercial backwater when it was finally ceded to the British in 1824. Malays, for whom Malacca was a tangible symbol of past glories, were brutally reminded of the realities of European control when the British demolished the great fort that had borne witness to so much history. In the words of Munshi Abdullah, a well-educated Malay-Tamil, "After its destruction, Malacca lost its glory, like a woman bereaved of her husband, the luster gone from her face. But now by the will of Allah it was no more, showing how ephemeral are the things of this world" (Hill, 63). In 1826 Malacca was joined to Penang and Singapore to form an administrative unit called the Straits Settlements, which became the base for the eventual imposition of British colonialism over the entire Malay Peninsula.

GLOBAL ENCOUNTERS AND CONNECTIONS:
The Malacca Heritage

During the fifteenth century Malacca grew from an insignificant settlement to become Asia's leading entrepôt. Whereas its Malay language, Islamic religion, and court culture established the basis for an emerging Malay identity, it was also renowned as a port where traders from all over the world were welcomed and cultural interaction was accepted and appreciated. Global connections created by trade and cultural exchanges linked it to other great cities of the early-modern world, such as Mecca, Cambay, Beijing, and Venice. For historians of Malaysia, Malacca's architectural legacy is a physical reflection of the best features of traditional Malay culture—a tolerance for difference, a willingness to recognize the abilities of any individual, regardless of racial origin, and the creation of an environment where all were welcome.

Today, ethnic relations in Malaysia are more fraught, but the multicultural heritage is still invoked as the basis of Malaysian society, and the government continues to foster the international connections that have contributed to a thriving economy and booming tourist industry. Furthermore, although we can only speculate about the ways Malacca might have developed without European intervention, its achievements and prestige under Malay rule means that it has a special status in Malaysia's national narrative. Malaysia's 1956 decision to announce its independence in Malacca rather than the capital Kuala Lumpur was thus highly symbolic. But Malacca is more than a monument to national pride, for it has also been recognized as a site of "world heritage" that all humankind should appreciate. At a time when ethnic, religious, and linguistic differences are so often divisive, this standing serves as a reminder not only of Malacca's architectural distinctiveness but also of the tolerance and adaptability that made it a unique "place of encounter."

ENCOUNTERS AS TOLD: PRIMARY SOURCES

The following two primary sources present both a local and foreign view of the city. The first, from a Chinese interpreter, describes the people and their environment in the early to mid-fifteenth century. The second dates to the early seventeenth century and describes Albuquerque's attack on Malacca from the Malay perspective.

Chinese Expedition to Malacca, by Ma Huan

This Chinese account of an expedition to Malacca in 1433 was written by Ma Huan, a Muslim translator and interpreter. In this capacity he accompanied the eunuch Zheng He, who led the Ming Dynasty's maritime expeditions dispatched to Southeast Asia, India, southern Arabia, and east Africa. Accounts of foreign places were not common in China at this time, and the Ming court therefore welcomed information about the geography, economy, and culture of distant places, particularly those with which the Chinese had tributary relationships. Published in 1451, his account of the places he had visited appeared in several subsequent editions and provides modern historians with important insights into the way China viewed the rest of the world.

- What measures did the Malacca administration take to safeguard the Chinese visitors' belongings?

- Why does Ma Huan give so much attention to specific products he saw in Malacca?

- What kinds of gifts would the Malacca ruler have taken to China to present to the emperor?

There is one large river whose waters flow down past the front of the king's residence to enter the sea; over the river the king had constructed a wooden bridge on which are built more than twenty bridge pavilions, and all the trading in every article takes place on this bridge.

The king of the country and the people . . . all follow the Muslim religion, fasting, doing penance and chanting liturgies.

As to the king's dress: he uses a fine white foreign cloth to wind around his head; on his body he wears a long garment of fine-patterned blue cloth, fashioned like a robe; and on his feet he wears leather shoes. When he goes about, he rides in a sedan chair. The men of the country wear the head with a square kerchief. The women dress the hair in a chignon behind the head. Their bodies are only slightly dark. Round the lower part they wrap a white cloth; and on the upper part they wear a short jacket of colored cloth. . . .

The land produces such things as incense, ebony, and tin. Incense is in origin the gum from a species of tree; it runs out into the ground; and when they dig it up, it looks like pine-resin or pitch. When you set fire to it, it flares up; and the foreigners all use this substance and set it alight to serve as a lamp. When they have finished building a foreign ship, they take some of this substance, melt it, and smear it in the seams, so that the water cannot get in; it is very effective. Many of the people in that the land collect this substance to transport it to other countries. . . .

There are two tin-areas in the mountain-valleys; and the king appoints chiefs to control them. Men are sent to wash the ore in a sieve and cook it. The tin is cast into blocks . . . every ten blocks are tied up with rattan to make a small bundle. In trading transactions they all take this tin for current use.

The speech of the people in this country, and their writings and marriage rites are somewhat the same as in Chao-wa [Java].

In the mountain wilds there is a kind of tree called the *sha-ku* [sago] tree. The people of the countryside take the skin of this article and, as is done with beans in the Central Country, they pound and soak it; after it has settled and been strained, the powder is made into balls the size of lentils; these are sundried and sold; they are called "*sha-ku* rice" and they can serve as rice for consumption. . . .

Whenever the treasure-ships of the central Country [China] arrived there, [the people of Malacca] at once erected a line of stockading like a city wall, and set up towers for the watch-drums at four gates; at night they had patrols of police carrying bells; inside, again, they erected a second stockade, like a small city wall, within which they constructed warehouses and granaries; and all the money and provisions were stored in them. The [Chinese] ships which had gone to various countries returned to this place and assembled; they marshaled the foreign goods and loaded them in the ships; then waited till the south wind was perfectly favorable. In the middle decade of the fifth moon [May 28, 1433], they put to sea and returned home.

Moreover, the king of the country made a selection of local products, conducted his wife and son, brought his chiefs, boarded a ship and followed the treasure-ships; and he attended at court [in Beijing] and presented tribute.

Source: J. V. G. Mills, trans. and ed., *Ma Huan* Ying-yai Sheng-lan: *The Overall Survey of the Ocean's Shores [1433]* (Cambridge: Cambridge University Press for the Hakluyt Society, 1970), adapted from 109–114.

Sejarah Melayu, by Tun Sri Lanang

This Malay account of Albuquerque's attack on Malacca in 1511 is taken from a long text commonly known as the *Sejarah Melayu* or "Malay Annals," which is considered the most important of all classical Malay works. The manuscript dates from 1612, although the bulk of the narrative was probably composed much earlier. The author, Tun Sri Lanang, was the Bendahara (chief minister) of the kingdom of Johor, founded by the refugee rulers of Malacca when they fled after the Portuguese conquest. His aim was to provide an account of the origins and history of Malacca kings for the benefit of future generations.

• How does the author remind his listeners of Malacca's greatness under Malay rulers?

• What is the role of the ruler in this battle?

• What kinds of differences can you see in the ways Malays and Portuguese fought?

• How does the author explain Malacca's defeat?

Now the city of Malacca at that time flourished exceedingly and many foreigners resorted thither. . . . Such was the greatness of Malacca at that time; in the city alone there were a hundred and ninety thousand people, to say nothing of the inhabitants of the outlying territories and coastal districts. . . .

After a while there came a ship of the Franks from Goa trading to Malacca: and the Franks perceived how prosperous and well populated the port was. The people of Malacca for their part came crowding to see what the Franks looked like; and they were all astonished and said, "These are white Bengalis!"

Around each Frank there would be a crowd of Malays, some of them twisting his beard, some of them fingering his head, some taking off his hat, some grasping his hand. And the commander of the ship landed and presented himself before Bendahara Sri Maharaja, who adopted him as his son and gave him robes of honor, as befitted his rank, while the commander for his part presented Bendahara Sri Maharaja with a gold chain.

And when the season came round [for the return journey] the commander went back to Goa, where he described to the Viceroy the greatness of the city of Malacca, the prosperity of the port and the number of the inhabitants. The Viceroy at that time was one Alfonso d'Albuquerque. When he realized the greatness of Malacca, the Viceroy was seized with desire to possess it. . . .

At the end of his term of office as viceroy d'Albuquerque proceeded to Portugal and presenting himself before the Raja of Portugal asked for an armada. . . . With this fleet he sailed for Malacca. And when he reached Malacca, there was great excitement and word was brought to Sultan Ahmad, "The Franks are come to attack us! They have seven *kapal* [general term for square-rigged decked sailing ship], eight *ghalias*, ten long *ghalia* [low-built warships using both oars and sail] fifteen *pencalang* and five *fustas* [fast ships using both oars and sail]." Thereupon Sultan Ahmad had all his forces assembled and he ordered them to make ready their equipment. And the Franks engaged the men of Malacca in battle, and they fired their cannon from their ships so that the cannon halls came like rain. And the noise of the cannon was as the noise of thunder in the heavens and the flashes of fire of their guns were like flashes of lightning in the sky: and the noise of their matchlocks was like that of ground-nuts popping in the frying-pan. So heavy was the gun-fire that the men of Malacca could no longer maintain their position

on the shore. The Franks then bore down upon the bridge with their galleys and fustas. Thereupon Sultan Ahmad came forth, mounted on his elephant Jituji. . . . Sultan Ahmad took Makhdum Sadar Jahan [his religious teacher] to balance him on the saddle because he was studying the doctrine of the Unity of God [a Muslim text] with him.

And the king went forth on to the bridge and stood there amid a hail of bullets. But Makhdum Sadar Jahan clasping the pannier with both hands, cried out to Sultan Ahmad Shah "Sultan, this is no place to study the Unity of God, let us go home!" Sultan Ahmad smiled and returned to the palace. And the Franks shouted from their ships, "Take warning, you men of Malacca, to-morrow we land!" And the men of Malacca answered, "Very well!." . . .

When day dawned, the Franks landed and attacked. And Sultan Ahmad mounted his elephant Juru Demang, with [one courtier] on the elephant's head and [another] balancing the king on the packsaddle. The Franks then fiercely engaged the men of Malacca in battle and so vehement was their onslaught that the Malacca line was broken, leaving the king on his elephant isolated. And the king fought with the Franks pike to pike, and he was wounded in the palm of the hand. And he showed the palm of his hand, saying "See this, Malays!" And when they saw that Sultan Ahmad was wounded in the hand, the war-chiefs returned to the attack and fought the Franks. . . .

And Malacca fell. The Franks advanced on the King's audience hall and the men of Malacca fled. The Bendahara was borne off the field, closely pursued by the Franks. And the Bendahara said to the man who was bearing him, "Hurl me against the Franks!" But his family would not allow this. Whereupon the Bendahara cried, "What cowards these young men are! If I was still a young man, I would die fighting for Malacca!"

Source: Tun Sri Lanang, *Sejarah Melayu or Malay Annals*, translated and edited by C. C. Brown (Kuala Lumpur, Malaysia: Oxford University Press, 1970), adapted from 151, 161–163.

Further Reading

Brown, C. C., trans and ed. *Sejarah Melayu or "Malay Annals."* Kuala Lumpur, Malaysia: Oxford University Press, 1970.

Cortesão, Armando, trans. and ed. *The Suma Oriental of Tomé Pires.* New Delhi and Madras: Asian Educational Services, 1990. Reprint of 1944 edition.

de Witt, Dennis. *History of the Dutch in Malaysia.* Petaling Jaya, Malaysia: Nutmeg Press, 2008.

Hashim, Muhammad Yusoff. *The Malay Sultanate of Malacca.* Kuala Lumpur, Malaysia: Dewan Bahasa dan Pustaka, 1992.

Hill, A. H. trans. and ed. *The Hikayat Abdullah.* Kuala Lumpur, Malaysia: Oxford University Press, 1970.

Hussin, Nordin. *Trade and Society in the Straits of Melaka: Dutch Melaka and English Penang, 1780–1830.* Copenhagen: Nordic Institute of Asian Studies, 2007.

Sandhu, Kernial Singh and Paul Wheatley, eds. *Melaka: The Transformation of a Malay Capital c. 1400–1980.* 2 vols. Kuala Lumpur, Malaysia: Oxford University Press, 1983.

Thomaz, Luís Filipe F. Reis. *Early Portuguese Malacca.* Macau: Macau Territorial Commission for the Commemorations of the Portuguese Discoveries, 2000.

Web Resources

Cheng Hoon Teng temple, www.chenghoonteng.org.my/.

Melaka and George Town, Historic Cities of the Straits of Malacca, UNESCO World Heritage Convention, http://whc.unesco.org/en/list/1223.

Melaka, Malaysia, Asian Historical Architecture, www.orientalarchitecture.com/malaysia/melaka/.

Index